BROWN
SAVIORS
AND
THEIR
OTHERS

BROWN
SAVIORS
AND
THEIR
OTHERS

RACE, CASTE, LABOR,
& THE GLOBAL POLITICS
OF HELP IN INDIA

Duke University Press   *Durham and London*   2023

ARJUN SHANKAR

© 2023 DUKE UNIVERSITY PRESS. All rights reserved
Printed in the United States of America on acid-free paper ∞
Project Editor: Bird Williams
Designed by Courtney Leigh Richardson
Typeset in Portrait by Westchester Publishing Services

Library of Congress Cataloging-in-Publication Data
Names: Shankar, Arjun, [date] author.
Title: Brown saviors and their others : race, caste, labor, and the global
politics of help in India / Arjun Shankar.
Description: Durham : Duke University Press, 2023. | Includes bibliographi-
cal references and index.
Identifiers: LCCN 2022048893 (print)
LCCN 2022048894 (ebook)
ISBN 9781478025092 (paperback)
ISBN 9781478020110 (hardcover)
ISBN 9781478027119 (ebook)
Subjects: LCSH: Altruism—Political aspects—India. | Altruism—Economic
aspects—India. | Public welfare—Moral and ethical aspects—India. | Social
stratification—Economic aspects—India. | Marginality, Social—Economic
aspects—India. | Capitalism—Social aspects—India. | India—Social policy. |
BISAC: SOCIAL SCIENCE / Anthropology / Cultural & Social | SOCIAL
SCIENCE / Ethnic Studies / General Classification: LCC HM1146 . S54 2023
(print)
LCC HM1146 (ebook)
DDC 305.900954—dc23/eng/20230411
LC record available at https://lccn.loc.gov/2022048893
LC ebook record available at https://lccn.loc.gov/2022048894

Cover art: *Global Shadows*. 2013. Digital. Courtesy of Arjun Shankar and
Nagraj Kumar.

Contents

III: URBAN SAVIORISM

IV: DIGITAL SAVIORISM

Preface: Encountering Saviorism

... I refuse to join them in performing the miracle—I will not say trick—of liberating the oppressed with the gold of the tyrant, and raising the poor with the cash of the rich.
—B. R. AMBEDKAR, *Annihilation of Caste*

The status of the "native" is a nervous condition introduced and maintained by the settler among colonized people *with their consent*.—JEAN-PAUL SARTRE, preface to Frantz Fanon's *The Wretched of the Earth*

A sweaty concept: another way of being pulled out from a shattering experience.
—SARA AHMED, *Living a Feminist Life*

PREMISE ONE: GLOBAL SHADOWS

Nagraj was one of my favorite ninth-standard students in Adavisandra school.[1] He was a curious student—what I later understood as a curiosity rooted in suspicion—and he asked question after question until he knew nearly as much about my research as I did.

I explained to him that I had come to Adavisandra to observe the practices of the education NGO (nongovernmental organization) Sahaayaka from the perspective of those who were at the receiving end of their interventions. Sahaayaka is a Bangalore-based organization working in thousands of rural schools, mostly in Karnataka state but also in Andhra Pradesh and Maharashtra. Sahaayaka's leadership comprised a group I call *brown saviors*—globally mobile savarna Indian-origin technocrats who had garnered excess racialized value for their technological capacities within the twenty-first-century global help economies.[2] These individuals had benefited from a longer global legacy of caste-colonial relations, with its intersecting (and sometimes contradictory) casteist and racist policies, which together facilitated the brown savior's eventual entrance into these help economies.[3]

I myself had landed in Adavisandra after traveling to a number of rural schools with my primary guide, Manoj, one of Sahaayaka's fieldworkers. The organization's fieldworkers hailed from Karnataka's villages and performed the daily tasks associated with Sahaayaka's form of rural uplift. Like Manoj, who had grown up just five kilometers away, Adavisandra's population is almost exclusively Hindu, "Kannadiga," and hailed from the Vokkaliga caste, the primary agricultural caste in South Karnataka and the second-largest agricultural caste in all of Karnataka state.[4] Adavisandra's economy is rooted in Karnataka's sericulture industry, producing silk cocoons that begin a silk commodity chain that leads to Muslim-majority factory towns in Bangalore's periphery before eventually connecting to the global silk market.[5]

In postliberalization and postautocratic India, agriculture is becoming less and less tenable for those living in Adavisandra, especially for those living on small plots of land. Because it is located only forty kilometers from Bangalore city, some of Adavisandra's agricultural land has already been bought up by the savarna global-urban middle class, who were taking advantage of the fact that many in the village were being forced to sell their land. For example, one Kannadiga brahmin family who had worked as engineers in Virginia for twenty years had purchased land in the village as a vacation home but had also started a "healthy, organic, sattvic" food business on their new property.[6] At the same time, *five* different NGOs were working in the village to support all those "in need." Based on these clashing phenomena alone, it seemed that Adavisandra was the right place to study the interventions of an NGO.

But as is the case with many fieldwork plans, my research agenda changed rather quickly when I arrived in Adavisandra. On my first day, the teachers at the school met me, heard that I was a former New York City schoolteacher, and said, without a hint of hesitation, "Oh, you are a teacher, we need some help, go teach." Their demand was jarring and made me exceedingly nervous, but I obliged. Over the course of the next year, even as I spent time with Sahaayaka staff and leadership, I also spent time in Adavisandra, filling in during periods in which students in the eighth and ninth standard did not have a teacher in their classroom. As a teacher, I began to take seriously that researching in this village might not be my most valuable purpose. While, at first, I did not know what to teach or how, eventually it became clear that I could use my training in visual anthropology and ethnographic film to teach students to use digital cameras, six of which I had brought with me during fieldwork. Over time I came to think of this endeavor as a participatory photography and film project, which generated thousands of photographs, some of which hang in Adavisandra school, others of which students took home to their families and friends, and a few of which hang in my family home in California.

Nagraj's interest in my research led him to ask more about my interest in photography and film, and eventually the image-making bug caught Nagraj as well. When he finally decided to take photographs, he took hundreds of photographs of objects—a frothing pot, a stove, a calendar, ceiling fans, a cat, a pomegranate tree, rice, a window, a spider crawling on the pink wall, a bottle of Pond's moisturizer, portraits of Hindu gods, spools of thread—but *never* a single shot of people. Not one. The closest he came was the shot you see in figure P.1, of his own silhouette in shadow. This image was one that we spent many days discussing while in Adavisandra and one that he offered to me for my research primarily because it showed his creative prowess *and* maintained his anonymity.[7] There was a particular danger Nagraj seemed to sense in the image, a visibility that the camera brought with it that he was not entirely

FIGURE 1. *Global Shadows*. Photograph taken by Nagraj, ninth standard, Adavisandra School. (Photo by Arjun Shankar and Nagraj Kumar)

comfortable with, and he was careful, therefore, not to photograph anyone in his family.

When I look back at Nagraj and his image-making practices, they remind me that the work of the anthropologist is as much about heeding the refusals of those who seek to remain in the "global shadows," and the political resistance that their opacity might allow, as it is about transparently revealing them to our readers.[8] This is why, after this preface ends, Nagraj, and youth like him, will sit mostly outside the frame while casting a long shadow.[9]

One day Nagraj wanted to take me to the hill near his home. I met Nagraj, and we wandered to the top of the hill together with six other children and looked around. Nagraj stared to his left, pointed to a small group of houses approximately two kilometers away, and said, "See over there. That was my village." He asked me if he could take a picture of his old village from the top of the hill with the camera, and I quickly agreed. It was after this simple gesture toward his old home that Nagraj and I finally began to speak about his past.

It had taken a long time for Nagraj to open up about his family and home. When I eventually learned more about Nagraj's life, I would begin to see his reticence as a necessary safety mechanism, a means of keeping his own unique and difficult story from emerging too quickly into the foreground.

While Nagraj now lived with his mother and grandparents in Adavisandra, he had previously lived in a village about four kilometers away. After our trip, Sripriya (my research assistant) and I went to Nagraj's house for lunch.[10] When we asked about Nagraj's father, Nagraj's mother said only that he had "died earlier" and that they had lost all of their farmland soon after his death. We did not press any further, the vagueness hinting that she, understandably, was not interested in speaking anymore about their past. In contrast, Nagraj's grandmother answered readily when I asked about their hopes for Nagraj's future. She told me that agriculture should "end with our generation . . . let him [Nagraj] study well and get another job." Literally any other occupation would seemingly do.

Later, as we walked away from his home together, Nagraj explained that his father had died earlier by drinking poison, a telltale sign that his father was another addition to the ever-increasing number of farmers' suicides in India.[11] Farmers' suicides have taken on a special place in the global imagination as one of the starkest examples of social disparity and suffering in India, unsettling the congratulatory tones accompanying India's supposed emerging world power.[12] There have now been over a quarter million documented cases of farmers' suicides in India over the past thirty years, rendering it one of the most tragic results of primitive accumulation in India's caste-colonial society.[13] During my own fieldwork, I encountered four instances of farmers' suicides, of which Nagraj's story was but one.

Suddenly and without warning, Nagraj began to reverse the flow of questioning and asked me about my own father, whom he knew by then had, like his own father, also committed suicide. He asked me to explain how and why my own father died, existential questions that connected the two of us. I felt nervous as Nagraj prodded further and further, feeling the weight of his questions and then feeling the weight of my earlier questions.

Nagraj smiled as he saw me sweat. He explained that he did not really want to focus on his life's tragedy any more than I did. Instead, he was more interested in telling me about his aspirations, and he told me that he wanted to be a lawyer so he could bring the people who caused violence like that done to his family to justice: suicide or not, he intuitively understood that something or someone else was to blame. The problem, as he conceived it, was systemic and social and not an individual pathology, deficiency, or failing.

Nagraj was also clear that he did not need "help" from anyone else in order to motivate himself. His life experience had given him the basis for his future goals. In fact, all this talk of help annoyed him.

"How did the thought of help come into your minds?" he asked.

He asked the question with irritation as much as curiosity. Nagraj was irritated because, for all the rhetoric of help, and even saving, no one seemed to understand what he was actually worried about or what he actually wanted for himself. Instead, Nagraj felt his reality was almost totally ignored because it was far too complicated, too implicating, and too systemic, not measurable in simplistic data analytics terms or scalable metrics, nor solved by poverty-alleviation strategies that reified a narrative of childhood incapacity and helplessness.[14]

Nagraj's critique also made me extremely nervous about what I was doing in the village and forced me to reflect on my own complicity in the projects that he was so ably critiquing. He compelled me to reframe how I conceptualized the politics of help in India by focusing far less on those who have been deemed in need or on the great benevolence associated with the savior class.[15] Instead, Nagraj's critique directed me to ask critical questions about who the individuals working for Sahaayaka actually were and why they were doing this form of help work in the first place. In the rest of this text, what I characterize as a *nervous ethnography*, I develop the analytic of the *brown savior* as a response to Nagraj's question, revealing the neocolonial capitalist regimes, racialized global histories, and graded caste stratifications that shape the politics of help in India.

This project is an experiment in nervous ethnography, a result of the twitchy, worried, agitated energy that has come with each stage of trying to tell the story of the brown savior.

This way of characterizing my experience of research might not be too surprising for those who know me best. My personality has been marked by nervousness, what doctors might view as an overactive sympathetic nervous system brought on by adolescent trauma that infuses the way I understand social interactions. Where others seem to make effortless connections and feel energized from sociality, I can recede into myself, perhaps performing enthusiasm but many times feeling isolated by the nerves that come with sharing myself with others. It has taken years to work through this, to recognize this instinct of mine and to enjoy the company of those whom I care about and who care for me. But it has also made my professional role as an anthropologist a kind of satire: How can one with all this nervousness do work that necessarily involves so much social interaction?

Nervousness, as Nancy Rose Hunt writes, "suggests being on edge. Its semantics are unsettled, combining vigor, force, and determination with excitation, weakness, timidity. Nervousness yields disorderly, jittery states, as in the *nervous wreck*, a *nervous breakdown*, or, as history has shown, a nervous national mood."[16] Thinking with Frantz Fanon, Hunt argues that an attention to nerves allows one to see our postcolonized world differently, as one in which the contradictions of colonization produced, in its aftermath, a jangling of nerves. This nervousness is a companion for those of us who recognize that we continue to live in neocolonial systems and want to combat them.[17] Worse yet, our nerves constantly fly out of control when we wonder to ourselves whether we might be loving and valuing all that which upholds this violent system.

I am thankful that ethnography has long been identified with neocolonial nerves, the embodied forms of emotional agitation that come with our body's somewhat awkward responses to the many stimuli associated with fieldwork in the aftermath of colonization.[18] Anthropologists are particularly nervous and sensitive about their craft given the discipline's neocolonial racist legacy, one that has been characterized by a radical Othering of and epistemic violence against peoples who did not fit into the neat confines of Euro-American epistemologies.[19] The constant drumbeat for more reflexive practice, for more considerations of power asymmetry, and for more critique of the entire anthropological project has served, at least for me, as a kind of balm, assuaging my nerves simply by calling out the very fact that we inhabit positions of violence. We've also reached a moment when these histories of epistemic violence may not feel so insurmountable, especially in a global-digital age when those we work with will inevitably have access to everything we've written about them.[20] They might even be producing counternarratives and challenging whatever stories we tell before we even get done telling them.[21] For once, we anthropologists might feel just a bit of the nerves that come with being so exposed, our ideas and theories up for questioning by the very people who purportedly trusted us enough to give us all of this information in the first place.

What is required, given the changing political stakes of anthropology, is a reappraisal of what we hope to gain from ethnographic research. For, even though anthropology and anthropologists have called over and over again for a reckoning with our nervous complicity in a violent history, what seems to have happened is that reflexivity has become "an excuse for political inactivity."[22] What I see more and more are lists of identity markers and quick commentaries on racial and gendered locations that actually have done little to subvert the anthropological impulse to study the Other. In fact, if anything, these insincere reflexive listings have only facilitated new types of Othering, an Othering that actually requires a facile description of encounter in which the anthropologist is strategically visibilized and therefore does not experience or share the discomfort that comes with being truly exposed with all their warts and flaws. Perhaps as important, these strategies to foreclose on nervousness have actually short-circuited the kinds of insights that arise when we have to sit and sincerely reflect on our discomfort.

Nervous ethnography forces me to reckon with the tradition of ethnographic fieldwork as a masculinist, ableist, racist project and with my own role in upholding this tradition. During our training, most every anthropologist has been told a story that lionizes the ethnographer who goes into the field; sees abject violence, poverty, and inequity; and comes home to tell the story in the most awe-inspiring of ways. This story of the ethnographic fieldworker traffics in a hypermasculinist ideology that sees distanced observation as valuable, and emotional anesthesia as courage. For those of us who experience anxiety, depression, stress, or any other mental or physical ailment, this version of fieldwork is both unrealistic and exclusionary. It prevents us from seeing ourselves in the figure of the anthropologist, but it also prevents ethnographic work from producing the range of insights that it otherwise might. Such ableist anthropology is also by definition antifeminist because it requires us to eschew, even ridicule, the ethics of care that a truly relational and embodied version of ethnography requires.[23] While I am nowhere close to recognizing and challenging the many ways that I might still uphold patriarchal masculinist values in my everyday life, a project that I know will continue till the end of my life, what I can say with clarity is that thinking with a feminist ethic of care while inhabiting a body assigned male at birth makes me nervous, especially as I become ever more aware of my own tendency toward valorizing hypermasculinist praxis and confront my own embodied (dis)abilities as central to how I can do my work.[24]

Here nervous ethnography takes its call from what Sara Ahmed has termed "the sweaty concept." For Ahmed, "sweat is bodily; we might sweat during more strenuous and muscular activity. A sweaty concept might come out of bodily experience that is trying. The task is to stay with the difficulty, to keep exploring and exposing this difficulty. . . . Sweaty concepts are also generated by the practical experience of coming up against a world, or the practical experience of trying to transform a world."[25] The task, as Ahmed has outlined here, is to be courageous enough to reveal those messy and vulnerable moments that made us sweat but also helped us to get closer to where we want to go personally and politically. Indeed, Ahmed is signaling to us that we are likely to have gone wrong, to have reproduced a politically unequal world in our research, when we feel too comfortable, when something resonates too quickly with us, or when our fieldwork somehow gives us too much pleasure or validates our worldview.

For me, sweaty concepts emerge when we, in the words of Bianca Williams, practice a "radical honesty" that renders us exposed, uncomfortable, and even ashamed as we push ourselves and our ideas in novel, politically grounded directions.[26] Nervous ethnography and sweaty concepts demand, as John L. Jackson Jr. has written, that we recognize that "the anthropologist is always a political actor in the everydayness of her practice (in a way that demands unpacking and explicit articulation) each and every time she sits at a community board meeting, watches a local rally, or asks the most idle of clarifying questions. The unit of analysis is not the anthropologist but instead the collision she is a part of—whether intended or not."[27]

All these collisions and the nerves they beget aren't meant to be set aside, nor should they freeze us, leaving us in a neurasthenic state. Nor are they supposed to become self-referential, a form of navel-gazing that keeps us so focused on who we are and what we are feeling that we forget that our job is to provoke difficult, politically transformative conversations. Our nervousness is supposed to produce in us a heightened sense of care as we reckon with how our positions shape what we can say about the social world, for better or for worse.[28] When we feel nervous, we must stop and try to figure out *why* we feel so damn nervous, and what might be analytically useful in these nervous encounters.

And then we might ask: What does all our nervousness generate? How do our nerves get us to care anew?

On Complicity

A nervous ethnography requires us to construct studies that hinge on an exploration of our complicity. Complicity makes us sweat because it forces us to acknowledge that the capital we've accrued has come at the expense of others.[29] Complicity requires that we cast aside our conceit of innocence, and, even more nerve-racking, it requires that we tell the story in a way that reveals our potential culpability.[30] A nervous ethnography, then, exposes the lost parts of us, when we misspoke or stayed silent, what that says about us and, only then, what that says about the world we are exposing in our texts. A nervous ethnography reveals more than we want to because we realize it is our ethical obligation to write about the power inequities we know best, because we benefit from them. In this sense, and in this sense only, nervous ethnography is an act of love that contributes to our liberatory impulses.

I have written elsewhere that it frustrates me to no end that we have so few white people who study their complicity in ongoing projects of white supremacy, and in anthropology we have very few people willing and able to study whiteness at all.[31] But when one thinks with nervous ethnography, it becomes obvious that these studies don't exist because such studies might implicate family and friends, because these studies feel too uncomfortable and do not allow for the psychic calming that comes with the belief (however constructed) that the people who are under our gaze are far away from who we are. Whether or not we eventually render "the strange familiar," it's the very notion that the strange is located elsewhere that traffics in "imperial pleasure," makes the research somehow more exciting and exotic, and short-circuits a reckoning with complicity, and therefore nerves.[32] In fact, for all the talk of reflexivity in anthropology, I rarely hear a story of why white people decide to study in China, or India, or Guatemala, or Sudan, even though these places seem so far from who they are. I've learned that these conversations don't happen because they would reveal that these people are complicit in our system of global racial capitalism, which, in turn, might mean they lose some of their capital in the process.[33] This is what allows the broader infrastructure of coloniality to remain comfortably hidden in anthropology (and many other fields as well), even now.

But I have also realized that the critique of the white anthropologist is also a kind of short-circuiting that has allowed too many like me to hide our complicity and therefore keep our nerves from jangling out of control. This study, as I have noted, is about a brown, transnational, savarna class of Indians who emerge as the brown savior—a class of Indians who are very much like myself. The academy in India and the academy in the United States are also both dominated by folks like me and the brown saviors in my study, brahmins and other savarnas whose dominant caste position translates into economic and social capital in both contexts.[34] We even have an entire wing of postcolonial studies that might be understood, at least in one sense, as the project of the brahmin intellectual elite romantically excavating the history of their feelings of loss vis-à-vis the white colonizer.[35] When savarna anthropologists have focused their gaze on India, they have either neglected conversations on caste entirely or presented findings that perpetuate the myth that caste is pertinent only in relation to the caste oppressed.[36] Rarely have savarnas come under deep anthropological study as savarnas, especially not by savarna anthropologists.[37] Instead, when savarnas have been studied by savarna anthropologists, they have most often been characterized through their urban, cosmopolitan, middle-class, linguistic positions, which reflect their caste position but are not called out as such. The continued and persistent critique of savarnas has been left to anticaste intellectuals, especially Dalit and Muslim intellectuals from the subcontinent and its diaspora, who, in most cases, already inhabit far more precarious locations in the academy. In so doing, many savarna scholars in the United States (and in the United Kingdom and in India and wherever else savarna scholars rest their heads) have short-circuited their complicity and trafficked in a narrative centered on their oppression as "post-colonized scholars" without dealing with the far more difficult task of understanding their role in maintaining global caste and white supremacy.[38] This truth might make it easy to "be frozen in guilt" because being a caste traitor is a much more difficult and nerve-racking task, a never-ending process of recognizing the new ways that one traffics in the same old forms of neocolonial savarna capital.[39]

On the Allure of and Repulsion to Brown Saviorism

To be quite honest, even the inception of this project is a story of brown savarna capital. In 2011, while a grad student, I, along with a colleague of mine, was approached by two men working for one of the biggest NGOs in India. They had come to the University of Pennsylvania to recruit people to help in the job of reforming Indian education. When we met, the two leaders were incredibly cordial and charismatic; they were well spoken, respectful, and ready to talk about the issues facing India. I was drawn to their stories about changing India, about *us* being keys to this change. "Come back and join us, we want you back there," they told us, almost matter-of-factly. I was intrigued, felt immediately connected to what these two savarna men were saying, and was uncritically flattered that they would think of me.

I had never, up till that point, had much interest in conducting research in India. I had gone to graduate school after being a ninth-grade teacher in New York City and was at the time more interested in studying the systemic inequities of the US education system than anything going on in India.[40] In fact, when I look back, it might be better to say that I was actually resistant to doing any work in India, as I had spent much of the fifteen years prior scrubbing India from my brain.

Up until the age of twelve, I lived an easy, middle-class savarna life in Northern California, part of one of the many savarna families who migrated to the Bay Area in the wake of Silicon Valley's technological explosion. While many of these families had moved to areas with large Indian and Asian populations, my family had moved to a town that was more than 85 percent white. Perhaps the sheer whiteness of the place produced a nervousness in my parents, because they were especially anxious to immerse me in "my culture," which amounted to a reproduction of brahmin life at home. At the time, I did not recognize the cultural norms I was being inculcated into as caste culture; however, that was indeed what it was.[41] These days I recognize myself as an embodied reminder that caste does not vanish in the United States. Instead, it travels with us, no matter how much some of those within our ranks would like that not to be so.[42] Mine, like that of so many savarna-born children of those who came to the United States in the 1980s and 1990s, was an incredibly privileged journey.[43] At the time, however, I was more interested in trying to find a way out from all my phenotypic and migratory difference, struggling just to deal with my place in a school that was clearly not made for a brown boy like me.

All that changed radically when my father took his own life just before my thirteenth birthday. Besides all the anxiety and nervousness produced by this kind of adolescent trauma, the effect of my father's suicide on my life was a form of extreme compartmentalization that necessarily meant keeping my work life safely away from everything having to do with family and home. The less people knew, the better for me. I could hide in plain sight and not have to face their looks of pity or shock. It also meant a disidentification with my father and therefore, in an almost cruel way, a disidentification with so many of the things that I identified with myself. India was one of those things. It is why I eliminated so much—language, religion, music, film, relationships—and why India is almost like a trigger for my most visceral nervousness.

While I am extremely proud of how my family and I have overcome, grown stronger and closer, and found many different kinds of meaning in the wake of our loss, the truth is that my ability to disidentify and find comfort in a brown America that was *not* savarna was itself a by-product of my caste capital, especially in the way it allowed me to grasp on to elite institutions of higher education for upward mobility despite all that was happening inside. My own trauma also allowed me to conveniently sidestep my own complicity in caste, race, and class oppression by cocooning myself in my own pain, a problem that I have only begun to truly understand and excavate.

At the same time, my instinctive and undoubtedly masculinist response to trauma has been an intense, hidden need to control: to control my environment, my time, my balance. Part of my compulsion to control has been a public image that performs a calculated form of eagerness and ease that hides any sign of emotional discontent. My writing, too, suffers from this need to control. Indeed, many may read this text—one founded on nervousness—and wonder why it might feel so controlled, even calculated and confident. But this is perhaps the point: nervousness is at once about living in a fraught world, being unable to control any of it, and struggling still to find some means of attaining balance and stability. My technique for coping with my nerves has been to hold on to the possibility that I can mediate whatever meaning is taken from this text in order to shield myself from what is to come. All this despite the fact that I know that these words will spill far beyond anything I can imagine, based on all the nervous energy of my readers. It takes a lot of nerve to write about our nerves.

This kind of contradictory trauma narrative and trauma response is not so unique in the brown world. In fact, I have heard so many brown folks tell me tales of trauma, anxiety, and nervousness that I have come to think of these affects as constitutive of the sense of brown. As Moon Charania notes, "Brown is a site of tactile anxiety lodged in sensation." This tactile anxiety is a result of a racialized contradiction "that creates unsettlement, discomfort. . . . Brown tells its own story, many stories, too many stories from too many places, spaces, geographies, and temporalities. Brown demands a border (even as it dissolves it), a nation (even as it leaves it), a moment of sovereignty (even as it renders it porous)."[44] Over time, I, like many of those who live under the sign of brown, have come to realize that these kinds of brown nerves can also unleash an intense sort of critical self-reflection, opening up space for unexpected solidarities and futures rendered otherwise

But for all my supposed nervous disidentification, control, and critical self-reflection, when these two savarna men from India asked me to come back, the entirety of my past came flooding forth again, maybe even flooded back with more force because of how long I had striven to erase it, and I immediately enjoyed the feeling of savarna paternal comfort that they were signaling could be mine. Perhaps what I saw in these folks who came to ask me to "go back and help" was that alternative path my life might have taken, one that might have led me back to India as a savior. It's certainly not that hard to imagine. Most of my extended family work in engineering, medicine, or finance, living the prototype of savarna-born Indian diasporic life. Many of them talk about going back to India to help the less fortunate, and a few have enthusiastically done so. And beyond my family, I know so many savarna-born Indian Americans, from California and elsewhere in the United States, who are ready to head back to India with their "marketable skills" to help those less fortunate than themselves. In another dimension, I, too, might have become one of these brown saviors, doubling down on the possibility of using my own skills to better the lives of those who were assumed to be ever so slightly like me.

Even in *this* dimension, as this project unfolded, there were many moments when I succumbed to the path of brown saviorism.[45] For example, I have noted already that even though I was supposed to have been studying the practices of the NGO Sahaayaka, my savarna instincts led me to work with those in rural India instead. The work of teaching in Adavisandra started as an unintended project in saviorism before changing as I was forced to reckon with all those in the school who refused my explanations for how and why I was there. Perhaps I might have completely succumbed to the compulsion to undertake brown saviorist research but for many people during my journey who stopped me and pointed out that I might be missing the point entirely and exacerbating harm. These included my students, teachers, friends, family, and colleagues, all of whom were able to see what was right in front of me and criticized that I was trying to fashion an alternative, more comfortable argument out of what should have been a story of brown saviorism. To all of you (and you know who you are), I say thank you once again.

These kinds of humbling, uncomfortable learnings have translated my nervousness into a form of critical engagement, reframing how I understood the rhetoric of folks like those NGO personnel who came to meet me during graduate school. I became intensely nervous about the insinuations attached to my body—my skin, my blood, my caste, my class, my professional skills—as a potential commodity in this help economy. And, over time, I have realized that it was precisely by following my nerves that I was able to identify all the sweaty concepts that have set the foundation of this project.

Most important, all this sweat and nervousness has led me to new ways of understanding my earliest encounters with Sahaayaka leadership, opening up conceptual space that foregrounds the complex raced, casteized, and gendered labor stratifications that emerged as brown saviors conducted their work. I turn to these complexities in the introduction to this book.

Introduction: Brown Saviorism

Racial capitalism—which is to say all capitalism—is a relation . . . that continues to depend on racial practice and racial hierarchy . . . and capitalism won't stop being racial capitalism if all the white people disappear from the story.
—RUTH WILSON GILMORE, in *Geographies of Racial Capitalism*, dir. Kenton Card

Poverty is not an effect of the brown world. The brownness of the world is partially known through the poverty that partially engulfs it.—JOSÉ ESTEBAN MUÑOZ, *The Sense of Brown*

India is not yet a nation. . . . Ambedkar has presciently observed that each caste is a nation in itself as each caste has its own caste-consciousness that did not help to form a fellowship of national feeling.—SURAJ YENGDE, *Caste Matters*

Sometimes an ethnographic project springs to life during the most mundane of social interactions. I had decided to attend Sahaayaka's monthly board meeting in Bangalore, India. There I was, half-listening, sometimes doodling in my notebook, and trying my best to glean something useful from the proceedings.

I had traveled to Bangalore, the "Silicon Valley of India," to study the practices of Sahaayaka, an education NGO that, at that time, was working in over fifty thousand rural schools in Karnataka state. Sahaayaka is part of the massive proliferation of NGOs in India over the past thirty years, what some have termed the *NGOization* of the voluntary sector. As the Indian state enacted ever more stringent forms of market fundamentalism after its liberalization in the late 1980s, the voluntary sectors—especially education and health care—increasingly saw the rise of the NGO. As of 2015, there were over three million

NGOs working in India, up from two million in 2009 and only twelve thousand in 1988. India now has the largest number of NGOs in the world, double the number of schools and 250 times the number of hospitals.[1]

Sahaayaka's programming centered on a whole slew of motivational techniques for children in rural schools. For example, Sahaayaka's fieldworkers, called *mentors*, would give motivational lectures about the need to do well in school and hand out small gifts and prizes—pencils, stickers, notebooks—if students reached preset goals for attendance, cleanliness, testing, grades, and the like. However, in the past five years Sahaayaka had increasingly been integrating new digital tools, data analytics strategies, funding initiatives, and partnerships with state governments into its organizational strategy.

At the board meeting, Sahaayaka's leaders were discussing how to improve their motivational programming and better help Indian rural children, whom they had determined were "the least looked after." The rhetoric of "looking after" kept ringing nervously in my mind when I first spied these words on Sahaayaka's website and heard the phrase repeated during the board meeting. It felt too paternalistic and too neocolonial. It seemed to reinforce many of the most intransigent global framings—in text, image, and film—of rural peoples as helpless, without agency, and in need of saving. Yet, in the postneoliberal era, these ideologies had been revised to imagine that this paternalistic form of care would produce hyperindustrious, entrepreneurial agents whose resilience and hard work would supposedly benefit them, their communities, the nation, and the global economy writ large. The juxtaposition of "motivation" with "looking after" therefore seemed to do the work of both reentrenching the importance of those who were doing the "looking after" and also signaling the responsibility of the marginalized to uplift themselves by shifting their "unproductive" emotional states.[2]

Despite my own misgivings, the crew of other people at the helm of this meeting were enthusiastically moving forward with the discussion. Sitting to my left was Krish, the CEO of Sahaayaka, a Kannada brahmin who had spent almost thirty years in the United States working in the technology sector before selling his company to join this education NGO.[3] Across from me sat Ajay, a Sahaayaka funder and global venture capitalist, a Kannada brahmin whose ownings included a vegan coffee shop in Bangalore and a resort on the outskirts of the city; and Srinivasan, Sahaayaka's founder, a Tamil brahmin whose forty-year career as a chemical engineer saw him traveling between India, the United States, Germany, and Brazil and who now spent half his time in the United States visiting his two children and grandchildren, who lived there permanently.[4]

Besides Sahaayaka's all-male leadership, there were three savarna, brown, diasporic personnel from a global development advisory organization founded in New York City that Sahaayaka had hired to conduct an impact assessment of the NGO. Gaurav, the head of the group and the "regional director of Asia," was joined by two diasporic Indian women: Shivani, a University of Pennsylvania graduate who was also a Teach for India alumna, and Sweta, a Yale graduate who formerly worked for JP Morgan Chase and traveled back and forth between Mumbai and San Francisco, which was closer to her hometown of Irvine.[5] Everyone spoke English with one another, and the ideas and concepts they deployed were all part of the most generic technocorporatist sensibility. Terms like "added value" were thrown around during the meeting to describe how the impact of an intervention should be assessed, while partnering with business schools, for example, the University of Pennsylvania's Wharton School of Business, was seen as a necessary asset.

At the time, I did not think much about *who* I was seeing in the room, perhaps because I was too much like those powerful people sitting all around me. I, too, am a savarna Indian American who has many relatives and friends doing similar types of help work. Being "too familiar" can sometimes prevent us from noticing that which is right in front of our eyes, especially when this familiarity is tied to capital.

Who, Exactly, Is in the Room? The Brown Savior
Is in the Room

Now, as I look back, there was and is something quite striking in the fact that those who were doing this help work were all "brown" people from the global savarna class.[6] Moreover, during the entire meeting, there seemed to be a clear, if implicit, assumption that everyone in the room had a special "primordial" knowledge of how to save those in rural communities in India, even if many of us had spent the majority of our lives in the United States or the United Kingdom. In fact, when I initially began fieldwork, many of the members of Sahaayaka justified their work along these lines, especially through blood talk. They even sometimes remarked that I was justified in my research because "it was in my blood," assuming that I, as a savarna diasporic Indian, had a racial tie to the Indian nation-state even though I had been born and brought up in the United States. My own silence and complicity in these kinds of "hemopolitical" arguments made me increasingly nervous, and initially I averted my analytic gaze, hoping that active neglect would calm me.[7] Eventually, however, I began to understand that these moments were the grist of my ethnography and that I would need to follow my nerves, no matter how difficult, if I was to figure out what was happening in the board meeting and how to understand the particular racializing processes that were unfolding in and through these help interventions. Over time, I began to develop a method of *nervous ethnography*, and with it I began to understand these hemo-political sentiments as a kind of racial compulsion that was driving global help work. At the very least, these hemo-political justifications, sometimes made explicit and sometimes not, served as part of a global racial common sense, a perception that fused "particular bodily traits, social configurations (national, religious, etc.), and global regions, in which human difference is reproduced as irreducible and unsublatable."[8]

In reality, how similar were the people at the board meeting to those they felt compelled to save? All of them were brahmins who had either grown up in the brahmin enclaves in South India before spending most of their young adulthoods learning, living, and working in the United States *or* been born and brought up in the United States as middle-class suburbanites. These groups, however different they might be, share racialized caste, class, and transnational linkages that place them within the growing global brown savarna class.[9] In contrast, the students these Sahaayaka personnel worked with in rural Karnataka were the children of relatively poor farmers whose ways of living were slowly being decimated as the city of Bangalore swallowed up its rural peripheries and as the privatization of education rendered government schools ever more devalued. Their lives, hopes, and experiences differed radically from anything that these Sahaayaka leaders knew while growing up with caste capital in India and were certainly far removed from what they learned while accruing more capital as brown elites in the United States.

Those who attended the Sahaayaka meeting were not exceptional cases. In fact, they epitomize the figure of the *brown savior*, part of a growing complex of savarna elites who are trying to use the social and monetary capital they have accrued during their time living, learning, or working abroad to start and run organizations that are intended to help those they see as less fortunate, most often in India but also sometimes in the rest of the postcolonized brown world. These actors have taken on a critical role in the reconstructed *help economies*, a term I use to describe the intersection of humanitarianism, development, and poverty-alleviation efforts.

Over the past fifty years, the question "Who is in the room?" has become one of the key representational vectors on which global multicultural, late liberal social change agendas have been constituted, assuming that those inhabiting particular racialized positions will solve the problem of global inequality by their very presence in positions of decision-making power regardless of their class position, political interests, or specific training and skills.[10] In particular, the help industries have sought to replace white people with people "of color" as a primary strategy by which to rectify the historical legacy of colonial racial capitalism's structuring of help in the Global South. If at one time the *who* of help relied on white/Other, West/East, First World/Third World, Global North/Global South binaries, these new actors seem to subvert these premises.[11] Instead, part of their ability to do this kind of help work relies on their historical relation to those nation-states on the wrong side of the global "color-line."[12] For example, Sahaayaka leadership did not seem to carry the baggage associated with Western-led development efforts in the Global South simply because they were brown, not white, even though, as I show, they reproduce and uphold many of the same racialized values and ideologies associated with *who* and *how* to help that have been passed down from the colonial period into the late liberal capitalist period.

In Sahaayaka's case, this racial dupe intersected with the history of brahmin and savarna ascension during the post/colonial period, during which caste-based exclusions and complicities produced a unique form of postcolonial racial and caste (read: white-brahminical) capitalism that influenced their particular strategies of help. As such, the NGO leaders I am discussing here emerge at the nexus of two intersecting processes of racialization: one associated with racist global developmentalism and white saviorism and the other associated with a distinct form of racialized casteism in India.

Savarna Technoracial Labor Capacity
in the Wake of Fascism

Sahaayaka's brown saviors did not explicitly consider or question any of the historical and systemic conditions that produced their ability to be in the room and enact change in the way they imagined. In fact, even though none of them had any experience or training in the help economies or the education sector, their interest in and ability to work in these contexts were built on a presumption of their "merit," the neoliberal ideal that sees individual success as based exclusively on intellectual capability and "hard work" rather than the accumulation of racial, gender, or caste capital.[13]

Even as they neglected any discussion of their own position as beneficiaries of systemic inequity in India and the United States, everyone in the room was excitedly encouraging Sahaayaka to change its interventions from the kinds of face-to-face encounters led by fieldworkers to a new phone app platform that Krish had been developing over the past year. Through the app Sahaayaka fieldworkers could log student data in a central database, allowing the organization to collect and aggregate student and school data, such as attendance and test scores. Krish was bringing his organization—and the education and voluntary sectors more generally—into the big data and data analytics revolution, the newest iteration in a long line of neocolonial technocratic methods by which to quantitatively "categorize," "predict," and "save" the world.[14]

Technological interventions had several advantages for Sahaayaka leadership. First, digital tools have been overvalued in the current global racial capitalist order, dividing the haves from the have-nots. Within this global regime of value, the digital has been seen as a kind of panacea for the rectification of social evils of all sorts, and therefore Sahaayaka knew that funding would accompany technological interventions. Second, these technological interventions were perceived as "neutral," apolitical, universal solutions to India's problems, and therefore Sahaayaka could make a moral claim to changing the entire system without having to get into the messy politics of position, history, or capital. This perceived neutrality and universality also had the added benefit of allowing Sahaayaka to imagine its interventions as useful *beyond* India in the future. Third, technological interventions played to the Sahaayaka leadership's strengths as former engineers, whose prowess with these tools has been perceived as a preternatural *racial* capacity of the savarna castes, especially brahmins. As I explain in more detail in chapter 2, Sahaayaka's leadership had benefited from a colonial and postcolonial history that had allowed brahmins to take on roles in the technology sectors.[15] At the same time, these digital capacities were perceived as "in their blood," allowing them to take special and central positions in the help economies.

Critically, between 2013, when I started my fieldwork, and 2018, when I conducted the last phase of my fieldwork, many NGOs came under attack after the rise of the far-right Hindutva (Hindu nationalist) regime led by Narendra Modi.[16] Specifically, the government was targeting international NGOs that they claimed were working at odds with state economic development goals by pointing out the government's human rights abuses.[17] In addition, the Hindutva state has systematically sought to attack those journalists, activists, and organizations that are seen as too liberal, too left, and too secular. In fact, terms like *liberal* and *secular* have begun to collapse distinct groups—left activists, anticaste organizers, protesters against anti-Muslim racism, technocrats, NGO workers, government officials who refuse to allow the constitutional system to collapse—under the weight of the constant hostility from a right-wing cadre who deploy these terms as pejoratives for any group that disagrees with them.[18]

Moreover, the Hindutva state has implied that any of these forms of dissent are at the behest of the "West" and are meant solely to delegitimize India's attempts to gain economic power and/or find pride in the "cultural" practices of Hindus after years of colonization.[19] In other words, the Hindutva state has appropriated the rhetoric of anticolonial struggle to justify its authoritarian policies, including its repression of human rights groups, activists, and critical NGOs. In fact, some within the right-wing cadre use the pejorative *brown sepoy* to castigate those who criticize the Hindutva state, insinuating that such people may have "brown skin" but are actually merely puppets for their white colonial masters.[20] In turn, this has made any critique that focuses on the secular, the liberal, or even the neoliberal tenuous, as many fear that these critiques will only further the Hindutva agenda and be appropriated by supremacists as further proof of the inadequacies of secular, liberal, and constitutional politics in India.

I myself have struggled to maintain a balance between sustained critique of actors who for the most part fall into the category of "liberal" and "secular" and the recognition that in the current climate in India such critique could be misused. Even the small possibility of my work being taken up by the right wing makes me *extremely* nervous. However, part of my project in this text is to show the continuities between late liberal political orders and the rise of fascist autocracy. As such, I have found solace in those scholars who teach that the potential for right-wing appropriation cannot and should not deter critiques of late liberal society, especially given the way that late liberalism, as the past ten years has made clear, can and does feed into fascism intentionally or unintentionally (even as it is seen as its opposite). Undertaking this type of study requires (1) a recognition and careful tracing of the specific ways that colonial forms of governance and valuation have transmuted in the late liberal capitalist autocratic period *and* (2) a specificity to the "liberal" institutions and the secular actors under study.[21]

In this case, my critique focuses specifically on the institutional politics of an Indian education NGO with US economic, political, and cultural linkages, which serves as a very specific form of liberal intervention with extremely unique implications vis-à-vis the rise of the Hindutva state. For example, during the early period of Hindutva ascension (2014–19), Sahaayaka actually prospered, expanding into more schools, creating partnerships with states beyond Karnataka and even beyond India, implementing its digital intervention strategy, and accruing more funding from donor agencies. This was at least in part because Sahaayaka's particular version of "liberal" intervention did not challenge state ideologies at all: it was an NGO populated by those who were perceived as "native" Indians, who effectively "browned" neocolonial technocratic development strategies even as they maintained strategically useful transnational connections to the United States. In fact, by 2018, shortly after the Bharatiya Janata Party (BJP) regime initiated the Digital India campaign, with its rabid emphasis on digitized solutions for India's future change, Sahaayaka would be hailed by Karnataka state and in India's national news media as the future "IT backbone" of Karnataka's education system. In this way, the nation-state was able to mask its fascist visions by leaning into a seemingly altruistic, apolitical, nativist technophilia.

In sum, let me emphasize once again that my exploration of Sahaayaka serves as a reminder *not* to view far-right fascist elements as somehow de facto in opposition to the secular/(neo)liberal subjects that fill the majority of the pages that follow. Instead, as I return to many times over the course of this text, the project of brown saviorism in India required the characters in this story to make pragmatic and fatal pacts in order to garner funding, expand, and intervene, which, however well intentioned, may have facilitated the very fascist projects that, on the surface, they were purportedly against.

On the "Primordial" and Feminized Labor
of the Surplus Fieldworker

All the talk of technological innovation and integration during the board meeting was especially jarring for me, given that my day-to-day travels seemed to have very little to do with anything that the people in the room were discussing. Just the day before, I had traveled some forty kilometers south from Bangalore to the village of Adavisandra with Suresh, one of Sahaayaka's fieldworkers, to visit a rural school. I had followed Suresh on many past occasions as he drove his motorcycle from school to school, cultivating in children a desire to pass their exams, to learn, to aspire, or even just to raise their hands when they were curious.

Nearly all the Sahaayaka mentors had family who worked in Karnataka as farmers, mostly from the Lingayat and Vokkaliga castes (Karnataka's traditional agricultural landed-gentry castes). In fact, one striking and important revelation of my work was the extent to which Sahaayaka's organizational structure actually only reproduced a historically situated gradation of caste laborers in South India, with brahmin elites at the top, followed by Vokkaliga and Lingayat fieldworkers at lower rungs of the organization, with very few Dalits and *no* Muslims in the organization at all. This fact was especially striking given that Karnataka's Muslim population is at least 12 percent, and the

Scheduled Caste population is at least 18 percent, both numbers that are higher than either the Vokkaliga (8 percent) or Lingayat (9 percent) populations.[22]

The fieldworkers came from a spectrum of class backgrounds, primarily because some of their families owned land while others did not. However, Suresh's cachet as a fieldworker was tethered to his perceived "primordial" knowledge of his native home and therefore the expectation that he had a special ability to connect with rural students because of a shared linguistic and cultural identity. This is why, at least initially, the mentors were the integral connection between Sahaayaka's headquarters in Bangalore city and the rural areas in which they worked.

But Suresh also saw his work in Sahaayaka as part of his own aspiration for economic mobility in the wake of India's massive urbanization and agricultural dispossession. Bangalore city, for example, has increased its population by over three times in thirty years, from 4 million in 1990 to over 12 million in 2020, while also growing threefold in physical size in the past twenty years. With Bangalore's expansion, those in its agricultural peripheries who once believed they could count on joining their traditional family occupations could no longer be so sure. Suresh felt the strain of all this change, especially because he had seen so many from his community left jobless. Where was all this surplus labor to go? For Suresh, the answer, as I discuss further in chapter 1, had been to join an NGO.

Suresh felt uncomfortable at the board meeting. He was the only mentor who had been invited to the proceedings and was very much at the periphery of the action despite the fact that he was at the center of interventions at these rural school sites. Even though he spoke five languages, English was by far the one in which he was least adept, and he strained to understand what was being said. From time to time, he asked me to clarify what he had heard, and then he would shake his head in exasperation when he fully comprehended what was being proposed.

On reflection, Suresh would tell me that he felt as if he had been considered valuable *only* for his supposed local-specific "authentic" knowledge as a son of a Vokkaliga farmer, limiting what his perceived capabilities were, what he might aspire for, and what positions he could hold in the organization.[23] Even when he was struggling to make ends meet, Suresh was expected *not* to be driven by economic aspirations because his work was seen as a form of community uplift that might be corrupted by any individual ambitions. This moral prerogative differed substantially from how the brown savior's moral ambitions were justified, even though both were supposedly helping their "kin." In the case of the mentors, their kin connection was no longer lucrative because, unlike the globality of the brown savior, their perceived skills and knowledge were inextricably linked to their knowledge of rural land and set the frame for the kind of affective labor they were expected to do.

Importantly, these racialized caste capacities for affective labor were also situated within a system of patriarchal capitalism, masculinizing the technocratic "rational" digital work of the brown savior while feminizing the relational, affective work of the mentor, rendering it less valuable and less translatable into monetary terms. This is why, whether or not brown saviors were assigned male at birth, in all the cases I observed, they reproduced masculinist values regarding technical capacity and patriarchal heteronormative hierarchies of labor value. At the same time, the feminizing of the labor of mentors was happening even as roles traditionally held by women were being replaced by this largely male NGO labor force. Indeed, Suresh's story pivots on Sahaayaka's organizational setup, which relied on the hiring of almost exclusively men, effectively invisibilizing the women who produce so much of the labor associated with traditional social reproduction (nurturing, caregiving, teaching, and the like). The few women mentors who joined Sahaayaka found themselves with even less possibility of upward mobility than mentors like Suresh.

One of Suresh's closest colleagues, Lakshmi, for example, had fought against the constraints of widowhood within the cultural politics of brahminical patriarchy in village Karnataka to achieve her position with Sahaayaka. She was now the sole breadwinner in her household in a village thirty kilometers south of Bangalore, taking care of her two elderly parents and providing for her nieces and nephews. Lakshmi, like Suresh, had imagined that working for Sahaayaka would be a stepping stone to further upward mobility rather than an end to her aspirational possibilities. However, as I discuss further in chapter 8, Lakshmi struggled to maintain her role in Sahaayaka given that, unlike Suresh, she was not able to drive a motorcycle up and down the rural hinterlands of Karnataka or into Bangalore city because of concerns for her perceived safety while on the road and instead had to take the bus, which limited both her ability to work at Sahaayaka's Bangalore headquarters and her exposure to Sahaayaka's leadership.[24]

But what irritated Suresh and Lakshmi the most was how quickly they were being pushed aside as Sahaayaka continued to integrate digital tools into their educational interventions. In their own framing of their situation, Suresh and Lakshmi expressed frustration and critiqued the fetishizing of these forms of digital labor that so profoundly influenced their perceived capacity to help. Regardless of how these new technologies were framed by the brown savior, Suresh and Lakshmi were certain that they were only incurring the wrath of the technological gadget. If they were to use any of these new technologies, they would merely input data based on the scripts they were given rather than learn how to use these technologies creatively. Whether explicitly stated or not, this capacity for technological work was not perceived as "in their blood," reinscribing a racialized caste hierarchy of labor: the brahmin transnational hailed for his intellectual and technical capacities as brown savior; the Vokkaliga agriculturalist recognized as useful for her bodily capacity and connection to the land as fieldworker.[25]

When I would reflect on this particular relation, I could not help but feel the shadows of the traditional colonial "native informant," whose role was almost entirely rooted in the binary opposition to the affective capacities expunged from the "technical," distanced, rational colonial master.[26] Yet now these colonial racialized relations were being reproduced within a global caste order in India, one that linked the "global" brown savior to the rural mentor. In this sense, Sahaayaka's praxis perpetuated a neocolonial form of stratification that allowed those with technical skills to accrue excess global value at the expense of all those people who performed the relational forms of affective labor that were necessary for organizations like Sahaayaka to subsist and grow in the first place.

Over the next few years, I continued to observe what was happening to Sahaayaka's fieldworkers, like Suresh and Lakshmi, in Bangalore and its peripheries, spending time in village schools across the region, while also meeting the Sahaayaka leadership when they were in Bangalore and in the United States: in, for example, Palo Alto, California; Boston, Massachusetts; and Philadelphia, Pennsylvania. In the juxtaposition between my urban-rural travels and transnational meetups, I began to see new theoretical starting points for my project. I started to understand what was happening in India's help economies in ways that moved beyond a reductive nationalist frame and instead situated these efforts within the current system of global racial and caste capitalism.

On the Racial Capitalist Politics of Brownness

For some, India and the savarna Indian subject might seem like a strange site for the study of *racial* capitalism, given that race as an analytic has rarely been associated with those from the subcontinent.[27] Part of the reason has been that critical analyses of race have been overdetermined by a "methodological nationalism" that focuses almost solely on the United States, and at best the Americas, and renders race "foreign" to places like India.[28] These boundaries have been reified through neocolonial academic disciplining and funding patterns that continue to neglect projects that transgress national borders to reckon with global racialized unfoldings and movements induced by colonialism that continue into the twenty-first century.[29] At the same time, the scholarship on postcolonialism in India, undertaken mostly by savarna scholars,[30] has focused on "the colonial wound" as an almost all-encompassing framework to understand postcolonial nation-building projects *without* incorporating a robust conversation on the ongoing impact of colonial racial categories on the subcontinent, especially as they intersect with caste in India.[31] As a corrective, I follow scholarship that takes seriously the colonial constitution of race and recognizes the continuities between the franchise colonial order and the racial dimensions of current inter- and intranational governing strategies, economic relations, and categories for differentiating populations.[32]

In particular, my study of global racial capitalism begins with W. E. B. Du Bois's classic insights in *Black Reconstruction in America*. While focusing on the historical potential of Black workers to bring about a worker-led democracy out of the violent plantation economies in the United States, Du Bois also understood that the freeing of labor was a global project. He wrote, "Out of the exploitation of the dark proletariat comes the Surplus Value filched from human beasts which, in cultured lands, the Machine and harnessed Power veil and conceal. The emancipation of man is the emancipation of labor and the emancipation of labor is the freeing of that basic majority of workers who are yellow, brown and black."[33] Du Bois's theorizing of surplus value and its extraction takes as a given that the primary labor force under colonial capitalism was "that dark and vast sea of human labor in China and India, the South Seas and all Africa; in the West Indies and Central America and in the United States."[34] In fact, for Du Bois, the so-called humanitarian impulses of the liberal West that were given by the colonizer as the reason for the abolition of the transatlantic slave trade (rather than the long and sustained rebellion of Black peoples in the Americas) actually propelled the exploitation of labor and the expropriation of land and resources across the world.[35]

In contemporary analysis, Du Bois's insights require that studies of labor focus on how specific peoples within the "dark proletariat" were and are produced and divided and come to occupy particular slots within global racial capitalist systems. Here I lean on Lisa Lowe's excellent characterization of racial capitalism, which suggests that "capitalism expands not through rendering all labor, resources, and markets across the world identical, but by precisely seizing upon colonial divisions, identifying particular regions for production and others for neglect, certain populations for exploitation and still others for disposal."[36] In Lowe's definition, colonial categories are always already racialized, linking particular bodies to a perceived (in)capacity for labor and therefore determining their potential exploitability and/or disposability.[37] In this sense, a study of racial capitalism captures specific dynamics related to the racialized stratifications of labor set in motion during the colonial period, including in places like India.

For me, placing *savior* in relation to *brown* opens up some of the contradictions associated with the quickly changing contours of the global racial capitalist stratification of labor as it relates to the help economies. While it is an underacknowledged aspect of the coloniality of power, colonial racial capitalism actually required an economy of salvation that demarcated racialized and gendered difference and hierarchy along the savior/saved binary. These racialized distinctions took on specific valences in the "brown world," which pivoted on questions of poverty and the regional distinctions that produced the (im)possibility for assimilation that continues to influence the trajectories of saviorism in these places. The racialized geographies of "brown" both set the conditions for ascension *and* occlude the operations of regionally specific forms of racialized power that produce brown saviors and their Others.

In fact, while I focus on the specific example of India and later show how current global racial orders occlude the operations of caste power in the Indian case, one of the most interesting phenomena I have noticed since beginning to write and speak on the brown savior is how many people from disparate places—Turkey, Pakistan, Algeria, Iran, Cuba, and Brazil (among many others)—find their own regionally specific versions of the brown savior. This is partially because the brown savior as analytic allows us to see how and why specific elite actors emerge from the postcolonized fold as those who are imagined to bring salvation even as others in the brown world remain "in need."

The particular racial descriptor *brown* has been used as part of the self-fashioning narratives of people from areas as disparate as Central and South America, the Caribbean, the Middle East, North Africa, and South Asia. Controversies over *brown*, especially with regard to *who* is brown, continue into the present primarily because the term is tethered to German, Spanish, Portuguese, British, and American strands of racist discourse that have brought much of the colonial world under their remit in contradictory ways.[38] As such, I draw from the work of Nitasha Tamar Sharma, who argues that understanding brownness requires us to follow the historical and political economic processes through which the category takes on racialized meanings.[39] As one example, in many parts of the Spanish and British postcolonial Caribbean, terms like *brown* and *browning* refer to the postplantation histories of miscegenation that resulted in a class of racially mixed peoples. Those who had undergone this process of browning sometimes found relative economic and political mobility within the Caribbean's colorist hierarchies that emerged out of the vagaries of violent colonial desire.[40]

By contrast, in the case I am concerned with, "brown" was first linked to India when late nineteenth- and early twentieth-century scientific racists began to include South Asians in the German color-based racial classifications of the late eighteenth century. This delineation as "brown" peoples became central to the self-fashioning narratives of savarna Indian elites as they began traveling beyond the confines of the Indian subcontinent during and after British colonialism.[41] In fact, because of the legacy of British colonialism and the ongoing emphasis on English education, terms like *brown* circulate quite often, especially in popular culture, and *brown* is an operative and expanding category both on the subcontinent and in the diaspora, especially (though not exclusively) among anglophiles.[42]

Despite these regional specificities and contradictions, because the coloniality of brownness impacted so many all over the world, it has connected these realms in imagined, if tenuous, ways. My conceptual framing of brownness draws, therefore, from the work of José Esteban Muñoz, who writes that "Brownness is vast, present, and vital. It is the ontopoetic state . . . of a majority of those who exist, strive, and flourish within the vast trajectory of multiple and intersecting regimes of colonial violence."[43] Muñoz is describing a capacious sense of brown that pivots on regionally specific, historically situated, yet affectively connected encounters with colonial and imperial power; the colonial wounds inflicted by these encounters; and the senses of self that emerge in and through these histories of encounter. Here brown is a racialized affective geography associated with the social, cultural, economic, and political "intimacies" of those living on continents touched by colonialism.[44] As one example from India, Jawaharlal Nehru, India's first prime minister, argued that "the brown, yellow and black races of Asia and Africa, [are] all hunched up more or less together. How far we of the last of these classes are from the heights where our rulers live."[45]

Brownness, in this conception, is not solely about phenotype, although that certainly is one dimension. Instead, I want to briefly evoke the idea of *brown blood* to bring focus to certain intimate dimensions of colonial racialization that are often overlooked and yet are constitutive of the sense of brown. One's blood is browned because of those intimate colonial encounters that create, in the words of Moon Charania, "unsettlement, discomfort . . . too close to dirt, mud, earth, shit, animals, nature" and too far below the heavenly racial purity associated with white colonizers.[46] In this sense, brown blood is the marker of distance "from the heights where our rulers live." However, unlike race-as-phenotype, race-as-blood evokes what is hidden, and therefore is exceptionally amorphous, easily mapping onto other markers of belonging along which global power operates, fixing unseen, yet predetermined, capacities for labor. The very invisibility of brown blood makes it so close, so intimate, so familiar and familial, so rigid, yet fluid, and so dangerous because of the potential that people might pass over to the other side unbeknownst. As I argue in chapter 2, my understanding of brown blood draws attention to the blood politics that began in the Old World, congealed in the New World, and continue to shape processes of racialization all over the postcolonized brown world.[47] In fact, as I discuss later in this introduction, these associations with brown blood are central to the purity/impurity politics of caste in contemporary India.

At the same time, within the current racial capitalist order, brown blood represents the possibility that the romantic ideas associated with assimilation might eventually come true. Here I am drawing directly from the work in anthropology that argues that midcentury discourses on racialization, especially in North America, sought to solve the problem of race through the romantic ideology of blood mixing that could, over time, "whiten" the blood of the body politic.[48] This ideology intersected with a global pedagogical assimilationist logic, most famously framed by British viceroy Thomas Macaulay, who in the 1830s endeavored "to form a class who may be interpreters between us and the millions whom we govern; a class of persons, Indian in blood and colour, but English in taste, in opinions, in morals, and in intellect."[49] That is to say, the inclusion of those with brown blood was actually intended to produce a global class of subjects who worked at the behest of white-colonial power. In this sense at least, brown blood is one way of making sense of the paradoxical position of those in the brown world who have ascended within (neo)colonial economies of salvation. I turn to some of these paradoxes in the next section.

On the Economies of Brown Salvation

As Nehru's statement earlier hints at, the postcolonized brown world was deeply enmeshed in the politics of saviorism, already seeing themselves as an underclass in need of development. Indeed, colonial racial capitalism required that the fetish of liberal modernity,[50] with its ideals of universal rights, technocracy, and the like, be tethered to a paternalistic "imperial initiative" that saw the colonized as not yet quite ready to govern themselves.[51] In this sense, the coloniality of power functioned by emplacing salvation as the never-achievable future potential for the brown colonized subject.[52]

These colonial roots of salvation found unique new forms in the post–World War II American reordering of things, in humanitarianism and development in particular, which initiated new powerful, capital-intensive international governing technologies. To justify outsider-led economic oversight of newly independent postcolonial nation-states, supranational organizations, like the United Nations, the International Monetary Fund (IMF), and the World Bank, further naturalized the rhetoric of impoverishment, intellectual incapacity, and civilizational lack through distinctions of developed/underdeveloped, Global North/Global South, and First World/Third World, thereby executing the trick of transmuting explicitly racist global discourses into cultural dog whistles and reifying the boundaries between saviors and those in need of saving.[53] In these conceptions, the discourse on poverty was an invention of the West meant at once to locate the problem in the postcolonized subject and also to erase the legacies of colonial exploitation/expropriation that had resulted in much of their lack. In this context, "the sense of brown," as Muñoz writes, is a racialized sign of economic and cultural impoverishment—*to be brown is to be poor; to be poor is to be brown*—and is marked by a flourishing despite the perceived deficiency and underdevelopment emplaced by (neo)colonial racial ordering.[54]

The Indian case is one stark example of the intransigent linkage between brownness and poverty. The British famously justified their rule in India and the extraction of its resources because of what they deemed extreme destitution and uncleanliness. The mark of abject impoverishment has continued ever since, with India continuously being characterized as one of the poorest and most unequal nations in the world. India's own 2012 Below Poverty Line benchmark places the number at 22 percent, a metric that has consistently been critiqued for arbitrarily lowering the perceived poverty rate while neglecting to address the massive increases in income and wealth inequality.[55] The poverty rate continues to be a brown smudge that cracks India's dreams of ascension to global superpower status. It is also a de facto justification for saviors who see themselves as having the appropriate skills to solve this problem once and for all.

Saviorist strategies continued to shift as part of the rise of neoliberal capitalism as the dominant mode of accumulation—which privatized social goods, facilitated the movement of elites, and saw a reentrenchment of inequality and protection of class power through mass militarization.[56] These reconfigurations also created the conditions for the major redeployment of financial resources to a growing circuit of capital, which I have characterized here as the *help economies*, producing niche markets that reproduced neocolonial racialized difference in order for funds to circulate and for interventions to be justified.[57] The rise of NGOs like Sahaayaka can be directly linked to this neoliberal rearrangement, which encouraged those elites from outside of the voluntary sectors to join and "fix" the social sectors.

These international rearrangements were linked to intranational unfoldings that had allowed certain classes of the previously colonized to take on central roles in the saviorist project. This class of global brown elites, drawn from the "old tyrants" of precolonization, was imagined as the inheritors of the project of salvation because they had appropriately assimilated into the ideology of modernity, liberal universalism, technocracy, and accumulation (what might be termed their "trickle-down" inheritance).[58] Frantz Fanon famously argued that elite colonized subjects sought to rectify their own feelings of deficiency by traveling to the metropole and imbibing the language, cultural norms, and values of the colonizer—that is, "they begin to speak like the white man" primarily because they understood that "you are rich because you are white, you are white because you are rich."[59] These brown elites were "deified" by those within their national contexts precisely because they had embraced the project of colonial modernity and therefore were expected to bring salvation to all their country people and, in some cases, to other postcolonized peoples perceived as "lower" on the racial hierarchy.[60]

In the Indian case, brown nationalist leaders were caste elites who had benefited from colonial rule, espoused colonial values, and made pacts with the colonizers to maintain their accumulative potential.[61] During the postindependence period, some of these figures—Nehru and the like—were deified as the fathers of the nation and undertook projects of "national development."[62] At the same time, these elites were sometimes criticized for their neocolonial developmentalist visions. For example, they were pejoratively called *brown sahibs* to denote their internalization of Western values, linked to a particular British education, English proficiency, and aspiration for civilizationalism.[63] The aforementioned brown sepoy updates the brown sahib figure by continuing to focus on elitism, English education (likely associated with the United States), and a supposed subservience to the West while suggesting these people are not authentically Indian enough and are, at best, misguided fools or, at worst, villainous traitors working against the rise of the Hindu state. These pejoratives foreground that "brown" as a shared neocolonial racial imaginary was fraught from its inception and continues to be so today.

Part of the operations of power that brown racialization masked was the fact that the promise of mobility and assimilation within white supremacist imperialism also required projects of brown expropriation rooted in anti-Blackness.

In this vein, Charania conceives of brownness as a peculiar and fraught *in-betweenness* in relation to both whiteness and Blackness.[64] She offers "brown-ness as a racial formation trapped in its own shifting specificities as one that, yes is 'coexistent, affiliates and intermeshes with Blackness' . . . but one that can also remain aloof toward, dismiss and extract from the global and diasporic field of blackness."[65]

Even during the postcolonial moment, the tense relationship between brownness and Blackness was already present in both its idealized form of solidarity and its fraught reinscription of racialized hierarchy. For example, the Asian-African (Bandung) Conference in 1955, for which Nehru was one of the primary organizers, was branded as the first significant attempt at creating solidarity across previously colonized countries in Africa and Asia. However, this particular attempt at global Afro-Asian solidarity was already enmeshed in racist and masculinist nation-building ideologies that relied on narratives that positioned Indian (and/or Asian) civilizations "above" African civilizations.[66] Famously, in one of the bulletins published during Bandung, the "brown man's burden" was enshrined as one articulation of the brown world's responsibility to help and support African nation-states along with exploited brown peoples from places like "Goa, Irian, Malaya, Guiana, and Cyprus."[67] Here the outlines of a specifically brown form of salvation began to take shape, imagining new spheres of influence in the formerly colonized world through which partic-ularly well-positioned brown peoples could consolidate their racial and eco-nomic power.[68]

However, unlike in this postcolonial version of brown racial in-betweenness, which remained grounded in the discourses on newly independent nation-states, in the case explored here the brown savior's rapid ascension sits at the nexus of the migratory patterns facilitated by the legacies of anticolonial strug-gle and the end of the Cold War, US multicultural imperialism, the rise of Third World superpowers, and the global connections forged in the digital age. This new racial capitalist order required a further reification of racialized dif-ference. Brown, as indexing a historical struggle against colonization and the fight against a perceived essential underdevelopment, inadequacy, and impov-erishment, does the work of "phenotypic [and blood type] homogenization."[69] This commodifiable form of brown a priori legitimates the brown savior as culturally authentic and therefore valuable, facilitating their power to deter-mine the course of salvation for "their communities" and other postcolonized ones as well.

The brown savior's value has been further enhanced in the global-digital age, when technological prowess has been linked to global ascension and has produced its own racialized politics. In fact, as I discuss extensively in part IV of this book, digital solutions are understood in mainstream discourse as morally superior, universal solutions that can be implemented anywhere in the world to solve the problem of global inequality.[70] This is why brown saviors chose digital projects as their method of salvation and why they were hailed within Indian nationalist discourses *and* in global ICT4D (Information Communication Technologies for Development) discourses.[71] In this sense, the brown savior's digital capacity provides further moral legitimacy and commodifiable value within the help economies.

As a result, the brown savior is a harbinger of a new global racial capitalist order that locates itself in the imaginary of a global transnational class, untethered from the racial topography of the West, who will purportedly sanitize late liberal global capitalism through their technological prowess. This new savior class is positioned to develop newly "browned" digital solutions to the problem of poverty while also supporting the fight against all those illiberal, "bad" brown Others deemed unassimilable. As I explore further in chapters 2 and 6, the US imperial war on terror intersected with the rise of Hindu supremacy in India to reinforce anti-Muslim racist ideologies. The false global perception of the "liberal Hindu" and the potentially "illiberal Muslim" shaped who the brown savior could be and what being a brown savior means for different religious groups on the subcontinent.[72]

As a reminder, India, and South Asia more broadly, is a place of immense regional, linguistic, ethnic, and migratory diversity, and there is a near-infinite number of ways to enter into the study of South Asian racialization. As a few examples, Sonja Thomas has analyzed the racialization of Syrian Christians in Kerala; Dolly Kikon has written on the racism experienced by northeasterners in relation to India's settler colonial regime; Mythri Jegathesan has located her study of Hill Country Tamils in Sri Lanka within the intersections of racial, gender, and caste histories of global "Coolitude"; Mariam Durrani has explored how Pakistani-origin youth negotiate the overlapping global histories of anti-Muslim racism; and E. Gabriel Dattatreyan has focused on the anti-Black racism experienced by African migrants in Delhi.[73] In migratory contexts, Vivek Bald has excavated the early migrations of Bengali Muslim sailors to the United States and their racialization upon arrival; Stanley Thangaraj has analyzed the racial politics of desi basketball players in the United States; Nishant Upadhyay has pointed out the complicity of the savarna diaspora in the North American settler colonial order; and Sareeta Amrute has revealed the racialized cognitive capacities that inhere in Indian bodies as they perform technocapitalist labor in Berlin.[74] Given my ethnographic context, I focus on the processes of brown racialization associated specifically with savarna Indians and their migrations to the United States, linked to their particular class and caste positions.[75] This particular form of brownness has become nearly hegemonic because of the immense capital accumulated by savarna Indian Americans and their ability to dictate the commodified form of brown that circulates globally. As such, in the case I present here, brownness should be understood in relation to specific processes of racialization associated with the global Indian "at the intersections of caste supremacy, brahmanism, coloniality, Islamophobia, and Hindu fundamentalism, all of which are calibrated through shifting capitalist political economies."[76]

On the Brown Occlusions of Caste

Commodified forms of brownness necessarily occlude other forms of racialized stratification that actually produce the brown subject's value. In the Indian case, this obfuscated form of value is related to their dominant caste positions. For example, Dalit feminist Thenmozhi Soundararajan has argued, "In embracing brownness as the key identity, they make their privileged positions of caste, class, immigration, and race— which would situate them in a position of not only oppression but also privilege — much harder to interrogate."[77] Soundararajan is pointing specifically to the legacy of caste supremacy, which has continued to allow for dominant-castes to maintain their social and economic positions.[78] This ongoing legacy of caste largely accounts for the brown savior's excess value in both India and the United States.

As I have already noted, most of Sahaayaka's organizational members were *savarna*, a term denoting those who came from any one of the four castes of the varna system (the Shudras, vaishyas, kshatriyas, and brahmins), as opposed to those from Dalit castes, who were the oppressed communities considered outside of the caste system, and therefore termed "avarna." In South India, in which this study took place, the primary divisions are typically among brahmins, Shudras (in Karnataka, these were mainly the Vokkaligas, Lingayats, and Kurubas, who were considered the "productive" agricultural castes, primarily as farmers and shepherds), and Dalits.

The relationship between race and caste has had a long and contested history. This makes sense, given that both race and caste have been technologies used to fix divisions and hierarchies of labor. In the Ambedkarite tradition, caste is understood as a precolonial system of brahmin supremacist legal-religious justifications for a hierarchic gradation of laborers codified in Hindu religious texts, maintained through hyperendogamy, and rooted in the exclusion and persecution of Dalits, especially through ritual untouchability.[79] In contrast, race emerged during the racist legacy of settler colonialism and the transatlantic slave trade, which sought to fix labor slottings by tying labor to notions of biologized bodily capacity linked to "blood" and "skin," and maintaining these racist slottings in legal frameworks rooted in anti-Blackness and Indigenous genocide.[80] The overlaps and tensions between caste and race were articulated in the 1930s by an anthropological school termed the "racial caste" school, led by anthropologists Allison Davis, Hortense Powdermaker, James Dollard, and Gunnar Myrdal, who sought to understand the race problem in the American South as an intransient "caste system." In *Caste, Class, and Race* (1948), Oliver Cox famously rejected this school of thought by arguing that race and caste *should not* be taken as commensurable categories of social differentiation given their very different historical emergences and regional enactments. He argued that race relations in the United States were better understood within the world historical emergence of capitalism and its tripartite system of labor-capital-profits.[81] In the context of India, B. R. Ambedkar argued just as forcefully that caste in India *should not* be understood through the logics of race because the "object of caste" was not to preserve "purity of blood."[82]

The debate regarding race and caste has returned to prominence recently with the acclaim for popular texts such as Isabel Wilkerson's *Caste: The Origin of Our Discontents*, which posits yet again that caste is a better way of understanding American racism than the category race while also arguing that it works in the much same way as caste in India and caste in Nazi Germany.[83] In works such as Wilkerson's, caste is used to evoke an invisible foundation for intransigent and inheritable hierarchies within national boundaries. While her text re-opens a useful and important conversation on caste as a global phenomenon, literature like Wilkerson's suffers from several shortcomings. First, this literature again fails to account for the way that class and labor play exceptionally important roles in theorizing *both* race and caste.[84] Second, Wilkerson's work (and Cox's earlier work as well) reifies a static and very limited notion of caste in India that does not recognize its dynamism and change, nor does it account for the fact that the very notion of caste has been forever changed by postcolonization.[85] Third, and related, this work maintains a simplistic nationalist view of how race and caste function and therefore neglects the far more complex, situated colonial and postcolonial histories of transnational movement that shape how race and caste have functioned in tandem.[86] In fact, such facile and rigid nationalistic boundaries between caste and race may actually facilitate casteist agendas that refuse to recognize the ways that Dalit activists have sought to position caste in relation to conversations on race in recent years.[87]

Let me be clear that I believe that a global caste critique can provide essential insights regarding the maintenance of intransigent and graded hierarchies of labor in many societies. Such an analysis would recognize the way that caste is founded on valuing/devaluing particular laborers based on the politics of purity/pollution and would focus on specific historical, migratory, and sociocultural instantiations of caste.[88] However, rigid, ahistorical, and nationally bounded ideologies of caste and race do little to help understand subjects like those in my study, who carry with them markers of India's caste system as they intersect with multiple histories of global racialization. The British in India determined which communities would play specific roles in the colonial bureaucracy based on what they perceived as the immutable labor capacities of different castes, effectively "racializing caste." Moreover, the word *caste* is a colonial term derived from the Portuguese term *casta*, which was used in the seventeenth century to describe the system of social stratification the Portuguese encountered in India. This term collapsed the dual systems of varna and jati and positioned them in relation to early European racial understandings of *limpieza de sangre*, or "blood purity."[89] Seen in this way, the preceding discussion of hemo-politics can be read as an example of the historical legacy of colonial encounter and the way conversations about kinship, caste, and the like have been refracted through processes of colonial racialization through blood purity/impurity discourses. Caste-as-blood took the question of caste "inside," the danger of caste impurity further tethered to maintaining the kinds of hyperexclusionary ritual and marriage practices that could prevent the potential pollution of dominant-caste blood. In turn, the legal and religious institutionalization of caste-based oppression was justified on the grounds of maintaining the blood purity of dominant-caste people who were supposedly "Aryan" and therefore actually white by ancestry.[90] Popularly termed the *Aryan myth*, this ideology proposed that brahmins and other dominant castes were actually just Europeans who had migrated to the subcontinent many years in the past.

While caste-as-blood purity became a justification for the maintenance of savarna supremacy in the Indian national context, it also reentrenched global hierarchies between white and brown. In, for example, the infamous case *United States v. Bhagat Singh Thind* (1923), which was meant to determine whether brown Indian migrants could receive citizenship in the United States, the court ruled that Thind's brown blood delegitimized his claims to citizenship. Thind claimed that he was "a high-caste Hindu, of full Indian blood, born at Amritsar, Punjab, India, a white person," despite the fact that he was actually Sikh, participating in the collapse of all South Asians into the category of dominant-caste Hindu in the United States.[91] However, US Supreme Court justice George Sutherland argued:

> It may be true that the blond Scandinavian and the brown Hindu have a common ancestor in the dim reaches of antiquity. . . . The type may have been so changed by intermixture of blood as to justify an intermediate classification. Something very like this has actually taken place in India . . . the vaunted purity of blood which the caste rules were calculated to perpetuate can scarcely have remained of more than a relative degree even in the case of the Brahmin caste.[92]

First, the "blond Scandinavian" and the "brown Hindu" are acknowledged to have a shared ancestry tethered to Aryanness. Second, the court enshrines the racialized category of "brown Hindu," which implies that brownness is separate from the category Hindu and can be attached as a descriptor for other ethnic or religious groups as well. Third, brownness is ontologically linked to the racial impurity associated with blood mixing, and, as I return to in chapter 2, the caste rules of brahminism are linked directly to an (unsuccessful) attempt at maintaining purity of blood.

Most important, the court case reflected the way that the dominant-caste pact with colonial white supremacy served to lock the dominant-castes into their position of brownness within global colonial cosmologies despite their best attempts to "purify" themselves of perceived brown blood and therefore maintain caste supremacy.[93] In turn, a blood-based discourse on caste stratification became a means for dominant castes to filter their own self-fashioning in and through the colonial logics of brown blood within which they experienced themselves as marginal. This feeling of marginality tethered to the blood is one way of reading the persistent need to "prove" dominant-caste Hindu ascension vis-à-vis the West.

At the same time, this global rearticulation of caste-as-blood actually occluded the materiality of caste oppression in India, which was based on the enshrining of graded labor divisions and exclusions through religion and law.[94] In fact, the protections emplaced by Ambedkar in the Indian constitution were intended to ameliorate this *material* legacy of caste violence and inequality, including through reserved quotas in education and government employment (this was itself a forced compromise owing to Gandhi's intransigent resistance to anything more).[95] However, these protections have largely rendered caste as a category perceived as pertinent only to nonsavarnas, and particularly Dalits, in popular media discourses. As a result, as I discuss further in chapter 5, savarnas, especially those at the higher rungs of the caste hierarchy, have been able to skirt discussions of their own caste positions, rendering themselves as the normatively unmarked "casteless" communities whose educational and occupational mobility has nothing to do with caste and is instead based solely on their merit.[96] This phenomenon has been especially true for those Indians who traveled to the United States, where caste has not been recognized as an operative form of discrimination until quite recently.[97] Mimicking this public erasure of caste position, scholarship on/in India has mostly neglected explicit excavations of savarna castes and their reproduction of casteist power asymmetries. In response, Gajendran Ayyathurai has argued for the field of critical caste studies, which "is committed to examining diverse cultural, religious, political, and economic mechanisms by which caste-power is produced and dispersed through a putatively inviolable caste structure."[98]

My project draws from and contributes to the critical caste studies school by revealing the ways that the NGO sector refracts problematic caste illusions/elisions, tracing the linkages between caste and racialized ideologies regarding who is capable of taking on global help work and who is still perceived as in need of help. As illustrated above, the brown savior most often emerges from the "casteless" globally mobile brown savarna capitalist class. Suraj Yengde explains, "The development-related model reinforces the unequal donor-receiver relationship, thereby permanently putting Dalit people at the receiving end—the lower end. . . . The handlers of such agencies and country/mission heads are invariably dominant-caste people."[99] Sahaayaka's leadership is one stark reflection of this caste- and class-based stratification within the global help economies.

Other caste communities, for example, those from agricultural castes who took on positions as Sahaayaka fieldworkers, were racialized quite differently within (neo)colonial systems of categorization. As I explain in more detail in chapter 8, the differentiations along urban/rural lines as they intersected with racialized caste position are yet another dimension by which to analyze the course of brown saviorism and the types of stratified labor that emerge in the help economies.

In Sum and What's to Come

What this discussion reveals, I hope, is that an excavation of brown saviorism requires careful attention to the overlapping and interlocking systems of power that produce brown subjects, whose positions are far more fraught than a simple rendering of the colonial wound can address. As Naveen Minai and

Sara Shroff write, "This is not just about whiteness. This is also about the ways in which racial, gender, [caste] and class privilege travels between global north and global south: white saviors, brown saviors."[100]

In the rest of this text, I provide seventeen short chapters, split into four parts, that rely on my sweaty, nervous ethnographic encounters to shed light on the story of brown saviorism in India and its role in racial and caste capitalist accumulation.[101] Through a process of unfixing, unsettling, and reframing, *Brown Saviors and Their Others* encourages a critical attention to the material histories, power asymmetries, racialized and casteized relationships, geographies of scale, and ethnographic unfoldings that tensely link the visions of transnational NGO leaders like Krish to the aspirations of fieldworkers like Suresh and the rural students who are at the receiving end of interventions. As with this introduction, I end each part with a short section called "In Sum and What's to Come" to transition to the next part of the book. While the short chapters and each part of the book can be read independently of one another, it is my hope that as you read, the synthetic distinctions I have made between parts and chapters melt into a series of overlapping, interconnected, and mutually constitutive arguments.

Part I, "Theorizing Saviorism," situates brown saviorism and the help economies within the workings of global racial capitalism.[102] In chapter 1, I explain how the help economies have become the solution to the problem of surplus labor in racial capitalist systems by functioning as markets for the saving of the dispossessed while also becoming potential sources of employment for some from within these dispossessed classes. In chapter 2, I situate the story of brown saviorism within a history of race, religion, and caste. I show how the bodily capacities of the Hindu and, more specifically, the brahmin are racialized with cognitive, technical, and spiritual capacities. These racialized capacities allow for the emergence of a class of savarna Hindus who ascend to the role of savior.

Part II, "Neocolonial Saviorism," foregrounds ethnographic examples that locate my analysis at the interface of neocolonial race, caste, and gendered relations as they influence Sahaayaka's praxis. In these chapters I focus on the way that particular racialized categories associated with colonial and postcolonial governance in India—poverty, nation, caste, gender, and religion—reemerge in Sahaayaka's institutional arrangement and, therefore, how brown saviors, mentors, and those who live in the villages outside of Bangalore imagine who should be helped and how. Chapter 3 excavates the long-standing racialized problem of poverty in relation to Malthusian population control theory. I show how, inadvertently, a neo-Malthusian logic is reproduced in and through the motivational strategies deployed by Sahaayaka. Chapter 4 focuses on the decisions made by Sahaayaka's brown saviors to partner with American universities and global funders, which allow the organization to accumulate resources only within the parameters of their global racialized slotting as brown Indians. Chapters 5, 6, and 7 focus on the neocolonial caste, gender, and religious hierarchies that hide in plain sight in the brown savior's supposedly universal technocratic interventions. Specifically, these three chapters focus on intraorganizational caste tensions, gendered stratifications of labor, and anti-Muslim organizational structurings that complicate the technocratic, data-driven operations of the NGO. Together, these five chapters show how Sahaayaka's interventions reinscribe neocolonial hierarchies within the governing structures associated with help.

Part III, "Urban Saviorism," focuses on the racializing processes produced as the brown savior travels along the urban-rural interface. Spatializing and territorializing my study in this way allows for a more concrete exploration of how the help economies function as part of the contemporary workings of primitive accumulation. In Karnataka the expansion of Bangalore has systematically led to the expropriation of rural land.[103] As I argue in chapter 8, the education NGO is a central terrain on which dispossession is negotiated. To reveal this unfolding process, I focus on the mentors, who sought ways to use the NGO as a form of mobility even as they were racially slotted into positions that rendered them largely immobile. Each of these chapters reveals the fraught position of the mentor, who challenges the brown savior even as they may actually reinforce the very same values in their strategies for mobility. That is to say, in some sense, the mentors wish to become brown saviors, too, and may produce new neocolonial cycles of stratification themselves.

Part IV, "Digital Saviorism," focuses on brown saviorism at the interface of digital proliferation. Each chapter in this part focuses on the ways that digital integration functions to (re)produce racialized division and allows brown saviors to accumulate ever more capital as they intervene in rural communities. Sahaayaka's excess value emerged as part of the powerful and totalizing imaginary of the digital as the solution to poverty in India. At the same time, the savarna diasporic Hindu has been perceived as having a preternatural capacity for technological innovation and therefore has taken on a leading role as the appropriate savior in this push toward digital versions of poverty alleviation. As I show in each of these chapters, Sahaayaka's digital solutions were never divorced from their historically constituted position. In fact, the digital future they anticipated had the potential to reinforce colonial, racial, postcolonial, postliberalization, and postautocratic structurings of help.[104]

I conclude by returning in "Against Saviorism" to my humble hope for this text: to unsettle, if ever so slightly, the project of global help in places like India by reframing it within the racial and caste capitalist enterprise. To consider the help economies as part of a global racial and caste capitalist system calls into question the foundation of global late liberalism's version of the moral good and, perhaps, opens space for a different way of relating to one another, one that is not founded on the necessary precondition that some people have excess value (to accumulate and to help) while others do not. I end by positing what a different "nervous" imaginary for change might be, especially at a moment when the power of the far right continues to gather steam in India and elsewhere.

I
THEORIZING SAVIORISM

The cumulative effects of decades of neoliberal reform have been a massive exacerbation of the inequalities of racial capitalism and its gendered divisions of labor.—SONIYA MUNSHI AND CRAIG WILLSE, foreword to INCITE!, *The Revolution Will Not Be Funded*

The Caste System . . . is a hierarchy in which the divisions of labourers are graded one above the other.—B. R. AMBEDKAR, *Annihilation of Caste*

There is much more to doing good work than "making a difference."
—TEJU COLE, "The White-Savior Industrial Complex"

1

GLOBAL HELP ECONOMIES

AND RACIAL CAPITALISM

It was February 2013, and I was still a few months away from embarking on my first extended field engagement in Bangalore. As part of my strategy to create goodwill, I had invited Srinivasan, Sahaayaka's founder, to Philadelphia during one of his many trips to the East Coast to visit his daughter, who lived in Boston. I enjoyed Srinivasan's company, primarily because I was inspired by the fact that he still had so much energy and enthusiasm for a man nearing eighty. In retrospect, I also felt a relationship to him because he reminded me of my own maternal grandfather, whom I had lost by the age of eleven but of whom I had fond memories. It was a somewhat nonsensical feeling because Srinivasan and my grandfather were really nothing alike: my own grandfather was very quiet, reserved, and cerebral, while Srinivasan was gregarious, politically engaged, and confident. Yet Srinivasan struck just the right chords of caste, linguistic, and paternal kinship, which facilitated whatever trust we had with one another. There is no doubt that I benefited from this unstated yet always present affective connection, a sense of communal belonging and trust that has also sustained networks of savarna accumulation in nearly every field in the United States.[1]

During Srinivasan's visit, he met with a few of the faculty and gave a lecture on Sahaayaka's program. After his day was over, Srinivasan, several of my colleagues, and I sat around drinking coffee at one of the coffee shops on campus and chatting before Srinivasan's flight out of the city. He was still exhilarated by his day of work, and so, as was his way, he began talking a mile a minute, repeating most of what he had already explained to us previously. This time, however, the informality of our chat allowed the rest of us to ask him more critical questions, and we wondered out loud about the panacea-like descriptions he was providing us. If we were to believe Srinivasan, he had developed an educational intervention that would solve India's rural crisis by motivating *all* rural children, regardless of caste, gender, or class position, to do better in school, pass their exams, get into college, and eventually get better jobs away from their homes. Srinivasan, like many other NGO leaders, had generated this salvation narrative as a way to prove his organization's worth in the ever more competitive help economies.

We began to push back a bit harder and started to make some systemic critiques that we wanted Srinivasan to address. For example, I mentioned several times that if *all* students in India passed their tenth-standard exams, there would simply not be enough jobs for even (generously) 10 percent of them and that, in fact, the system as set up required a differentiation and hierarchy of labor, required that many children *not* graduate from secondary education and *not* join the formal economy, required that many people lose their lands and livelihoods and sense of community, even if a few were able to benefit from interventions like his.[2] I wanted Srinivasan to address the processes of "neoliberal-cum-neocolonial dispossession," which seemed to be a premise for his whole project, capturing the way that strategies of accumulation continued to violently separate human beings from land and resources but also from their forms of relationality, even as the NGO sought to help these people who had been dispossessed and therefore, in a perverse way, actually benefited from their dispossession.[3] I also wanted Srinivasan to explain why *he*, as a cosmopolitan, savarna former engineer, should be the person in charge of change.

At first, Srinivasan acknowledged the truth of some of our claims, even noting that the best-case scenario was one in which Sahaayaka became obsolete because the people they were working with no longer needed them. But then he shrugged and dismissed my critique by explaining, "Sure, what you say may be true. But that is a problem still very far away, so we can worry about that later. For now, the goal is to get more children to stay in school and graduate from tenth standard. That is the *urgent* matter." Srinivasan got even more persistent when we provided research that showed that youth in India were stranded after leaving their traditional agricultural livelihoods and completing secondary education. They were *already* "waiting" for a moment when jobs might become available to them.[4] The systemic critique, we argued, was necessary now, more than ever, and the liberal reformist vision of educational mobility seemed but a distraction.

The whole conversation made me nervous, both because I was, at the time, terribly conflict averse but also because these disagreements risked all of the cachet I had built up over the previous few hours. I had developed a selfish, possessive, extractive streak when it came to my research, and it would take me three long years to disentangle myself from this ideology. At times, this would mean that I stayed quiet, made compromises, and smiled when I should have frowned and disagreed. But in this case, so early on, I had done the opposite, perhaps because I was around much more ethically driven colleagues. The result was a nervousness I did not enjoy.

To his credit, Srinivasan listened and thanked us for our insights. Perhaps he acquiesced because of his own misgivings about his project and his recognition that he might have been making compromises despite the fact that he saw himself as a "Marxist on the inside" after having witnessed massive worker exploitation in his earlier industrial-sector jobs. Ultimately, we changed the subject without things getting more heated, though the ideological lines had been drawn.

As I think back on that interaction from so early in my research, I have come to realize that Srinivasan's claim held a certain seductive quality, relying on the seemingly obvious moral value associated with the ideology of "at least I am doing something *now*," while pushing off more difficult systemic critiques till later. Srinivasan's paternalist vision of help reminded me of Cynthia Enloe's argument that "later is a patriarchal timezone," in which those men with power make decisions based on the rhetoric of immediate need, which ultimately devalues issues related to gender, race, caste, and capital and therefore leaves the redress of these issues suspended in a time always yet to come.[5]

Srinivasan is certainly not alone in this paternalistic approach to helping others. For many of the more elite students whom I have taught in institutions of higher education in both the United States and India, joining an NGO seems like a better alternative to corporate work and a legitimate way of doing something good for those elsewhere in the world. Perhaps this is why the same students who are eager and ready to learn about and critique racial, caste, and gendered capitalism's devastating effects in housing, education, health care, citizenship, incarceration, and the like many times freeze when I level these same critiques at the help economies. When I am met with these reactions, I explain that no one I have encountered who works for NGOs, Srinivasan or others, does this work because they intend to do harm. In fact, in most cases, they are deeply dedicated to the work they do and the need to create a better world.[6]

The sheer scale and emotional stakes associated with the help economies make critiques of them exceptionally fraught, despite the fact that all of this attention to helping Others has made almost no perceptible dent in global poverty and inequality.[7] Currently, nearly one in three people worldwide give to a philanthropic organization, taking for granted that providing aid is a necessary social good. In addition, supranational organizations, NGOs, and philanthropic networks have mushroomed, with NGOs growing to over ten million, with a total economic impact equivalent to the gross domestic product (GDP) of the fifth-largest country in the world.[8] Narratives of poverty, destitution, and helplessness and images of suffering are being generated and circulated at ever-increasing rates, only exacerbating the urgency with which people all over the world feel the need to help.[9] We are, for better or worse, in the age of the nonprofit-industrial complex, an entire economy of help that requires funds, labor, and new subjects who are deemed in need.

But the help economies are, like any other institutional arrangement, political, and regardless of any emotional attachments, there is utility to interrogating the relations of power that produce their conditions of possibility. I encourage my students by quoting Oscar Wilde, who wrote many years back, "It is much more easy to have sympathy with suffering than it is to have sympathy with thought."[10] I explain that Wilde is pointing us toward the affective dimensions of the savior complex, a psychosocial condition that emplaces a compulsion to help Others based on the urgency to rectify suffering, the conceit that one has the tools to rectify such suffering, and the belief that one can quantify the success or failure of one's attempts at mitigating suffering. These kinds of psychological impulses are part of what Savannah Shange terms a "libidinal economy" because they discipline "the desire for freedom into a quantifiable goal" and short-circuit more difficult forms of critical questioning regarding the material conditions that produce social suffering in the first place.[11]

Most often, this kind of critique has been leveled at white saviorism and has been tethered to a critique of the "industrial complex" it has produced, precisely because the historical unfolding of saviorism is rooted in the white colonial missionary complex.[12] However, given the global spread of saviorist ideologies and institutions, the whiteness of the savior complex may, as I have suggested, actually now be linked to brown skin/blood. In trying to explain why this complex has unfolded in the way it has, I draw explicitly from theories of racial capitalism rather than theories that emerge from within the dominant late liberal discourses that have largely monopolized the terms on which global help work can be imagined.[13]

On the Need for a Racial Capitalist Critique of the Education NGO

While there are many different types of NGOs with diverse practices and goals, I am primarily concerned with the NGOs that draw funds from multinational corporations, include transnational actors, and therefore function as nodes along which "global capital flows."[14] This type of NGO has had an exceptionally important role in shaping how the help economies are imagined.[15] Sahaayaka is one such NGO, garnering funds from large multinational donor agencies (the Michael and Susan Dell Foundation, Cisco, Target, Mindtree, and Coca-Cola, among many others), partnering with state and national governments, and privileging transnational actors at the highest levels of leadership and trusteeship.

When NGOs like Sahaayaka have been critically analyzed by anthropologists and other critical social scientists, whether they've been headquartered in India, the United States, or elsewhere in the world, there has been a tendency to see these institutional actors in straightforward neoliberal terms. The dominant story is that NGOs have filled the void left as state governments have absconded from their responsibilities to their citizenries over the past twenty years—especially in health care and education—as liberalism's social welfare prerogatives have been replaced by neoliberalism's free-market fundamentalism and mass privatization.

This story makes quite a bit of sense, especially in India, where the liberalization of India's economy in the late 1980s has seen massive increases in the capacity to accumulate (for specific individuals and the nation as a whole) even as national inequality has also risen sharply.[16] In this particular narrative, the rise of education NGOs like Sahaayaka, and the brown savior more generally, dovetails with the privatization of the Indian education system over the course of liberalization, which linked the private school with modernity, globality, and class mobility, especially in its evocation of English as the language of mobility and, therefore, the most valued medium of instruction (replicating colonial cultural ideals for the neoliberal era).[17] The result has been, predictably, the slow decimation of the government (public) schools, which have been economically dispossessed as their cultural value has also diminished. Statistically, the shift from public to private education has been striking: now almost 50 percent of school-age students in India go to a private school, double the percentage in 1978.[18] This massive shift, in turn, has also made government schools a ripe arena for outside "help" by NGOs and NGO leaders who exemplify the postglobalization regimes of the private sector "value-add": namely, those of financial capital, transnational capital, and digital capital. Figures like Srinivasan fit snugly into this analysis, as they possess the right kinds of capital necessary to take on leadership roles in these privatizing industries.

But what neoliberal critiques of the state-NGO nexus in education and other sectors cannot explain is how differentiation and hierarchy are produced and operate in and through these industries, especially as it pertains to the question of *who* makes up varying labor forces and how this labor is organized. Moreover, such critiques do not ask *how* NGO labor exploitation, and the crisis of surplus labor more generally, might actually be linked to historical and contemporary forms of land expropriation and dispossession rooted in settler colonial praxis and ongoing strategies of primitive accumulation.[19] Attention to racial capitalism can provide some answers to these questions.

Racial capitalism as an analytic focus has been largely absent from theoretical engagements with the twenty-first-century help economies.[20] This lack of attention to racialization, labor, and land dispossession in scholarship on the help industries is quite surprising given that it has become almost taken for granted that development and humanitarian intervention—two of the most well-known forms that the help economies have taken—ought to be characterized as "colonialism in disguise."[21] Indeed, the open secret of nearly all humanitarian and development campaigns over the past seventy years is that they have focused almost exclusively on previously colonized peoples, many of whom have been dispossessed as part of histories of imperial and colonial oppression, and that "racial meanings reproduce a distinction that sustains a power differential necessary for the justification of [development] projects."[22] Despite these critiques, a 2020 study by Kamna Patel showed that the three major development studies journals included only thirty-two articles that mentioned race over the previous thirteen years and that even fewer, less than twenty, critically engaged conceptually with theories of racialization.[23] As Adia Benton argues, many scholars still deploy the "notion of the 'human,' differentiated only by the (binary) terms defined by the humanitarian encounter—victim/savior, beneficiary/provider—with little regard to the kinds of social distinction between humans, like race, that precede and are intensified by the humanitarian encounter."[24] Moreover, in separate engagements with race and development, Uma Kothari and Denise Ferreira da Silva both argue that the lack of attention to race in development discourse occludes and even naturalizes racialized extractivism along First World/Third World and developed/underdeveloped binaries.[25]

For example, critics of developmentalist reason, most prominently the post-development school of thought, pointed out that the sudden "discovery" of abject lack, poverty, and "cultural backwardness" in the postcolonized brown world was a convenient reassertion of the former colonizers' economic, moral, and cultural superiority and, therefore, capacity to help Others. These critiques revealed the way that highly technocratic language and moral claims to alleviate suffering obfuscated the reality of norms and value judgments that largely amounted to a new form of Western cultural and economic imperialism. In turn, postdevelopment critics, Arturo Escobar in particular, called for a resistance to Western interventions in the brown world and argued that "local agency" should be allowed to assert itself to solve their own problems.[26]

Somewhat ironically, this form of critique actually reinscribed a binary opposition between the West and the rest, rich and poor, outsider and Indigenous, global and local, and essentialized the ahistorical idea of the poor and Indigenous as radically distinct, different, and naturally opposed to the West. Here "poor" and "Indigenous" are identities that, by definition, collapse all internal differences and represent a radical politics. As important, the problematic construction of "the local" as somehow separate from the rest of the world belied the fact that, especially in the brown world, colonial encounters had produced migratory patterns and changes in cultural norms and values that rendered impossible any authentication of a "pure" local cultural sensibility.

As such, the slippery identitarian question of *who* was part of the local became the means for inadvertent neocolonial reproduction. On the one hand, the local seemed to valorize those from areas considered as "primitive" within colonial racist cosmologies, who were supposedly less exposed to modern capitalism, again reinscribing their primordial difference. This rigid identity-based characterization of the local poor was too easily appropriated by development agencies, producing the image of a hyperindustrious, resilient impoverished laborer tethered to the land whom organizations simply needed to collaborate with in order to bring them properly into the circuits of capitalism.[27] In some sense, Sahaayaka, and especially Srinivasan, had imbibed this particular register for interventions, arguing consistently that one had "to go there"—had to go to the community—to figure out the actual needs of people and ways to help them, which, on its surface, seemed to be a much better strategy than explicitly impositional forms of intervention. Ultimately, however, as I will discuss further in chapter 4, "going there" still functioned to radically separate Sahaayaka from those they were helping and to facilitate Sahaayaka's already well-planned agenda for rural uplift.

At the same time, given the way the West's universalism was positioned against the colony's "provinciality," the "local" became associated with any racialized group originally from the colony, including those brown saviors I am considering in my study.[28] As Escobar noted in later reflections on postdevelopment critique, these dynamics of the local actually brought into visibility a class of "transnational expert communities whose training, interests, tastes, and economic and political goals coincide enough to keep the development actor-networks going and well-oiled."[29] Here, of course, the brown savior's racialized difference is tethered to a perceived nativity and "local" legitimacy that allows for their ascendance within the help economies. Even worse, the valorized production of "local knowledge" has been easily folded into the golden myths of autocratic regimes in India, who argue that their oppressive Hindutva policies and populist cultural impositions are merely a means to bring back "local"—glossed as "Indigenous"—values and ideologies destroyed by a history of colonization.

In sum, the postdevelopment critique was too readily appropriated by those with very different political agendas because it remained stuck in Manichean representational models that did not truly grapple with the materiality of exploitation/expropriation tethered to specific categories—including race, gender, and caste—that shape developmentalist accumulation.

The Materiality of Racial, Caste, and Gendered Capitalist
Critique of NGO Labor

While my argument is not intended to fetishize the primacy of race and racialization as a global analytic to study the help economies, racial capitalism, as I deploy it here, draws from the legacies left by those intellectuals who recognize that capitalist accumulation, from its inception in settler and franchise colonialism and the transatlantic slave trade, relied and relies on racialized differentiation and hierarchy, not as an epiphenomenal characteristic, but as constitutive of its very unfolding.[30] These theorizations take the ethnographic study of capitalism in a different direction, focusing attention on, first, the processes by which "internal" differences within colonies (caste, for example) are racialized and, second, the way these racialized differences and divisions are accumulated and organized as "precincts of value and limited value" in order to determine the labor hierarchies within the formal economy, who must remain outside these formal labor relations as disposable labor, *and* whose land and resources can be taken without compensation.[31] Kalyan Sanyal, for example, has argued that neocolonial capitalism *cannot* include all people as formal workers because of the strain this would cause on capitalist economies and the curtailing on accumulation this would mean.[32] We might say that capitalism relies on a stratified differentiation predicated on primitivizing communities (hence the *primitive* in *primitive accumulation*) or, in the words of Michel-Rolph Trouillot, predicated on producing new savage slots.[33] This was a premise that Srinivasan was unwilling to acknowledge in the discussion described earlier in this chapter.

In late liberal capitalist societies, and especially in India, the help economies have been one way to deal with the problem of those "edge populations" that have experienced the brutal effects of dispossession.[34] On the one hand, the help economies function by creating niche markets based on the very fact that certain populations are deemed outside of formal capitalist relationships and therefore are in need of saving. As Nagraj pointed out with frustration in the preface, his rural precarity and his age seemed to be an excuse for outsiders to help him whether he wanted their help or not. At the same time, the help economies have also become one partial solution to the problem of surplus labor, employing particular precincts of precarious labor to watch over those deemed "outside." As Suresh's story in the introduction indicates, NGOs have become a venue for economic and social mobility for those who previously lived and worked in agricultural communities. By conscripting those like Suresh into their inner workings, the help economies serve to legitimize racial capitalist social relations by providing the illusion that they can solve the internal contradictions of capitalism through uplifting those who have been (purposely) left out or dispossessed, even though ultimately it exploits these new classes of laborers.

Differentiating these surplus labor populations within the help economy requires the production of a necessary *antirelationality* between "saviors" and their "Others." In stressing the way that the savior/saved binary functions as a constructed form of antirelationality, I am drawing from the work of Ruth Wilson Gilmore and Jodi Melamed, who argue that racialized inequalities are reproduced through "technologies of anti-relationality," by which "forms of humanity are separated (made 'distinct') so that they may be 'interconnected' in terms that feed capital."[35] In this case, the savior/saved binary evacuates other forms of relationality such that the *only* important and operative distinction is that between one's capacity to save Others because one is highly productive and one's capacity to be saved because one is deemed economically unproductive. Such reasoning relies on the occlusion of the historical, political, and economic violence that implicates these variegated saviors in the dispossession of those who are in need of saving, development, poverty alleviation, and the like.

For example, Walter Rodney's *How Europe Underdeveloped Africa* situates the ideologies of development within the global imperial regimes of extraction that have produced so much global poverty. While Rodney is speaking about the specific historical processes by which Europe enslaved people and expropriated resources from the African continent, his monumental work sets the foundation for a broader understanding of the ongoing neocolonial developmentalist project and the way that this project produces inter- and intranational racialized differentiations tethered to the need to accumulate.[36] In particular, Rodney's work signals the way that the savior/saved binary continues to operate by hiding itself within the ubiquitous twentieth-century discourses regarding the developed/underdeveloped and linking itself to reformists who, like Srinivasan, believe they are doing radical change work even though they do not critique the material histories that uphold neocolonial capitalism or their positions within these material histories.

Kalpana Wilson's work draws Rodney's insights into contemporary discussions of how global capital, labor, and race continue to shape developmentalist reason.[37] In particular, Wilson explicitly points to the ways that the significant increase in global inequality has produced a regime of "human" development and poverty alleviation that focuses on the very same racialized populations who had been left out of colonial projects and later national economic prosperity and are therefore in perpetual crisis, culminating in globally influential initiatives like the 2015 UN Sustainable Development Goals. Within this regime, ideas of self-reliance, sustainability, capacity building, added value, and empowerment draw together development and humanitarianism and become, in the words of Jemima Pierre, part of the implicit "racial vernaculars of development," organizing bodies into those who can provide aid and those who cannot.[38]

The INCITE! Collective's *The Revolution Will Not Be Funded* explicitly articulates the systemic processes of what they term *the nonprofit-industrial complex*, which works in parallel to the carceral state, managing and controlling dissent by channeling activism into careerist projects that work at the behest of the state apparatus and by allowing the veil of philanthropic altruism to remain intact.[39] But the INCITE! Collective also warns that a critique of the nonprofit-industrial complex requires further attention to would-be victims and would-be saviors, along with the gradations of labor therein, as they emerge from historically situated racialized and gendered relationships. One set of humans who have been characterized as having "limited value" and have been targeted for saving have been so-called Third World women and children.[40] This racist and sexist cosmology begins with the famous premise outlined by Gayatri Chakravorty Spivak, in which "white men save brown women from brown men."[41] Here saving so-called brown women assumes the extreme patriarchy of brown worlds and occludes the functioning of white supremacy and colonialism. Over the past forty years, the politics of saviorism on the subcontinent has drawn on these lasting colonial legacies and intertwined them with American imperial interests. Specifically, the US war on terror has justified itself by arguing that it will also "liberate" Muslim women and girls, who are supposedly experiencing exceptional oppression within an essentialized Muslim patriarchy.[42] Shenila Khoja-Moolji has argued that these forms of saviorism focus on the idealized education of the Muslim girl, who will become a change agent for social liberalism, economic growth, the end of terrorism, and even population control.[43] Such discourses find cognates in India with regard to rural women and girls. In this case, the empowered poor rural girl will find economic mobility, educate her children, and crown India as a truly liberal democracy. In these cases, scholars have shown how elite-led interventions construct "racialized women in the global South as saviors, while promoting the notion of self-sufficiency."[44]

The illusion that brown women and children must be taught to tether their "superhuman" resilience to strategies for accumulation in order to save their communities necessarily obscures the fact that these groups already do so much unrecognized, yet essential, global labor. Here I draw on the large body of feminist critiques of capitalism, Sylvia Federici's, Maria Mies's, and Gargi Bhattacharyya's works in particular, in which capital accumulation relies on the erasure of global gendered labor. This is why the theorizing I undertake in this text takes gendered and racialized difference as mutually constitutive of processes of accumulation.[45] There is no racial capitalism that is not always already gendered racial capitalism.[46] But the associated point I want to emphasize, as I did in my earlier discussion of Suresh and Lakshmi in the introduction, is that the help economies translate traditional social reproductive functions (including those like social welfare schemas, which are purportedly part of the function of the state) into productive markets—with employees, funds, and infrastructure—while also demarcating individual labor value through neocolonial ideologies of masculine and feminine praxis. The stark contrast between Srinivasan (or Krish), as a masculinized, rational, technocratic worker, and Suresh, as a feminized, affective care worker, is one ethnographic example of how the savior/saved binary hinges on and reproduces a gendered, racialized, and casteized form of antirelationality.

Perhaps surprisingly, only recently has caste become an important consideration in the NGO sector in India. In fact, before the early 2000s, caste was almost completely excluded from development discourses. For example, the 2015 Sustainable Development Goals include race and gender discrimination but not caste-based discrimination. Interventions by NGOs related to caste began to take shape after Dalit activists argued that caste should be considered on the development agenda under the rubric of claims for Dalit human rights.[47] These activists brought the NGO sector in line with broader social movements, which required a move away from the abstracted, autonomous, "poor" individual who was the normal focus of NGO intervention to a focus on the particular historical process of exploitation experienced by caste-oppressed groups.

However, David Mosse has argued that the continued neglect of caste in the mainstream help economy discourses is partially because caste has been considered *outside* of political economic relations, thus delinking it from the considerations of poverty and socioeconomic disparity that undergird the logic of the help economies. Instead, caste was associated with either the "cultural" realm of religion or the invisible purity politics of blood, rendering it an internal matter outside of international accountability protocols, or positioned within formal governance, focused on quotas, reservations, and other civil-society mechanisms internal to the state.[48] When caste did emerge within the help economies, it either was subsumed into other categories, like rurality or gender exclusion, or was likely to center, as Suraj Yengde argued, on an essentialized figuration of the hopelessness of Dalits.[49]

Most strikingly, in his conversations with the World Bank, the United Nations, and other aid agencies in Delhi, Mosse found a "marked *nervousness* surrounding the issue of caste. Among bureaucrats and nongovernmental organization (NGO) workers, the degree of openness to the topic was often a reflection of the caste identity of my interlocutors."[50] Here Mosse is pointing to the fact that dominant-caste communities who work for NGOs are much less likely to discuss caste and, when they do, are likely to experience nerves. Nerves, as I have argued earlier, emerge in these discussions because these personnel are confronted with their complicity and the way that their neglect of their caste position in India's caste society might belie their great benevolence.

These characterizations mimic many moments I observed with Sahaayaka. What I noticed most frequently was a willingness to speak about caste in the abstract or, more specifically, as it pertained to issues perceived as distant from NGO personnel or NGO praxis. For example, during Srinivasan's visit to Philadelphia, he gave an entire lecture on caste in relation to Sahaayaka's work. In this lecture he railed against the caste-based discrimination in villages, pointing to the fact that toilets remained uncleaned because of a caste-based purity politics that required that the cleaning of toilets be performed only by specific Dalit communities. In his lecture Srinivasan used these observations of caste to show the way that his, and by extension Sahaayaka's, work was building awareness and pushing against these oppressive systems.

In contrast, Srinivasan had nothing to say about the caste stratifications within his organization, nor did the organization's explicit mission have anything to do with caste. Instead, as I have mentioned, the organization focused on the generalized categories of rurality and poverty (and sometimes girls).[51] Not surprisingly, when caste did come up in relation to Sahaayaka's praxis, as I discuss in chapter 5, the leadership was exceedingly nervous because it complicated the simplistic vision of doing good from this "universal position."

What I hope is clear at this stage is that the help economies rely on labor stratifications that produce the victim who is in need of saving, those from the victim classes who might join the NGO labor force as exploitable labor, and those classes that rise to the status of savior.[52] As such, the critical questions questions are *who* can become a savior and *how* one becomes a savior: What historical processes, accumulations of racialized difference, and mobility regimes allow for actors to imagine themselves as those who should take on leading roles in the help economies' global labor force?[53] These questions set the stage for the next chapter, in which I draw out some of the historical intersections of race and caste that allow Sahaayaka's leadership, and those like them, to ascend to the role of brown savior.

2

THE RACIAL POLITICS OF THE SAVARNA HINDU

(OR THE WOULD-BE SAVIOR)

The unique form of brown saviorism I address in this book emerges from a history of racialization at the nexus of colony, nation, religion, and caste. In this chapter I focus on the racialization of the Indian, Hindu, and brahmin, who are perceived to possess preternatural spiritual and technological capacities.[1] These perceived racialized capacities have allowed these subjects to take on prominent roles in the help economies and shape their directions.

Race and racialization were far from my mind when I was first conducting my fieldwork in India even though I had already noticed the ubiquity of "blood talk," had seen the way that caste and religion were caricatured through racialized discourse, had theorized the NGO as reproducing colonial categories, and had often read the famous lines of Thomas Macaulay I cited in the introduction, who sought "to form . . . a class of persons, Indian in blood and colour, but English in taste, in opinions, in morals, and in intellect."[2]

As I read Macaulay's statement now, the conflation of blood and color only seems to further reveal the way that blood talk was and is already "in color." At the time, however, it was as if I could not process India as a place where race mattered, no matter how many times I had obviously racialized encounters or read about this colonial history of "blood" and "color." I, like so many others trained in the Orientalist university, perceived India, and the world, through the categories already conferred on it by the colonizer, which largely disallowed a discussion of race or racialization in the regions both east and west of the Americas.

FIGURE 2.1. Redacted image of a human cranium labeled "Hindu of Bengal." Housed at the University of Pennsylvania Museum of Archaeology and Anthropology in Philadelphia, Pennsylvania. (Photo by Arjun Shankar)

That started to change in 2015 when three of my colleagues and I were wandering around the basement of the University of Pennsylvania's Museum of Archaeology and Anthropology, trying to find our way to a room purposely hidden away from the roaming public. Somewhere in this basement, we were told, we would find one of the largest collections of human crania in the United States, gathered by the racist scientist Samuel Morton in the early 1800s.

Morton is considered one of the founding members of the phrenological school of racist science. He measured crania and falsified craniometric data to prove his theories of polygenesis (different origins of different races).[3] Morton believed that his findings would allow him to construct a perfect, systematic typology of global race and, just as important, prove the superiority of the so-called Caucasian race.

The collection has been in the possession of the Penn museum since 1966 and has been the source of much controversy.[4] However, despite the fact that I was trained at Penn, I had somehow never actually seen this collection before. I had been absent when the collection was discussed during my Intro to Archaeology class and was not required to take Physical Anthropology.[5] I had also somehow never taken a class in the one classroom of the museum in which a portion of the collection had been displayed until 2020, when graduate student protests finally resulted in the collection being removed from public view entirely.[6] And so, as I approached these crania, I had no idea what I was really getting into.

I was there to look at these crania only because I had naively agreed to lead a film project about the collection and the history of scientific racism. The film was intended as part of a broader educational effort to figure out how to deal with these human remains given their sordid legacy. The museum had already created a new public exhibition on the history of scientific racism, and it was in the process (at the time) of putting together a series of public seminars on science and race.

It's hard to describe the feeling of being surrounded by human remains. On the one hand, most of us postcolonized subjects have been trained to think of the dead as "not living," as "of the past." This distancing allows researchers to justify the study of the dead. But if you let your mind wander ever so slightly out of the colonial imaginaries of life and death and learn from the many Indigenous scholars who tell us quite differently, you remember that you are seeing people's ancestors and that many people experience these ancestors as still living lives. You remember that the collection itself is a story of lives lived in exceptionally horrific conditions. These realizations hit so fast that the experience of being in that room with those crania can be suffocating and nerve-racking.

But if sitting in a room full of human remains was disconcerting, making a film about human remains was even more so. Given my own training as a visual anthropologist, I knew all too well that images can reproduce the most racist forms of representation.[7] How were we going to depict these human remains without reproducing this kind of violence?

We struggled with this question for a long while, and at times I thought that we should not show any human remains on-screen. In the end, though, we did show some of these human remains, and we did our best to contextualize the collection in a way that could educate youth about the ongoing history of scientific racism. I'm still not sure we made the right decisions. Notice that I have redacted the entire image of the human cranium in this chapter (figure 2.1), a more respectful way, I hope, of representing these humans who are someone's ancestors.[8]

When we first entered that room full of crania, however, we were far away from these difficult conversations about film, race, and human remains. Instead, we were walking around nervously, staring at these humans and trying to decipher the labels that had been affixed to many of them: things like "Negro Born in Africa" or "Child Six Months Old." In one row I spotted a series of thirty or so crania that were labeled with some variation of "Hindu of Bengal," and I could not stop lingering on them, feeling somehow drawn back again and again as we paced the room. I finally turned to one of my colleagues and blurted anxiously, "What the fuck is a Hindooooooo skull?!?" I stretched out the last syllable to mock the early colonial scientific racist spelling of "Hindoo" while also masking my nerves, which were starting to jangle out of control. Ultimately, I kept returning to this question: What, exactly, is a Hindu skull? It began my journey to rethink what I had learned while I was in Bangalore and to theorize the brown savior as a decidedly racialized figure who was and is positioned within a colonial story of the racialization of religion and caste.

On the Racial Conflation of the Hindu, Indian, and Brahmin

A number of anthropologists have sought to understand the relation between race and religion and, more specifically, the ways religion was and continues to be racialized. Junaid Rana, for example, has argued that Christian clashes with Jewish and Muslim (sometimes glossed as Moorish) peoples in the "Old World" between 1300 and 1500 were the basis for differentiations that located the problem with the latter two groups in the impurity of their blood, an impurity that could never be eliminated even if these peoples converted to Christianity.[9] In turn, Rana argues that the cultural practices associated with these religious groups became the fodder for their racialization, especially because these groups could not be easily differentiated by phenotype alone. As such, this early history of racialization included from its inception criteria and characteristics beyond phenotype.

Even as the Abrahamic faiths were being racially differentiated among themselves, the generic category of the "heathen" became a racialized figure both in the "New World" in encounters with Indigenous peoples, *and* in the East, as colonizers were encountering Hindus in their travels. These groups were collapsed by many early missionaries, for example, Cotton Mather, who in *India Christiana* (1721) grouped the "heathens" of India and America into one category and wrote, "The promise made unto OUR SAVIOUR, I will give the Heathen for thine Inheritance, and the Uttermost of the Earth for thy Possession."[10] As he made blatantly clear, the heathen was a primary site for salvation, and in contexts as diverse as the Americas and the Indian subcontinent, missionary zeal was deployed to civilize the heathens by teaching them the precepts of Christianity.

While "India came to America by mistake," the collapse of these extremely different peoples was essential to the colonial cause.[11] The conflation of the "brown Indian" and the "red Indian" was a by-product of European imaginaries of the "Orient" that facilitated a global project of colonial expropriation. As Shaista Patel argues, extending the work of Chickasaw scholar Jodi Byrd: "The figures and histories under the metonym of 'Indian,' as Byrd notes, were 'flexible and indiscriminate,' and 'signified non-Western or anything that was 'East.'" Just like the Moor was a referent for everything expellable from European purity and referred to several different groups of people, "Indian" too was a fluid categorization of Europe's Others.[12] In describing the Orientalist discourses that collapse India and the "New World," Patel reveals how settler and franchise colonialism required a *global* racialized image of the Indian in order to justify itself.

Paradoxically, the Hindu slowly morphed from the position of Indian heathen to European ancestor as European Christians sought to construct an origin completely separate from Semitic (i.e., Jewish) or Moorish (i.e., Muslim) peoples. This is why, in *Crania Americana* (1839), Morton's treatise on his scientific racist findings, he wrote several pages dedicated to the "Hindoos" and characterized them as part of the "Indostanic family of the Caucasian Race."[13]

Morton believed that the Hindu was related to the European even though he sought to discover a taxonomic basis for their essential difference. He, like many other Orientalists, found the essential difference of the Hindu race in their religious practice and the caste system. He writes at length:

> The Hindoos are among the oldest nations of the earth. Their present civilisation, with its institution of castes—their religion, which is Brahminical—and their language, which is Sanscrit, may all be traced to an antiquity of nearly three thousand years. . . . They appear by nature to be a mild, sober and industrious race, warm in their attachments and fond of their children. But their love of the marvellous, fostered as it is by a fantastic religion, is almost without a parallel among nations. . . . The Brahminical religion of the Hindoos is essentially idolatrous. . . . The castes are four great divisions or classes, each designed to be isolated and exclusive in all its relations. They are, 1st, the Brahmins, or Priests; 2d, the Rajahs (or Kishatrias), or Soldiers; 3d, the Vaisya, or merchants and cultivators; and 4, the Sudras, or subordinate cultivators, who are, in fact, the slave population of Hindostan. Each of these tribes is subdivided into several more, of which the number is uncertain. This singular thraldom prohibits all intermixture or association of castes: yet notwithstanding the severest social and bodily penalties, the impure or mixed castes are very numerous; for of these the Pariahs alone are said to constitute one fifth of all the people of India. Inferior, if possible, to these are the Pallis of Madura, and the Puliahs of Malabar, whose touch is defilement even to a Sudra. . . . [T]he Brahmins, and perhaps the Kishatriya and Vaisya castes were originally a race of northern conquerors of fair complexion; while the Sudras and other inferior tribes were an aboriginal and darker race.[14]

In his discussion Morton is conflating several categories, including those of India, the Hindu, the brahminical religion, and the caste system. While the term Hindu had emerged in the thirteenth century to refer to those who lived across the Indus River, Morton was drawing from the British, who mapped the term onto the cultural and religious practices associated with brahminism. This simplistic mapping of India onto Hindus and brahminism would continue to remain operative, reflecting the idea of India as the "home" of the Hindu and those who followed the brahminical scriptures.

But Morton also brings together two other critical elements in the racialization of the Hindu. First, he locates the essential quality of the Hindu in their "love of the marvellous," linked to their "fantastic religion." As I argue, the idea of the Hindu as exceptionally religious, superstitious, and/or spiritual would continue into the twenty-first century. Importantly, this Hindu brahmin figure, as Patel writes, was "constructed as genteel and honourable in opposition to barbaric Muslims" and the "loathsome" Ethiop, which allowed Europeans to valorize their encounters with this supposedly mild, industrious, and hyperspiritual group of Hindu Indians, while maintaining their anti-Muslim and anti-Black cosmology.[15]

At the same time, Morton gestures toward the racialization of caste, by claiming that brahmins, kshatriyas, and vaishyas are fair-complexioned outsiders while the Shudras and "other inferior tribes" are darker. Here Morton is drawing explicitly from the German strand of racist science initiated by Johannes Blumenbach. This strand of racist science was furthered by the Orientalist philologist Max Müller, who spent his career studying and translating Sanskrit texts and, in so doing, postulated a link between European language families and Sanskrit. These linguistic studies facilitated and reinforced the "Aryan theory of race," a hegemonic mythology in the early twentieth century in which lighter-skinned, savarna Hindus had migrated from Europe to the subcontinent and had conquered it and were therefore "white" as opposed to the indigenous populations (termed Dravidian) of the subcontinent.[16] Caste differentiation, in this conception, was meant to maintain the purity of the Aryan conquerors despite the fact that Morton notes that "the impure . . . are very numerous" in India.

Scholars on the Indian subcontinent also drew on and contributed to this scientific racist legacy. For example, in *Caste and Race in India* (1932), the brahmin sociologist G. S. Ghurye (also known for being the mentor of sociologist M. N. Srinivas), argued that there was a relationship between race and caste and sought to prove it by deploying the scientific racist measuring techniques developed in the United States. Ghurye focused on measuring crania, nasal cavities, and all sorts of other phenotypic characteristics as proof of a clear race/caste relationship. In his interpretation of his data, Ghurye postulated that "the state of things can be the result only of such regulations that prevented the possibility of the Brahmin blood being mixed with aboriginal blood."[17] Here Ghurye is articulating the logics of caste through the language of blood, effectively racializing the conversations on caste and mapping the colonial ideas of blood purity onto caste-based exclusion.

While anticaste leaders such as B. R. Ambedkar argued that caste *should not* be seen through this racial logic, many savarna nationalists took up the idea that one's caste reflected biologically immutable capacities and proved savarna racial superiority.[18] For example, the Hindu supremacist nationalist leader Lokmanya Tilak wrote *The Arctic Home in the Vedas* (1903), in which he argued that the savarna castes were originally Aryan people who migrated from the Artic some eight thousand years earlier, explicitly mapping Vedic hymns and astrology onto this imagined movement.[19] In writing this text, Tilak was in conversation with Max Müller and William F. Warren, the president of Boston University from 1873 to 1903, revealing the extent to which scientific racist discourses were circulating globally.

Romila Thapar further elaborates on how the Aryan myth translated into the savarna-led nationalist movements, writing:

> These views coincided with the emergence of nationalism in the late nineteenth century in India, articulated mainly by the middle class, which was drawn from the upper caste and was seeking both legitimacy and an identity from the past. Origins therefore became crucial. To legitimise the status of this middle class, its superior Aryan origins and lineal descent was emphasised. It was assumed that only the upper caste Hindu could claim Aryan ancestry. This effectively excluded not only the lower castes but also the non-Hindus, even those of some social standing. Aryanism therefore became an exclusive status. In the dialogue between the early nationalists and the colonial power, a theory of common origins strengthening a possible link between the colonisers and the Indian elite came in very useful. For early nationalism, Aryan and non-Aryan differentiation was of an ethnic and racial kind, but was also beginning to touch implicitly on class differentiation.[20]

While I am not concerned with the facticity of the claim of Aryanism (an excavation that I think is anywhere from irrelevant to outright dangerous), Thapar's analysis reveals the way that class, race, and caste were linked in the Indian nationalist project, creating an alliance between white colonizers and savarna elites, which ultimately allowed for the upward mobility of savarnas in binary opposition to everyone else, including Dalits, Muslims, and the rural poor.[21]

On the Racialized "Brahmin-Essential" Strategy
of National Uplift

Somewhat paradoxically, even as early Hindu supremacist leaders like Tilak were arguing that brahmins and other savarnas had come from the Arctic, they were also simultaneously emplacing the seemingly contradictory idea that the imagined Indian state was the natural and deserved homeland of the Hindu.

Through such rhetoric, savarna Hindus were "indigenized," and their anticolonial independence movements could also be seen as a means to finally bring forth an explicitly Hindu nation that had been erased through years of "outside" rule by Mughal and British colonizers. This ideology has been perpetuated in India over the past one hundred years, which has provided a precedent for the current Hindu supremacist regime's appropriation of "decolonial" and "Indigenous" discourse as justification for its fascist claim to power.[22]

Taken from this perspective, the emerging Indian nation was actually a construction of "the Brahmin-essential self." In fact, even though the emerging nation was explicitly articulated as a pluralistic, secular democracy, Jawaharlal Nehru himself conceived of India as a brahminical vision mirrored by the West, stating, "For the West also brings science and science brings food for the hungry millions. But the West also brings an antidote to the evils of this cutthroat civilization—the principles of socialism for cooperation, and service to the community for common good. This is not unlike the old Brahman ideal of service, but it means the brahmanization (not in the religious sense, of course) of all classes and groups and the abolition of class distinctions."[23] Nehru's ideology has often been viewed as anticolonial because it involved nonalignment with the West and included pseudosocialist policies and rhetoric. However, despite his nonalignment stance, he still believed in the technocratic, scientist nation building project of the colonizer. At the same time, Nehru's quote suggests a fetishizing of the brahmin as the moral vanguard for India's postindependence uplift. He remarks explicitly on the "Brahman ideal of service" and calls for the brahminization of India as a means to erase class divisions. Here Nehru occludes the materiality of caste supremacy while evoking the character of the brahmin as morally superior. Nehru also displaces religious and caste markers onto cultural practice, which implicitly racializes the cultural characteristics of the brahmin, allowing him to argue for the brahminization of India even as he suggests that this phrase is not being used "in a religious sense."

Still, the idea that brahmins would become the vanguard for this technocratic nation building vision was not obvious and was actually a by-product of the brahmin's changing economic and occupational mobility during British colonial rule. In the eighteenth and early nineteenth centuries, brahmins were considered solely as the bearers of the Hindu scriptures and were constrained by this perceived religious zealotry. This spiritual "cognitive" restriction meant that they were incapable of technomaterialist work because it had traditionally been associated with the "manual" labor of lower castes. In fact, during the early colonial period, the British brought over their own engineers and scientists with the assumption that Indians, and brahmins in particular, did not have the capacity for engineering.

However, Ajantha Subramanian argues that as urbanization and industrialization created the necessity for local skilled labor, dominant-caste men gained access to colonial education and were conscripted into white-collar technical jobs (now deemed "conceptual" rather than "manual").[24] Over time, as these jobs became increasingly valuable and valued, the technological industries in India became the almost-exclusive purview of brahmin men. The result was a new racialized stereotype that associated brahmins with the innate cognitive capacity to be science and technology experts. Practically, this meant that occupations that were previously barred to brahmins, and that would have historically resulted in the loss of caste position, could now be joined as long as one maintained appropriate blood ties through hyperendogamous exclusionary practices predicated on who one was allowed to touch and not touch. It also meant that caste-as-blood was inherently gendered, making the labor of maintaining caste tradition the purview of (cisgender heterosexual) women in the patriarchal household even as (cisgender hetereosexual) brahmin men were exposed to new occupational and cultural possibilities.[25]

Nehru's quote also points to the way that brahminization was seen as community service that would solve the issue of poverty and "the hungry millions" in India. The problem of poverty had become a focus for nationalist leaders, especially as it was linked to the agrarian question and, in some cases, the issue of caste, given that many Dalit castes continued to work for landed agricultural castes. In opposition to the rights-based approach espoused by Ambedkar, elite Hindu reformers saw the issue of caste oppression as a spiritual and cultural problem that could be rectified only through the paternalistic "uplift" of Dalits, which had the advantage of drawing them into the Hindu fold during the nationalists' fight for independence.[26] Mohandas Gandhi became the ultimate symbol of this form of Hindu salvation in his "Harijan uplift" ideology. Harijan was a word that Gandhi coined for Dalits that meant "God's children"; it was roundly criticized by Ambedkar and other anticaste leaders as a patronizing project of charity that sidestepped the real political and economic violence faced by Dalits.

Importantly, Gandhi's form of uplift and service relied on the discursive force of the singular racialized caricature of the brahmin, which presented him as a priestly man who abstained from material impulses (the earning of money, sexual practice, and the like) and therefore did good works in the world without any expectation of reward (enshrined in the idea of Hindu dāna that

Nehru is evoking in his discussion of brahmin service).[27] This racialized idea of the brahmin was passed down along with the idea that, for savarna reformers, formal political means of social change were less important than extrastate reforms, which might be one reason that specific NGOs led by those perceived as "native" and implementing brahminical-technocratic strategies for uplift are able to proliferate so quickly in India. Practically, this approach to service required patronage, and Gandhi advocated for "trusteeship" as the solution, in which the rich became trustees who would paternalistically watch over the poor. Gandhi himself garnered funds from several rich businessmen, including the billionaire G. D. Birla, for his uplift initiatives, causing the activist Arundhati Roy to facetiously remark that Gandhi should be considered India's earliest "corporate sponsored NGO."[28]

Race, Caste, and Transnational (US-Centric) Reorderings

These racialized assumptions ossified as savarnas moved abroad in larger numbers in the mid-twentieth century. If at an earlier moment savarna elites would have looked toward Britain and the old empire for new opportunities, as the twentieth century unfolded, their eyes now turned to the United States as it replaced the United Kingdom as the center of imperial power in the post–World War II period.[29] The Hindu had already emerged as a unique category in the United States during the late nineteenth century as part of the aforementioned scientific racist turn, which linked the "brown" Indian to the "red" Indian.[30] At the same time, in common parlance in the United States, the category Hindu served as a catchall term for *anyone* from the Indian subcontinent. As Junaid Rana writes, this meant that Hindu was used to refer to people from Bangladesh, India, Pakistan, or Sri Lanka *and* collapsed all religious groups from the subcontinent—including Sikhs, Christians, and Muslims—into this category.[31] The result was a further global entrenchment of the idea that India was a Hindu nation, which erased any differences among those who were migrating and reinscribed the savarna Hindu Indian migrant as the "true" representation of India.

Savarna migration was facilitated by mid-twentieth-century immigration reform in the United States—most notably the 1965 Immigration and Nationality Act—which allowed for the integration of high-skilled educated technocratic workers from the subcontinent, a self-selection bias that furthered the racialized caste-colonial history that privileged brahmins, and savarnas more generally.[32] Hindu Americans were folded into the "model minority" narrative, which had initially been used to valorize Asian Americans and was a "convenient way in which to reproduce anti-Blackness."[33] While their model status was linked to their aforementioned educational pedigrees and economic mobility, Hindu Americans also benefited from the global representation of Gandhi as the "nonviolent" anticolonialist, which became iconized in the United States through the figure of Martin Luther King Jr.[34] This seemingly preternatural capacity for nonviolence, also linked itself to the perceived excess spirituality and duty-bound service of the brahmin, a perception that was amplified as a group of spiritual gurus—including Osho, Baba Ram Dass, and Paramahansa Yogananda—moved to the United States and began proselytizing to (mostly white) Americans.[35] This racialization actually mapped itself onto *all* Indians in the United States,[36] "brahminizing" them even as many different communities carried their own culturally specific caste, regional, linguistic, and religious identities with them.[37] Ultimately, this historical legacy produced the possibility that these Hindu Americans could eventually be ideal saviors given this perceived racialized capacity for selfless, nonviolent service.

At the same time, Hindu Americans were slotted in with other "brown" subjects in the United States. Stanley Thangaraj, for example, argues, "South Asian Americans are read through and against other 'brown-skinned' subjects, such as Latinos, Southeast Asians, and Middle Easterners, who are lumped together as a result of their illegibility in the black-white racial logic."[38] While in one respect Thangaraj is right to regard brownness as illegible, in another respect brownness was actually romanticized: blood mixing and assimilation were imagined as rendering race obsolete and finally allowing the American experiment to be achieved, as long as, of course, everyone had become brown in blood but white "in taste, in opinions, in morals, and in intellect."

India's liberalization in the late 1980s and early 1990s only enhanced the savarna Indian subject as the model brown subject.[39] India as the so-called largest democracy in the world—a framing of the nation-state that was saturated with global value—also became one of the largest and most aggressive advocates for free-market capitalism, boasting the largest number of billionaires while consistently maintaining gross domestic product (GDP) growth rates of over 6 percent during the early years of economic liberalization. This kind of economic liberalization facilitated further friendly relations with the United States, which resulted in the entrance of many more Indian technocrats through the H1B visa policy, especially in engineering and computer science, to fill these burgeoning fields in the United States. In turn, (mostly savarna) Indian Americans have the highest median household income in the United States, an astronomical $116,000.[40] This excess accrual of capital became further associated with Indian American "genetic" dispositions for "knowledge," even linked to things like prowess in the US Spelling Bee.[41]

Legal frameworks, such as the Overseas Citizens of India (OCI) scheme, have facilitated the production of this transnational racial subject. The OCI was devised for people of "Indian-origin" who were eager to remain connected to the Indian nation even while residing permanently abroad. From a state perspective, the scheme was a response to the fear of "brain drain," in which India's highest-skilled workers were moving elsewhere, and was a method to facilitate the "reverse flow" of money, ideas, and people back to India from abroad.[42] Although an OCI cardholder must still have a visa, the cardholder is conferred a "forever" visa when they receive their card, and thus a citizen of another country—the United States or Britain, for example—can freely enter India without having to apply for a visa each time. The OCI cardholder "as flexible citizen" and therefore "exception" serves to optimize the functioning of multiple neoliberal states (the United States and India in this case), facilitating market-driven development through global Non-Resident Indian networks. But the OCI is also premised on a particular racial logic of "blood" that assumed a kin relationship between those outside of India and those within the nation-state. This set of economic and legal frameworks has allowed for excess racialized capital to be attached to the bodies of savarnas who were born in the United States *or* who were born in India but had moved away from India for education or work: distinct groups that have been collapsed into the single category of Non-Resident Indian to signify their blood ties to the subcontinental area siphoned off post-1947 as the Indian nation-state came into being.

In the Indian case, it is important to emphasize again that this racial logic only truly benefits savarna Hindus. For example, Indian-origin Muslims, especially those who have any family member with "Pakistani ancestry" (almost inevitable given the history of partition), have been systematically erased in this version of blood, nation, and religious belonging.[43] In fact, this racialized narrative of savarna ascension relied on an active distinguishing from, and therefore reinforcing of, the racist stereotyping of the Muslim subject produced as part of the global war on terror, which dovetailed directly with anti-Muslim sentiment in India. This exclusion of Muslims is tethered to a discourse on security and terrorism that positioned Indian Muslims who lived abroad as potential "terrorists and criminals" who were therefore seen with suspicion. This also has allowed for censure of those diasporic Indians who voice dissent against the Indian state, especially those who speak against India's anti-Muslim policies, including the National Register of Citizens (NRC), the Citizenship Amendment Act (CAA), and the militant occupation of Kashmir.[44]

Finally, the massive overvaluation of the digital in the late twentieth century became an essential regime of value that facilitated savarna Hindus' accumulation of global wealth and racialized distinction. In India between 2013 and 2019, there was a 68 percent increase in the number of wireless internet users, which represented a growth from 220 million to 696 million.[45] Within this regime, savarna men, and brahmins especially, who had already ascended as the techno-cognitariate during the postcolonial period, were again conferred excess capital. In India those who went to elite engineering institutions, for example, the Indian Institutes of Technology, had gained global cachet and were seen as the drivers for India's future growth. Not surprisingly, the majority of those who attended such schools were brahmins, who saw themselves as both meritorious and naturally gifted entrants into these elite universities despite their massive historical accumulation of caste capital.[46]

In turn, savarna men were able to convert their caste capital into modern forms of global "casteless" capital while reproducing the racial myth that savarna Hindus had the unique cognitive capacity to fix any of society's ailments through their technological capacity. This technological ascendance coupled with the hyperendogamy characteristic of caste created what Michiel Baas has termed the "IT caste."[47] Crucially, the perceived racial capacity for spiritual practice was mapped onto the information technology (IT) caste as they moved globally. Sareeta Amrute, for example, has shown how Indian IT workers were racialized by the white German managerial class in Berlin as having sage-like qualities.[48]

These racializing processes came together with the global help economies through the proliferation of global ICT4D (Information Communication Technologies for Development) initiatives, which became the technological answer to the problem of poverty in the brown world, especially in places like India.[49] Here, finally, the brown savior fully emerged, seeking multiscalar systemic interventions to revamp areas like education that were deemed in need of saving owing to their bureaucratic inefficiency and lack of digital infrastructure. For example, Nandan Nilekani, the billionaire former CEO of the Bangalore-based tech giant Infosys, undertook the massive Aadhaar project, which was intended to create a biometric ID for all 1.2 billion Indian citizens, even as he founded the EkStep Foundation, which developed software that was intended to tackle the issue of illiteracy.

Similarly, Sahaayaka had sought to intervene in and restructure the educational system in India through motivational programming for rural children *and* through the integration of a new, scalable platform for data collection, storage, and analytics into Karnataka's educational bureaucracy. But Sahaayaka's influence extended *beyond* the confines of India. For example, they had become a model for interventions in other regions in the brown world, such as the Maldives. Krish, the CEO, had also been asked to consult with Gooru, an education technology company led by a number of Indian American former Google employees working both in Redwood City, California, and in Pune, India. While I discuss this further in part IV, what these interventions reveal is the way that the brown savior has capitalized on the global circulation of their perceived spiritual, cognitive, and technological capacities over the past twenty years.

Part I Is Done: In Sum and What's to Come

Together, the two chapters in part I create a conceptual framework that positions the help economies within global racial capitalist regimes while helping us to understand the historical emergence of the brown savior. In particular, I have argued that understanding the help economies requires an attention to savior/saved binaries not as obvious, taken-for-granted, ahistorical slots but instead as a by-product of situated histories of encounter. My analysis carefully attends to the labor differentiations along lines of "value" and "limited value," which intersect with perceived essential differences regarding one's capacity for labor based on race, caste, and gendered position. Such an analysis requires an empirical excavation of the specific histories and political economic relations that produce these differentiated labor slottings. Therefore, in chapter 2 I focused on the specific historical genealogy of the savarna Hindu as would-be brown savior. I briefly attended to how the brown savior ascended because of the accumulation of racialized differences over the colonial, postcolonial, and liberalization periods. The inscription of racialized religious and caste value, tied to their spiritual, transnational, and technocapitalist labor capacity, allowed brown saviors to gain excess labor value within the help economy.

In part II, I turn to my fieldwork engagements with Sahaayaka to illustrate what brown saviors do with all their accrued capacity to save Others and the contradictions that emerge therein. Specifically, I reveal the way that the practices of Sahaayaka's brown saviors are actually predicated on neocolonial ideologies, values, and imaginaries.

Specifically, each chapter focuses on a different vector of neocolonial racialized difference. As is by now a well-known fact, colonial governance required the fixing of differences in the colonies, utilizing these racialized distinctions to determine particular labor roles within the colonial regime. I characterize the forms of racialized difference I analyze in each chapter of part II, as neocolonial because they have been shaped by these earlier colonial demarcations of difference as they relate to labor capacities. For example, as I have already noted, the brahmins' precolonial role as priests was fixed as a perceived exceptional cognitive capacity that determined their labor slotting in the colonial government and explains, in part, their ascendance within the help economies. Similarly, I show in chapter 3 that the conception of poverty embedded in much of the NGO work in India, including in Sahaayaka's intervention, is connected to and reproduces colonial understandings of the poor as both an inherently unproductive population and a destabilizing force. Such ideas were passed down as part of the governing strategies in postindependence India and have continued to pervade the assumptions undergirding help work, including, perhaps surprisingly, literacy campaigns and Sahaayaka's motivational strategies.

Similarly, labor distinctions associated with the West/the rest, dominant caste/oppressed caste, (cisgender heterosexual) man/(cisgender heterosexual) woman, and Hindu/Muslim trope on the binaristic, immutable logics emplaced by colonial and imperial powers and influence the kinds of strategies Sahaayaka employs as part of its uplift efforts. To be sure, oppressive religious and caste distinctions existed *before* colonization and have been weaponized anew within India's Hindu supremacist autocracy. However, as a number of scholars of India have shown, these categories operated in distinctive ways postcolonization. As such, each chapter in part II, pays careful attention to how these neocolonial differentiations have been reproduced within the help economy and dictate the particular form of saviorism I observed during my fieldwork. As the reader moves between chapters, I hope it will become clear that these neocolonial distinctions are deeply imbricated in one another, especially when it comes to determinations regarding how Sahaayaka should do its work.

Importantly, neocolonial forms of differentiation are occluded in the technocratic liberal assumptions embedded in help work. In other words, Sahaayaka was characterizing its interventions in universal terms abstracted from those differences on which material inequity is predicated. This is itself a neocolonial governance strategy that assumes interventions should and would be beneficial to *all* people within a nation-state independent of their position within it even as, paradoxically, these interventions reemplaced neocolonial distinctions and exclusions.

II

NEOCOLONIAL SAVIORISM

All reform consists in a change in the notions, sentiments and mental attitudes of the people. . . . If new notions are to be inculcated in the minds of people, it is necessary to give them new names. To continue the old names is to make the reform futile.—B. R. AMBEDKAR, *Annihilation of Caste*

One has to deal with those who manipulate the system and those who are either agents or unwitting accomplices of the said system.
—WALTER RODNEY, *How Europe Underdeveloped Africa*

Colonial and postcolonial power is always exercised with the agreement and support of some portion of the colonized society. It is crucial to continue studying by what means active or passive consent to policies of dependency are obtained.—FRANÇOISE VERGÈS, *The Wombs of Women*

POVERTY'S MOTIVATIONAL DOUBLE BIND

(OR NEO-MALTHUSIAN VISIONS)

I was wandering around the village of Adavisandra with my research assistant Sripriya and ten of my eighth- and ninth-standard students. It was a lazy Wednesday, and we had spent the past few hours inside a classroom because these students, who on a normal school day would be in school, had no place to be. They had stayed back in Adavisandra while their classmates had gone on a five-day school trip to visit some famous sites in Chennai and Tiruchirappalli. I felt compelled to do something, would-be savior that I was, so I volunteered to teach them about some topics outside of the standard school curriculum. One of the Adavisandra teachers, Manjunath, handed me the keys to the primary school building with relief, thankful to have a dilemma averted.

For me, these keys made me nervous because of the responsibility they represented but also because of the capital they evinced. The key is a tool for unlocking that which is hidden; it can evoke neocolonial anthropological dreams of unmediated transparency, complete consent, and the superhuman capability to crack a cultural code and discover the essence of some otherwise mysterious cultural system.[1] I knew my power to wield the key was a by-product of capital—as male presenting, as brown, as savarna, as Hindu, as American, as well educated, all of which unlocked this school to me despite the fact that I had been there only for a few short months and really had no substantive reason I should be trusted with so much power. Hesitatingly or not, I had deployed my status as brown savior, with unfettered assumptions of access traveling with me just as they did with those Sahaayaka personnel whom I intended to study.

Even though I was disturbed that my students could not join their peers on this field trip, my students did not seem to be. As we walked around Adavisandra after our makeshift class, they told me that "of course" they would have loved to go on the trip, but of course they could not. They explained matter-of-factly and *very* slowly, probably because they felt I could not understand what they were trying to tell me given my own class position, that *they were the poor* and that they did not get the opportunities that others did. But they were not cavalier or fatalistic about any of this; instead, they were despondent, assessing the wrongs and structural inequities that had produced all of this unfairness for them. A few of the students in the ninth standard started to talk about their aspirations, which they linked directly to the problem of poverty:

SRIPRIYA: Why do you want to be lawyers? Where did that determination come from? What injustice is going on around here?

KRISHNA: Politicians are bribing. . . .

INDIRA: It is the rule of the rich here, the poor don't get justice in the court. They're buying the law with money, the poor are not getting justice at all.

JAYANTI: Corruption . . . politicians. They're draining everything.

Indira connected her aspiration to become a lawyer with the injustice wrought against the poor in India when the rich "buy" the law with money. The narrative about corruption in India mediated the issue of classed inequality, injustice tethered to the fact that the state apparatus was only meant to serve the "rule of the rich." For Indira, the success of the rich did not confer moral authority; quite the contrary, it signaled their likely exploitative and extractive behaviors, the fact that they were "draining everything" and leaving nothing for anyone else.

But as we continued walking, the students were less clear about how exactly to change the system beyond their own personal aspirations. When pressed, they started to speak more mechanically, less passionately, even clinically, as if they were reading from a textbook. They started again by telling me that *they* were the poor and that *they* were in need of development, evoking one sense of brown that continues to shape life in places like India.[2] As they chanted these words, I could not help but hear them reckoning with how it feels "to be a problem," a constant sense that they knew they were the ones that were to be surveilled, managed, and reengineered.[3]

Eventually Jayanti and Pallavi considered one solution to the problem:

SRIPRIYA: ... what improvements are required in the society?

JAYANTI: First, our country should develop.

PALLAVI: ... There should be a law of only one child per family ...

SRIPRIYA: And then?

PALLAVI: Population will decrease.

SRIPRIYA: ... and then?

PALLAVI: Illiteracy should be erased, and everyone should be happy.

In this case, Jayanti and Pallavi conflated the problem of national development with individual underdevelopment, an idea that has become the ubiquitous racialized position for the "Third World" brown poor. Moreover, they were parroting these developmentalist ideologies and linking them to population control, assuming that their own individual decisions to have children or not should be regulated by the government and were the key to improving India.

In fact, Jayanti and Pallavi's comments reflect a long history of colonial concerns over overpopulation, which infiltrated the strategies for development within nation-states like India. What I want to argue in this chapter is that, somewhat more paradoxically, these ideologies actually shape NGO actions, from literacy campaigns to empowerment, by implicitly focusing on the wasteful, unproductive practices of the poor that ought to be eliminated. For example, as I will show, ideas like "motivation," a key tenet of Sahaayaka's empowerment-based interventions, do the work of disciplining students toward goals that implicitly are marked as making them more productive citizens but that also might actually further exacerbate their potential for dispossession.

The Malthusian History of Population Control and the "Wasteful" Poor

Historically, the fear of overpopulation, especially among the poor, was one of the most critical concerns within colonial racial capitalist systems. Thomas Malthus famously feared the expansion of the poor population in Britain, witnessing the French Revolution and fearing that the same revolutionary impulse would arise in Britain as well.[4] In Malthus's reading, the greatest threat to the elite classes was the latent revolutionary potential of the poor, who might recognize the ills done to them and overthrow those exploiters in power. Malthus's instinct makes some sense as even in the preceding stories told by my students, their first explanation for their poverty was to correctly point to the immoral accumulationist tendencies of the rich, backed by the state, a recognition that sets the basis for their own interest in fighting a system that treats them unfairly.

Importantly, in the Malthusian framing, the latent capacity for uprising is not primarily based on the experiential knowledge that comes with facing injustice but is actually more akin to a racialized characteristic of the poor, a capacity that cannot be easily expunged from their blood. In fact, Malthus's theory was that the poor would be eradicated by massive disasters (famine, etc.) if they were not restrained from social welfare, from marriage, and from giving birth; he couched his claims in moralizing rhetoric about those deemed "deficient," "unfit," and "unindustrious." Here impoverished British men and women were perceived as lacking the appropriate moral disposition to procreate. As such, Malthus's ideas reinforce the fact that colonial racial capitalism as a system began with the project "to differentiate—to exaggerate regional, subcultural, and dialectical difference into 'racial' ones *within* European states."[5] At the same time, these ideas were also emplaced in the colonies: for example, Malthus deemed Native tribes in America especially unfit for procreation because of their "constant labor" and "libertinage" and determined that brown Indian women were prone to "passion for men," which, in turn, caused overpopulation, famine, and mass death.[6]

But even as fears of overpopulation in Britain were mitigated in the eighteenth and nineteenth centuries because of the migration of more and more of the British poor to its colonies, neo-Malthusian ideas were reenforced with colonial subjects.[7] As Kalpana Wilson has written, "Colonial officials like Lord Lytton, the Viceroy of India during the famine of 1876–1879 in which up to 10.3 million people are estimated to have died, invoked Malthusian principles to justify his refusal to prevent these deaths."[8] These neo-Malthusian ideas continued into the post–World War II period as one of the key tenets of developmentalism, linking population control with national economic productivity.

In these discourses those living in the homogenized "brown world," abjectly poor and forlorn, also were unable to withhold their excess sexual urges. Family planning programs and sterilization campaigns proliferated across the previously colonized world, predicated on the biomoral assumption that "nonwhite women were having too many babies and were thus the cause of underdevelopment and poverty."[9]

In 1952 India was one of the first countries to implement family planning programs, claiming that by lowering fertility rates and slowing population growth it could propel its national economic development. This strategy was heavily backed by global donors, particularly the Ford Foundation, which spent $35 million globally (and $20 million in India) on such campaigns from 1952 to 1975.[10] Infamously, these programs came to a head in the 1970s under Indira Gandhi's Emergency, when many poor men, especially from the oppressed castes, were forced into sterilization.[11] Family planning programs have continued in India, with the one shift being that such sterilization campaigns now focus more squarely on poor women, only exacerbating the way that "the management of women's wombs . . . illuminates the coloniality of power."[12] Indeed, the idea that the poor cannot or should no longer procreate makes possible the conditions for them to no longer exist (their literal extinction), which, in turn, makes their land and properties available for productive use, a classical example of expropriation in racial capitalist societies.

Despite all its obvious antecedents in eugenicist histories, the move toward population control continues to be viewed as a compelling solution to the world's poverty problem. For example, population-control initiatives are encouraged by global development agencies like the Bill and Melinda Gates Foundation and through the 2020 UN Sustainable Development Goals, which argued that overpopulation is one of the key issues contributing to environmental degradation and global climate change.[13] Here, pointing to overpopulation among the poor as the reason for economic ills, environmental ills, and social ills does the work of, yet again, placing the problem of poverty at the feet of the poor while also placing those in power on the moral high ground—not just in relation to their greater capacity to reason but also in an embodied and biological sense. This naturalized distinction, in other words, allows the liberal agent of change to maintain their comfortable and powerful position as savior by locating the problem in those who purportedly need to be saved through the disciplining of their sexual urges.

Perhaps as important, Jayanti and Pallavi linked population control *with illiteracy*, suggesting that these two characteristics of the human, being uneducated and overpopulating, must be eradicated simultaneously through the reshaping of the impoverished body. In this conception, what is assumed is that the learning of letters will result in a reengineering of the human being such that wasteful and unproductive codes of conduct, including sexual urges, will be replaced by more productive forms of being. This is why part of the argument for universal literacy in India has been that higher literacy rates can predict a decline in fertility, solving the problem of surplus unproductive populations in a conjoined way: making those who cannot be expunged more productive while also leading these people to eventually stop reproducing. In this sense, population control and the eradication of illiteracy are two sides of the same coin within racial capitalist systems, working in tandem to strategically eradicate a lack of productivity among those deemed a priori as surplus.

Yet liberal saviors' moral conviction that such policies are the solution to the problem of poverty clashes against the actuality that human beings, rich or poor, should not be compelled into following other people's rules as to how they use their bodies. In fact, for the liberal savior, *forcing* people to do what is "in their best interest" is too distasteful, too obviously colonial, and therefore the savior cannot rely on force without losing their moral superiority and turning into what they see themselves in opposition to: the fascist. Therefore, the liberal savior chooses to toe the tricky line between convincing and compelling, and in many cases it is quite hard to tell the difference. This, I argue, is the liberal savior's conceptual double bind when it comes to the problem of poverty alleviation.

One solution in India has been to provide external incentives, particularly monetary incentives for sterilization. However, it would be even better if the poor would just internalize these messages and produce this change under the illusion of self-driven decision-making. Here the problem becomes a pedagogical one, not in the traditional sense of teaching people particular skills or ideas, but in the sense of making people believe in the moral good of their bodily disciplining. The task, in other words, is affective and not cognitive. The liberal savior is constantly seeking the key to beget this affective change, what Michel Foucault might have termed a "technology of the Self," which would unlock the poor's capacity to plan their families, imbibe the right educational ideologies (especially pertaining to literacy), and mimic the values of those in power unquestioningly.[14] Pallavi and Jayanti's generic, memorized responses to the question of development are one example of how this disciplining can occur over the course of years of education. However, this magical key still proves quite elusive given that most people, including children like Jayanti and Pallavi, are quite a bit more skeptical of the agendas of the savior than the savior would like them to be.

Empowerment and Motivation

The discourse of empowerment was one clever solution to this problem that emerged within the help economies, which sought to promote projects of self-help, self-care, and self-development, under the premise that this would ultimately bring those who have been left out of the successes of economic growth into its folds. As I noted in chapter 1, "neocolonial-cum-neoliberal" saviorism actually requires the dovetailing of paternalistic modes of intervention with the production of hyperindustrious would-be capitalists.[15] For example, Aradhana Sharma writes, "Empowerment now exemplifies neoliberal ideals of personal capacity building and self-governance. . . . Currently, empowerment is a mainstream, transnational development strategy widely used by NGOs and states alike. This translates into a problematic bureaucratization, hierarchization, and professionalization of empowerment as an expert intervention, which can work against the very spirit of equality and justice that empowerment is supposed to connote."[16] In this sense, empowerment can serve the purpose of seemingly promoting agentic possibility and future self-realization, while also ultimately bureaucratizing the problem of poverty and linking the problem to market expansion without addressing the many systemic bases for economic inequity *or* providing government-led social welfare schemes.

Sahaayaka's brown saviors had a variation on this empowerment strategy in their programs to "motivate" children. While Sahaayaka chose not to challenge standardized curricula or the way teachers taught their material, they highlighted that their interventions sought to change how students felt and acted. Krish, the CEO, tried to describe this motivational affect to me, telling me, "I just feel it when I go in. I know it already before I do anything else. If it's a motivated school, you just feel that. And I've been trying to figure out how to explain that to anyone else." Krish believed that harnessing this motivation was the key to changing rural life, unleashing a child's ability to improve their attendance, test scores, and investment in their learning. This was why he called Sahaayaka's program the *prerana program*, a Kannada word that could be glossed as either "motivation" or "inspiration."

This idea of motivation was part of what had endeared Sahaayaka to the Karnataka state government and international funders alike, giving them immense power because of the tantalizing allure of changing the entire education system through just a few small tweaks to a student's emotional state. For example, in praising Sahaayaka's motivational program, the state project director of Sarva Shiksha Abhiyan wrote, "A number of organizations, public and private, have been working to improve learning outcomes by creating innovative Teaching and Learning Methods (TLMs). However, these can only bear fruits fully if students are interested in what they are learning and 'pull' the inputs. Despite recognition of this (including from the Gates Foundation), innovations in creating student 'demand' for learning inputs have received scant attention."[17] In this statement he articulates the key to unlocking student potential as someone or something "pulling" (not forcing) students to take up the values and ideologies disseminated by those in the education system. Here motivation takes on a magical quality, the key to unleashing a massive amount of energy toward the goal of educational attainment. The idea was especially intriguing to the state government because it entailed very few resource inputs and was therefore cheap, a crucial consideration in neoliberal governmentality. That is, students would learn the appropriate skills and dispositions without building new schools, adding more teachers to classrooms, providing more curricular tools, or requiring any of the other educational resources that have traditionally been viewed as the primary method by which those who were underachieving might be helped. In this sense, motivation, like many of the discussions of empowerment, was completely abstracted from questions of inequity and was therefore an ideal intervention mechanism within development's "anti-politics machine."[18]

Perhaps in the most literal sense, motivation is the reason for a body's movement, an explanation for why we make the decisions we make. Madhu, a new hire at Sahaayaka, struggled to fully articulate what motivation meant, but she was quick to stress the importance of *intensity*:

> Let's look at cricket. So, when you are in the stadium, the sense that you feel, or the intensity in which you are engaged, is different than when you are watching on the television. It's very, very different.... Now I'm not talking about intensity in just one sense, it can be positive or negative.... I am looking at rewards and incentives. As a child who is thinking, "I am going to get a star, I love the fact that I am going to get a star," my intensity is going to shift to the event that is leading me to success.... When you look at motivation, intensity is all about "what am I feeling" and "why I am feeling." Because my "why" is changing, and my feelings change based on the structure; if the structure has not changed, I am still feeling the intensity, but I am feeling a negative intensity . . . and that is also quite intense.

In Madhu's articulation, affective intensity is a foundational building block for motivation. This intensity is about the body's relation to the environment, in this case how students experience their classrooms. As Madhu specifies quite clearly, it is the particular structures within the classroom that set the stage for the increase in affective intensity, either good or bad.[19] The challenge, then, was to *direct* intensity toward the standardized curricular goals that Sahaayaka had determined for students.[20] As important, Madhu's reference to the cricket stadium suggests that intensity is collective. Students in classrooms feed off each other's intensity of experience, and as they do, they shift their actions within these spaces.[21] Those shifts, in turn, are intended to produce more affective intensity, creating an endless loop.

In trying to show how this motivation was produced, Krish took out a sheet of paper on which he had designed what he had termed the "learning tree." Set in black and white, the tree was broken down into boxes, each of which included a standard learning goal in mathematics. "You know," he started, "we kept coming back to the issue of children tracking their own progress. To get them to be self-motivated instead of externally motivated. And we realized stuff like this, the tree, especially in a book they could keep, could really help with that." He then pulled out a sheet of colorful stickers, intended for students to stick one by one into each section of the tree until they had completed the entire page.

I sat in class and watched students meticulously place these stickers in the appropriate position. But even as they each did this individually, there was also a collective intensity that they generated.[22] One student held up his notebook, and others followed suit, each building further intensity until there was a palpable need to do more, get more answers correct, so that they might produce more of this result. In stark contrast to the directed production of motivation by an outsider, these students were generating these affective intensities themselves. In turn, they were motivating themselves to sustain their school activities, finish math problems, and move through the curriculum.

The tree was a metaphorical analogy of growth. In this case, the analogy of the tree reproduced the vague yet ever-present relation among human development, the goals of state/national development (in this case evidenced by the fact that standardized curricula set by the state shaped the goals of the learning tree), and the idea of the organism. In other words, Sahaayaka's model was reproducing a kind of structural-functionalist biomoral politics, in which society—like a tree—had parts that made it whole, parts that, if they functioned just right, would both help individual students be successful and also produce a classroom community and a school community that were optimally motivated and in sync toward the goal of bettering society.

What the tree analogy regenerated was another version of a developmentalist (read: civilizational) progress narrative. The teleological end point, in this case, was the completion of the tree, which represented students' shared and singular progress and growth. This meant that all of this affective intensity toward student motivation was not a way to get students to think more critically about what they were learning, about whether it was relevant to their lives in villages in Karnataka or not, or about the system they were in. In fact, that kind of free thinking was detrimental to their motivation, "pulling" them in a direction that might beget some questions regarding whether or not learning these skills would actually allow them upward mobility.

Indeed, this motivation was actually meant to steer students away from the kind of questioning that was already part of these students' daily lives, as evidenced in Jayanti and Pallavi's comments earlier in this chapter. Many students resisted the formal schooling system because they understood that the system as currently constituted would never support them. And, statistically speaking, they were right. As I noted in chapter 1, a brief scan of job possibilities revealed that if every single child in India completed tenth standard, less than 10 percent could get jobs. This structural constriction meant, in fact, that questioning the system in which they lived and/or finding alternative livelihoods was a rational choice. Yet value was placed solely on a singular math and literacy education, which drove them further away from their families' traditional agricultural occupations and lands. The implication is quite striking: if there are no jobs and students are being convinced and trained with skills to leave traditional livelihoods for these nonexistent jobs, then they are actually being set up for their own demise, dispossessed through educational attainment in ways not so dissimilar from those Malthusian strategies of population management. Motivation, in other words, might be considered an ideal technology for racial capitalist expropriation.

Seen in this way, Sahaayaka's motivational techniques may have more in common with another, more notorious version of motivation. During the Emergency in India, and afterward, the government had hired "family planning motivators" whose job was to convince the poor to get sterilized. These mediators functioned to create the illusion that the government was providing a choice and that those who were getting sterilized were being "motivated" by monetary and moral incentives.[23] Perhaps the brown savior's interventions were unintentionally doing something similar: by motivating (or empowering) students toward educational goals that sit perfectly within India's version of (under)developmentalism, they sustained the circuits of accumulation through dispossession under the guise of free choice, monetary possibility, and moral fervor.

This push toward motivation was not unique to India: Krish excitedly wrote that the Maldives Education Department had approached Sahaayaka about their work: "Interesting day sharing Sahaayaka's motivation and technology programs with delegates from Maldives Edn. Dept. and realizing our programs may actually benefit kids there too! Maybe Maldives in 2018 . . ." Here motivation signals the future potential of a global racial capitalist order led by the brown savior.

Yet Sahaayaka's expanding influence in the brown world should not be taken as their "natural" or obvious position within the global help economies. Instead, their influence over the brown world is historically situated in neocolonial hierarchies of labor value related to the Indian's perceived slot within a post–World War II global economic reordering that still largely maintained the binary between, in Michel-Rolph Trouillot's terms, the "West" and the "rest." In turn, these neocolonial racialized labor hierarchies played out in how Sahaayaka saw the role of the Indian worker, where they looked for expertise and funding, and how they reasoned about why they, and not others, should be the ones helping "on the ground."

In the next chapter, I turn to these neocolonial global labor hierarchies, their influences on Sahaayaka's multiscalar relationships with US-based business schools and Karnataka's government schoolteachers, and the "fatal" contradictions therein.

4

FATAL PRAGMATISM (OR THE

POLITICS OF "GOING THERE")

I sat on the dusty steps of a government school in early 2013, after one of my first school visits in South Karnataka. I was still adjusting to the pace of the encounters: following a mentor onto the school grounds; noticing the green, orange, and white of the Indian national flag painted on the pillars and walls; shaking hands with the headmaster and several teachers; sitting in a make-shift office with metal cabinets everywhere, a picture of Mohandas Gandhi on the wall and a chalkboard with the school "strength" (number of students) scrawled across it; straining to understand the headmaster while he discussed the many issues he and his students faced; trying in vain to refuse the mix of biscuits, tea, and small bananas that were given as a show of respect but that were playing tricks on my stomach after the third or fourth go of it; and running into two or three classrooms to speak to children, before quickly exiting behind a mentor out of the school and back toward the street. Each visit generally took no more than forty-five minutes, and I would come away from these quick forays into the classroom always wishing I had noticed more, especially when I looked at the blank pages of my notebook, which shamed me with their barren lines.

In these early years of Sahaayaka's growth, Srinivasan himself would go from school to school, speaking with headmasters, teachers, and students and trying to forge personal, lasting relationships that he believed were fundamentally unique. Unlike other NGO personnel, who would come, talk for a few minutes, make many promises, provide some basic educational tools, and leave, Srinivasan wanted to show the people he worked with that he was invested in these relationships by returning again and again and again. "You have to *go there*," Srinivasan would quip anytime I would see him. "You have to see what is happening *on the ground*." These explanations were also couched in Srinivasan's visceral distaste for government bureaucrats, who he argued were making decisions in faraway central offices without a care for the needs of their constituencies.

I often remember the critical pedagogue Paulo Freire when I am trying to understand Sahaayaka's brown saviors, especially Srinivasan. Freire argued that educational reformers working from within the system are "resigned fatalistically to neoliberal pragmatism . . . while considering that [they are] still 'progressive' pedagogically and politically."[1] This fatal pragmatism takes hold because reformers cannot imagine challenging the economic and political systems that produce inequality (or if they can imagine it, they do not believe such change is practical). Instead, they work within the system, hoping that those incremental changes they seek to make will erode the broken institutions about which they voice so much displeasure. Srinivasan was an almost classical version of the fatally pragmatic educational reformer, railing against capitalism, bureaucracy, and the like, even as he undermined his own progressive ideals in his attempt to make "strategic" decisions. This was mainly because Srinivasan's belief in "going there" contradicted the practicalities of Sahaayaka's goal to efficiently scale up its interventions. One of the organization's primary metrics for assessing impact was to track the increase in the number of Sahaayaka-affiliated schools, drawing from the managerial logics that Srinivasan and the other heads of Sahaayaka had learned during their time working in for-profit engineering industries. Scaling, in turn, required agreements with state governments, funding from corporate donors, and increased organizational bureaucracy, all of which undermined any altruistic visions Srinivasan may have had. How was one to "go there" when the numbers of places to go kept growing?

However, Freire's conception of fatal pragmatism does not quite capture a neocolonial figure like Srinivasan, primarily because it cannot reckon with the way that these pragmatic neoliberal decisions and determinations of value were and are based on specific histories of global racialized, casteized, and gendered labor relations. That is to say, not everyone can or will make the same fatally pragmatic decisions, because they have been positioned differentially in the historical accumulation of global labor value. The question of *who* was required to go *where* structured the brown savior's strategy for intervention and, as I will show, only reproduced neocolonial hierarchies of West/rest, expert/nonexpert, moneyed/nonmoneyed, on which global racial capitalist relations had been founded.

On the Perceived Problem with the Indian's Labor Capacity

In particular, Srinivasan's decision-making strategies were based on his previous work experience as a part of India's rising managerial class during the 1980s and early 1990s. Before 2007, Srinivasan had worked for the Indian manufacturing company Bharat Heavy Electricals Limited (BHEL) for over thirty years, a company whose growth signaled India's emerging technological prowess on the world stage along with the brahmin's rise within the postcolonial technocracy.[2] Srinivasan was nostalgic for that time, when he would travel abroad—to Berlin, São Paulo, Moscow, and many sites in the United States—learning, negotiating, and developing new global standards for chemical manufacturing. There was one story Srinivasan loved to tell, one that I heard for the first time while sitting with Srinivasan after this school visit to Harohalli. "You know the problem with Indians?" he would start, as if it were an unquestionable truth that there was, indeed, a fundamental, essential problem with Indians:

> See the Japanese and the Germans, even the Americans, they understand how to follow directions and produce. Indians are not like that. . . . If you give an Indian worker some directions, for example, you specifically ask him to put a blue ball in a white basket, he may follow for a while. But then he may run out of the white baskets, and he will think, "well, why don't I use these blue baskets?" He won't think to himself, "well, maybe there is some reason why the instructions were given as such." Instead, he will simply start putting blue balls in the blue baskets. Then, you know, the entire factory will have to shut down for two weeks because,

as it turns out, the ink from the blue baskets results in some chemical reaction that erodes most of the equipment. . . . See, the Indian will not follow instructions properly. Instead, he will think to himself, "Yes, let me try and figure out some other method." And that will lead to disaster.

Admittedly, when I first heard Srinivasan's words, I didn't think too much of it. On its surface it all seemed innocuous, even irrelevant, to the project of help Sahaayaka was undertaking. However, as Srinivasan repeated this story over and over again during the next several years, I began to situate this story within the legacy of racial logics that fused "particular bodily traits, social configurations (national, religious, etc.), and global regions, in which human difference is re-produced as irreducible and unsublatable."[3] In this case, Srinivasan imagined and produced an "Indian race" based on a masculinist and ableist relationship between personhood and nation that predetermined the bodily capacity to follow directions properly (or not).[4] Even more important, the mapping of identity that Srinivasan described became the taken-for-granted basis for ra-cialized differentiation and hierarchy in which Indian men remained "behind" the Americans, the Japanese, and the Germans, whose ability to follow direc-tions was of higher value in the world economy.

For those savarna men like Srinivasan who grew up in the years just after India's independence and worked in the industrial sectors, this racialized feel-ing of Indian inadequacy was linked to the cultural politics of post-Fordist in-dustrializing societies. Workers following rules in a step-by-step fashion—the classic assembly-line model—was essential to the efficient production of goods and, in turn, the nation's potential for economic growth and excellence. The need to discipline the male worker has been caricatured and theorized exten-sively in the literature on post-Fordist societies. Antonio Gramsci, for example, argued that capitalist production required moralizing cultural frameworks for how men should comport themselves inside and outside of work, in their con-sumption (of alcohol, food, etc.), the nuclear family systems they upheld, and their sexual practices.[5]

As important, Srinivasan's articulation of Indian deficiency was classed, gendered, and casteized, locating the issue specifically in the male, nonbrah-min, Indian labor force, that is, those men who were expected to receive and follow directions given by brahmin (or perhaps dominant-caste) managers, like Srinivasan himself. The impossibility to fully regulate and discipline the body of the nonbrahmin male worker resulted in Srinivasan's anxieties, which lami-nated themselves onto a masculinist performance anxiety regarding India's ability to achieve on the world stage.

This conception was foundational to why Srinivasan was so insistent that he should commute to schools to speak with students and headmasters as frequently as possible and provide moral framings for why students should act differently both at home and in school. In turn, he desired to produce students who would be appropriately disciplined such that they could join the growing labor force. He also desired to prove that they could be successful with just the right kind of help from those like him, as his experiences allowed him to see beyond the vagaries of "the problem with the Indian." This is why it was he, and not anyone else, who should "go there."

Sitting on the steps, he continued:

> I used to tell headmasters (HMs), "I can make you deliver not because I am better than you, you are a far better teacher than me. I mean, I don't even know how to teach so there is really no comparison! But the issue is that you don't know what you're capable of doing." . . . You know, the first school I took in Harohalli, I told the HM that all students must pass their SSLC exam.[6] And he told me, "No, no, four cannot pass." And I told him, "Absolutely no, you have to make them all pass," and you won't believe, in four months they made all the students pass the exam. "Afterward, they all said, "O nimminda aithu" (Because of you it happened), and of course I told them the credit goes to them, but they said something very interesting in response, they said, "You are the guy who made us realize we can do it."

In his own telling, those Srinivasan worked with—the rural, less affluent, non-brahmin, government-school headmasters—believed their own achievements must be due to him instead of their own work. Moreover, in this story, the labor hierarchy was maintained in that the practice of asking for help had been completely imbricated with the feeling of inferiority, evidenced in the idea that these headmasters "don't know what [they are] capable of doing" and needed someone to explain that they were capable. Here Srinivasan's description required the erasure of the headmaster's agency. Instead, the basis for success or failure was the headmaster's ability to push himself and his body to its limit based on the demanding presence and regulations of the manager.

At the same time, the labor hierarchy was maintained because of Srinivasan's perceived capacity to discipline, manage, and increase the outputs of those around him. This was partly due to his years of managerial work, which was tied to his travels abroad and exposure to those who were *not* Indian. While these travels were predicated on his caste capital as a brahmin technologist, this global exposure and cosmopolitan travel also did the work of diluting the brownness of his blood: he was still brown, of course (as will become clear in the next part of this chapter), but not quite in the same way as these headmasters who had never gotten the chance to travel outside of India. This perceived racialized difference between local headmaster and brown savior was critical in emplacing value hierarchies that gave Srinivasan legitimacy and made his words hold power over those he encountered in schools.

In this sense, Srinivasan's explanation actually contradicted his ideas about going and learning from those teachers, students, and headmasters in rural schools. On the one hand, the need to manage those he supposedly was learning from was pragmatic, based on the assumption that these local headmasters needed his skills and his motivational techniques in order to improve the life chances of students. On the other hand, these assumptions and the strategies they evoked proved fatal to Srinivasan's progressive imaginations because they only reinscribed the binaristic value hierarchies between outsiders and those "on the ground" that Srinivasan had so adamantly wanted to push against.

On the Labor Value of US Managerial Experts
and Its Inverse Relation to "Going There"

If Srinivasan's global exposures, managerial prowess, and caste capital convinced him that he had accumulated the appropriate capacities to discipline those within these school contexts, they also differentiated his value from those of the United States' managerial class. In fact, the transnational alliances he sought placed him in fatal pacts with capitalist interests in the West.

For example, Srinivasan sought to legitimate Sahaayaka through partnerships with overvalued entities in the United States, including corporate funders, US-based NGO leaders, and academics who sat in Ivy League institutions. Srinivasan's logic was pragmatic: he needed global legitimacy in order for Sahaayaka's program to grow and sustain itself. In fact, later he would admit that his main reason for replying to my initial emails inquiring about doing research with his organization was because he had wanted to have a stronger relationship with the University of Pennsylvania, knowing that a partnership with the university would increase his cachet both in the Indian national context and abroad. He craved these partnerships despite the fact that he did not put much stock in the knowledge produced in these spaces, especially as it pertained to Indian education. "They [North American university scholars] don't know anything about what is going on at the ground level," he would tell me with a high level of self-righteous indignation. It was a paradox that continuously emerged in Srinivasan's discourse and one that Srinivasan could not extricate himself from because he was so invested in the kinds of scalable models of growth that he could accomplish only through an association with a particular constellation of powerful figures within the global knowledge economy. It was why, in other words, Srinivasan's pragmatism was fatal; he was making concessions that would ultimately leave him in a compromised position.

But while sitting on the steps of Harohalli showing me his program, Srinivasan was not at all concerned with these pragmatic compromises. In fact, he was rather proud of them, and when he would talk to me about my own relationship with Sahaayaka, he would frankly tell me, "See, I don't mind telling you, actually we are just using one another. Right now, you being here is very useful, so we want you. Of course, you want to learn about education here, so we can help with that." This particular approach to our relationship was fraught, as on several occasions Srinivasan asked me to help validate the organization's impact on children. It was the difficult position that I, like other anthropologists working in the development space, found myself nervously navigating: How was I to maintain my scholarly integrity while I was developing relationships that had moved far beyond mere participant observation, affectively entangling me in the inner needs and desires of the organization and its members? Ultimately, I never published anything about Sahaayaka's program for them, though I did work on a white paper early in my fieldwork that is a constant source of self-criticism. That decision was one of many examples of my own fatally pragmatic decision-making in exchange for access that continue to haunt my fieldwork.

Srinivasan's attempts at leveraging his connections did not stop with me. In 2013 he arrived in Philadelphia and negotiated a (brief) partnership with the University of Pennsylvania's Wharton School of Business. He had contacted a white woman professor in the business school, and the professor, while overtly enthusiastic, was not all that interested in Sahaayaka's program per se. Instead, she saw an opportunity to leverage this relationship so that her students could study the NGO sector as part of their final capstone "field" projects to obtain their MBAs. While Srinivasan was excited about the possibility of working with Wharton, I was more skeptical, wondering to myself who was using whom.

The professor put Srinivasan in conversation with three master's students in the Wharton program, who were tasked with developing an "exit strategy" for Sahaayaka. The question of exit is a problem for NGOs that seek to scale up, given that funding is always limited and that expanding to new spaces meant that already existing school sites needed to be divested from. For Sahaayaka, the question was how to know whether a school in which they had been working could now sustain (or motivate) itself without any further direct intervention.

After their initial meeting, the students agreed to work with Sahaayaka via conference call held once Srinivasan went back to Bangalore. I sat in on several of these conversations between Wharton students and Srinivasan, conducted from a small office in the Wharton building at the university. The entire set of polymediated interactions—conference calls, emails, PowerPoint presentations, and Skype chats—centered on the premise that these media forms could facilitate Wharton students' virtual space-time travel to Karnataka, an adequate proxy for real on-the-ground observations of the organization.[7] Moreover, each call was predicated on the assumption that the students were "managerial experts," thanks in no small part to their Wharton branding, while Srinivasan played the role of the humble, grateful NGO novice from the brown world. Unlike the authority with which he talked to headmasters in schools, these interactions dripped with deference and hyperbolic gratitude. Hearing twenty-one-year-old US business students talking authoritatively to a seventy-year-old man who had spent almost thirty years of his life in upper management would always make me bristle, reeking as it did of neocolonial power relations. But when I mentioned this to Srinivasan, he almost scoffed at my naivete, chalking it up to my youth and lack of awareness of how things *really* worked. As he explained it, this was a necessary method of interaction when working across these massive differences in geopolitical power that was premised on the ongoing legacy of US imperialism.

I kept a copy of the "deck" that the students created, an artifact of Srinivasan's early attempt at university-based legitimacy. Because none of the students had ever gone to India, much less worked directly with an NGO, their solutions to the problem of exiting schools were abstract and generic. They gave several examples from other NGOs, though none of the examples were drawn from the Indian context, and two of the three NGOs they had chosen were not working in education. Ultimately, Sahaayaka never found any use for any of the recommendations and was still struggling to find a way to exit schools during my time conducting research. Still, Srinivasan sent an enthusiastic final email to the professor of the course in which he claimed that (1) the recommendations would be of "immense value" to Sahaayaka; (2) the collaboration between Wharton and Sahaayaka should be formalized; and (3) Srinivasan would be willing to have any number of meetings to make this happen.

Later Srinivasan admitted that he had never really intended to use the recommendations from the students but rather wanted to use the project to solidify a relationship with Wharton that could result in some kind of funding in the future. However, Srinivasan never got a response from anyone from Wharton after the end of the course, the endless possibilities fizzling out as soon as the students had gotten the "field" experience they needed. The MBA students came away from their project having their own illusions of "immense value" reinforced, legitimating that the American capitalist classes sitting in the seats of prestige with no experience in any of the actual pertinent fields should still be looked to for advice by those subjects struggling to change impoverished, "developing" societies. Srinivasan's request for institutional help actually became a form of labor he was providing for these students free of charge, a conveniently discovered "native informant" who could allow students to "go there" without having to leave the safety of the ivory tower. In the end, Srinivasan's pragmatism proved fatal because his own understanding of global value actually made it impossible for him to follow his own ideas regarding who had knowledge and who did not. While he insisted that one could only learn what to do by "going to these places" and learning from those who experienced struggle firsthand, he systematically sought advice and resources from those who had no interest in "going there" at all.

However, even as the question of "who" was required to go "where" revealed the incessant overvaluation of the West by the savarna brown savior, it also revealed that the brown savior required that those from the West *not* be able to go to the places in which they were intervening if the brown savior intended to cultivate their own power in these places. To put a finer point on the analysis in this chapter, one key takeaway is that the dominant castes in India require the white/brown, West/rest, US/India binaries in order to become the experts on and "spokespeople" for India, the poor, the rural, the marginal, and the oppressed castes on a global stage.

In the next chapter, I take this caste critique of savarna brown saviors further, locating their power in their ability to "abstract" themselves from the problem of caste even as caste hierarchy operated in nearly every aspect of their interventions.

5

THE CASTE OF LIBERAL INTERVENTION

Whether implicitly or explicitly, caste is part of every page of this ethnography. I have noted, for example, that the leadership of Sahaayaka was almost exclusively brahmin and that my own easy access to the organization was, at least in part, linked to our shared caste identity. Perhaps more strikingly, every single member of Sahaayaka's board of trustees was an elite brahmin, only one of whom was a brahmin woman. There is a long history of such savarna networks of corporate trusteeship, most famously the billionaire G. D. Birla's monetary backing of Mohandas Gandhi's "selfless" lifestyle during the nationalist period.[1] Such "trust" networks are built on the unstated assumption that intracaste communities are blood kin and therefore can be trusted both interpersonally and monetarily. These global caste networks have, in turn, been largely exclusionary, limiting the ability of those who are not savarna to access such networks and, therefore, find means of mobility both in India or as they travel abroad.[2]

Yet, despite these obvious facts, caste had always been a relatively absent topic in my dialogues with Sahaayaka leadership. Krish, Sahaayaka's CEO, rarely discussed caste or his own caste position, admitting that he could see that his own social situation had given him a lot of benefits without ever stating explicitly that it was due to his caste. This was partly because Krish had managed to transform his "caste capital into modern capital" as he had traveled to the United States, enhanced his technological prowess, and found his way into a leading role in the help economy.[3]

The organization did not keep data on caste; however, Krish was starting to reconsider this stance because he would end up discovering the castes of students anyway. For example, one of Sahaayaka's early motivational strategies was to take ten of the most successful students in their network of schools (based on exam scores and/or attendance) on a trip to New Delhi. For the students involved in the trip, it would be the first time they had traveled so far on the train, and therefore it would be a source of excitement and pride. "The funny thing," Krish told me, "when we took students on the Delhi trip, the SC [Scheduled Caste] students would get 75 percent off their rail tickets, so we would get to know after the fact anyway."[4] After finding this out, Krish realized that caste information might be quite useful to measure the success of Sahaayaka's intervention, another demographic metric to map against attendance, test scores, and so on. Such information, he explained, might help the organization determine its impact on SCs, while also better targeting student populations who were in need. In this type of categorical attention to caste, caste is abstracted from embodied experience and is instead associated solely with a government category that could "fix" itself epiphenomenally on certain people's bodies and not on others'. In this case, Krish was becoming comfortable tracking caste as category and as data while keeping caste safely abstracted from his embodied historical position, even as his caste networks facilitated his success.[5]

This notion of caste is so embedded in the framework of Indian political sociality to be taken almost as a given. As Satish Deshpande argued, the commitment in the Indian constitution to redress caste included specific caste reservations in governance that also filtered into institutions of education and higher learning.[6] While these constitutional requirements have been absolutely necessary for redressing the ongoing legacies of caste atrocity, they have increasingly and explicitly been reframed as "antimeritocratic" to bolster the Hindu supremacist crackdown on anticaste struggle. At the same time, this constitutional legacy has also meant that those who claim SC or Scheduled Tribe (ST) status were more likely to identify themselves within these categories as a means for political and economic mobility. By contrast, those who did not partake in this state-initiated caste categorization—namely, the dominant castes—have been able to see themselves as "outside" of caste, allowing them to imbibe the universal liberal values associated historically with whiteness while seeing their successes as merited and self-actualized. As Ajantha Subramanian writes, "There is no question that many upper castes think of themselves as modern subjects, or at least as subjects with sincere commitments to universalistic ideals of equality, democracy, and rationality. At the same time, they are able to inhabit a universal worldview precisely because of a history of accumulated privilege, a history that allows them a unique claim to certain forms of self-fashioning."[7] In the help economy, part of savarna self-fashioning was the ability to invisibilize their caste position while deploying the neocolonial liberal ideals of universality, equality, and paternalistic care they had inherited.

In the rest of this chapter, I draw out some of the contradictions embedded in brown saviorism when the savarnas' caste position is explicitly visibilized and they are no longer able to characterize their interventions as casteless.

Prevention of Atrocities, the Marking of Dominant Castes, and the Potential Loss of Savior Status

I started to think more deeply about how the brown saviors' intervention intersected with their modern caste capital when I met with Srinivasan sometime in the late fall of 2014. A few months earlier, Srinivasan had received a call from the inspector of the Jayanagar police station in Bangalore just as he had embarked on a trip to Coimbatore, Tamil Nadu, asking him to return to Bangalore immediately.[8] The inspector explained that one of the Sahaayaka mentors had accused Srinivasan of caste-based discrimination and SC/ST harassment under the Scheduled Castes and Tribes (Prevention of Atrocities) Act, 1989. This act was meant to protect SCs and STs from violent acts by dominant-caste groups.[9]

In his telling, Srinivasan was at the mercy of the law despite the fact that he believed he had done nothing wrong at all. Srinivasan was filled with anxiety; he had never had to go to the police station before, and he knew that if he went to the station, he would be required to show up in front of a magistrate within forty-eight hours, meaning he would most likely have to stay in a jail cell overnight. "In all my life," he admitted, "I never knew what it means to be in that situation. It is the one case where I am guilty until proven innocent. I have to prove that I am innocent, the other guy does not have to prove that I am guilty."

Srinivasan was pointing out and critiquing one of the primary tenets of the Prevention of Atrocities Act: that those from SC/ST communities can come forward anonymously if necessary, and a First Investigation Report can be registered against any person without a preliminary inquiry. All of this is to protect those who are at continuous risk of violation in India and to provide one of the very few legal statutes in which Dalits are believed a priori. Dalit communities have rarely been given adequate forms of protection in India, despite the fact that an atrocity against a Dalit by a non-Dalit happens every sixteen minutes. The Statement of the Objects and Reasons for the 1989 act lists a number of atrocities, including the fact that "of late, there has been an increase in the disturbing trend of commission of certain atrocities like making the Scheduled Caste person eat inedible substances like human excreta and attacks on and mass killings of helpless Scheduled Castes and Scheduled Tribes and rape of women belonging to the Scheduled Castes and Scheduled Tribes."[10] Given the extent of and sheer repulsiveness of these atrocities, a stronger form of protection was and is necessary.

Yet this same tenet has been viewed as draconian by dominant-caste objectors because it seems to them to violate the basic habeas corpus freedoms of the accused and therefore one of the most cherished "universal" freedoms in (neo)liberal democracies. The "violation" of liberal freedoms comes into focus when those in power risk the loss of capital. That is to say, the claims to being violated begin when "universal" freedoms do not serve the interests of the powerful quite so easily because they suddenly collide with the attempt to rectify the wrongs wrought by an axis of domination from which they have historically benefited. This is partially why the situation of being "guilty until proven innocent" is so disconcerting.[11]

By 2018 the fight over the constitutionality of the act had made it to the Supreme Court of India, and the court banned any immediate arrest of a person accused of insulting or injuring a SC/ST member. This ruling was, in the court's justification, "to protect innocents from arbitrary arrest."[12] But I was most transfixed by the language of the plea filed in the Supreme Court, in which the plaintiffs argued that the court "cannot remain a mute spectator to the abuse of law as we are living in a civilised society and there were many growing instances of misuse of this act."[13] I kept getting caught in this phrase—"we are living in a civilised society"—a phrase that says so much. The rhetoric of civilizationalism was being used to argue that the Prevention of Atrocities

Act was actually somehow uncivilized because it did not protect those dominant castes who might be accused of a crime and thus kept India from living up to the precepts of liberal democracy and entering fully into modernity. By extension, those who utilized this act—that is, SCs and STs—must be uncivilized, a turning of the act's purpose on its head. In this rhetorical move, what all in India ought to want is to uphold "universal" liberal values, even if these values have rarely, if ever, protected those facing atrocity.

But for all this talk of the violations of the rights of those wrongfully accused, Srinivasan's situation got resolved rather quickly. Soon after his initial call, Srinivasan got a lawyer who helped him through the process, talked to the inspector, and conveyed the message that "this guy is part of a genuine organization and he has been working for children in government schools for years." Eventually he went to the police station and signed a statement saying the same, and the officer explained to him that it "had become a standard practice for people to misuse the SC/ST act to harass others." The case went away almost as quickly as it appeared; all that liberal anxiety of being wronged, of being subject to the abuse of power rectified by a shared regime of value that was predicated on the assumed altruism associated with Srinivasan's role in the help economy. In this instance, his capital came from his altruistic merit as savarna savior, which simultaneously performed the work of demonstrating his caste entitlement. Indeed, what must be emphasized is that Srinivasan both claimed universal liberal values and asserted the need to protect Dalits *until* efforts to do so implicated or impacted him. In other words, what was most disconcerting for Srinivasan was that he might actually lose his status as savior when his caste capital no longer allowed him to remain an unmarked, universal subject.

This example is also perhaps why B. R. Ambedkar wrote almost ninety years prior, "As a rule, I do not like to take any part in a movement which is carried on by caste Hindus. Their attitude towards social reform is so different from mine that I have found it difficult to pull on with them."[14] Throughout the early twentieth century, Ambedkar had been constantly in conflict with savarna reformers, like the Arya Samajists of the Jat-Pat Todak Mandal.[15] Ambedkar was to address them with the speech that would one day become the book *Annihilation of Caste*, but he never gave the speech because of the Mandal's unwillingness to listen to words that would have meant a true reckoning with the entire edifice of savarna Hinduism. Ambedkar's speech was too much for these reformers because it was too implicating and shattered the facile belief that one could destroy the caste system simply by changing whom one shared a meal with or whom one married. Instead, Ambedkar had suggested it was the entire system that produced casteist sentiments and that therefore the only way to bring about a change in sentiment was to "destroy the religious notions on which caste was founded."[16] But Ambedkar was also thinking in the civilizational terms of his time as well, working through the pragmatic democratic ideals of his mentor John Dewey to challenge the supremacist ideals of the savarna Hindu: it was uncivilized to maintain centuries of material oppression and violence, uncivilized to continue to justify a system that did not destroy the entire structure of caste. And annihilating this system by any means necessary was the first and foremost agenda for any society that was truly interested in democracy, secularism, liberalism, or "reform." The focus of this approach to justice is to "people" justice and specifically point at those who continue to maintain and benefit from liberal systems of inequity and violence, without abstracting from these specificities.

Such social justice agendas look quite different from the kind of casteless reform espoused by Sahaayaka and organizations like it, which do not identify any of the particularities of caste violence anywhere in their institutional practice or point toward the people who are perpetrators of such violence. What we might say, then, is that Sahaayaka's version of reform, in the words of Edward Said, seeks "to obliterate the role of classes [and castes], the role of economics, the role of insurgency and rebellion."[17] When one works within a system of power, perhaps this neglect of power is to be expected.

Globalizing the Brown Savior's Liberal Erasure of Caste-Based Discrimination

I became certain of the global foundations of this liberal ideology later, when I sat with Krish and Ranga one afternoon in 2017 at one of the newest bars in Bangalore. We bonded through this ritual of beer-as-homosociality, and Krish and Ranga traded stories of their exploits back when they worked together in Texas. They rued that no matter how many new bars opened up in Bangalore, these bars simply did not feel like the places they used to frequent. Ranga had just returned to Bangalore after living for thirty years in Austin, Texas, where he had gone to school and then started his own design tech firm. He had known Krish for many years and, after moving back home to help out with his elderly parents, had decided to join Sahaayaka at Krish's behest.

But as one beer turned to two and then three, the topic returned to the moment when the organization leadership was accused of caste-based discrimination. Krish seemed to start just where Srinivasan's version ended: "Yes, me and Srinivasan had to go down to the police station, and they told us that one of the mentors, Gopal, had filed a complaint. Apparently one of the mentors, Shiva, was giving him a hard time, telling him he shouldn't do this or that. But we didn't even know that he was SC . . ."

I am struck here by the displacement of the caste problem onto the mentors. If Krish and Srinivasan are "beyond" caste because of their own casteless capital, the mentors are decidedly not. In this case, Shiva's caste position as a Yadav becomes the primary focus of the discussion. Yadavs have traditionally been an agricultural caste group who have worked to improve their social standing through a process of brahminization, claiming a descent from Yadu and from Krishna, which they argued conferred on them kshatriya status. In this sense, what Shiva seemed to be doing was following a model in which, as Ambedkar writes, "Each caste takes its pride and its consolation in the fact that in the scale of castes it is above some other caste."[18] The incident reflected the way that the direct labor of upholding caste has been left to nonbrahmin castes, only furthering brahmins' ability to remain outside of caste even as they draw capital from their caste-based networks and movements.[19]

When I talked to Shiva about this later, he was ashamed about what had happened. Shiva began to reflect on his own life in Andhra Pradesh and confessed that caste "has always been part of his family" and that he had explicit conversations with everyone in his family about how they could prove their caste was "the best of all of them." This valorization was a tangible means by which to articulate and therefore feel his mobility along an axis of caste domination. Of course, Shiva was not the only one. Most of the mentors, for example, Vishnu and Suresh, from the Vokkaliga or Lingayat caste groups, also explained that they had been told stories of their caste's supremacy and that they had never felt it was something they should not be proud of.

Shiva admitted that he had poked fun at another mentor because of his dress and eating habits, though he refused to go into more detail and claimed that mostly he was trying to educate his fellow mentor, only "trying to give him tools that would make him more effective." In his articulation Shiva was explicitly mapping caste embodiment with one's potential to be an effective member of Sahaayaka. In other words, Shiva's story tangibly revealed how participating in the help economy's form of mobility was "characterized by an 'expanded reproduction' of caste prejudice."[20]

And yet what facilitated this reproduction of caste prejudice within the organization was the brown savior's own dismissal of caste. Ranga did not think at all about his caste position despite the fact that he himself was a member of the dominant Reddy caste community of Andhra Pradesh.[21] Before Krish could finish explaining, he blurted out, "Why does this matter? Who cares?

What is the benefit to continuing to focus on caste? Now, I know we may not agree about everything, but at least we can talk, we can have a dialogue about this." Krish tried to reply, not quite agreeing with Ranga's sentiments, but his discomfort and nervousness rendered him nearly mute. I, somewhat shocked at the directness of Ranga's assertion, reacted viscerally, pushing against Ranga's claims, only for Ranga to reply, "Yes, yes, I may have a more conservative stance than you, but [the] point is still that we can dialogue." Ranga's statement left me tongue-tied, evincing my embodied complicity despite my vocal disagreement: "we" could dialogue because we both were on the same side of a "civilized," respectable sociality tethered to our caste capital.

Ranga was first and foremost emphasizing his own perceived liberal, caste-less subjectivity, a privileged position that allowed him to believe "he did not see caste" and that had congealed in his travels over his many years in the United States and now made the conversations about caste in India seem foreign and backward to him. Ranga was also mimicking conservative discourses on caste that suggested that it was the continued emphasis on caste—and not historically produced caste capital—that had maintained caste inequity. But most important, at least for me, was Ranga's explicit reference to "dialogue," which implied that those who were bringing up caste over and over could not have a dialogue. Instead, it was Ranga and those like him (or me) who could have these dialogues, presumably because we were not irrationally consumed with caste. In this sense, then, Ranga's global travels had only reinforced the neocolonial values associated with unmarked, respectable, civilized discourse that sought to occlude the historically and regionally specific categories of power that differentiated those who had the power to effortlessly dialogue from those who did not.

However, lest one conclude that Ranga's remark—"Why does this matter?"—could possibly be true in the United States, I want to return to the beginning of this chapter, in which I mentioned Sahaayaka's trusteeship and funding. One of the funders whom Krish had come in contact with through his savarna tech networks in the United States was Cisco Systems, a technology company in California's Silicon Valley that had started a massive undertaking in India as well. Cisco has been a favorite of the Hindu American community because it has hired many people of Indian origin who have migrated from India and/ or grown up in the United States while also being hailed as one of the top 100 most diverse workplaces in the United States. In 2020, however, Cisco came under new scrutiny after a Dalit American was discriminated against by two savarna managers who knew him from their time going to school at the Indian Institutes of Technologyy (IIT) and saw him as less meritorious and less skilled because he had supposedly found mobility owing to India's reservation system.[22] However, caste was not a protected category in the United States, and so until this case, caste-based discrimination in the United States had continued mostly in silence, facilitated by those savarna tech folks, like Ranga, who claim that they really don't see caste.

Clearly, as Ambedkar teaches and as the examples above reveal, invisibilizing caste while benefiting from the capital of caste networks did nothing to reform "the sentiments and mental attitudes" of these men as they traveled abroad or when they came back home to help in India.[23] This is why I see Sahaayaka and the brown savior more broadly, not as an abstract, universal, Western form of masculinist savior discourse, but as one that intersects very clearly with the emergence of globalized brahminism.

Moreover, given that the discussions in this chapter were all between brahmin *men*, I hope it is clear that this form of brown saviorist practice is deeply masculinist. However, as I suggest in the next chapter, this form of saviorist practice relies on the appropriation of global women's and girl's empowerment discourse as it intersects with the historical unfolding of brahminical feminism. Such discourses mutually reinforce class- and caste-based ideologies regarding how help work should be done and what outcomes brown saviorist interventions can produce (and for whom).

6

HINDU FEMINIST RISING AND FALLING

I was about two hours into nervously scanning Facebook in 2016, unable to disconnect even though I was fully aware that the algorithm was latching onto me, pushing forth stories that hit my dopamine receptors and provided the thrill that also made my nerves jangle and my eyes burn.

Just as I decided it was time to log off, sometime around two in the morning, I noticed that Sahaayaka had posted an announcement:

> Rural women are the key agents for achieving the transformational economic, environmental & social changes required for sustainable development, though they are the ones with very limited access to quality education & health education. . . . Keeping this in mind this Women's day we announce the launch of Girl Empowerment Program . . . which

will focus on the holistic & overall development of underprivileged girls, in the age group of 15 to 25.

I nervously clicked on the link to the full story and discovered that Sahaayaka had just received funding from the Michael and Susan Dell Foundation to launch a program focused specifically on girls' education. At first, I was perplexed. Sahaayaka leadership had never in my time conducting research with them shown any specific interest in girls' empowerment, nor did their intervention cater to the fifteen-to-twenty-five age group.

But perhaps I should not have been so perplexed. Girls'/women's empowerment is one of the largest areas for NGO funding in the Global South. A brief scan of NGO projects in India, and South Asia more broadly, inevitably leads to the conclusion that poor women and poor girls are exceptionally oppressed, in need of immediate and urgent interventions. In the past twenty years, scholars (almost always working under the sign of woman within the unstated division of gendered academic labor) have focused on and critiqued this construction of the fundable empowered girl in contemporary global help economies and have shown how girls and women have been characterized as the ideal groups to change families, communities, and nations as a whole.[1] Women are seen as preternaturally capable because they are "natural" caregivers, the locus of social reproduction within the heteropatriarchal family.[2] In this heteropatriarchal organization of care work in the global help economies, empowering Third World girls is not just a moral good but the most efficient way by which poverty in brown worlds like India might be alleviated.

Sahaayaka's rhetorical move is quite similar to this hegemonic global discourse on women's empowerment. By saving "rural women," we save society from its ills "in perpetuity"; therefore, girls' empowerment is "sustainable development." Here "economic" development is linked to the environment, imagining women as essentially closer to nature and more likely to do the work of saving the environment because of their natural need to care.[3] Somewhat paradoxically, women's ability to sustain environmental change in this cosmology is conflated with their ability to learn how to accumulate wealth—as if the environment, which has been decimated by the excesses of colonial masculinist extraction, will now be saved using the same logics as long as these logics are proliferated by women. However, for women to become these agents of change, they must be developed "holistically" by organizations like Sahaayaka when they are still young. The undertaking seeks, then, to socially engineer girls who will want to beget the appropriate types of economic and environmental change when they are women (with funds delivered by Dell, of course).

The current emphasis on girls and women, and Sahaayaka's opportunistic new program, does not come from nowhere. As Shenila Khoja-Moolji writes, if one was to take the specificity of help economies seriously in South Asia and the Global South more broadly, "we would begin . . . not with the present moment—where poverty is portrayed as a 'given' and girls as 'superheroes' who will deliver societies from it—but with a look into the past in order to examine how we got here. This would lead us to explore the histories (and legacies) of colonization in the global South."[4]

But if much of the historical focus has sought to understand the colonial constructions of the Third World, brown, or South Asian women as in need of help and as potential superheroes, much less focus has been given to how brown women of the bourgeois classes have entered into, exacerbated, and reshaped these same help narratives regarding brown girls and women. Specifically, given how constitutive patriarchy and caste have been to how empowerment has been articulated in India, it is not surprising that global savarna women, as much as global savarna men, have been staunch advocates for global help projects and have taken on roles as brown saviors all their own.[5] Savarna Indian women as the perceived bearers of tradition and maintainers of community— both in the Indian national context and in the diasporic context—have been prone to inernalizing a particular form of racio-ethnic logics, which, in turn, has drawn attention to uplifting and/or empowering impoverished women on the subcontinent.

For example, in Sahaayaka, the few women members of the leadership, while not the heads of the organization, came from the transnational South Indian brahmin class—well traveled and well educated in technocratic fields— which facilitated their entry into help work and influenced how they saw the value associated with their work. Moreover, the savarna women from other development organizations who worked with Sahaayaka were also well traveled and well educated in technocratic fields, influencing how they understood their special roles as change agents.

In the rest of this chapter, I turn to the historical and ethnographic specificities of these savarna brown women as they relate to the work of brown saviorism. This version of savarna brown saviorism captures the revolutionary potential of feminist activist projects within the nonprofit-industrial complex, privileging caste elites and channeling the work of help in directions that facilitated their own accumulation without challenging the intersections of systemic forces (capital, caste, and gender) on which women's oppression is based.

A Short History of the Perceived Labor Capacities
of Savarna Indian Women

Historically, colonial discourses in India focused much attention on saving women from a perceived oppression, presupposing that patriarchy and sexism were no longer operative in the white Western metropole. In India the British were especially disturbed by the plight of Hindu women, in practices like sati, child marriage, widow isolation, and rampant illiteracy. These practices were used as examples of Indian society's exceptional backwardness and primitivity, justifying the British civilizing mission through an attention to women's uplift.

These ideas about India circulated across the world, traveling between colony and metropole while also circulating to the emerging US empire. Famously, in *Mother India*, the US Indophobe Katherine Mayo (1927) wrote, "The infant that survives the birth-strain—a feeble creature at best . . . must look to his child-mother for care. Ignorant of the laws of hygiene, guided only by the most primitive superstitions, she has no helpers in her task other than the older women of the household, whose knowledge, despite their years, is little greater than hers."[6] Then, later, Mayo continues:

> Rich or poor, high caste or low caste, the mother of a son will idolize the child. She has little knowledge to give him, save knowledge of strange taboos and fears and charms and ceremonies to propitiate a universe of powers unseen. She would never discipline him, even though she knew the meaning of the word. She would never teach him to restrain passion or impulse or appetite. She has not the vaguest conception how to feed him or develop him. Her idea of a sufficient meal is to tie a string around his little brown body and stuff him till the string bursts. And so through all his childhood he grows as his father before him, back into the mists of time.[7]

The assumptions underlying Mayo's critiques were that (1) *all* Indian women, regardless of caste, were impoverished and uneducated; (2) all Indian women suffered from the social ill of child marriage, and they were therefore nothing more than girls themselves (a conflation that continues to be operative today); (3) Indian children suffered terribly owing to this "primitive" lack; (4) superstition, racialized as inherent to Hindus, was a stark example of their backwardness that emplaced them in a different time; and (5) the primitive child-woman inculcated the norms of an exceptional patriarchal oppression through her rearing of little brown boys.

Mayo used these claims to argue that India should not be given independence and that the only way to save these poor, oppressed girls/women was through continued British rule. In this racialized gendered politics, the white woman, while understood as inferior to her white male companions, could *still* demonstrate her supremacy across racial lines (both intra- and internationally). Mayo's book was iconized by many development agencies and organizations in the United States, producing the interlocking frameworks for US global developmentalism, poverty alleviation, and girls'/women's empowerment, even becoming required reading for the Peace Corps in India for a large portion of the twentieth century.[8]

These portrayals of Indian society and the plight of women became a stinging rebuke and rallying cry for liberal elite savarna Hindu reformers, who called for banning polygamy, child marriage, and sati while also advocating for widow remarriage. While some reformers were influenced by their experiences with British missionaries and education, Hindu social reformers sought to justify these reforms by rereading Hindu sacred texts, arguing that many of these practices, especially sati and the denial of widow remarriage, were *not* present in ancient times. This argumentation sought to revitalize Hinduism by "proving" that Hindu practices were not inherently antiwomen.

At the same time, as Third World feminist scholars have made clear, the construction of the Indian woman subject during the postcolonial nationalist era was inherently tied to women's role as the bearers of cultural norms and traditional familial practices.[9] Anticaste feminists have linked these forms of patriarchal value to caste supremacy, revealing the ways that caste supremacy filtered into the discussions of what constituted the appropriate traditions that women needed to uphold (linked to savarna Hinduism) and which women were to be uplifted in order to create a more egalitarian, "civilized" society. In turn, reformers fought for educational opportunities, rights to property, widow remarriage, and divorce for dominant-caste Hindu women while neglecting the rights of other religious and/or caste groups.[10]

This attention to savarna women set the stage for how uplift would occur within education settings. Even as anticaste reformers such as Jyotiba Phule, Savitribai Phule, and Fatima Sheikh had advocated for women's education *and* the education of the oppressed castes as early as the mid-1850s, the majority of Hindu reformers focused their energies on dominant-caste women's education *not* to promote their occupational or economic mobility but instead to strengthen the patriarchal caste system, emphasizing that educated dominant-caste women would be better mothers to their children and wives to their husbands.[11] These reform efforts came into conflict with the ideas of nationalist leaders more influenced by the British suffragists, for example, Jawaharlal Nehru, who believed that empowerment and uplift ought to be premised on producing economically independent women. Ultimately, this allowed for dominant-caste women to attend newly opened women's colleges in India, travel abroad to attain education, find new job opportunities, and chart territory for further savarna feminist economic and political mobilization.

What I want to emphasize here is that the central contradiction in the emergence of a savarna women's uplift project in India (and abroad) was between the maintenance of a Hindu heteropatriarchal family structure and the types of economic and occupational mobility afforded to dominant-caste women in the twentieth century, a problematic that was only further exacerbated as savarna middle-class women ascended and migrated in much larger numbers in the era of economic liberalization. Not surprisingly, then, similar tensions between economic mobility and heteropatriarchal structuring traveled with those savarna Hindus who moved to the United States in the twentieth century.[12] Amy Bhatt, for example, has written about the struggles faced by women who were educated as engineers and then came to the United States to join their male partners through H-4 family unification visas. She shows how these women, while interested in getting jobs in their new country, were unable to do so in many cases, resulting in their "housewification."[13]

Here I want to argue that the NGO solves the contradiction between savarna Hindu heteropatriarchy and occupational mobility because NGO labor was and is perceived as a form of feminized care work. Therefore, working for an NGO did not undermine the social reproductive role of women. Indeed, this version of feminist care has a long history in postcolonized India, as dominant-caste Hindu women, like their Victorian counterparts in Britain, had been able to join social work fields, especially in projects to help the poor.[14] Over the course of the latter half of the twentieth century, savarna women who had access to prestigious degrees and occupational skills, especially women who were part of the "IT [information technology] caste," deployed these skills within the help economies because these economies were sufficiently tethered to the market as to be considered a higher-status form of labor. At the same time, the NGO as "care work" allowed for maintaining, and even hailing, Hindu feminine sensibility while leaving unchallenged savarna women's position in relation to their partners (who invariably continued in traditionally technocratic sectors) or within their families.

In this sense, savarna Hindu women's mobility through entrance into the help economies served to allow for their accumulation of capital in two senses: in terms of actual economic accumulation and in terms of the accumulation of sociocultural capital as the appropriate type of cisgender-heterosexual women. This form of accumulation required the maintenance of difference and hierarchy between them and those they were helping, that is, the poor, impoverished, and incapable. In other words, the ability to accumulate relied on a kind of naturalized order of status and work that saw the women working in higher positions in the NGO as more capable of affecting change because they inhabited the positions of being transnational, technocratic, marketized, feminine, and Hindu.[15] These positions, it should be emphasized, did not allow these savarna Hindu women to break from their expected position within leadership hierarchies (none of the women I met held posts in the highest strata of their organizations) or allow them to challenge the basic roles in heteronormative Hindu households.

Savarna Women, Help Work, and Questions of Mobility

Take, for example, my encounters with Swati and Sweta, whom I met when they came to a Sahaayaka board meeting to do an "impact assessment"—a scene that I describe in the introduction. They had flown in from Mumbai just to consult with Sahaayaka for two weeks, a period that was, apparently, long enough for them to understand the organization's praxis and give detailed feedback on what needed to change.

One evening, Swati and Sweta met me for a drink. They wanted to find out what, if anything, made Sahaayaka worth funding. "We're doing this as a favor, actually we're basically doing this pro bono. In education there aren't the same direct returns as in other sectors, and there's limited growth and funding potential anyway, so we aren't really in this to make any money," they explained, elaborating that it was only because the Michael and Susan Dell Foundation had asked that they were there at all. I was meant to hear in these words their great benevolence in making time for an organization that did not neatly fit into a profit motive, but what I actually heard was that the accrual of capital was the foundation from which these women considered the value of labor.

I asked them why they had chosen to join this sector. Swati was a graduate of the University of Pennsylvania who was also a Teach for India alumna, and Sweta was a Yale graduate who had formerly worked for JP Morgan Chase and who traveled back and forth between Mumbai and San Francisco, which was closer to her hometown of Irvine. They admitted that they had left *much* higher-paying jobs to join the "social sector," and they were much less miserable now that they were "doing good." The corporate sector, Sweta said, was cold and impersonal, and she had felt out of place. This juxtaposition again centered the great benevolence of their act, the emphasis on leaving "much higher-paying jobs" signaling the sacrifice they had made for the good of Others. At the same time, they also eschewed the coldness and misery of the pure masculinist profit motive for a softer version of accumulation that sought to produce social impact.

For Swati and Sweta, these aspirations were tethered to their positions as upper-middle-class savarna Indian women. Swati was clear on one point, "women have to use their power differently," a phrasing that implied she was speaking for *all* women but that actually reflected the rhetoric of global sisterhood that accompanied a form of "femo-neocolonialism" associated with the ideologies of upper-class, cosmopolitan, well-educated women.[16] She started to explain what she meant by unexpectedly citing Chitra Banerjee Divakaruni's novel *The Palace of Illusions*, a reinterpretation of the Indian epic the Mahabharata, told from the point of view of Panchaali, the woman who became the wife of all five Pandava princes. The tale is intended as a savarna feminist critique of the original epic, illuminating the unequal position of women within traditional Hindu society and within the Hindu scriptures. Both Swati and Sweta had fallen in love with the novel, using it as an example of the changing position of "brown women" in contemporary society, in which the privilege to tell their stories was also the privilege to help others. Sweta and Swati's argument relied on two foundational conflations. First, the epic Hindu texts stand in for a generic Hinduism that invisibilizes the way that these particular stories are indicative of savarna caste culture. Second, the slippage between brownness and the specificities of savarna Hinduness was striking, assuming one for the other in a way that seemed to imply that savarna Hindu stories, ideas, and practices could be assumed as useful and easily applicable to a broader project of brown salvation. In this subtle, but very powerful, set of conflations, caste-cultural forms are assumed as invaluable within the hierarchy of "brown" tools for social change.

As we talked, both Sweta and Swati voiced a kind of malaise, and as we moved from two drinks to three, they began to voice some deep doubts about exactly how impactful they really were. Swati, especially, seemed emotionally drained as we talked about their jobs. She suddenly asked, of no one in particular, "Is anybody really helping at all? Are we really saving the world?" On the one hand, these women had "altruistically" chosen this path over alternative, more financially lucrative options. Yet if their work was not bringing about social change, then why choose this path at all and eschew greater financial possibilities in the first place?

When I asked why Swati had left teaching and why she would not go back, she fell silent, almost shocked by the question. Of course, she finally said, she would not go back to a profession in which her work was poorly compensated even if her impact was greater. Social reform was great but only if it fit the appropriate confines of her class position. In some sense, this visceral reaction to the slight possibility of downward mobility also fit into the logics of girls' and women's empowerment, which is predicated on the singular goal of bringing more women into the circuits of accumulation. Swati's emotional response had two implications. First, if women's empowerment is predicated on the generic category "women" finding economic mobility, then it is inconceivable that any woman who had gained such upward mobility should ever be expected to lose any capital. Such loss would by definition be antithetical to women's liberation. Second, and by extension, this version of women's empowerment also rendered impossible any conversation regarding material wealth redistribution or labor revaluations that could emphasize the importance of social reproductive work over productive work and might therefore challenge the logic of racial and gendered capitalist ordering.

The Labor of the "Good Brahmin Girl"

But if Swati and Sweta's understanding of the help economies was related to their particular positions with a global development organization, those savarna women working for Sahaayaka every day had very different experiences and ideas regarding their work. Just a few days later, in Sahaayaka's Bangalore office, I sat and listened to two women speak to me about why they had decided to join Sahaayaka. Madhu, in her late twenties, had joined Sahaayaka after a stint working for Wipro, an Indian technology company, and then with Teach for India, while Rekha, in her mid-forties, joined after moving back to Bangalore from Virginia, where she and her husband had both worked as IT professionals. As I mentioned in chapter 3, Madhu had been hired to develop Sahaayaka's motivational programs. Rekha, in turn, was hired to help develop the digital infrastructure for Sahaayaka's projects.

Rekha explained that she had had a great job in "the States," but when she decided to move back to India with her husband, she had a hard time finding a job in technology again. When she heard about Sahaayaka, it allowed her to volunteer at first and then work part-time, enabling her to use her skills as a technology professional without shirking her responsibilities to her family, which was growing, with two young children at home and her husband's parents now living with them. But she also told me she was enamored by the prospect of her work making direct impacts in a way she had not felt in the past. Rekha's job allowed her to maintain heteronormative labor obligations while also utilizing her technology skills, thus resolving the contradiction that had arisen with her reentry into more traditional reproductive obligations in India after living and working in the United States.[17] Crucially, the NGO prevented the housewification that might have otherwise occurred, and Rekha expressed her thanks to Krish repeatedly during the conversation for giving her the opportunity to do her job.

When I asked Madhu about her life, about why she ended up in the help sector, she began with her time as an engineering student. "You know," she says, "I was a good brahmin girl . . ." She laughed, and I, too, laughed nervously as I acknowledged that I knew exactly what she meant: a good brahmin girl marries a good brahmin boy, gets a white-collar job in engineering or medicine (or maybe in education), and maintains her caste-cultural identities by remaining (sufficiently) vegetarian, while participating in the brahmanical art forms (Bharatanatyam, Carnatic music, etc.). Madhu had followed through on this particular ideal, marrying a brahmin man who worked in software engineering and becoming an engineer herself. Unfortunately for her, two years into the undertaking, she found herself unfulfilled with what she was doing:

> I started looking elsewhere, and, you know, I decided to start to volunteer at Teach for India, just to see what it was. And I loved it. . . . So I thought, okay, I can do this for two years, and then I will do an MBA or something. So I quit Wipro, and it was strange, my boss, he asked me very worriedly, "Are you sure you're making the right decision? Do you think this is good for you?" I guess not many people make this change.

Madhu transitioned from Teach for India into one NGO, STIR, which produced motivational tools for teachers, before joining Sahaayaka in 2016. Initially, when she made the move from Wipro, Madhu perceived her career as a teacher as a stopgap measure, thinking she would do this for a few years before getting an MBA and returning to an occupation that would be more suitable to her class and caste position.

Even as Madhu talked about enjoying the work she was doing, she could not help but return several times to her relationship with her parents. She sighingly explained that her parents were incredibly unhappy with her. "It was a literal cold war," she remarked. "For them it was a complete failed stage. And I used to try very hard to convince them. But then I realized I cannot. They will not understand . . ." She drifted off as she said this, her face revealing her struggles to convince her family that working in the social sector was a worthy job for someone with her educational pedigree and social background. The evocation of a cold war, a melodramatic and hyperbolic way of describing her relationship to her family, evoked the way that being a perceived class traitor can rip apart one's established familial relationships. This clash of values—economic and sociocultural—structured how Madhu felt about her work, pricking her with doubt as to whether this type of work was what she should be doing and for how long.

It also shaped how she did her work. On the one hand, she seemed to have a moral fortitude when she discussed her educational work and the needs of children. She repeated, as if a mantra: "education fails all stakeholders." But then, as she spoke, her altruistic call toward educational change flattened, cracking under the weight of her social position and social relations. She described the work that her husband did as an engineer, explaining that he made casino equipment that he sent abroad. It was a less-than-altruistic endeavor, and she seemed to know this but spun it anyway: "He is always saying, what is my impact on India, if I am building technology for casinos, how am I making an impact? Because if others go to casinos and I make money off of them, then I am helping India's economy grow." Her savarna moral universe followed his: whatever increased India's national gross domestic product (GDP) was morally justified, and, therefore, the furthest this accumulationist moral imaginary might go was to the edges of the nation's borders. Here I also want to mark that Madhu's sentiments might not be so different from Swati's, Sweta's, or Rekha's: all of them had decided to participate in help work within the confines of India and within the confines of accumulation, despite their very different migratory trajectories.

Madhu's social position also continued to reproduce a belief that she could do something different in the future. She mentioned, as if obvious, "If I look at going back to software—if I'm going to go back to telecom, I'll ask: who is it reaching out to, how is it helping the end audience?" For Madhu, then, to be part of the help economy was a choice that had given her essential learnings regarding her ability to enact change. If in her previous stint as an engineer she was meandering and without purpose, now she had discovered that the value of her work stemmed from asking the question: How does this impact those at the receiving end of interventions? In the end, the ability to ask and answer this question gave Madhu a kind of power she might never have felt, a power that came out of both a feeling of moral superiority—that she was making an impact that justified her exit from the technology sector in the first place—and a conviction that she now had the skills and ability to make an impact in *any* field, for *any* audience, even if they were not those most disenfranchised by the systems of inequality perpetuated in India. For a good brahmin girl, these perhaps were not small victories. But for students in rural schools, whom Sahaayaka was purportedly in the midst of empowering, one wonders how much these victories mattered.

In sum, the role of savarna women in help economies shows how racial and gendered capitalism actually accommodates and requires the incorporation of those deemed adequately different into new labor slots as long as they do not challenge the raced, gendered, classed, and casteized boundary logics for accumulation. In this case, the boundary logics associated with the heteronormative gender binary and acceptable forms of casteized gendered labor stay remarkably stable despite the supposed transformations brought about by the inclusion of savarna Hindu "brown women" in the help economies.

Such inclusions also require the absolute exclusion of those Others deemed largely unassimilable. In fact, what is also made clear in this chapter is that all those women who were incorporated within Sahaayaka were Hindu, implicitly reflecting how inclusion/exclusion functions along gendered Hindu/Muslim lines. In the next chapter, I make this religious boundary line explicit by showing how the institutionalization of Hindu supremacy functions to determine who can take up roles in the labor hierarchy of brown saviorism in India and who cannot.

GATEKEEPERS (OR THE ANTI-MUSLIM

POLITICS OF HELP)

I was driving on the Mysore Road, away from Bangalore and through the industrial towns that dot the main road. I was with Sarathi, a Sahaayaka mentor I
had just met. I held on too tightly to the back of his motorbike and, sensing my
nervousness, Sarathi tried to lighten the mood by joking, "You are Arjun, and
I am your charioteer." The joke was a reference to the Mahabharata, the Hindu
epic in which Arjuna, one of the five Pandava princes, was led into battle by
Sarathi (another name for Krishna), a god in human form. In this scene, which
transpires at the climax of the epic and initiates the central conversation of
the *Bhagavad Gita*, the best-known philosophical and religious text of Hinduism, Arjuna begins to doubt his cause: he doubts whether he should continue
with war, a war in which he will have to fight cousins, teachers, friends, even
one of his own brothers. He asks Krishna, who he does not yet know is a god,

why he should go about this vile act. The answer to this question is the basis of the *Gita* and has resulted in millions upon millions of pages of exegesis, debates, controversies, songs, poems, dances, sculptures, paintings, and so much more.

For whatever else the *Gita* might be, it is one of the two or three texts that function as Hinduism's "proof" of its intellectual, philosophical, and spiritual contribution to the world, garnering such global recognition that it has become a key tool for legitimating the current Hindu supremacist project in India. For example, when Narendra Modi made his first trips around the world, he gifted *The Bhagavad Gita according to Gandhi* to US president Barack Obama and gifted a different version of the *Gita* to Japanese emperor Akihito. In his quoted text on the back of the book, Modi wrote that the "Gita is India's biggest gift to the world," conflating caste Hinduism with India and placing it in a new position of supremacy among any number of potential "gifts" from India to the world (the Taj Mahal, for example).

Sarathi giggled at his metaphor, and I tried to play along as best I could, not ready to tell him that this kind of comic relief did not resonate with me in the way he thought it might. Instead, it made me nervous. Laughter has a cultural politics all its own, setting the boundaries of inclusion, in who will get the joke but, more important, in who is allowed to hear the joke in the first place. If, in some cases, anthropologists share a sincere laugh with their participants "in the face of certain death," as a way to remind ourselves that life has a glimmer of light even in the face of precarity, in this case, hearing the joke and sharing a laugh signaled our collusion and my complicity: two Hindus, perceiving themselves as godlike figures, entering another world to save those in need.[1]

After a few more minutes of unpleasant banter, Sarathi and I drove under a bright green sign "LAND OF TOYS, CHANNAPATNA," which signaled that we were close to our final destination. Channapatna, a town in Bangalore Rural District, approximately sixty kilometers south of Bangalore city, is known for its toy industry, which was started sometime during the rule of Tipu Sultan ("The Tiger of Mysore") in the eighteenth century, when he brought over Persian toy makers to train local artisans. The industry provides the outward-facing character of the town, and as we drove, my eyes lingered on the toy stores on both sides of the street selling colorfully painted wooden toys—tops, dolls, and decorative scenes from the Ramayana and Mahabharata, including many versions of the Arjuna-Krishna chariot scene. The industry was protected by the World Trade Organization (WTO) as a "geographical indication" (GI), a trademark that created a special global market value for products from this region. Channapatna also was a Muslim-majority township, with over

60 percent of the population identifying as Muslim, mostly of the Mahdavia sect, founded in India by Muhammad Jaunpuri in the fifteenth century.[2] This history and these contributions to India, like many of the histories of Muslims in India, are being erased as a revisionist mythology re-creates India as an essentially Hindu nation, *especially* in Karnataka, where the Hindutva regime's influence increased immensely between 2013 and 2020.

There Sarathi and I were, in the midst of this historic area, about to disembark and see one of the largest Urdu-medium schools in Channapatna, attended by many of the Muslim children in the region. I had wanted to observe these schools for quite some time, but each time I was led to other schools in Sahaayaka's networks, more Kannada-speaking, more Hindu, and more traditionally rural. The question was why.

Secularism, Technocracy, and the Reproduction of Structural Inequality

One of the first things I noticed in my fieldwork with Sahaayaka was that brown saviors considered themselves secular, liberal, and nonpartisan, and they therefore eschewed any explicitly Hindu-based arguments for social change and were explicitly against the Hindu supremacist ideas that have become a touchstone of contemporary Indian politics. For example, members of the Sahaayaka leadership were no fans of Modi, the Bharatiya Janata Party (BJP), or any of the other figures who represent the current anti-Muslim politics in India.

On its surface, this seemed to indicate that Sahaayaka's liberal leadership was in direct opposition to the BJP Hindutva regime. This perception was seemingly furthered by the fact that Sahaayaka's leadership valorized the figure of A. P. J. Abdul Kalam, a Muslim and a former president of India. On their website Sahaayaka claimed that Kalam was really the entire reason for the organization's mission, explaining that Kalam had told the organization to focus on rural schools in 2002 because they were "the least looked after." In 2013 Sahaayaka brought Dr. Kalam as the chief guest for its tenth-anniversary celebration, and his presence at the celebration was the pride of almost everyone within the organization. A poster of Kalam hung in the Sahaayaka main office, another reminder of his influence on the organization's activities.

As I return to below, Kalam's technocratic position was quite a bit more fraught: he was a nuclear scientist, most visibly involved in the Pokhran tests, a series of five nuclear bomb explosions meant to symbolize India's "ascension" as a global superpower and further move into mass militarization, and he was actually elected to the presidency by the National Democratic Alliance in India, a coalition government led by the BJP. At the same time, Kalam was a strong advocate for development through education. For example, in *Ignited Minds* (2002), Kalam wrote, "The development of education and healthcare will yield benefits of smaller families and a more efficient workforce. It is the key to employability and social development."[3] Because of words like these, Kalam was the appropriate figure to be valorized and followed by the Sahaayaka leadership: a good, technocratic liberal subject whose religious background did not play a central role in how he conceived of India's future and who was able to create "unity" across the political spectrum.

This technocratic, liberal stance had only been furthered as Sahaayaka's leadership traveled between India and the United States, imbibing this ideology as it manifested in both contexts in the age of neoliberal, unmarked, "universal" discourses. Practically, as I have mentioned, this meant that Sahaayaka resisted any claims to helping or providing specific access, skills, or teaching to any religious, caste, or ethnic community in particular, including Muslim children, despite the fact that many of the largest schools in which they worked were majority Muslim. Krish, for example, explicitly argued that Sahaayaka had to work with the Indian government because it was the only way the organization could procure funds and continue to work in schools, resulting in interventions that were completely unmarked and focused on "helping all" while never specifying any community in particular.

This universalizing method of neoliberal intervention only served to reproduce structural inequities tied to a racialized Hindu supremacy because the brown savior's refusal to explicitly recognize social stratifications of power also rendered them completely unable to address similar questions within their organization. For example, I had always been baffled that Sahaayaka had not hired even *one* Urdu-speaking Muslim from around Karnataka to join their intervention, especially given that the organization's strategy had always been to partner with communities and intervene with the help of those mentors who had a stronger understanding of particular "local" contexts.

In Karnataka at least 12 percent of the population is Muslim, with many concentrated in the large towns, like Channapatna, where they work in primarily nonagricultural occupations and own less land than the nonbrahmin savarna (Vokkaliga and Lingayat) farmers in the region. And yet all the Sahaayaka fieldworkers, called *mentors* by the organization, were Hindu, and most of them (with few exceptions) spoke Kannada, the dominant regional language, and could not speak Urdu, the language commonly spoken by Muslims in the region. This limited the mentors' ability to work in the large Urdu-medium schools in South Karnataka's towns that were under their supervision. In many cases, they did their work in these schools mechanically, just as a bureaucrat would (as if to tick off a box on their checklists), without forging the strong affective connections they did elsewhere; or, in some cases, they steered away from these schools altogether, even though these schools were just as low performing as their Kannada-speaking, Hindu counterparts, reinscribing the fact that these schools and students were outside of the fold.

This was a critique I brought forth to Srinivasan and Krish on several occasions, and it was readily acknowledged as a problem with the organization's overall structure and employee demographics. However, no change occurred in my time in the field. This was primarily because the majoritarian, generalizable, quantitative terms that Sahaayaka used to measure success or failure necessarily resulted in an emphasis on the largest segment of the "local" population first, most of whom invariably attended Kannada-medium schools. The construction of the "local" in majoritarian terms itself reproduced social stratification. Further, in the selection of only Kannada speakers whose families had worked in the agricultural sector, it was assumed that those who could help develop Others were *not* from Karnataka's Muslim communities but from Karnataka's Kannadiga population.

This position only reinforced already existing gendered racist models of Muslims in India, which were folded into a spatialized discourse in India that situated Muslims as somehow outside the national fold and therefore outside the logic of "kin" relations that implicitly undergirded the brown saviors' version of help.[4] As I argue here, in the context of Karnataka, this racialized Hindu nationalism also worked along linguistic lines, rendering Kannada speakers, who were also more likely to be Hindus, as both worthy of being fieldworkers and worthy of help, as opposed to the Urdu-speaking Muslims in the region.

The Everyday Practices of Anti-Muslim Racism

We got off Sarathi's bike, and I scanned the surroundings. In most ways, I saw very little difference from other schools. Children were scampering around, eyeing me with a special kind of curiosity; teachers were going about the business of getting their students settled down; and the headmaster welcomed us into the school. Sarathi and I spent about forty-five minutes at the school, during which Sarathi encouraged the students to "do well" and handed out pencils and erasers to a few students who had answered correctly the math questions he had written on the board, a cause for momentary excitement.

What I also noticed was the speed with which Sarathi and I left the school. Generally, when we were about to leave a school, I would observe so much

affective connection: the smiles, hugs, and teasing that constituted the mentors' connection to the schools and communities in which they worked. However, in this case there was no stopping to talk with teachers about their day
or week, no groups of students that Sarathi had made a connection with who
hovered around him, no jokes about their studies or inquiries about their families. Instead, once the job was done, we were immediately off. It was subtle,
almost imperceptible, except in juxtaposition with other school observations.

Afterward, Sarathi began talking about the students, trying to describe his
perceptions of the sociopolitical world in which these Muslim children lived.
Sarathi sighed as he explained that the Muslim students in the school were
"difficult" and that they did not take their education seriously. Sarathi listed
the many ways in which those from the Urdu-medium schools in Channapatna
were "backward": boys from these schools dropped out early to join family
businesses; girls were expected to marry and leave school before completing
tenth standard; and none of the students bothered to learn Kannada "properly." In Sarathi's telling, these kinds of deficiencies were specific to Muslim
populations in the region, evidenced by his specific remarks about their lack
of Kannada proficiency, which were indicative of the racialized prism through
which he saw Muslim students as inherently disadvantaged. This linguistic difference has been used as a cudgel to argue that Muslim populations
in Karnataka have participated in their own "self-ghettoization," blaming
these communities for not assimilating enough into the Kannada norms and
attributing their lower achievements in education and economic mobility to
"cultural" sensibilities that limited their ability to learn "market-linked languages" in India.[5]

Sarathi began to expand his racist cosmology, away from the specificities of
the school and toward a more general discussion of Hindu-Muslim relations in
India. Because his job was to take me around, he wanted to make sure I got the
right impression about Karnataka and Sahaayaka's program. He started by as-
suring me that in these South Karnataka regions where he was working, there
were few, if any, Muslim-Hindu problems. However, he admitted, in Manga-
lore, a city on the west coast of Karnataka, there had been a lot of problems,
and even in his hometown in North Karnataka, there had been some problems
of "Muslim boys harassing Hindu girls." I started to argue, questioning his
framing of the problem and inquiring how it could *only* be Muslim boys harassing Hindu girls. But he insisted, suddenly remembering that I might not know
the real story of what was happening in India because of my many years in the
United States. Sarathi began to take on the role of teacher, slowly explaining
the "real" story to me. In trying to highlight how he saw the issue, he ended

with the seemingly straightforward, even lighthearted fact that "not all Muslims are terrorists, but if it is a terrorist, then it is a Muslim."

He grinned at me afterward, pleased with his turn of phrase, and giggled to himself, looking at me with expectant eyes that suggested that I, too, was now privy to this truism, a fact that should also somehow be funny. The racist joke, in this context, was supposed to function as a social connection, a signal that Sarathi and I shared the same beliefs and values. But Sarathi's pleased giggle turned into a nervous laugh when I did not smile back and then turned into a steely-eyed stare when I changed the subject.

Sarathi's case demonstrated the way that many mentors viewed educational possibilities through the lens of racialized religious, gendered, and linguistic difference. This positioning manifested affectively, in how they played their roles as the gatekeepers of the help economy: in who they decided could and should access the values they had been given a privileged role in disseminating. In making his decisions as a gatekeeper, Sarathi was relying on a specific form of gendered anti-Muslim racism to make sense of his work with Urdu-speaking Muslim students.[6] In the Hindu supremacist mythology propagated over the past 150 years, Muslims in India have been characterized as outsiders and invaders who are also depicted as chauvinists and sexual deviants, penetrating "women-as–Hindu nation," which, in turn, preemptively justified the violence against Muslims by the state.[7] In this racist neocolonial cosmology, the Hindu man is striving against the Muslim man's perceived violent hypermasculinity and the Hindu man's supposed effeminate docility.[8] This perceived crisis of Hindu masculinity has been percolating for at least a hundred years and has been one affective foundation for Hindutva reemergence. In fact, in recent years Hindu iconography has become increasingly hypermasculine. For example, Hanuman, the monkey god valorized in the Ramayana and historically depicted as genial, has been increasingly depicted as angry, aggressive, and militant, which has reached iconic status within the circles of young Hindutva men after being praised by Modi.

Sarathi's racist and masculinist reconfiguration also linked this history of anti-Muslim racism with the American imperial global war on terror.[9] Here, rather than merely drawing on the trope of the Muslim as hypermasculine outsider and invader, Sarathi was drawing on a racialized discourse of Muslims as terrorists in India that is situated in the post-9/11 era but more specifically after the 2008 bombings of the Mumbai Taj Hotel, which has produced India's specific form of the global "racial infrastructure of the terror-industrial complex."[10] This racist ideology has facilitated the increased anti-Muslim racism seen throughout the country, evinced by the Delhi pogroms in

February 2020, the citizenship policies of the National Register of Citizens (NRC) and the Citizenship Amendment Act (CAA), and the hijab ban in Karnataka in 2022.

Finally, Sarathi's case also showed how these discourses played out specifically in how fieldworkers racialized Muslim *youth*. On the one hand, Muslim women and girls have been seen in India, and globally, as the subjects who are in greatest need of saving as part of the moralistic framings of the global war on terror.[11] At the same time, Muslim boys have been perceived as beyond saving, already potential terrorists within the ongoing spread of the "terror-industrial complex."[12] This racist figuration deemed Muslim boys as already adultlike deviants.[13] Sarathi explicitly pointed to the potential deviance of the Muslim boy, who, by the nature of his capacity "to harass Hindu girls" and his potential for terrorist activity in the future, no longer could be helped. When juxtaposed with Sarathi's earlier generic description of Muslim boys as likely to join family businesses, it became clear that Sarathi saw Muslim boys as already adultlike and outside of the educational fold, potential threats to those like him. Muslim girls, in contrast, were agency-less caricatures in his characterization—only likely to marry—and therefore, in this racist imaginary, they, too, could not be saved, even if they might actually need saving, because they were trapped within an imagined, exceptionally unjust Muslim patriarchy. In this sense, Sarathi was participating in a process of primitivizing in order to empower himself as a gatekeeper for Sahaayaka's interventions.

I knew this was not the position of every Sahaayaka mentor. Suresh, for example, was one of the very few mentors who knew Urdu, and he spoke passionately against the anti-Muslim racism in India. Other mentors also expressed concern that Urdu-medium schools seemed to be falling further and further behind despite the fact that the mentors continued to go to these schools to motivate these students.

But the issue here was *not* whether any individual Sahaayaka mentor was anti-Muslim or not. The issue was that it was left to them to make these arbitrary determinations in the first place. Indeed, Sarathi's process of gatekeeping was occurring even as the brown saviors themselves were completely invisibilized in the story, the blame for any wrongdoing placed at the feet of the individual mentor who acted in an immoral way. Even as Sarathi was reproducing racist anti-Muslim stratification in his interventions, the brown savior could persist in an ignorance facilitated by the neoliberal impulse to quantify, remain neutral, and unmark their interventions. This meant that mentors might get trained on how to fill out a data sheet or analyze test scores and school attendance, but they were not trained on how to identify their own bias and the particular needs of any of the communities they were working with. In an environment that was and is already anti-Muslim, it was likely that interventions would therefore reproduce anti-Muslim ideologies. At best, this meant Muslim children were not given the specific kinds of assistance that might have been useful to them as they sought mobility within India's racial and caste capitalist ordering, and, at worst, it meant that Muslim children were treated as deficient outsiders as interventions unfolded. It was in this sense that Sahaayaka's brown saviors, in their technocratic, neoliberal understandings, perpetuated the racialized disenfranchisement of Muslims in India, despite their rhetoric and supposed political views to the contrary.

To take this argument further, one especially important implication of the above analysis is that technocracy, one of India's colonial inheritances for governance, works equally well under authoritarian and liberal regimes and actually blurs the lines between these regimes. In fact, just like Sahaayaka, the BJP government articulates many of its claims through the rhetoric of universal, technocratic economic development, the means for the nation to continue to accumulate capital.

Given this analysis, the figure of Dr. Kalam also changes in significance. Just like Sahaayaka, the BJP has embraced Kalam by highlighting that he was a scientist and missile technologist whose technocratic secularism seemed to diminish his Muslimness. In fact, controversy ensued in 2017 after Modi unveiled a memorial to Kalam on the second anniversary of his death and placed an

FIGURE 7.1. Memorial to former president Dr. A. P. J. Abdul Kalam in Rameswaram.

engraved *Bhagavad Gita* next to him (figure 7.1). While eventually other texts were also placed next to Kalam, in this instance the BJP used the figure of Kalam to construct an ideology centered on technocracy that reinforced the binary between the "good" secular Muslim who also embraces the teaching of India as Hindu and those "bad" Muslims who practice their faith too overtly and therefore do not seem to embrace India's techno-Hindu society.

Part II Is Done: In Sum and What's to Come

What I have tried to show in part 2 is how particular colonial racial distinctions are rearticulated and mobilized in contemporary help work in India. Specifically, I have tried to draw out the way that neocolonial intersections of poverty, nation, gender, religion, and caste produced labor distinctions that determined how Sahaayaka's praxis unfolded. To be sure, these are not the only neocolonial categories of governance that are operative and important in India. However, these were the categories that emerged specifically in my ethnographic work with Sahaayaka and therefore are the categories that I sought to visibilize here.

I have also tried to show how these ongoing neocolonial labor differentiations actually challenge Sahaayaka's organizational rhetoric as working as part of the "anti-politics machine" in which interventions are apolitical, technocratic, and unmarked. In some ways, my analysis here further substantiates work like that of Lisa Lowe, who shows us that liberalism, despite its guise of universality, requires exclusion.[14] In fact, I have shown that technocratic praxis reproduces these neocolonial exclusions, blurring the lines between the (neo) liberal and the overtly fascist.

While part II's analysis remained grounded mostly at the level of neocolonial categories of institutional governance, part III recognizes that contemporary racial and caste capitalist systems require *spatialized* and *territorialized* distinctions to determine appropriate sites for expropriation and exploitation. Therefore, especially in chapter 8, I draw out the ways that material dispossession in India was produced on the racialized lines of urban-rural distinction. In the rest of part III, I focus on the position of the mentor within these spatialized processes of expropriation/exploitation. This analysis focuses on the mentors as they negotiate their positions between rural/urban and the organization. On the one hand, the mentors' experiences are situated within the violent expropriations of agricultural land that relied and rely on the racialized labor slotting of rural people. At the same time, the mentors imbibe aspirational imaginaries of economic mobility and ideologies of moral conduct that drive them to join the NGO and the project of brown saviorism.

This part of the book therefore focuses on the contradictions and moral dilemmas that emerge at the nexus of the mentors' simultaneous aspirations to find a way toward economic mobility while also doing what they consider morally valuable work. I draw here on Leya Mathew and Ritty Lukose's work on "pedagogies of aspiration," which "proposes that liberalisation [in India] has generated an expansion of aspirational trajectories that require and necessitate forms of self-fashioning [which] must be understood in terms of the uncertainties and precarities of generating social reproduction and mobility."[15] In part III, I analyze the mentors' aspirational precarities under the rubric of "Urban Saviorism" to draw attention to the way that Bangalore city, urbanity, cosmopolitanism, and globality (as tethered to the city) mediate their attempts at mobility within the education NGO sector, the moral contradictions that emerge, and their resistance to the constraints they face. In each chapter, the city, and its relation to the rural, hovers in the background, spatializing the analysis of aspirational precarity experienced by the mentor class.

III
URBAN
SAVIORISM

The rural-urban interface is the territoriality of liberalization, the space within which the regime is re-making itself, and the region whose boundaries are being redrawn through these rural-urban conflicts.—ANANYA ROY, *City Requiem*

The movement of capital across and through rural land follows similar rhythms of disinvestment and revaluation. . . . Rural economies, no less than urban manufacturing and service centers, are integrated into broader economic flows, via transnational social divisions of labor . . . and global consumption regimes.—RUTH WILSON GILMORE, *Golden Gulag*

What we understand today as globalization . . . has been facilitated by the reconfiguration of capitalism and by the transmission and reproduction of deeply embedded social hierarchies and prejudices rooted in a past character-ized by territorial concepts of belonging and notions of civilization that both generated and were generated by racial inequalities.—DEBORAH THOMAS AND M. KAMARI CLARKE, "Globalization and Race"

THE ROAD TO ACCUMULATION

I am looking at some old field notes, scratch marks on the page that I can barely discern. I can make out two names, Raj and Lakshmi, underlined twice, though both lines look more like squiggly strikethroughs than anything else. On that particular day, I was sitting with Raj on the bus, traveling out of Bangalore on the Kanakapura Road. The ride was bumpy, and I jumped up and down in my seat as we slowly inched out of the city through all the noisy, messy traffic that defines Bangalore's twenty-first-century growth.

Bangalore, once a sleepy garden city in South Karnataka known for its cool temperature, has famously been recast as the slowly overheating "Silicon Valley of India."[1] Over the past twenty years, Bangalore has become a hub for global technology companies, an IT (information technology) city that has seen a massive influx of people.[2] The city's population has doubled, rising from

5.1 million in 2001 to 12 million in 2020, while also tripling in physical size as it seeks to make room for the ever-increasing number of companies and people, both from across the globe and from neighboring areas, who continue to migrate to the city seeking opportunities, sometimes imagined and sometimes concrete.[3] As it has grown, Bangalore has quickly enveloped the villages that surround it on its south, east, and west, agricultural land now rebranded as industrial satellite towns.

At the same time, global economic policies have systematically disenfranchised those living in agricultural areas, only exacerbating the tendency in contemporary India to emphasize industry over agriculture. In India, and Karnataka specifically, as more and more economic resources have been pushed toward city centers, many in villages must now seek new occupations as their traditional livelihoods no longer provide them living wages. In other words, the relationship between Bangalore and its rural surrounds is but one manifestation of the urban-rural conflicts that mark twenty-first-century global accumulation. As Ruth Wilson Gilmore reminds, the urban-rural interface is a key spatial "edge" on which global racial capitalist accumulation occurs, both in terms of questions of expropriation and in terms of dealing with the problem of "surplus labor" that emerges through racialized processes of primitive accumulation.[4]

In this context, roads like the Kanakapura Road might really be "roads to accumulation," paths that not only facilitate the movements of products, people, and ideas but also place massive constraints on who can partake in the prosperity of a rapidly globalizing Bangalore.[5] Infrastructures reflect "mobility regimes," producing some subjects who can move more freely and quickly, while simultaneously presupposing and reproducing "immobile Others" who are stuck because of their positions within neocolonial histories of marginalization.[6] For whom are infrastructures built, and to what ends? Whose movements are facilitated, and whose are not?[7]

Bangalore, Agricultural Land, and a Colonial History
of Primitive Accumulation

One way this question might be answered is by thinking with the cultural politics of Bangalore versus Bengaluru. The city, whose name had been changed to Bangalore during the colonial era, was renamed Bengaluru in 2014 after nearly ten years of planning.[8] The imaginary of Bengaluru evokes a critique of "Westernization" and technocapitalist globalization linked to a Kannada-linguistic nationalism that sought to produce an "authentic" Karnataka. At the same time, focusing energy on the cultural politics of naming merely submerged and did little to address the material conditions that continue to dispossess the poor, especially the rural poor.[9] As such, in my own text, I have maintained the usage of Bangalore to recognize that the city has actually only continued to function as a neocolonial city, rife with expropriation and exploitation.

Rural populations around Bangalore have long recognized the unevenness and unfairness tied to urban expansion projects and the new infrastructures associated with them, protesting constantly against their dispossession. For example, one of the earliest manifestations of these ongoing urban-rural tensions occurred in 1995, when a protest, pictured in figure 8.1, broke out in front of a newly opened KFC on Brigade Road, in the heart of Bangalore city. The most powerful protesters during the KFC incident were the Karnataka Rajya Raitha Sangha, one of the most influential and vocal farmers' associations in India, who objected to the global commodity chain bypassing local producers. For them, the Brigade Road's new KFC was concrete proof that they had been pushed off the road to accumulation. It took nearly ten more years before KFC expanded to the rest of India, the initial controversy giving the corporation pause about India as an emerging market.

FIGURE 8.1. Photograph of protests at KFC in Bangalore, 1995.

Similarly, a protest erupted in 2007 against the BMIC or NICE road-building project. The Bangalore-Mysore Infrastructural Corridor (BMIC) was primarily sponsored by a US-based investor, NICE, whose ambition was to create a series of circular highways on the perimeters of Bangalore along with a highway that would connect Bangalore to its closest neighboring city, Mysore. The land around the highway was taken under eminent domain laws for new residential enclaves, which displaced farmers, denuded seven thousand acres of forestland, and drained eight lakes.[10] Farmers protested the road project and demanded better compensation for the land that had been taken for the road, the return of the excess land that was taken for the residential enclaves, and the construction of service roads to connect villages that had been divided by the expressway project, making the transportation of goods between villages hazardous.[11] These types of farmers' protests only proliferated in larger and larger numbers as 2020 came to a close, during a time in which rural unemployment reached a forty-five-year high under a Modi regime that continued to remove state protections for farmers.[12]

Infrastructure projects in liberalized India are connected to earlier colonial land-use policy, which also focused on a solution to the agrarian question in India.[13] As David Lloyd and Patrick Wolfe argue, new modes of accumulation heralded under neoliberal privatization "emerged from an earlier moment of enclosure and dispossession" marked by British colonial strategies of land commodification and settlement.[14] The British, realizing that most of India's population lived in agricultural communities, recognized that their extractionist interests required a reengineering of India's agricultural laborers' relation to the land. The oft-discussed colonial zamindari, ryotwari, and mahalwari tax revenue systems were attempts by the British to unleash the productivity of the land by conflating the natural right to property ownership with the commercializing of agriculture. They encouraged farmers to use the land to produce maximal surplus value in the shortest period of time by giving some of them rights to property ownership *and* by creating tax models that required farmers to produce surplus if they wanted to have any chance to pay their taxes and still survive.[15]

As already hinted, the NICE road project and the expropriation of agricultural land hinged on the continued application of these colonial logics, specifically a reading of eminent domain in the Land Acquisition Act of 1894, originally written under British colonial rule. Eminent domain laws are a classical example of primitive accumulation, allowing the state to expropriate land from those who are not producing the highest-possible value from the land and therefore are not working toward the goal of accumulation. Here we can read the British colonial project as a settler colonial project that was passed on to those savarna, brown subjects who had imbibed the modernist values of the colonizer and actually took on the role of settler.[16] White skin or brown skin, the settler has never left India.[17]

In postindependence India, the Indian state continued to focus on the "agrarian question," as the Indian peasantry's use of agricultural land was still perceived as unproductive and wasteful, marking India's premodern, backward past and preventing it from developing the Nehruvian vision of a technocratic future.[18] The green revolution in India, for example, released the surplus value of agricultural land by integrating technological tools into farming, including high-yielding-variety seeds, tractors, irrigation facilities, pesticides, and fertilizers.[19] However, as the agrarian question continued into the postliberalization period, two primary changes occurred: (1) unleashing surplus value required the agricultural sector to further integrate into circuits of global capitalism; and (2) using land for agricultural purposes was now no longer seen as the most productive use of many of these lands, especially those closest to rapidly expanding urban centers. The results of these changes were the kinds of state-corporate land grabs that farmers have been protesting.[20] In some sense, as Utsa Patnaik has written, the postliberalization period in India has actually reverted to a more draconian form of land expropriation because now, as with the NICE project, the state "enters into collaboration with the giant transnational companies in this new process of primitive accumulation."[21]

The Mentor, the Crisis of Surplus Labor, and the Racialization of Rural Difference

While we rode down the Kanakapura Road, Raj sighingly explained that the city was swallowing up more and more villages every day. Raj's role was as Sahaayaka's "liaison," the connective tissue between the leadership in Bangalore and the mentors who traveled all over village Karnataka. Raj, like many of the Sahaayaka mentors, had grown up in one of Bangalore's surrounding villages and had come to Bangalore, like many of his colleagues, searching for a job that might improve his economic possibilities. Before joining Sahaayaka, Raj hadn't done any previous work in the NGO sector. He had been a film curator in Karnataka, putting together small, local Kannada film screenings for those in the Bangalore area. Given this background, Raj never thought he would find himself doing this job. However, film curation, especially the curation of indie films in the Kannada language, was not paying the bills, and so when he stumbled on the opportunity to join Sahaayaka, he had thrust himself into his new line of work. This perspective gave him a special insight into how the NGO sector worked for people like himself and the Sahaayaka mentors, especially in the wake of land expropriation and dispossession. But he was also quite pragmatic and contemplative about all these tensions, and as we slowly rolled down the road, he confided, "If you live in a village and you want to get out, there are not many other good options for employment but joining an NGO. If you are in a town or city, then OK, maybe you can find something, but in a village what else can you do?"

Raj was suggesting that for those rural peoples who have been left out of India's largely urban-centered economic growth, the NGO was one of the only ways they could imagine mobility for themselves. The NGO, in other words, rather than a purely altruistic project, was imagined as their "road to accumulation." Most of Sahaayaka's mentors had grown up in villages all over Karnataka and witnessed firsthand the growing difficulties that farmers were facing as the agricultural sector had been decimated in India's push toward urban-focused economic development. These mentors had received BEd, DEd, or BA degrees and were looking for jobs away from their native villages thereafter. In this case, the NGO played a critical role in the project of accumulation as it addressed the problem of overeducated rural surplus labor that was "waiting" for jobs that did not exist.[22] However, the mentors' incorporation into the NGO sector was also limited by their racialized, casteized, and gendered positions, all of which relied on historically situated ideologies regarding rural peoples' capacities for labor.

In the colonial period, for example, the determinations of the value of land, wasted land, and permanent settlement also required distinctions among those who were living on the land, valuations that invariably naturalized differences and determined who had the right to land and who were considered disposable surplus populations. Judith Whitehead, for example, has argued that "the division of lands in India into state forests, on the one hand, and privatised farm or commercial land, on the other, was accompanied by racialised divisions based upon two axes. First, there were evolutionary typologies that differentiated 'tribes' from 'castes' and, second, Orientalist exoticism, which, in turn, divided various castes from each other."[23] These racialized divisions reified rural peoples based on their supposed capacities for economic productivity, which relied on already existing graded caste hierarchies and gendered social relations in village India. In turn, this also dictated the various forms that the British civilizing mission would take by distinguishing who was in need of what type of civilizing and development. In Karnataka, emerging landed gentry caste groups, especially Vokkaligas and Lingayats, were deemed to have the appropriate capacity for permanent settlement and agricultural cultivation and were encouraged by the British in these areas through law and education.[24]

In postindependence India, village life was perceived as the "primordial India," the truest form of Indianness that was lost not only through industrial development but also as savarna Indians, especially brahmins, moved to urban centers and/or abroad. The mythology of India was also filtered through a strong Gandhian cultural nationalism, which reinforced binary oppositions of village/city, agriculture/industry, and true India/outside civilization. The village became the locus for authentic cultural knowledge that had not been sullied by the vagaries of colonial encounter, globalization, and economic change, as evidenced by the many anthropological village studies in the postindependence period, which reified Indian society as a system of rurality and caste.[25] The village in some sense became the locus of Bharat, "the Sanskrit term for nation as ancient soil but also referring to the masses of 'real India' as both locus of cultural difference and developmental problem."[26] This imagined rural India was a racial imaginary, in which the village and the villager were static, unchanging, untouched by the benefits of economic transformation. At the same time, under the technocratic vision of Jawaharlal Nehru, the village (and the villager) was also seen as the site most in need of paternalistic development, given their perceived backward practices and incapacity for technological, modern techniques. In this sense, the Indian state inherited the racial politics of the British colonial civilizing mission in their approach to rural development.

The brown savior was, in some sense, the next inheritor of this racialized view of the village, primarily because rural India continues to have a special place in the hearts and minds of the diasporic and bourgeois savarna Indian elite because they, too, have imbibed the nostalgia for rural India as authentic India, while also imbibing the view of rural India as outside of the sphere of economic productivity and technocratic capacity. Taken this way, Sahaayaka's rural uplift agenda, especially in its statement to focus on the rural as "they are the least looked after," can be situated in this history of racialized rhetoric regarding India's villages, dictating both how the project of saviorism was conceived by savarna elites and how mentors were slotted into labor positions in the organization based on their racialized caste positions as those who were "closest to the land" because they were traditional (but actually colonially emplaced) landed gentry.

For example, the incorporation of the mentors into Sahaayaka stemmed from the idea that their particular "funds of knowledge" were valuable—*funds of knowledge* being a term that has been used to "denote a strength-based perspective, seeing a richness of history within economic marginality and the contours of a fertile cultural landscape along streets marked by perceived scarcity."[27] While the attention to funds of knowledge was seen as an essential critique of earlier deficiency-based paradigms of those who had been dispossessed, when taken up as a guiding principle for the help economies, the funds-of-knowledge approach reveals itself as something else: it considers the value of personnel *only* for their supposed local-specific funds of knowledge, limiting what capabilities they are perceived to have, what they might aspire for, and what positions they can hold in any organization.

In this case, Sahaayaka mentors were seen as incredibly valuable to the workings of the organization primarily because they were perceived to be the bearers of authentic rural knowledge. While not all of them worked in their "native places," the Sahaayaka fieldworkers worked in areas whose demographics they could understand, at least to some extent, both linguistically and culturally, which, as I discussed at the end of part II, was part of the reason they were hired by Sahaayaka. This was an imagined set of authentic ethnoracial identities related to Kannada, Hinduism, caste, and agricultural work that stood in binary opposition to the position of the brown savior. In this sense, the fieldworkers were being produced as racialized subjects in relation to the managerial, modern, mobile, technocratic brown savior class. As important, it was assumed that this ethnoracial, primordial knowledge was an essential source of exchange value for fieldworkers, and therefore objectifying themselves became their most precious source of potential value.[28]

In some sense, the mentors represented the very same populations that have been the target of, and even benefited from, the racialized agrarian question in the colonial and postcolonial periods, but that had seen harsher economic conditions in India's liberalization era.[29] However, unlike those who were protesting the loss of their livelihoods, in many cases the Sahaayaka mentors had already given up on their traditional occupations, which, in turn, led them to the NGO. Here the mentors' relative educational mobility, linked to their caste positions as traditional landed gentry, coupled with their desperation for work in the postliberalization period, actually facilitated the growth of the NGO sector because, as Raj noted, they had few other options available to them.

For the mentors, their shifting occupational aspirations were never without ambivalence and/or misgivings, as I would hear from the Sahaayaka mentors who would rue that they had been forced to work away from their families and in environments that looked little like the open, green, quiet landscapes of their youth. They would complain about their long hours on the road, in buses, on motorbikes, or, if fortune was in their favor on that day, in a car, traveling back and forth between Bangalore and villages in other parts of Karnataka state; sometimes to Sahaayaka field offices 40 kilometers away from Bangalore in Ramanagara, 60 kilometers away in Kanakapura, or 250 kilometers away in Hubli-Dharwad. However, what they complained about most was a seeming cap on their ability to move up in the organization. They constantly wanted more authority, more training, higher salaries, and larger roles in Sahaayaka, which they were somehow unable to get despite their best efforts. These were the contradictory "feelings" associated with urbanity: the feeling of loss of land and livelihood, hopes for a better future, aspirations just out of reach. For the mentors, the city became a place of constant toil; never-ending, interminable movement; new life possibilities and slow, smoggy deaths.

Gendered Labor and Mentor Mobility Regimes

These aspirations for urban mobility were situated in a regime of neocolonial brahminical patriarchy, which further stratified the mentor class based on gendered positioning.[30] I began to recognize this later in the day, after Raj took his leave and I decided to stay back at the Sahaayaka field office in Kanakapura. One of the mentors, Lakshmi, requested that I accompany her on some school visits, and so, not two hours after my last bus ride, I found myself sitting on the bus again, this time with Lakshmi.

Lakshmi was one of Sahaayaka's longest-tenured mentors, and she was one of the very few women who had the role of mentor in the organization. I had known Lakshmi for almost three years, and yet our relationship did not really begin during the first two. When the men had taken an aggressive interest in me, coming over to shake hands, ask questions, and offer their help, Lakshmi was in the background, speaking only when I initiated conversations, what I perceived as the class- and caste-based gendered social relations that were continuously being reproduced in the organization. It had taken time for Lakshmi to position me, to get over a suspicion that I might be there to do more harm than good. Even when we finally started to speak more frequently, she would still text me after each of our conversations to remind me not to report what we talked about to Sahaayaka's leadership. I always assured her that I would not, and with each approving smile emoji, we developed a tenuous trust.

Perhaps it was because we passed her village on our way that she began to talk to me about her life and why she had ended up joining Sahaayaka. Her family lived in a village of approximately five hundred people in an area of Karnataka that had produced three of Sahaayaka's mentors. She still stayed in her native village because there was no one to take care of her mother and father. She had one brother who lived in Bangalore, but "he has no interest in taking care of our family, but I do," she told me with a hint of resentment in her voice. While her brother and most of the Sahaayaka other mentors were able to work without worrying about their families, having wives to do this domestic labor, she was forced into all of this domestic labor, falling prey to the cultural expectations of women as nurturers and caregivers, not just of children, but of elders as well.

Then she asked me, changing the topic, "Arjun, one thing, do you like Indian girls or foreign girls?" I paused, taken off guard by her question, before nervously stumbling through an ill-thought-out response. Thankfully, before I got too far, Lakshmi, seeing my visible nervousness, interrupted, "It is okay. People in India won't accept girls from anywhere else. In India, people do not have an open mind." It was a judgment on the country that also doubled as an explanation for her own plight. "Already I am *broken*," she said. It was a phrase that I did not quite understand, and I asked her to clarify. She told me that seven years earlier, her husband had passed away, after only three months of marriage. She was now a widow, and she had decided that she would never remarry given the incredible stigmas against widow remarriage still present in her village. By falling in line with this ideology of streedharma, or appropriate female conduct, Lakshmi had accepted her plight within the brahminical patriarchy.[31]

Lakshmi then admitted that she did not know if she would have ever joined Sahaayaka if she hadn't lost her husband so young. It had forced a different reckoning with getting a job and making enough so that she could survive alone while also taking care of her parents. That was why, when she found the opportunity with Sahaayaka, she was so eager to join. The salary was good enough, and she could continue to live in her village while doing her work. For Lakshmi, the NGO was a road to economic security.

I am scrolling through the notes I've taken from this conversation in my notebook, still struggling to discern them. The very strain of discerning them jogs my memory, and I am taken back to the moment when Lakshmi looked at me and laughed as I was struggling to take these notes on the bus. She had pulled out her own notebook and showed me how she used her elbow and knee to brace against upcoming bumps, and began to write, neatly and confidently.

Unlike the other mentors, who drove to schools on scooters, Lakshmi almost exclusively took the bus to make her school visits. Lakshmi had ridden the bus every single day for four years, usually two or three times a day as she traveled from school to school, and these rides were a part of her in a way I could not quite capture. Even though she had a scooter that she used for short, local commutes, she did not ride her scooter from school to school because, as she told me matter-of-factly, it was too unsafe for women to do so, especially when traveling over long distances and off main roads, where many village schools were. Instead, Lakshmi oversaw schools that were close to the main Kanakapura road, from which bus travel was possible. She was thankful that Sahaayaka had been willing to accommodate her, but she also knew that the fact that she could not ride a scooter constricted her movement, keeping her safely confined in the space between the Kanakapura field office and her village home.

Her physical immobility had also confined Lakshmi's mobility within the organization. All the other mentors were able to travel to Bangalore frequently, to show initiative by taking on more schools farther away, and to obtain professional development in Bangalore or even in North Karnataka. They partook in a slew of other activities that increased their "value" and could potentially allow them to get more pay or move up the organizational ladder. These activities were almost completely foreclosed to Lakshmi, and I never once saw her in Bangalore or in any of the many mentor workshops that I went to all over Karnataka. Instead, she stayed working in the same schools for the entire time I observed her working for the organization.

This did not mean that Lakshmi did not have desires or aspirations for the future. Far from it: Lakshmi was sculpting an array of possible futures that could function in relation to the constraints she faced. She had started to set aside just a bit of money every month, a few rupees that represented the possibility for a change later. When I asked her what she wanted to do, she told me at first that she wished she could find a job in Bangalore somehow. I asked her if she was interested in an education job in the city, but she said no, she wanted a job in the private sector with a "company." I asked her in what type of company exactly, and she replied that she would prefer to join a "computer" company.

I did not immediately respond, sitting with the thought of all the barriers to Lakshmi's dreams. Seeing my face, Lakshmi smirked, "You think I don't know computers? Or you think I won't do it?" I shrugged nervously, embarrassed that she had so easily caught the skepticism on my face, and replied that of course I thought she could do it. But then she herself stopped and reminded me, though perhaps it was more a reminder to herself, that traveling to Bangalore would be too hard while she had to take care of her parents and that she would have to improve her English skills quite a bit before she could ever imagine getting one of those kinds of jobs. Instead, she told me, "I will build a computer center in my village." She went on to explain that she wanted to start an internet center for the children in her village because they had so little access to training and expertise. She thought she could use her skills and learning from her time in Sahaayaka to help them and change the future possibilities of her village drastically.

Here Lakshmi was imagining that she could use the capacities she had developed during her time with Sahaayaka as a means to mobility without the need for physical movement, eschewing her slotting in the racialized, casteized, and gendered hierarchy she was ensconced in. Perhaps more important, Lakshmi's aspirations also reflect the way that her participation in the NGO and her exposure to the brown savior had cultivated her "entrepreneurial citizenship." She had, as Lilly Irani argues, "become an 'agent of change,' an ideal worker, an instrument of development, and an optimistic and *speculative citizen*. This citizen cultivates and draws what resources they can—their community ties, their capacity to labor, even their political hope—into the pursuit of entrepreneurial experiments in development, understood as economic growth and uplift of the poor."[32] Becoming an entrepreneur seemed as if it might be Lakshmi's way to tap into the road to accumulation even as she helped those in her village, a way of bridging her economic ambitions and her social obligations. But Lakshmi's aspiration for entrepreneurial uplift was far more precarious because she was not already comfortably situated within the circuits of capital. The question, then, was whether this imagined entrepreneurial future was actually attainable or whether this cultivation of aspiration was merely a way of preventing Lakshmi from joining those, like the protesting farmers, who had decided that these offerings of upward mobility were but a dupe.

In the next chapter, I extend this discussion of mentor mobility and the spatialization of their racialized and gendered labor slottings by focusing on the kinds of moral assumptions placed on mentors by the brown savior. I turn to a Sahaayaka training session for mentors, one of the many that Lakshmi was unable to attend, to show the kinds of assumptions that influenced who the mentors should be, why they should do their work, and where they should learn the appropriate skills to do their work.

URBAN ALTRUISM/URBAN CORRUPTION

About two months into my time in Bangalore, I got a call from Srinivasan inviting me to a retreat he had planned for some of Sahaayaka's mentors in Hubli, "Chotta Mumbai," a small city of approximately one million people near the coast of North Karnataka and bordering Maharashtra, approximately 450 kilometers from Bangalore to its east and 550 kilometers from Mumbai to its north. Hubli was the second-fastest-growing city in Karnataka, now considered a single conurbation with its neighboring city of Dharwad, whose center was some twenty kilometers away. Hubli-Dharwad is an example of the material changes wrought by late capitalist urbanization in postcolonial nation-states, expanding and connecting second-tier cities to one another even as first-tier cities, like Bangalore, market themselves as "global."

The retreat, Srinivasan told me, was intended to remind the mentors of their role in implementing Sahaayaka's programming. Srinivasan lamented that the mentors had become far too concerned with money, salary dreams that he believed were far more than "the market would bear." "That is all they are concerned about," he told me. "They need to develop their skills and managerial talents. Learn first, then maybe money will come later. It is sad, they were not always like this . . ." On the one hand, Srinivasan's phrasing locates the problem temporally, implying that there was some moment in the past when the mentors were working purely altruistically, doing their work because of a commitment to Sahaayaka's mission and as a form of uplift for their communities. At the same time, Srinivasan would remark that the mentors from North Karnataka, associated with a higher degree of rurality, had not yet "been corrupted" like their counterparts from South Karnataka, who spent more of their time in and around Bangalore city. In this imagination, ideas about corruption and altruism were spatialized, mapped onto region and proximity to the city, which, in turn, spurred on Srinivasan's own anxieties regarding his personnel.

This use of territorial concepts of belonging also regenerated racialized casteist hierarchies regarding the Sahaayaka mentors, whose caste position was linked with particular capacities to labor. Mentors were slotted into a graded hierarchy that valorized those mentors who labored altruistically for the good of their native village people, mimicking the figure of the idealized caste laborer who did their work unquestioningly because it was their duty and role in society. But this idea of "being corrupted" or being "less pure" also evoked ideas of the noble savage that attached a romanticized nobility to an indigenous person's supposed static tie to the land and "simpler" way of life. Mentors could maintain their respectability (read: nobility) within this framework only if their aspirations were never tied to monetary rewards or movement away from their land. In other words, the brown savior displaced and occluded the mentors' economic needs through this racialized rhetoric of altruism and selflessness, a rhetoric ultimately geared to generate affective attachments to the organization's moral valuations that held "on-the-ground personnel" to their jobs as an immobile labor force. The irony was, of course, that the fieldworkers' "demands for economic development and equality [were] delegitimized" even though the brown savior's entire value was accrued because of the economic and physical mobility that allowed them to take on the role of saving Others.[1]

At the same time, the brown savior felt a paternal moral obligation to prevent the mentors from being corrupted, a reproduction of previous paternalistic development relations (read: civilizing missions) that began with the assumption that those with power needed to help the ignorant and easily corruptible Other.[2] The retreat was one way for Srinivasan to perform this obligation by teaching the mentors how to avoid the city's corruption and what their appropriate conduct and skills should be. Here a kind of neocolonial logic undergirded Srinivasan's paternalistic relation to the mentors, in the sense that "righting and purging of various forms of 'waste'—unruly conducts, things, and natures (in short, matter perceived as out of place)—was a central . . . aspect of" his mission.[3] Paradoxically, purging wasteful and corrupt conduct required moving away from the village and into the city, despite the fact that the city was precisely what Srinivasan had claimed was a corrupting force. The difference, of course, was that Srinivasan could steer the mentors in the appropriate direction, teaching them what they needed to learn while steering them away from those values deemed inappropriate to their positions.

In the rest of this chapter, I show how Sahaayaka leadership slotted mentors into gendered spatial arrangements—in their residential living and travel obligations—that assumed that their moral and occupational growth must occur somewhere beyond their traditional homes. I reveal how these characterizations and expectations only doubled, tripled, and quadrupled the mentors' labor, while also channeling their aspirations toward (impossible) saviorist dreams.

On the Reengineering of Mentors and the Doubling (and Doubling and Doubling) of Labor

I accepted Srinivasan's invitation to attend the retreat and bought a 10 p.m. bus ticket from Bangalore to Hubli, curious as to what it was that Srinivasan had planned for the mentors. Six hours on a sleeper bus can feel like an eternity, especially if one has a weak stomach or bladder, and I stared out the window, trying to distract myself, squinting through a dirty window to see if I could get a glimpse of the landscape as it flew by. It was the middle of June, a time when the rains were just starting to change the earth from brown to green, but through the dirty window I couldn't tell much of a difference as the entire world took on a gray-brown tint.

After six hours in the bus, I reached Hubli station, awaiting Suresh. I had known Suresh for two years, having met him during my first trip to Bangalore, before he moved away from South Karnataka and back to Hubli, which was near his native village. When I left him in 2013, Suresh was a bachelor of twenty-four, just getting ready for marriage. Back then, both his English and my Kannada were terrible. Now his English and my Kannada had improved, though his English more so than my Kannada. I hadn't seen him since and was very much looking forward to catching up with him.

Suresh drove up on his motorbike, and I jumped on. When I asked Suresh about his family, he told me excitedly, "I have just had a baby, a baby boy!" I congratulated him, and he explained that his wife and child were not with him as she was with the baby at her parents' house for the next six months while he stayed in the Sahaayaka office. He admitted that he missed his family dearly but said that he would make a trip to visit them the following week after finishing some of his work with Sahaayaka.

Suresh had taken charge of all Sahaayaka schools in Hubli-Dharwad and Pune, a city approximately 450 kilometers to the north of it. He seemed unfazed by the added responsibility, telling me that he was becoming more and more interested in training and expansion. "I am working with Anand on professional development," he said. "I am still not used to meeting HMs [headmasters] and teachers and presenting our vision. I want to develop this." It was clear that over the three years since I had seen him last, Suresh had identified a set of skills that would make him better at "helping" others, including public speaking, the ability to break down interventions into digestible numbers, and the capacity to make a PowerPoint presentation. Suresh knew rural schools intimately, and yet, in order to "communicate effectively" with those working in rural schools, Suresh felt the need to learn skills that actually relied on the ability to *abstract* and, ultimately, transmit a generic template of what change should look like across all the schools in which he worked. In other words, Suresh's culturally specific knowledge was wasted if it could not be translated into a universalizable form.

To learn these skills from Sahaayaka's brown savior class, Suresh had to make monthly trips to Bangalore, traveling six hours each way even as he continued to do his work in Hubli and Pune. He calculated that he was traveling by bus or car for almost forty hours in some weeks. This urban-rural distinction was marked on Suresh's body, in his tired eyes and lack of sleep, in the doubling of his labor, and in the constant movement that kept him away from his family and produced an incessant longing for them.

The Sahaayaka field office in Hubli took up the lower two stories of a house, along a street of residential homes all built in a similar style: cement walls, white or off-yellow; gray stairs that remain unpainted; lacquered wood doors (though I can't claim to know the wood type); and gates in the front. A row of seven motorbikes lined the narrow driveway, leaving almost no room to scoot by and into the flat.

I followed Suresh past the bikes and into a narrow set of rooms behind the house. There were several mattresses in one room, and Suresh explained that some of the mentors (all male), including himself, were staying there at the moment. He would continue staying at the Sahaayaka office until his wife finally came back from her parents' house some six months in the future.

Many of the Sahaayaka field offices had this same dual function, being used both for the day-to-day administrative work of the mentors and also as make-shift hostels where the staff could stay on a temporary basis. The advantage to living in the office was that mentors could save money while living in urban areas where their salaries would otherwise make living nearly untenable, especially while also having to pay for expenses for their families back in their native villages. They were also able to access computers and the internet, something most of the mentors could otherwise access only on their phones.

The lack of demarcation between private and public in these quasi-home, quasi-work spaces was a visible challenge to any assumed separations of the private from the public. It reflected the role of the NGO itself, an entity never quite sure of its status between the private sector and the public sector.[4] On the one hand, Sahaayaka worked in government schools, regulated by the stipulations of their memoranda of understanding with the government. On the other hand, their funding still came largely from the private sector, limiting the scope of their work to that which funder agencies decreed. There was a hypervisibility and surveillance of the mentors that came with this dual scrutiny, and it was reflected in these types of social spaces that kept the mentors in ready reach of Bangalore-based Sahaayaka administrators, donors who wanted to know what their funds were being used for, and government officials who wanted to make sure that Sahaayaka never overstepped its agreements. But this hypervisibility also required a literal break from familial and other personal relations, clustering the mentors in a homosocial space that assumed their primary identity and role was as an employee of the NGO. In so doing, Sahaayaka was able "to achieve an optimal regulation—an equilibrium of internment and circulation—of . . . human bodies with their dispositions and desires" channeled toward organizationally exchangeable value.[5]

Seven men, between the ages of twenty-four and twenty-eight, sat together, drinking coffee, eating biscuits and idlis, and watching the TV9 Kannada news. I went around with handshakes for those who I did not know and hugs for all of those mentors whom I was meeting again after a long while. Eventually, we made our way out of the office and crammed into a mid-1990s Suzuki "Carry Van" that was far too small to carry ten grown men.

We traveled for twenty interminable minutes until we reached the Taj Gateway Hotel-Hubli, part of one of the most famous hotel chains in India, started by the Tata family in the early 1900s, where the retreat was to take place. The Taj Gateway is a comically grand caricature of twenty-first-century urban architecture. It was built along the four-hundred-acre Unkal Lake, in the middle of seven acres of palm trees, and included the most "world class" of accommodations: meeting rooms, a lavish "Western" cuisine (pancakes, pastas, salads) with an "Eastern" touch (idlis, sambar), a gym, an Olympic-size pool, and high-speed WiFi throughout the premises. At the Taj, I could feel the neocolonial city come to life, ready to colonize minds.

None of the mentors had ever seen, much less been to, the Taj Gateway Hotel, and when we arrived there was real excitement as they looked around. We walked into an all-glass meeting room that overlooked a pool and sat down. We all shivered inside, the AC turned too high for those not used to anything but a fan.

Speaking in a mix of Kannada and English, Srinivasan welcomed everyone with magnanimity, clearly taking great pleasure in the fact that the mentors were visibly in awe of the space he had chosen to run this retreat. The next six hours were a cacophony of discussion, mentors shouting ideas, going through workshop activities, and having several speakers give lectures on organizational development. But what stayed with me for a few days afterward was the beginning, when Srinivasan asked each mentor to explain what the organization's mission was and what the biggest problems were for the organization. The mentors went around, and as they began to speak, Srinivasan interrupted and critiqued, taking up much of the space in the room with his hypermasculinist rejoinders to whatever the mentors would posit: "Sir, the problem is headmasters"; "We don't have time to travel to so many schools"; "Sahaayaka is working with the community"; "We have too much paperwork, so we cannot spend as much time in the schools as we want"; "It is very difficult to work for so little pay, sir"; "Plant school gardens—do a village case study—run a reading program"; and so on and so forth. By the end, Srinivasan was visibly frustrated, particularly because the mentors were not able to replicate one another's responses to his question. For Srinivasan, rather than an indicator of the mentors' immense capacity for ideation and commitment to bettering the organization, these responses were damning evidence that the mentors had lost sight of the organization's singular mission because they had been corrupted by dreams of money.

As the day moved on, Srinivasan took on a more active pedagogical role, giving mentors assignments and suggesting skills that ought to be developed.

He rummaged in his handbag and pulled out a copy of an English-language text, *Turtles, Termites, and Traffic Jams: Explorations in Massively Parallel Microworlds*, written by Mitchel Resnick (1994). The book had a strong following in the mid-1990s and advocated decentralized approaches to organization building in which every member of an organization played an agential, synchronous role in helping the organization reach its goals. Then he took out a copy of Dale Carnegie's (1936) *How to Win Friends and Influence People*, a book that has become synonymous with a particular kind of bourgeois aspiration for the postcolonial middle class in India.[6] "You all need to read these books," he encouraged. "I know it will be difficult at first. But even if you read fifteen pages, slowly it will come." While Srinivasan was supposedly asking mentors to develop their skills and take on more proactive decision-making, he was actually asking them to reassess their values. By mapping English onto "the technical domains of society and economy," he was implicitly producing a neocolonial division of labor that mimicked a program of civilizing.[7] Srinivasan knew that the mentors did not read or speak well in English, and therefore his ask would be difficult for them, especially because their day-to-day jobs in schools actually did not require the use of English since they were mostly speaking to teachers, headmasters, and students in Kannada- or Urdu-medium schools. This meant that they were expected to learn these skills in their free time, outside of their time in schools, doubling their labor while also diminishing the value of the essential labor they were already doing in schools despite the fact that their culturally specific knowledge was why they had been hired in the first place.

Yet civilizing did not just begin and end with the forceful request to learn technical skills in English. It also required imbibing the cultural values that were presented in the Taj hotel. For example, after our meetings Srinivasan invited the mentors for dinner at the Taj's famous buffet, which includes hundreds of dishes, including a mix of pastas, salads, soups, and desserts. Commensality here is intended as a form of neocolonial reengineering, changing what the mentors valued as they encountered and learned the culinary etiquette and tastes of the global elite classes. The mentors poked at and ate the food politely, though slowly and without much enthusiasm. Suresh confessed that he had never had pasta before, which he had been excited about at first, but then, as he took his first bites, he kept saying the taste was "interesting," a sentiment that was, for me, a polite euphemism for "not very good."

When the meeting finally ended, we jumped back into the van and ran to the nearest local hotel (a very different kind of hotel), located approximately five minutes away, where we ate chicken biryani, vegetable biryani, and chicken masala fry and drank Kingfishers while talking about the day's meeting. The bar was dark and musty from smoke, with large screens covering the windows, but no one minded, happy to be in a much less foreign and more comfortable space. Suresh joked about how they could finally eat *"real* food," and I was reminded that taste buds aren't that easy to colonize.

The next day I took an all-night train ride back to Bangalore with Suresh and several others. These long train rides had become a normal part of their daily routines, and they inculcated me into the journey's most important elements: talking endlessly, playing pranks on one another, stealing a few swigs from a bottle of beer, and finally dozing off one by one when they had no more energy left. I finally arrived in Bangalore sometime around five in the morning and waved goodbye, dazed and very, very, tired.

On Economic Need, Moral Obligation, and Impossible
Dreams of Saviorism

The next time I met Suresh was almost five months later, during one of his many trips to Bangalore. We had spoken on the phone only once, very shortly after the retreat, when Suresh, having taken seriously Srinivasan's request, had attempted to read some of the texts that Srinivasan had recommended. He asked if I would help him with some of the vocabulary, and I assured him that I would help. I never heard from him again, taking that as a tacit indicator that the attempt at reading Resnick's text had come to a halt, perhaps because the daily labor obligations were too high or because Suresh did not experience the immense "added value" the book was supposed to provide in his work and life.

Suresh looked tired, bags under his eyes, his usually well-ironed shirt creased from hours sitting and sleeping on a bus. We talked on our way to a tea stall, and I found out that he had come into Bangalore just for the day to attend a meeting and was leaving to return home on the 5:30 p.m. bus. It left us only a little more than two hours to talk. Time was fleeting for Suresh as he scrambled to learn as much as he could as fast as he could, to move up the NGO value chain.

We finished our tea and started walking. A girl of about eighteen stopped us and tried to hand me a piece of paper, which I instinctively refused. Suresh, on the other hand, grabbed the paper immediately and started reading it. "INTERESTED IN MAKING MORE MONEY, CALL US." A call center was looking for people with English and basic computer skills interested in working for them.

I watched as Suresh read the advertisement, carefully folded the paper, and put it in his pocket. "Why keep that?" I asked, before thoughtlessly blurting out in one of my many class-inflected stupors, "It's a waste." Suresh chuckled and confessed, "I need one extra job. Do you know of anything, Arjun? Something that I can do from home in the evening?" I told him I didn't know of any jobs but asked why he needed another job when he was already working for Sahaayaka.

"The pay is only 18,000 rupees, and it's not enough. When I was a bachelor, it was fine. But now I have my wife and also a child. It is much harder for me now. I don't know what job I can find." When I asked him why he didn't just change jobs entirely and leave Sahaayaka, his response was direct and, to my surprise, more confrontational than I expected. "I've made a commitment. For at least five years I want to do my work and improve schools. I cannot leave it just like that. They have made me the coordinator for all of Pune as well, and that is a big thing. I don't want to leave just like that."

This was the perplexing dilemma that I found many of the Sahaayaka mentors facing. Suresh was completely invested in the cause of educational change as a moral prerogative, without which his past seven years of work were rendered meaningless. This unquantifiable feeling of moral responsibility to the cause, the organization, and the schools and communities he worked with overshadowed his financial hardship. Moreover, being "from there," that is to say, from a village like those he served, doubled the moral obligation, merging the obligation to the organization with the obligation to his native fellows. This produced a Sisyphean paradox, at least for those mentors who bought into this vision, pushing toward utopian goals that were never achievable but so ethically binding that mentors kept working toward them.

At the same time, Suresh's experience ran almost diametrically opposite to Srinivasan's racialized caricature of the mentors. Rather than being "corrupted," as Srinivasan had argued, by money and proximity to the city, Suresh's struggle was to find a way to *stay* with the organization because he believed in its altruistic ideology despite the fact that Sahaayaka was not providing the basic salary necessary for him to take care of his own relations. Paradoxically, then, this form of altruism created a situation in which mentors were unable to help their own families even as they were supposedly working for the NGO precisely to help people like those in their own families.

Suresh explained that he had an alternative solution to his problems. "I'm starting my own NGO," he exclaimed. Suresh seemed to want to replicate much of what he was doing with Sahaayaka, except instead of being a mentor, he wanted to be in charge, to take on the role of savior and thereby resolve the contradiction between altruism and economic mobility. "We started it a few years back. Will you join it? You can be on the board!" I gave a nervous nod, feigning enthusiasm without giving a commitment, balancing those bounds of friendship that had developed as we'd gotten to know each other beyond the confines of work and research, but that still pivoted on my capital as would-be brown savior.

As we tried to think through how Suresh might go about developing his NGO, our conversation turned to a young Indian American named Chaand who had started an NGO in Bihar. I told Suresh about how Chaand had taken a year off from the University of Pennsylvania to start his organization, about how he had raised thousands of dollars of funding through a Kickstarter campaign, and how he had managed to get his organization running by the age of twenty-three. "Twenty-three!" Suresh was almost in shock, before getting noticeably more somber. "He's twenty-three and already has his own NGO. I'm already twenty-seven. And still . . . nothing. Maybe I will go back to my village." It was Suresh's shame that caught my attention. Suresh's aspirations had been reshaped during his time as a Sahaayaka mentor, the possibility of creating his own NGO representing the ideal end to all of his learning in the organization. This aspirational expansion had also produced the perception that Suresh was on an equal footing with people like Chaand, an illusion that obfuscated the major material differences tied to a web of financial, educational, national, transnational, and caste power relations. Because Suresh defined difference only in terms of age, the locus of blame rested with him alone, his lack of hard work and skill development, producing shame at his perceived underachievement. Suresh explicitly mapped his feelings of underachievement in relation to the possibility of going back to his village. The village, in this characterization, was a space and time where his aspirations would go to die.

Two years later I met Suresh, and he told me with resignation that his NGO had stalled. "We found that all the members, they had other jobs. We could not afford to quit and take risk." he said. "We are dependent always. Here I am dependent on Sahaayaka. There we do not have land, so if we are going back, then we have to work on someone else's land. There is no freedom."

If Suresh had joined the NGO thinking that he might be more independent than he had been previously while working on his family's land, he had realized that working for the NGO had actually produced only a new form of dependence. For Suresh, freedom was tethered to an imaginary of economic independence, whether that were because one owned enough land to grow crops for oneself or because one owned an NGO that allowed one to accumulate enough to live without worrying about risk.[8] However, Suresh's idea of freedom also required the ability to accrue wealth while maintaining one's sense of altruism in the process, crystallized in the aspiration to create his own NGO. Here Suresh is providing a theory of saviorism that fits exceptionally well into accumulationist ideologies, eschewing any redistributionist possibility in favor of a neoliberal self-actualization that locates problems and solutions in individuals, even for those whose material conditions render this accrual nearly impossible.

Suresh's argument makes clear the NGO's function within India's current version of primitive accumulation, fusing expropriation and exploitation in a way that relies on the fact that those who experience its harshest conditions still must believe in the system. Such an interpretation is not meant to blame or place responsibility on those like Suresh who are struggling to find a means of mobility in a system that is designed to produce dispossession. Instead, as I have argued, processes of expropriation require the simultaneous cultivation of particular types of aspiration and labor expectations within organizations like Sahaayaka. I turn in the next chapter to one of the starkest examples of this contradiction, focusing specifically on farmers' suicides in India and one mentor's reckoning with his own future in relation to this form of tragic loss.

10

A GLOBAL DEATH

One day in late August, I stepped off the bus and looked around, awaiting Manoj. "Hi, Arjun, how are you?" he yelled, bringing his motorbike up alongside me.

Suresh once told me, laughing about his relationship with Manoj, "I love him, he is my friend, but he is too serious. He does not like to have fun." By not liking to have fun, Suresh meant that Manoj never drank or smoked with his colleagues, never stayed out late, admonished anyone who slacked off on the job, and also disliked most of the films (Kannada or otherwise) that the other mentors watched. Later Manoj would explain that he didn't like these movies because they had too many "bad elements" in them—drinking, sex, and the like—which he found immoral. Manoj had also recently given up eating meat, a decision that was grounded in the casteist cosmologies of brahminical cultural mores.[1] For Manoj, his vegetarianism and abstinence from alcohol were a means by which he could differentiate himself from the rest of his peers and realize an upward mobility that he associated with these brahminical practices.

Manoj was quiet as we drove together on his motorbike, responding to my questions politely but rather abruptly. Usually he was asking hundreds of questions about the United States, about my research, and about my family. At first, I didn't really notice, lost as I was in my own overwhelming sensory experience.[2] I began filming on the way, letting the bumps of the road jostle my small handheld Sony, futilely attempting to shoot footage that would, during viewing, somehow seem more akin to that moment of lived experience: the beating of the sun against our uncovered heads, the quick swerves that kept us from hitting especially large potholes, the slowing as we passed a goatherd leading his goats or as a group of schoolchildren left school. I was a clumsy, timid cameraman, holding on to the rear handlebar a bit too hard and squeezing my legs tightly against the sides of the bike until there was a slippery film of sweat against my thighs.

Just before we reached the school, Manoj stopped his bike and turned around. "Arjun, I want to tell you something." "Haan Manoj, tell me." "My father died." I put down my camera, the interest in capturing lived experience instantaneously eradicated from my mind. "Manoj, what?? When? Why didn't you tell me sooner?" "Just a few days back, when you were gone." "What happened? Was it sudden?" "Yes. It was suicide." Manoj let out the last word—*su-i-ci-de*—slowly, as if his mouth still hadn't gotten used to saying the word.

My sadness mingled with nerves until I let loose an embarrassingly incoherent string of words and questions. "Why are you here working still? Why do we need to go to school?" Manoj shrugged: "It is okay. It is my job, my duty."

We rode slowly for the last half kilometer, stretching time to experience this solemn intimacy together for a few moments longer. I asked some questions about his mother, about what he needed to do next, and then, as my nerves slowed down, reassured him as best I knew how, tapping into my own small cave of past experience with loss: "Try not to keep thinking about why. You will never have an answer, and it will only drive you crazy." It dawned on me then that Manoj had joined me on this day in order to distract himself from the all-consuming grief that comes with tragic loss. I did not ask about his father again during the rest of our trip. Instead, we both quietly immersed ourselves in the daily work in the school.

Traumatic events, especially the experience of losing a loved one in the way Manoj had, seem to carry with them a kind of affective immediacy that makes explanation and theorization feel insensitive or impractical. Indeed, my own interaction with Manoj reflected this need to experience death in its affective immediacy: in my instinctive closing of the camera, in my hesitation to accept Manoj's insistence on working, and in my declaration that Manoj need not think about "why" his father's death had occurred.

But understanding *why* social suffering occurs, including tragic events like suicide, matters. *Why* matters because attending to the material conditions of social suffering helps us to dislodge the incessant need to individualize, pathologize, and locate blame in those who are experiencing suffering and instead pushes us to think about suffering as rooted in political, economic, and historical phenomena. *Why* matters because it shifts our temporal analysis away from thinking about a tragic event as an end in and of itself, instead leading us into the past and, as important, *into the future*, broadening our gaze to recognize the complex ways people weave new forms of life after death.[3] Such an excavation requires a sincerity and honesty that does not valorize or vilify the choices of those who are making sense of and coping with tragedies that might be beyond our own comprehension. Exploring the *why* of social suffering should produce, as Roseann Liu and Savannah Shange write, a kind of "thick solidarity that is, a kind of solidarity that mobilizes empathy in ways that do not gloss over difference but rather push into the specificity, irreducibility, and incommensurability of racialized experience."[4]

In the rest of this chapter, I further analyze my interactions with Manoj to get at the *why* of farmers' suicide in India and its afterlives. I begin by highlighting the colonial (dis)continuities with current agricultural dispossession before exploring how global regimes of economic and cultural value shape the meanings, decisions, and hierarchies produced in the wake of tragic loss. In Manoj's case, tragic death is linked to a devaluation of agricultural labor that produces in Manoj an impulse to separate himself from his village community and find ways to link himself to "global" communities—a process that also requires him to valorize those like the brown savior. Somewhat paradoxically, as I show, this affective process also creates the conditions for his suffering to be abstracted from the specific political economic relations that produce it.[5]

Primitive Accumulation and Farmers' Suicide as Social Pathology

Manoj's father was a farmer who had worked his entire life in a small village in Ramanagara District, thirty-five kilometers south of Bangalore. He owned a small plot of land, approximately one hectare in total, on which the family had attempted to grow reshmi (silk), the crop that has been designated as the most lucrative within Karnataka's export economy. Unfortunately, as Manoj's father discovered, reshmi, unlike other local subsistence crops like raagi (finger millet), could produce surplus value only when grown on a much larger scale. And so the family's land never produced any profit, and Manoj's father was forced to labor on neighboring land, picking silk cocoons and doing any odd jobs available in the area. Eventually, with debt and depression mounting, he took his own life. His father's tragic disposability also meant that Manoj's family had been primed for dispossession. For example, in the weeks following his father's death, Manoj sold off his family's goats and was thinking about when, rather than if, he should sell the land that was left.

Utsa Patnaik has argued that farmers' suicide is the starkest reminder that India's market liberalization of the 1990s was actually a continuation of earlier colonial strategies of primitive accumulation. She writes that farmers' suicides recall:

> the primitive accumulation of capital . . . in Europe during the 16th and 19th centuries. . . . But the 21st century is not the 18th and 19th century: the peasantry of the global South has nowhere to go if it is dispossessed, in contrast to the dispossessed peasantry of the North, which migrated in vast numbers to the New World. . . . No mass peasant suicides owing to debt took place before 1991. . . . [I]ndebtedness-driven farmer suicides started from 1998. Total recorded farmer suicides between 1998 and December 2008 were 198,000; specifically debt-driven suicides have claimed over 60,000 peasant lives over the last decade.[6]

Patnaik provides a historical-materialist *spatial* theory of primitive accumulation that relies both on expropriation of agricultural land and on the expectation that surplus populations will move away from this land. Her argument hinges on the fact that the surplus peasants in Europe during the years of industrialization, while dispossessed in large numbers, were able to migrate out of Europe, thus solving the crisis of surplus labor in early modern capitalism. However, unlike in these earlier colonial-industrial years, even as Indian farmers are driven ever more into debt, they have virtually nowhere to go. The result is the massive number of farmers' suicides in India, now counting more than a quarter million.

While I agree with Patnaik's general argument, I would provide two qualifications. As I have noted previously, farmers in India have actually moved in large numbers to cities, including to Bangalore. While it is true that their likelihood of economic mobility has remained low, at least conceptually, the city has been conceived of as one solution to the crisis of surplus. Moreover, neocolonial racial capitalism does not solely function through disposability. Rather, it creates graded stratifications that produce some possibilities for mobility for surplus populations based on their ability to internalize neocolonial values. Here material changes brought on by economic dispossession, including the loss of life, might also facilitate psychosocial changes for those left behind, in what they aspire for and dream about.[7] These types of changes work not on the intellect but on the affective level and have the potential to further ossify the social stratification produced by expropriation.[8]

The next time I visited Manoj was two weeks later at the Sahaayaka field office. Manoj had not missed work even once since his father's passing and, if anything, was even more diligent with his tasks than he had been before. For Manoj, being productive may have been a distraction from his grief, but it was also indicative of a late capitalist subjectivity, in which his capacity for labor functioned to reinforce his sense of self and regulate his emotions.

The compulsion to work meant that he had already finished all his work for the day by the time I arrived, and so we sat in the Sahaayaka office making small talk with Lakshmi until the workday came to an end. He began to name places in the United States—Niagara Falls; Chicago; Washington, DC; Snake River (a place I myself had never heard of)—that he wanted to go to. As he kept naming more places, Lakshmi joked, "Oh Manoj, your ambitions! I just want to move to Bangalore!"

Lakshmi and Manoj had grown up in neighboring villages just kilometers apart. Lakshmi, like Manoj, had struggled and, like Manoj, had used her job with Sahaayaka as a means for economic mobility. However, Lakshmi's aspirations were quite a bit different from Manoj's, and her joke revealed the way that neocolonial capitalist aspiration was and is inherently gendered.[9] Even though both were seeking mobility through their roles in the help economy, horizontal (spatial) and vertical (economic) mobility were differentiated based on their gendered positionings: Manoj spent much of his time in Bangalore learning from Sahaayaka leadership, even as Lakshmi stayed mostly closer to her village. For her, the freedom to move to Bangalore was as significant as the idea of flying abroad, if not more so.

Eventually Manoj and I left the office, waved goodbye to Lakshmi, and began to drive toward Manoj's home. On the way Manoj told me more about his father: "Because we owned only very little land, my father had to work as a day laborer. He would pick reshmi leaves on other people's land, climb trees and pick coconuts, etc. For this he would receive two hundred to three hundred rupees. But in the end he would use a lot of it on alcohol." He paused to talk more about alcohol in his village. "Younger people now go to wine shops in the towns, but the older people, like my father, drink sarai. It is the local drink. I have thought many times, 'Why? What is the need?' But my friends, colleagues, all are drinking. You should tell them not to." I stayed silent when Manoj asked me this favor, feeling nervous at Manoj's insinuation and the way it marked me. Manoj was imagining that I somehow had both the appropriate moral sensibility and the authority to admonish other mentors. Here, the "capacity to save" those whose practices were deemed immoral was mapped onto the fact that I was part of the global, savarna class.

Manoj continued on, not realizing my discomfort. "My father didn't drink too much when I was in school, but soon after I started my job, my father's drinking increased a lot." When I asked why, Manoj said he didn't know. He concluded the same way when asked about his father's suicide and added, "It is a hard time for all farmers now, my father was only one example." Manoj's characterization of his father's passing was not couched in any language of individual pathology. Rather, Manoj framed it within a set of agricultural relations and in a manner that did not isolate his father's suicide as mental illness or render it "to be the exclusive fault of individuals who are sociopathic, criminal, or, at best, irresponsible or organically sick."[10] In so doing, Manoj was able to make links to, and implicitly theorize suicide within, a set of economic, political, and social processes he witnessed within his community.

Entrepreneurial Virility and Distancing from Agricultural Labor

Eventually we ended up at Manoj's family home. As we walked in, he pointed to a small, closed room just inside the front entrance of his house: "This is where my father died." Manoj and I commiserated on the passing of our fathers—the specificities of how they had taken their own lives and how we had each dealt with the aftermath—before he finally suggested that we go for a walk around his village.

As we walked, Manoj told me about it: "There are eighty families in the village, like my own. It has been very difficult for the farmers here, costs are high and profits are low, even for silk. The people are going through a very difficult time, and most of them are not interested in changing at all. Only four members from my class ever left the village for a BEd or BA," he continued, "and then another five or six left to Bangalore to work as laborers." I asked Manoj if he would ever think about going into farming, and he bristled. "No. No. No. Never." In making this statement, Manoj was noting the struggles of agricultural workers and his own deep anxiety about ever doing such labor, a form of labor that he had seen take his father and that had slowed his own professional growth. In this sense, I read Manoj's bristling as indicative of his fears of losing his "entrepreneurial virility," economic destitution intersecting with emasculation.[11] For Manoj, agriculture was linked directly to this type of masculine loss, leading to alcoholism, debt, and a diminishing self-worth that would end in suffering and/or death.

Perhaps to make his point even clearer, Manoj differentiated himself when he talked to me about his village and his community, referring to "they" or "them" rather than "we" or "us." Here, distinguishing himself from his fellows was the psychological effect of these neocolonial processes of dispossession. Primitive accumulation required not just the expropriation of land but the internalizing of neocolonial values, specifically through valorizations of one's capacity to change and leave behind those who supposedly did not possess the appropriate kinds of values to change their circumstances. Manoj made this claim quite explicitly, characterizing his fellow villagers as unchanging and static.

In other words, Manoj's socially situated theorization did not actually produce a sense of resistance to the economic, political, and social processes that facilitated dispossession. Instead, it allowed him to valorize himself and his decisions as someone who had succeeded within the system as it was currently constituted. I asked him how it was that he ended up wanting to get an education and move out while most of the other students hadn't done this at all. Manoj answered:

> At that time there was a lot of pressure from my family. We were told it was best to get money faster and help financially rather than continue with education. I fought with my father about that. Even though the cost for Pre-university course (PUC) college was only five hundred rupees, my father wouldn't pay. My grandmother finally gave me the money to go to school. But then my sister was married at eighteen, and so expenses were too high.

He chuckled sadly, then continued, "I never took dowry in my own marriage. But that is why, first, before getting my BEd, I worked at an industrial plant for four years. My parents had no education. But with me and my wife both with degrees, it will be much easier for my children." Here Manoj focused on the specifics of his battles with his family, his deep desire for change and growth, and the way he fought the odds in order to succeed and leave the traditional family occupation. This kind of "bootstrap performativity" required that Manoj see himself as different from (even better than) his own family, relying on his willfulness and natural talent, coupled with his discomfort with illiberal gender norms, like dowry and child marriage, which he marked as a particularly sinister form of village backwardness.

I realized later that I had inadvertently facilitated this framing through my form of questioning, by asking him why it was *he* and not others in his village who had somehow made it "out," reflecting my own colonized valuations of life and labor. This persistent need to know why Manoj had striven to achieve upward mobility was itself a neocolonial haunting, what Elizabeth Povinelli argues is "a way of holding those who suffer accountable: 'Look, this one had the will to lift herself up by her bootstraps.'"[12]

But both Manoj and I were forced to reckon with our elitisms when we stopped to watch a friend of Manoj's work, one of the few members of his village who had also gotten his BEd. He slowly took silkworms off a bed of mulberry leaves and placed them, one by one, on the chandreki, the woven bamboo platform on which the silkworms spin their cocoons. During this process a small boy walked out and smiled at us. Manoj introduced me and said, "He is from America. Do you want to go to America?" But before the boy had a chance to reply, his friend, without looking up from his work, cut the boy off, "Yes, yes, but what good is that to us? Who will give him a job there?"

If Manoj relied on a bootstrap narrative, it was his friend's critique that suddenly brought forth the lie. Manoj's neighbor, too, had completed his bachelor's degree in education and had had dreams of leaving the village. The difference was one of luck: he had failed to land a job and therefore had been forced to return to his village. In asking the question of labor, his friend recognized the impossibility of finding adequate compensation for one's labor in a global elsewhere that systematically devalued their lives and work. He, unlike Manoj, did not want to spread a lie to younger children, a dupe propagated by those with power that made people believe that following the expected educational trajectory within the system would result in global mobility. Thus, framing Manoj's story as one of success and willfulness occluded the real structural inequities that shaped both Manoj's life and the lives of those in his community.

A Thesis on a Valuable Death and the Imaginaries of Travel

When we got back to the house, we ate lunch in a somber mood. Manoj mentioned his father again, now grappling with how his friend's critique had punctured his earlier framing of his father's resistance to his education. Perhaps, Manoj surmised, his father may have had legitimate reasons for not believing in the value of an education that gave very little guarantee of mobility for those from the village.

As we finished, Manoj perked up. "Arjun, have you heard of Charlie Chaplin? You know *Modern Times*? Have you heard about his life?" I was a bit confused by the question, but I replied that, yes, I knew who Charlie Chaplin was, but I knew very little about him beyond his films.

Without notice, Manoj jumped out of his chair and ran into his room. I followed him, and he looked for a book on his bookshelf. He pulled out a book, written in Kannada. "This is an autobiography of Charlie Chaplin." I looked it over, a book of about ninety pages that Manoj had bought on a trip to Sapna Bookstore in Bangalore. "You know, Charlie Chaplin's life was so hard. He suffered a lot. Even he struggled as a child. He never had a father, and his mother, she became crazy. He got divorced three times. He saw two of his children die. The government forced him to leave the United States." Manoj paused and thought before he continued, "One thing that is the same everywhere, stay home or go far away, everywhere you will find hardship. Always hardship."

At first, I was captured by Manoj's theorizing of hardship and found solace in the idea that everyone experienced suffering, whether a movie star or a fieldworker from an Indian village. I, too, wanted to see parallels in suffering, in, for example, my own journey with familial suicide and Manoj's. This sentiment was so evocative, in fact, that it took me years to realize that Manoj was dealing with the contradiction revealed by his friend, who had let him know that there was no use looking to America or seeing oneself in relation to those so far away. By universalizing hardship and suffering, Manoj did not have to reckon with the specificities of the many material forces that differentiated the hardship of farmers like his father from other incommensurable forms of hardship experienced by those living in other places and other times.

Manoj got up again and grabbed his computer. "I have always been interested in space travel," he told me. "I want my children, either girl or boy, to become astronauts." As proof, he shared a clip he had downloaded off of YouTube, a clip from TV9 News, a local Kannada television network, about Kalpana Chawla, the first Indian American astronaut and the first Indian woman to have gone into space. Chawla was born in Karnal, India, before migrating to the United States to complete her master's degree in aerospace engineering from the University of Texas at Arlington in 1982. The news story was about her tragic end, her death as part of the 2003 Space Shuttle *Columbia* disaster, in which seven crewmembers died.

After her death she was memorialized both in India and in the United States. Seventy-Fourth Street in Jackson Heights, Queens, was renamed after her as Kalpana Chawla Way; a dormitory at the University of Texas at Arlington was named Kalpana Chawla Hall in 2004; a planetarium bearing her name was opened in Haryana (figure 10.1); and, closest to Manoj's home, the Kalpana Chawla Award was instituted by the government of Karnataka in 2004 for young women scientists.

I asked Manoj afterward whether he wasn't afraid that his children might die like Chawla if they became astronauts. He looked at me with no concern.

FIGURE 10.1. Kalpana Chawla Memorial Planetarium in Kurukshetra, Haryana.

"We all die somehow sometime. Some at sixty, seventy, some earlier. But even now, ten years later, I remember her. Do something great even if death follows."

Manoj introduced the figure of Chawla to underscore what might be considered a "valuable death" in a mass-mediated globalizing world. For him, like many others, memorialized death was no longer confined to traditional physical sites of burial and cremation but also included virtual places.[13] Chawla's death was a worthy death because she had done "something great"—gone to space and died in the process—remembered by a global digital public through a process of mediatization, in the local, national, and global media coverage of Chawla's death, and digitization, in the news reports uploaded onto (and downloaded from) YouTube, accessible to anyone on the internet. This framing also revealed the class-based inflections of such moral economies, taking as a given that access by a global digital public was of more import than access by those who lived only walking distance away. In other words, a valuable death was one recognized through global-digital circulation, and a less significant one was "local," leaving people like Manoj's father invisible in the wake of their struggles to survive, unless they became the unique subject of a film or news story.

Perhaps most important, Manoj identified with the figure of Chawla because of her ethnoracial tie to India in a globalizing context. Purnima Mankekar argues that mediatized circulations of "transnational public cultures" produce sometimes contradictory forms of affective affiliation and belonging to racialized global "Indian" identities.[14] In this case, the circulation of Chawla's image on Kannada media networks as an "Indian abroad" did not merely affect those who lived in migratory contexts, such as the United States, but also had an equally powerful affective impact on those who continued to live in India, in this case those living in rural Karnataka.[15] These ethnoracial connections were part of a "global racial common sense" that Manoj readily embraced in trying to make sense of the death of his father and differentiate himself from those who had remained in his home community.[16]

This globally circulating valorization of the Indian abroad is also one of the reasons the brown savior is recognized not only by those in power but also by those whom they hire for fieldwork positions. The brown savior's access to village communities and their ability to enact change within these communities hinge on and are facilitated by the fact that to be modern, to be well traveled, to have gone abroad and come home, produces value both in life and, as Manoj explained, in death. This particular valuation of life and death is also, importantly, what made Manoj such a good fieldworker and the perfect subject to join an organization like Sahaayaka and "motivate" those from villages all over Karnataka. Unlike others in his village who had eschewed neocolonial liberal aspirations, Manoj still believed in the project of brown saviorism and was eager to change those who grew up like him.

A few months later, I received an excited message from Manoj on Facebook. He wanted to talk urgently, and when I received his call, he told me that he had finally obtained an Indian passport. Manoj had been working hard to figure out the paperwork, wade through the bureaucracy, and collect the funds to achieve this dream. But then Manoj sighed, "I thought I can go anywhere now, but . . ." He finished by explaining that getting a visa to the United States was exceptionally difficult and that the prices for flights were far too expensive. He had decided that instead he would fly to Bangkok, a place that was cheaper to fly to and where a visa was easily attainable. "Maybe someday . . ." he told me wistfully, not willing to give up on his dreams of travel despite this most recent encounter with neocolonial capitalism's arbitrary stratifications of mobility.

Manoj's struggles for international mobility also take me back to Utsa Patnaik's attention to the differences between colonial and current forms of primitive accumulation. As she noted, in the seventeenth, eighteenth, and nineteenth centuries, the expropriation of agricultural land was premised on the fact that the white working classes could move elsewhere because the world had been rendered largely borderless to European subjects within the racist political economy of empire. Now the nation-state functions as the major fulcrum for expropriation; passport regimes allow the citizens of former and current imperial regimes in Europe and United States to move freely while binding and holding the expropriated classes of the brown world in place. As such, neocolonial passport regimes maintain the separation of the brown world from the rest, allowing for people like Manoj to travel within it—in this case from India to Thailand—while making sure that the white world is not contaminated by their brown presence (unless, of course, the white world suddenly has a need for a cheap and unprotected labor force).[17]

At the same time, Manoj's story reveals the way that internalized value hierarchies are required for the subsistence of the saviorist racial capitalist project, specifically as these hierarchies pertain to the value of agricultural labor and rural life. In the next chapter, I provide a further elaboration of how graded stratifications and hierarchies get reproduced by mentors at the village level as they participate in the brown saviorist project.

THE INSULT OF PRECARITY

(OR "I DON'T GIVE A DAMN")

Shiva was bored and in need of an adventure. He called me and planned for us to spend a Sunday together near the Ramanagara Sahaayaka office. He met me in front of the office, wearing a pair of gray jeans and a white polo shirt. He had posted several pictures of this particular getup on Facebook, with the addition of a pair of sunglasses; pictures which showed him sitting fashionably on a hill overlooking a lake. Shiva never dressed in the standard slacks and long-sleeved collared shirts that the other mentors wore, eschewing that uniform for clothes that revealed his unique confidence, style, and swagger. This confidence also showed in Shiva's constant contact with Srinivasan, Krish, and the rest of the Sahaayaka management team, with whom he would eagerly share feedback about the program and even level critiques when he felt something needed to be changed.

These abilities were themselves a by-product of his relative capital within the graded caste and class stratification of Sahaayaka mentors. Unlike many of his fellow mentors, whose families owned no more than one or two hectares of land, Shiva's family, part of the Yadav caste community, owned over twenty and was generally prospering in his native village, located at the Andhra Pradesh–Karnataka border.[1] His family's economic stability had allowed Shiva to try his hand at employment beyond the agricultural sector without the stress of having to tend his family's land *or* having to give up the aspiration to a future in agriculture. For Shiva, unlike for most of his fellow mentors, agriculture was not a dying industry; it was and continued to be flourishing, as much an opportunity for financial success as any other occupation. When he became frustrated with his work, he would tell me casually, "It doesn't matter for me. I can always go home to my native place and work."

Shiva's confidence also emerged in his ambitions for the future, especially in how he saw himself within Sahaayaka. He, unlike most of the other mentors, saw his rise up the managerial ranks as inevitable if he just kept strategizing to find small advantages over his peers. He believed he, too, would eventually be in the room with Krish, Srinivasan, and other NGO leaders, making decisions that would lead to massive social change. In this sense, Shiva, like Suresh, aspired to become a brown savior.

This aspiration toward brown saviorism created perplexing and sometimes harsh ways of establishing value, status, and hierarchy primarily because these saviorist aspirations came into conflict with the realities of Shiva's material precarity. On the one hand, Shiva was frustrated by his inability to maintain his superior status in encounters with those from villages in India and, on the other hand, Shiva recognized that he could not quite attain the excess value, sometimes associated with whiteness and other times with Americanness, he conferred onto the brown savior. In turn, Shiva's aspirations sometimes became the basis of frustration, indignation, and resentment when he inevitably recognized the unfairness of the system he was working within, a system that required both ethical compromise and the devaluation of his labor.

Precarity, Hierarchy, and the Pedagogy of the Insult

On that Sunday afternoon in Ramanagara, Shiva started the conversation, as he had many times before, talking about his aspirations: how he wanted to expand the car service his brother had started, how he wanted to become a politician back in his village, how he felt drawn back to his family's farmland, how he wanted to move up Sahaayaka's corporate ladder, and, most often, how he wanted to start his own NGO for the education of gay men in Karnataka. Here I was reminded of a joke Raj had made to explain the current state of things in India: "Everyone in India wants to start their own NGO." Given my interactions with the Sahaayaka mentors, I could see that Raj's joke was rooted in truth.

But the kind of NGO these various actors imagined for themselves was also an indicator of their position within saviorist hierarchies and the spheres in which they had relative social and cultural capital to help Others. As I have argued throughout this text, Sahaayaka's brown saviors constructed rural up-lift projects based on motivational, digital strategies precisely because of the way that these projects positioned them in altruistic and valuable terms. In this case, Shiva's imagined project was quite different. I asked Shiva several times about why he had chosen to focus on gay men. Shiva shrugged and told me that he had noticed that the men from "that community" were being kept out of education. The universalized figure of the "gay man," not marked by other forms of difference, especially racialized, caste, or religious difference, functioned strategically within Shiva's saviorist imaginary. First, the generic gay man was, by definition, excluded, outside, and in need of help by a het-erosexual "insider" who could benevolently bring him into the normative structures of society through education. Ever more frequently in India, this imagination of the gay subject is a way for the aspiring heterosexual liberal sub-ject, like Shiva, to prove his tolerance, modernity, and progressive politics.[2] In proving his exceptional tolerance, Shiva was also able to imagine himself mov-ing up the sliding scale of value in the saviorist hierarchy. At the same time, the juxtaposition between Shiva's ideas regarding gay men's education and the earlier ideologies espoused by Sarathi regarding the education of Muslim youth in chapter 5 also revealed the fact that saviorism required a distinction between an appropriate precariat who could be helped and a population who was deemed beyond helping within India's accumulationist project.

After some good-natured jokes about my future—rejoinders about whether I would get married, to whom, and when (all of which assumed a compulsory heteronormativity)—Shiva transitioned to his other favorite topic, strategiz-ing as to how to get his salary increased by Sahaayaka, from 12,000 to 18,000 or maybe even 20,000 rupees. For Shiva, it was not just what such money could buy but how it would reposition him within Sahaayaka's organization and, more broadly, within the world of India's help economy. We would think together, deciding what he should ask for and how to word emails in English.

One of Shiva's special hobbies was learning languages, so these strategy ses-sions also served as an opportunity for him to improve his English. When he was bored of strategizing about his job, he would entertain me by reciting poetry in each of the languages he knew well: Urdu, Hindi, Telugu, Kannada, and Lambadi.

Our discussion was suddenly interrupted by a boy, perhaps sixteen or seventeen, who knocked on the door and then walked in, carrying in his arms two large boxes filled with plastic food-storage containers. He was selling these containers door-to-door, a version of the traveling salesperson that persisted in these parts of Karnataka. Shiva started talking to the boy, asking what he wanted and what he was selling.

He grabbed the containers, thankful for the distraction, and started heckling the boy, speaking in Telugu, Hindi, and (to a lesser extent) English, all languages the boy did not understand. He threw the dishes in the air to "test" the boy's claim that the containers were "unbreakable." When the boy tried to bring up the price of anything, he made counteroffers that were absurdly low—a hundred rather than a thousand rupees—until finally the boy grabbed his wares in frustration and started walking out. The interaction unsettled me, but two things were clear: first, Shiva saw his position as somehow above that of the salesboy; and, second, Shiva could not afford the products as currently priced.

"You are just making fun!"

The boy's accusation changed the tenor of the conversation. Shiva felt bad and grabbed a few of the plastic containers in a feigned attempt to realistically consider them. He asked my input and inquired whether I wanted any, to which I gave an emphatic no. And so Shiva handed the containers back and apologized before deciding to give the boy a few last pieces of advice: "If you want to sell, you should not be afraid, and you need to speak clearly. Stand up straight. You will sell much more." After a few more gestures, comments, and a word of encouragement, the boy left.

During the boy's visit, I could not help but notice Shiva's need to reinforce his position within a set of rural social relations. Given his training with Sahaayaka, Shiva saw himself as distinct from those like the salesboy, who had not "reached" the educational and professional positions that were, at least implicitly, perceived as more valuable and as a mark of upward mobility. Yet Shiva's need to belittle this boy revealed the precarity of his imagined higher status. Insults reveal much about the people who insult, especially regarding the circumstances in which they feel their social status is challenged. In this case, Shiva insulted the boy when he was unable to afford the goods that were being hawked, a realization that brought into focus the fact that, for all of his aspirations to upward mobility, he was still really not so different from this boy.

The insult was intended to reassert the hierarchy that had been threatened by this realization. However, once the boy recognized that he was being mocked and explicitly pointed it out, the insult no longer functioned as a powerful reentrenchment of hierarchy primarily because Shiva had not believed that the boy would or could explicitly mark the insult as an insult when he was trying to sell products. Subsequently, Shiva's apology recognized the insensitivity of his taunting, but it did not shift how he saw his status in relation to the boy. Instead, Shiva again asserted authority by teaching this boy using a register that he used during his school visits. His ability to distinguish himself was a by-product of this pedagogical prerogative, interactions—both formal and informal—in which he was afforded the opportunity to show his learning by teaching others how to be better and how to improve their own standing as he himself had.

The Racialized and Gendered Image of Social (Media) Mobility

Soon after, Shiva and I jumped on his bike and made our way out to our school visits. "I want to take you to the top of one of the hills close by," Shiva told me, explaining that we would first go on a school visit before hanging out. Anytime I thought of the hills in Ramanagara, I thought of the famous Bollywood film *Sholay*, which had been filmed on one of the many hills that dotted the area around Ramanagara and which people reminded me of at almost any possible opportunity. Someone, noting my foreignness, would ask my name, why I was there, then transition smilingly into, "Oh . . . you know, *Sholay* was filmed here." And so I could almost see Gabbar Singh shouting at the top of his lungs as we passed through on Shiva's bike. *Sholay*'s fictional world centers on the village of Ramgarh, which is meant to stand in for all Indian villages. As M. Madhava Prasad writes, anthropologists, in seeking to fictionalize the names of villages, also traffic in *Sholay*'s version of essentializing the village, representing the villages in which they have conducted their fieldwork as the quintessentially Indian village.[3] I often think that anthropological representations of the village are nothing more than poorly rendered movie scenes, and I have also often wondered whether I, too, traffic in this form of essentializing, especially when it was so clear that each of these villages was too infinitely complex to be captured on the page. The question made me nervous and was partly why I had tried to avoid the representational politic of the village entirely, hoping to stay far afield of this clichéd history of the anthropologist by moving my attention to new sites from which to traffic my badly rendered movie scenes.

We reached a large school that was nearly empty, except for sixty "failing" students whom Shiva had "motivated" to come to school on Sunday to get extra academic help. Seeing Shiva in these classrooms, I could see the confidence he gained from mentoring, the reason he wanted to work in education and make an impact on students' lives. The classroom frenzy when Shiva entered was palpable, with students running to the front of the room to greet him and raising their hands to answer questions.

Shiva told me during a break, "See, I was talking to the children and telling them how they needed to study harder, pass tenth [standard]. How they need to learn English and science and math. I could see that they were believing in me, in what I was telling them. They really look to me. I am their role model." Then, more exasperated than outright angry, "Globalization? What is this globalization? . . . How, if we are supposed to carry these words to students, to motivate them, how can we be making next to nothing? What can we tell them?"

It was not that Shiva did not enjoy his work or did not see its altruistic possibilities. The problem was that he, unlike Sahaayaka's leadership, was tasked with doing so much affective labor, and yet these aspects of his job never translated into any further compensation. Like other forms of feminized affective labor[4] like caregiving, child rearing, and nurturing, which are construed as "outside" formal economic processes and seen as social obligations that are not economically productive, Shiva's labor was not being tangibly translated into monetary capital. This is why "doing good" and participating in the world of help were always in tension with his socioeconomic aspirations. For Shiva, "globalization" represented the economic mobility and autonomy he was unable to attain, which would have allowed him to change his future based on his own dreams and desires.[5] He was disconcerted by the contradiction between his own position and what he was telling his students.

Still, Shiva was extremely proud of the students' attendance, and he finally confessed that he had convinced them to come by telling them a special guest (me) would also be coming. He was even more excited because a journalist from a local Kannada newspaper would be documenting the event. I was completely taken off guard, not realizing until that moment that Shiva had planned the day's entire event around my presence and that I was about to be paraded into the classroom as more than just an observer.

I walked into a classroom of students who were sitting silently and waiting for a grand speech. The students were most interested in "America," having been prepped by Shiva earlier in the day, and so they asked about what kinds of foods were eaten, how far away it was, and what sports were played. When they found out I was a teacher, they asked specific questions about the education system in the United States, how different it was, and whether I "liked" America or India better. These questions had become commonplace for me, and my answers did not last long. Eventually, when the classroom went silent, Shiva grew anxious: "Listen, he has come from far away, you should not waste his time. Ask questions." The students and I had not developed any rapport, and so we stumbled through a few more responses together before closing the session.

What was quite clear was that Shiva's goal was not necessarily student learning. Instead, Shiva had planned this event because he knew that it would garner him visibility beyond the school site. Sure enough, a few weeks after our trip, Shiva called me excitedly and said, "Arjun, you and I are in the newspaper!" Much to my own chagrin, there we were, pictured talking to students with a story about Sahaayaka. I started to sweat as I stared at my photograph, wondering what this revealed about me and my research, and then handed back the newspaper clipping without saying a word.

Shiva had recognized that his upward mobility was less about the *actual* impact or outcomes in these schools and far more about his ability to make his work visible beyond the classroom. This required that Shiva make his global networks, and the concomitant capital tethered to them, visible to those in his local networks. My presence was valuable because it signaled that he had been able to orchestrate the presence of a non-Kannada-speaking global Indian, "proved" by my photograph in the newspaper. This made Shiva's intervention seem more significant and effective and allowed him to potentially be seen as a brown savior himself. However, the photograph was more than just proof. Shiva had been able to orchestrate media coverage that placed me, the outsider, in front of the camera and *not* the students. This subversion became a site of pleasure, evidenced by Shiva's palpable excitement about the way that he had orchestrated the entire scene and accumulated additional social capital in the process.

This was not the first time Shiva had taken advantage of opportunities to develop his global network to improve his status in Sahaayaka and the rural communities in which he worked. Sahaayaka had sought many different international partnerships in order to legitimate their programs. While they had mostly targeted the United States, which, as I have noted, set the stage for my own relation with Sahaayaka, European universities had also sent students to Sahaayaka to conduct research. In every case, the mentors were tasked with the actual labor of showing these people, whether donors or university students, around, which was a job outside of their normal tasks but was pitched as an opportunity for "professional development."

For example, Shiva explained, "Some girls from Belgium came to see Sahaayaka's program. They were studying education from the university, like you. And while they were here, I learned some French." Later he showed me Facebook pictures of one of the women, a blond-haired, blue-eyed lady wearing an apron and holding a plate of food, with the caption "Belgium meets India #tikkamasala."[6] Then he added, "Now if I go to Belgium, they are there. They have already said that I can stay with them anytime. See how pretty she is." Shiva's encounters with these women and his ability to sustain these relationships over social media allowed Shiva to imagine himself as someone who *could* go to Belgium. This capacity for potential global mobility gave him an enlarged sense of value. As important, by commenting on these white women's beauty, Shiva marked his own mobility in relation to India's colonized standards of white desirability, especially given these women's "Aryan" features, that is, blond hair and blue eyes. It was not that Shiva would actually be able to go to Belgium or be in a romantic relationship with these white women. Rather, the very fact that these white women whom he deemed beautiful continued to be in conversation with him marked his newfound standing in a neocolonial raced and gendered global order.

Global Hierarchies of Disposability and the Reentrenchment of the "Backward"

As we left the school, one of the schoolteachers, Ragu, started to speak with Shiva, inquiring as to where we were going and why. On hearing that we would be walking to the top of the nearby hill, he eagerly asked to join. We walked up the hill together, a massive single stone, some three thousand feet high; the sun was beating on our heads as we climbed a jagged staircase from which the entirety of the Ramanagara taluk was visible below.[7] Once at the top, Shiva told Ragu of all his aspirations, as he had with me many times in the past. Ragu was taken aback and impressed by all the ideas, only stopping to question whether Shiva could, in fact, do everything he said.

Ragu himself had a very different story to tell about his path to teaching in rural Karnataka. He spoke well in both Kannada and English, revealing his educational pedigree. He told us that he had been a chemical engineer working with a pharmaceutical company in Bangalore. After working for five years, he had quit, disillusioned with the work he had been doing.

How could I go on working there when I could see what was happening? Just polluting the environment, making money, and for what? When it comes to drugs, I know how many cause horrible problems, and if I know what is happening, how can I continue working there? I don't want to live in Bangalore. I would much rather stay here, away from the smartphones and all of the junk. Everyone is just looking at their phones all day.

Then, a bit later in our conversation, "Please do not take offense, but the Americans don't want to test their drugs on their own people. So they come here and do it to the poor." I took no offense, though I recognized that Ragu was marking me as a stand-in for the evils of American imperial expropriation.

Ragu's critique bundles the undesirability of Bangalore city with the overreliance on technology, accumulation, and US imperialism. Those with power in Bangalore were facilitating environmental decay and human disposability, inhabiting a particular slot in the global racial capitalist apparatus, which determined whose bodies were valued and whose bodies were deemed disposable.[8] Ragu had witnessed how American drugs were tested on brown Indian bodies, which he understood had been deemed an acceptable human cost given the potential for corporates in *both* America and Bangalore to accumulate wealth. This racialized disposability sat in almost direct contrast to Shiva's near-utopic pleasure at forging global connection, revealing those attempts at mediatized visibility and mobility as a mask for massive inequities.

It had been six years since Ragu had left his job in Bangalore and started working as a teacher, and yet his struggle with his decision was still evident so many years later. He repeated the same statement six times during our ensuing discussion: "People keep asking me always, even my mother, why I had left. How I could leave such a job. But I tell them 'I don't give a damn.'" Ragu had eschewed that which he ought to have desired within a regime of value that simplistically ranked bioengineering in Bangalore over teaching in the village. He now felt like a kind of alien, ridiculed by those closest to him and constantly having to justify his choice of becoming a teacher.

Ragu's sentiment—"I don't give a damn"—was his emotional response to these systemic inequalities. In some sense, not caring was his way to find some distance from his feelings. Yet this feigned apathy could not hide the deep well of anger and resentment. Ragu had made what he considered a truly altruistic choice, and yet he had been socially castigated for it.

This self-pity morphed, at times, into regret that he had become a teacher and had to teach students. Ragu would tell me how "backward" the students were and how difficult it was to make them learn anything. He articulated his own sense of self-worth by suggesting that he was still not like his students because of his own educational attainment and previous occupation. By emphasizing these distinctions, Ragu actually served to reinforce the graded stratification and hierarchy between urban and rural India. For however much Ragu had critiqued and sought not to participate in the exploitative global racialized capitalist order he had seen in Bangalore, he, like Shiva, could not help but resort to the insult as a way to claw himself up a value hierarchy when his status had been so thoroughly undermined.

What continues to stay with me from my interactions with Shiva and Ragu is just how difficult it is to change our strategies for dealing with a world that we recognize as deeply unfair. Instead, Shiva and Ragu felt compelled to perform a type of altruism that reentrenched the assumption that their actions were founded in righteousness even as they inevitably reified hierarchies of value in the process. In the next chapter, I continue to critique this line of saviorist reasoning by attending to Sahaayaka's corporate partnerships and the mentors' critique of these partnerships. The analysis to come should bring us back to one of the basic premises of this text: that saviorist interventions seem to do less for those who need help than for those who do the helping.

AC CARS AND THE HYPERREAL VILLAGE

Starting in 2010, Sahaayaka had been aggressively growing its global funding base, procuring long-term funding from the Michael and Susan Dell Foundation, NDTV (New Delhi Television Limited), Coca-Cola, Target, and Cisco Systems, among others. These funding sources had resulted in a total Sahaayaka annual budget of over five crores (approx. US$1.25 million), making it one of the largest NGOs in India that was not directly linked to a parent corporation.[1]

I asked Srinivasan how Sahaayaka had managed to procure funds from such a diverse set of sources to sustain their programs, but before I finished my question, he cut me off:

Krish has agreed to some partnerships that I hate. I cannot stand them. You know he has partnered with NDTV/Coke, that Support My School campaign? You must have heard of it, the commercials come on television all the time. I don't know why he has agreed, but when I asked Krish, he just said, "What is your problem? We will only try it for a year." And besides, he keeps asking where will funding come [from] if we don't accept these offers. But I tell him, "so what if we lose this funding, we'll find other sources that will match our vision."

As INCITE! has argued, funding is and has been the Trojan horse within the NGO sector. The NGO as a partner got corporate funding that allows "corporations to mask their exploitative and colonial work practices through 'philanthropic' work."[2] Just as important, funding also determines the course of global saviorism, structuring stratification by determining who gives funds, who gets funds, for what, and how.[3] In this case, Srinivasan's major concern was that Krish had begun to manipulate Sahaayaka's program to fit the needs of funders.[4] This was unacceptable to Srinivasan, who had made his entire mission about rural uplift through decentralized mentor-led motivational techniques.

As such, Srinivasan had a major problem with the NDTV/Coca-Cola partnership given that none of the objectives of the initiative had much to do with Sahaayaka's motivational programming. The Support My School campaign focused on "revitalizing neglected [government] schools in rural and semi-rural areas" through infrastructural projects that would, theoretically, allow children to access toilets (especially girls), clean water through rainwater harvesting, sporting equipment for physical education, a library, and a "clean" school environment.[5] Srinivasan was critical of the entire campaign, from its focus on school infrastructure to its model for funding. "I do not understand what they are seeking to do. Shouldn't they at least talk to someone on the ground before building more toilets? Why are they asking for donations when Coke and NDTV have so much money? I refuse to go to any of these schools. I will not set foot in them."

It is Srinivasan's last phrase, the visceral emotional response to the continued relationship with NDTV/Coca-Cola, that I cannot forget. No matter the benefits of getting funding through the program, Srinivasan was unable to set foot in schools that he had spent the past seven years cultivating relationships with because he could not face the contradictions inherent in Sahaayaka's changing priorities.

In the rest of this chapter, I want to explore the implications of Sahaayaka's partnership with NDTV/Coca-Cola in order to further excavate the kinds of "deliverables" imagined as useful by those within the help economy and the reality of their "impact" (or lack thereof) on those at the receiving end of these interventions. Here I want to underscore again the paradoxical relationship between saviors and their Others, in which the perceived beneficiaries of programs are actually those from whom value is extracted. Simultaneously, these kinds of extractive interventions are also meant to emplace new "hyperreal" aspirational trajectories on those at the receiving end of these interventions. These cycles of imagined, yet materially negligible, impacts place the mentors in contradiction, wanting to do real social change work while knowing that these kinds of interventions are nothing but optical illusions.

Hyperreal Philanthropy and Savarna Benevolence

Despite all of his misgivings, Srinivasan still encouraged me to go to the schools funded by NDTV/Coca-Cola, and eventually I set up a time to visit with the mentors. Before I left, I got on the internet, looking through the many pages of the NDTV/Coca-Cola Support My School campaign website, a philanthropic collaboration between NDTV, one of India's largest broadcast networks, and Coca-Cola, the global beverage giant, which had fifty-six bottling plants in India, having started expanding into the Indian market in 1993, very early in India's liberalization. Coca-Cola's practices in India have been controversial because of their neocolonial land-use practices in which they exceed the legal limits for groundwater extraction and pollute the environment with toxins.[6] Perhaps to respond to these controversies and to manage its social image, Coca-Cola has undertaken a series of "sustainability" projects: "initiatives that reduce our environmental footprint, support active, healthy living, create a safe, inclusive work environment for our associates, and contribute to the development of the communities where we operate. Some of the Company's flagship community development programs include the 'Support My School' program, the 'Parivartan' retailer training program, women empowerment program as a part of the global 5BY20 campaign etc."[7]

The initiatives listed by Coca-Cola reproduce the dictates of neocolonial patriarchal capitalist giving, focusing on women, children, and retail training to get the poor further into the circuits of markets while leaning in to the liberal rhetoric of environmental sustainability that will somehow be facilitated by Coca-Cola's continued accumulation.

On the Support My School website, the words "500 Schools Revitalised /#Supportmyschool Mission: 1000 Swachh Schools" were featured prominently, scrawled in lettering meant to resemble the writing on a chalkboard.[8] The reference to *swachh*, which I return to in chapter 17, mimics the national campaign toward a "Clean India," while "revitalized" schools was meant to reference the success of NDTV/Coca-Cola's intervention. Here the agentic description of the philanthropist—the person who was doing the revitalizing—served "to reify the binaries between the rich and the poor in that the poor become dehumanized objects of pity, while the rich (ironically) become powerful subjects whose putative humanitarianism is extolled."[9]

On the right side of the website, I stared at a small picture of three schoolchildren holding up pictures they had (presumably) drawn with the caption "Thank you. Your contribution will help shape the future of many children," then "CLICK HERE TO DONATE." The images of children on-screen, smiling and asking for funds—somehow simultaneously endearing and pitiable—were meant to pull at an individual user's heartstrings, implying that a person's decision to donate or not would have a direct impact on these children's future. Here the campaign structured the savior/saved relationship around the perception of personal responsibility for impact.

I was most struck by the polymediated worlds that together facilitate aid—the Twitter hashtags providing links to the Support My School Facebook page with videos and images but always leading back to the main site, with simple captions like "Here is how you can help."[10] The strategy relied on the knowledge that web-enabled individuals do not function on a single platform or within a single media world but rather traverse across them. However, while one could begin in any media space—for example, on Twitter—the campaign's marketing strategy was actually intended to minimize choice, strategically advertising on each media platform to lead back to the originary website and its request for donations and limiting the kinds of rich interactive possibilities that have come to characterize Twitter, Instagram, TikTok, and the like.[11]

The whole design of the site was a spectacle: a scrolling top bar that moved between pictures of celebrities—in this case Anil Kapoor (a Bollywood film star who gained global notoriety for his role in *Slumdog Millionaire*), Aishwarya Rai Bachchan (former Miss World winner and Bollywood megastar), and Sachin Tendulkar (perhaps the greatest Indian cricketer of all time), standing with schoolchildren on a stage, smiling and saluting, on a brightly colored podium (figure 12.1).

When I clicked on a link to a telethon video, I was faced with an immediate sensory overload: Bollywood music blasting, children dancing in unison, and Sachin Tendulkar standing in the middle, smiling amid the music to signal the launch of the campaign. A panel of celebrities sat on a stage in California, the first event of the campaign meant to bring the powerful savarna Indian American diaspora into the philanthropic fold. The panel was followed by a montage of journalistic-like reporting in which a narrator explained the many challenges that children faced all over India. Later, Sachin Tendulkar taught a few

Jana gana mana...dil se

FIGURE 12.1. Redacted screenshot of NDTV/Coca-Cola campaign featuring Anil Kapoor, Aishwarya Rai Bachchan, and Sachin Tendulkar. (Photo by Arjun Shankar, originally from NDTV/Coca-Cola Support My School Campaign, https://www.ndtv .com/supportmyschool)

children how to swing a cricket bat. Aishwarya Rai Bachchan joined Tendulkar onstage to provide a check to a child named Hema, described with a caption in English as a "Rickshaw Driver's Daughter" who "Couldn't Even Afford School Fees." That was followed by a musical performance by a three-year-old musical prodigy who played the drums for Aishwarya, whom he apparently idolized.

In all these examples, the emphasis was on the celebrities' exceptional capacity, both their talent in their field and their ability to do good.[12] The juxtaposition between Rai Bachchan and the poor children who idolize her rendered Rai Bachchan a hero, visually troping on a history of neocolonial humanitarian and developmentalist imagery in which salvation was linked to the benevolent "First World" figure gleefully centered within a frame along with those impoverished Third World figures they have encountered. In this sense, the celebrity global Indian's encounter with the child takes on a racialized character when understood relationally and as situated in this history of image making.[13] First, the telethon relies on the obvious visual mapping of the light-skinned brown savarna celebrity with the darker-skinned brown rural child, which epidermalized success, beauty, and money.[14] At the same time, and as important, the celebrity's racialization was linked to their connection to institutions of global capital (NDTV, Coca-Cola) *and* their cosmopolitan travels (sitting in California while launching this telethon for rural India). These differences between the celebrity and the rural child were then linked to differing capacities: the celebrity to exceptional heroism and benevolence, and the rural child to need, idol worship, and indebtedness.

Soon after, there was a long and very serious discussion of school playgrounds between Sachin Tendulkar and Rahul Bose, an Indian rugby player and film actor. Bose reflected in English:

> I was thinking about what NDTV is doing. . . . I learned more on the playground than I did in the classroom. . . . I learned in the playground that everybody is equal. These are things you can talk about in a classroom, but if you give a playground facility in a school, you are actually creating . . . you're telling the children to go out there and discover the things that they otherwise won't.

The playground, as perceived by Bose, was a place where all children could learn about equality through personal discovery outside of the classroom. This theory was predicated on a politics of nostalgia, marking an imagined time when schools were places with beautiful facilities that allowed all children to play and have profound insights about the world. The implication was, of course, that there had been a demise in the quality of the government school and that playgrounds were no longer sites at which children could do this kind of learning. The politics of nostalgia therefore served to valorize India's past. At the same time, this nostalgic idea occluded the fact that the savarna classes had absconded from the government school system in India at precisely the time when Scheduled Castes were joining public institutions en masse and when the state had begun to neglect government schools with the rise of the privatized school system. In turn, occluding these systemic changes allowed a doubling of valorization, especially when savarna philanthropists then "gave back" to a government school by creating a playground that resembled the school of their imagined past.

However, at the time I was watching this footage, I had very few of these thoughts in my mind. If anything, I forgot my own experiences of India's schools and my understanding of history, taken as I was by the hyperreality produced in this particular digital philanthropic space. For Mikhail Epstein, hyperreality is "a phantasmic creation of the means of mass communication, but as such it emerges as a more authentic, exact, 'real' reality than the one we perceive in the life around us."[15] Additionally, Umberto Eco argues that "the . . . imagination demands the real thing and, to attain it, must fabricate the absolute fake."[16] Thinking with Epstein and Eco's ideas prove helpful, as they describe the effect of the NDTV/Coca-Cola telethon, which painted a picture that felt more complete, fuller, better than the reality itself, unsullied by actual hardship, complex social relations, and educational inequity. This hyperreality offered viewers possibility and, perhaps, what the "real" reality had already become under the guidance of the NDTV/Coca-Cola campaign's revitalization efforts.

Of course, this "unreal circulation of values" determined what digital publics believed were just causes and how these causes could and should be imagined.[17] In this instantiation, the telethon was intended to "liberate" the viewer from necessary action in social justice endeavors beyond the donating of funds.

"They Came, Then They Went" and Hyperreal Aspirations

Armed with this information, just a few days before the new year, I visited three of the eight schools that were initially selected for the NDTV/Coca-Cola program, accompanied on my trip by two of the Sahaayaka mentors, Vishnu and Shiva. At first, they wondered out loud why I wanted to go to the schools at all, explaining that they had hundreds of pictures taken during the two days when NDTV/Coca-Cola showed up at the schools to "revitalize them." They scrolled through pictures on their laptops, and it seemed, for a moment, that the mentors, too, had been drawn into the hyperreality of the two-day event.

I realized within the next hours that the mentors had actually tried to dissuade me from going to these schools because they themselves did not want to waste their time when they had so much work to do and were uninterested in the NDTV/Coca-Cola campaign, believing the project to be completely irrelevant. "Why do you want to see?" asked Vishnu. "We just stood for a few hours, and they came. There is nothing there, they came, then they went."

At the time, I did little to reflect on the unequal labor relations that had facilitated my research, insistent as I was on getting as much information as I could during my time in the field. Whether or not the mentors wanted to spend time with me, in almost every case, my presence and research produced another layer of work for them, more time on the road, more questions, more tasks that had nothing to do with their jobs. At the same time, the mentors had no choice but to comply, given that the Sahaayaka leadership had requested that they assist me. In retrospect, perhaps I should have decided not to pursue the "valuable" information I had so eagerly sought.

I was first taken to a school with beautiful murals painted on every wall. These murals were part of the NDTV/Coca-Cola project, along with a number of other small pieces of school beautification: a jungle gym, a garden, a water-filtration system to get clean water, new toilets for both girls and boys, and a new recreation room furnished with a table tennis table. On two pillars of the school were a set of pictures of great sports stars in India, one of which showed the smiling face of Sachin Tendulkar.

The headmaster showed me around the school. He was especially proud of a garden in the back that included cages for birds and trees and flowers that had been well maintained. Then he pointed over at the two bathrooms, though he did not venture over to them. I sauntered over on my own and looked in, only to find them unused, the toilets covered in mud, the smell so suffocating I could barely set one foot inside to snap two photographs. The headmaster grabbed me as I came out and directed me back toward the main office, but I noticed that there was water leaking across the floor in a neighboring classroom. I asked him about it, and he took me inside, reluctantly explaining that they had been given a water-purification system but that the system had failed, instead leaking water all over the floors, making the classroom unusable for daily instruction. He did not know how to fix it, and he had tried to contact someone to help him, to no avail. "I think we will have to throw it [out]," he said with some finality as we walked out.

Vishnu explained the problem with the NDTV/Coca-Cola campaign in two sentences, emphasizing his earlier comments. "See," he said, "if the school was already good, then they maintain the new infrastructure. If not, then they don't." He continued, telling me that the school we were at was, in fact, already a good school. Yet, even at a school that aimed to maintain its infrastructure, there was only so much that could be done. For NDTV/Coca-Cola, "revitalizing" a school meant coming for a few days, making it over by dropping off a few shiny new toys, and leaving, none of which allowed for sustainable change, which would have included, at the very least, check-ins with the schools and educational programs that could help schools understand how to sustain the new infrastructure. In contrast, these few hours of celebration were suspended in time on their website, a moment of joy produced for all potential donors to witness and facilitating the accumulationist projects of NDTV/Coca-Cola.

The headmaster finally took us upstairs to a room, locked so that no one could come in unless explicitly given access. I noticed seven students peeking at us through the window, so I called them to come and join us as we entered the room. Inside, along one wall, was a row of books in steel cabinets, and the students ran over and grabbed some books to read when we entered. At the far end of the room, as brand new as the day it was given, stood a table tennis table, ready to play, though it did not seem to have ever been touched (figure 12.2).

I love table tennis, and I wanted to play, so I asked a few of the students if they would like to join me. They moved gingerly, eager but also hesitant. I held a racket expectantly until I realized that no one would join me. When I asked the headmaster why no one would play, he told me simply that they did not know how to and that they had never been taught. It dawned on me then that the table tennis table was set in place by brown saviors who had imagined what should be useful and fun to those at this school based on what they themselves found useful and fun. They, like me, must have loved table tennis.

FIGURE 12.2. Table tennis table at Kannada-medium school in Karnataka. (Photo by Arjun Shankar)

But it was not as if the table tennis table did not do any work within this school space. It sat as a showpiece and was meticulously cared for, carrying a high symbolic value defined and imposed by NDTV/Coca-Cola's mission. In this sense, the table tennis table was experienced as its own hyperreality for this school community, just as the website might be for those who viewed it: the table tennis table, while still potentially usable as a table tennis table, functioned instead as a facsimile. As a playable piece of equipment, it was useless for students who did not know how to play the sport. But as a facsimile, "it emerges as a more authentic, exact, 'real' reality" than that which is part of the everyday functionings of the school. "Real" reality here is equated with the lives of those who left the table tennis table behind, which ought to be aspired to by these rural children.

AC Cars and Breaking with the Altruistic Impulse

The absurdity of the NDTV/Coca-Cola program was, as I have said, not at all lost on the mentors, and over the next few weeks, they began to explain to me that these new collaborations reflected poorly on Sahaayaka's leadership. For example, a few days after my school visits, on New Year's Eve, I was sitting on the roof of the mentors' shared home and drinking as the clock struck midnight. As we sat, Vishnu pulled me over to where he was sitting. He wanted to say more about our day at the NDTV/Coca-Cola schools and started talking angrily about the future of Sahaayaka. I could see his eyes burning with hurt as he spoke: "These people in their AC [air-conditioned] cars don't care. They are always telling this and that, but they don't do anything. They sit there and talk and talk and talk, but have they seen what we do? I told them this is wrong approach, this won't work. But they will not listen. They will not come down. They will not understand."

As he spoke, Vishnu no longer distinguished between Sahaayaka's leadership and the NDTV/Coca-Cola campaign. For Vishnu, the AC symbolized those who sat in Bangalore, unwilling to come anywhere near the schools unless they were comfortably driven in cars with AC. It symbolized elitism, lack of understanding or care, even incompetence, linking these traits to upper-class, urban, cosmopolitan caste elites. These brown saviors liked to "talk and talk and talk" about the problems facing people and about how to change them, while safely and comfortably separated from their actual experience of daily life.

But even worse, Vishnu was especially hurt because he had actually believed in Sahaayaka's message, and he felt duped by this obvious move away from the ideals he had believed in. Vishnu's family had worked in a nearby village as farmers, but they had so little land that they were not able to sustain themselves on farming alone. His father and mother had both ended up as laborers, working in the reshmi fields and doing their best to make ends meet. It had been a struggle, and Vishnu never forgot that he had not been able to go to college for several years, until he could pay his tuition fees himself. He had come to Sahaayaka with the promise of changing situations like his own in mind, believing that educational attainment was the only way out. But just a few months after our talk on the roof of his home, Vishnu would quit his job, tired of all those people who were pontificating from the safety of their AC cars.

The next time I met Vishnu was in 2015. It had been a year since he left Sahaayaka, and he now worked for a new NGO, this time in the health-care sector. "I do work with the eye now," he explained. "It is very interesting work. Very different from Sahaayaka, but I have learned very fast how to deal with the industry." I met him at his home, only recently rented in a small third floor flat in the town of Ramanagara. He was incredibly proud of his new flat and had requested that I come so he could show me around. His wife and newborn child were there, and they welcomed me with wide smiles as I entered. Before I even sat down, Vishnu was ready to show me his brand-new flat-screen TV, the couches, and the new washing machine that he had purchased recently. His new job paid more, and he was incredibly happy with this experience of upward mobility.

Vishnu had called several of the other Sahaayaka mentors, including Shiva and Suresh, and they entered the house and marveled at Vishnu's new appliances and complete change in demeanor. At first, they were almost shocked. Vishnu had been adamantly against accumulating material wealth, one of the few Sahaayaka mentors who believed in doing his work because of its supposed inherent moral good. In fact, Vishnu had previously chastised the other mentors for their seemingly brazen lack of commitment. The contrast between that Vishnu and this new one was too much for the other mentors to bear, and they burst out laughing, playfully, if also enviously, poking fun at him for the transition from someone who was an adamant moralist to a pragmatic moneymaker. They made this division quite clear in their jokes, suggesting that one could not be both at once.

Vishnu chuckled, as if they had been unable to understand something really quite simple that he had realized. He responded by lifting his right hand to his shoulder, palm facing away from his body, as if to make a sign of the Abhayamudrā.[18] At the same time, he lifted his left hand to his stomach, hand flat, palm up, and began wiggling his fingers back and forth, as if to say, "Pay me now." This juxtaposition was striking, a symbol associated with spiritual attainment placed in direct relation to the explicit request for monetary compensation. "For us," he said reasonably, "there is no other way." *One has to be pragmatic*, Vishnu was suggesting. *The brown savior always is.*

Part III Is Done: In Sum and What's to Come

In part III, I have sought to reveal the kinds of contradictions that emerge in the help economy at the nexus of expropriation and aspiration. These chapters reinforce that the brown savior complex seems to extract exceptional amounts of labor value from those marginalized individuals within its ranks even as it purports to lift the same marginal communities from their supposed economic servility.

More important, by focusing on the mentor class in the help economy, these chapters draw attention to the spatial and territorial arrangements that reinscribe racialized stratification within the help economies, including through the imagined and real production of boundaries among urban-rural, national, and global value, boundaries that in many cases are by-products of colonial spatial distinctions. At the same time, these chapters have teased out the relationship between labor hierarchies in the help economies and the primitive accumulationist strategies that produce surplus labor. Indeed, one premise of this part of the book is that the help economies function as one solution to the crisis of surplus labor. However, I have shown that functioning as the conduit for surplus labor requires that those who join the help economy imbibe the value hierarchies that produce their dispossession in the first place. This contradiction is what so many of the mentors struggled with and negotiated.

In part IV, I move my attention to one final sphere within which to analyze how the help economy functions as part of racial and caste capitalist systems: namely, through the project of what I term *digital saviorism*. By way of entrance into the discussion that follows, I want to return to the "hyperreal" image of the table tennis table in this chapter. While my discussion focused on the table, some of the more perceptive may have noticed a computer monitor sitting on the floor, just to the left of the table. The computer, unlike the Ping-Pong table, is not on display. Instead, it has been cast aside completely, hidden on the floor, waiting to be discarded. We might surmise that the computer can no longer function as a facsimile—an aspirational imagining just out of one's own attainment—in an India in which technology is all around, whether in a city or in a village. Especially since the rise of Narendra Modi's Digital India movement, a technological future is now anticipated: it is no longer a fantasy but an expectation, a future that most people believe is nearly here. Such constant attention to technology's anticipatory possibility makes sense given that the stories told in this ethnography center around Bangalore, the iconized harbinger of India's digital future as "Start-Up City."[19] Given this context, a computer that cannot be used, unlike a Ping-Pong table that cannot be played on, is useless, a symbol of failure to actualize what already should be.

Digital anticipation also has meant that those who possess digital skills accrue excess value, including in the help economies. In the case presented here, because its leadership was largely tech-savvy, Sahaayaka was able to ascend rapidly, joining the ranks of those who were pegged to lead social change agendas in India. In the next part of the book, I turn to the kinds of digital strategies Sahaayaka deployed and show how these strategies may actually facilitate new material forms of racialized and casteized stratification.

IV
DIGITAL SAVIORISM

...tech designers are erecting a digital caste system ...—RUHA BENJAMIN, *Race after Technology*

An app will not save us. We will not sort out social inequality lying in bed staring at smartphones. It will not stem from simply sending emails to people in power, one person at a time.—SAFIYA UMOJA NOBLE, "Social Inequality Will Not Be Solved by an App"

As digital labour becomes more widespread across the uneven geographies of race, gender, class, [caste], and ability, and as histories of colonialism and inequality get drawn into these forms of labour, our imagination of what these worlds contain similarly needs to expand.—SAREETA AMRUTE, "Of Techno-ethics and Techno-affects"

13

DIGITAL SAVIORS

I drove to Cupertino, California, in 2015 to meet Krish, turning off I-280 North just a minute away from one of Apple's main headquarters. Northern California was where I had grown up and where I came to remove myself from the world of research, immersed instead in the worries associated with taking care of family. I had learned to safely compartmentalize my home from a young age, and as a result California was a place stuck in time, bounded and kept away from all else in my life. I thought the ethnographic impulse to separate "here" and "there" would make life easier for me. Yet here I was, my wish to keep my familial and professional lives in safe compartments but a pitiable figment of my imagination in the global-digital age.

Of course, given the project I was undertaking, the idea that home could be separated from my work was naive from the start. The Bay Area is the center of

Silicon Valley's project of technocapitalist accumulation, which also happened to be one of the centers of the savarna technocrat's upward mobility in the United States. The California I drove through looked nothing like the California of my youth. If, way back when, I grew up in a nearly all-white middle-class neighborhood on the peripheries of the Silicon Valley boom, now everywhere I looked, I saw brown savarna families enjoying the fruits of their technocratic educations as they or someone in their families worked at Facebook, Uber, Google, Apple, Yahoo, or any of the other technology companies that have taken over the Bay. From their midst, ever more brown saviors will emerge.

When I finally saw Krish, it took us a few minutes to get reacquainted, sitting together in the three-room apartment he had rented. He confessed that he had taken a hiatus from Bangalore partly because he wanted to make sure his daughter got her US citizenship and partly because he needed some distance to rethink Sahaayaka's program. Since its start in 2002, Sahaayaka's vision for educational reform in India, as I have detailed earlier, had relied on direct face-to-face "motivational" encounters between mentors and children in schools. But Krish had tired of this way of thinking about Sahaayaka's educational interventions, feeling that the organization was stuck in the past rather than anticipating its future. He had decided that it was time to change, and if he was going to stay on with Sahaayaka, he was going to bring the organization into a new educational paradigm bolstered by his unique technological know-how.

Krish was using his time in the United States to observe those organizations that were devising technological solutions to the problem of educational inequality. For example, Krish was working as a consultant for Gooru, an educational technology (edtech) company started by former Google employees based in the Bay Area. The company had created a learning platform that they believed would revolutionize how teachers could teach and how students would learn. Smart technologies, new learning interfaces, and a whole slew of other digital tools were all part of Gooru's big technological fix, which they had begun to test in field sites both in the United States *and* in India. The name of the organization, Gooru, evokes the idea of the Hindu spiritual guru, and, not surprisingly, many of the members of Gooru's leadership were Non-Resident Indians (NRIs) whom Krish had gotten to know in California's savarna American technology circles.

Krish started to explain in more detail what he had been doing with his free time in the United States: "I've been visiting a ton of schools in the United States, mostly in East L.A., where these guys started to implement their programming. I've learned a lot. One, I really don't know if the challenges in India are that much different than those in the USA, same problems of inequality, lack of resources, etc." If, at a different time, Krish might have idealized the United States and its education system, his research was telling him that the problem of educational inequality was a global one.

Yet much was left unstated in Krish's recognition of the global inequality he was witnessing in his travels between India and the United States. For example, given that East L.A. is over 97 percent Latinx, Krish's use of "East L.A." was actually a racialized code for Latinx communities in Los Angeles, who have been deemed one of the brown communities most in need in the United States. In placing East L.A. in relation to those he worked with in India, Krish was actually imagining a version of the brown world inextricably intertwined with the problem of economic inequality and poverty. Gooru's intervention and their construction of brown marginality also trafficked in an implicit anti-Blackness by both completely neglecting Black populations in and around Los Angeles (or in the world for that matter) and targeting brown folks as the appropriately assimilable Other, more easily integrated into these new technological education systems.

At the same time, Krish was able to imagine solutions to the problem of brown poverty without reckoning with regionally and historically specific systemic forces because he understood technologies as apolitical, neutral fixes. This conceit of neutrality allows those who build such technologies to see these universal tools as a panacea to solve any problem, sidestepping the more difficult task of challenging racial and caste capitalist systems on the basis of historically emplaced and reproduced inequity. This is why an organization like Gooru could deem their tools equally useful and easily integrated in two contexts more than eight thousand miles apart, one of many "new digital infrastructures of poverty relief" that are "rationalized by a call for efficiency, doing more with less, and getting help to those who need it" anywhere on the planet.[1]

If the global brown underclasses were at the receiving end of these kinds of infrastructural innovations, it was the technological overlords who decided what problems ought to be solved and what "fixes" would solve these societal ills. These powerful decision-makers, as Ruha Benjamin warns, "are erecting a digital caste system, structured by existing racial inequities that are not just colorblind. . . . These tech advances are sold as morally superior because they purport to rise above human bias, even though they could not exist without data produced through histories of exclusion and discrimination."[2] In Benjamin's argument, the supposed neutrality of technology allows those who can create these technologies to characterize themselves as morally superior because they transcend existing forms of exclusion in their interventions. Fittingly, Benjamin uses the phrase *digital caste system* in a very broad sociological sense in order to focus attention on the extreme intransigence of the stratifications that are being produced between those who have the power to create new technologies and those who do not—an intransigent stratification that is ever more global in scope and scale.

Taking Benjamin's insight as a departure point, I will show in the following chapters how the brown savior's technological productions facilitate their accrual of global power in their ability to determine both what problems ought to be solved and what tools ought to be created to solve these problems. In turn, these strategies may only further entrench already existing stratifications in racial and caste capitalist societies.

Technophilia, Technopanacea, and Solutions
"Imagined in Their Heads"

In India the rise of the digital brown savior has been made even more visible since the early 2000s, *especially* in the help economies. If the 1990s brought India's liberalization and if the aftershocks resulted in an "end of poverty" discourse that recognized that market fundamentalist reforms in India had actually produced higher levels of poverty, the mid-2000s overlaid a new attention to digital integration as the driver for India's development and social reform.[3]

The most massive of these initiatives was Narendra Modi's Digital India movement, which sought a three-pronged goal of creating digital infrastructure, delivering digital services, and developing digital literacy.[4] In a far-ranging speech in front of California's Silicon Valley's top CEOs, Modi emphasized, "I see technology as a means to empower and a tool that bridges the distance between hope and opportunity. Social media is reducing social barriers. . . . We will connect all schools and colleges with broadband. Building I-ways are as important as highways. . . . We want to turn our villages into smart economic hubs and connect our farmers better to markets."[5] Notice that Modi uses the metaphor of the highway—the road to accumulation—to make sense of digital connectivity. Digital India, in this construction, carries with it an unquestioned moral efficacy because it is the *only* means to develop and educate India and uplift all those who have been left out of India's economic growth, with a specific focus on rural India.

Soon after Modi's speech, none other than Mark Zuckerberg, CEO of Facebook, changed his Facebook profile picture to include the colors of the Indian flag, part of a massive social media campaign to promote the Digital India movement (see figure 13.1). He included a status update that read, "I changed

FIGURE 13.1. Mark Zuckerberg changed his Facebook profile picture to support the Digital India campaign.

my profile picture to support Digital India, the Indian government's effort to connect rural communities to the internet and give people access to more services online. Looking forward to discussing this with Prime Minister Narendra Modi at Facebook today."[6] In many ways, it makes sense that Zuckerberg would ally himself with Modi's tactic of digital uplift given that he has consistently sought to frame Facebook as a social good because of its capacity to connect people, despite the fact that the content being shared on the platform might do more harm than good.[7] In the case of rural India, Zuckerberg is assuming, like Modi, that technological connection will lead, by definition, to rural uplift. Here, again, a digital solution to the problem of rural poverty need not reckon with more difficult questions of land speculation and expropriation, debt economies, and the like.

Zuckerberg's meeting with Modi also demonstrated the new brown savarna–white alliances that were emerging as digital saviors ascended from the Indian diasporic ranks, especially since many had strong connections back to India, with nostalgic dreams of developing rural India in particular. As India's liberalization facilitated the movement of the caste privileged, these diasporic technocrats were folded into a narrative that characterized them as ambassadors for India on the international stage, forging more global connections even as they maintained their affective sense of "Indianness" and Indian pride.[8]

The result has been a kind of paradox: on the one hand, the brown savior's technologically mediated ascension served as a kind of reinscription into a narrative of national belonging no matter where in the world they were living; on the other hand, it has functioned as a form of whitening, allowing some brown saviors to exponentially accrue value because they no longer had to locate themselves in their undertakings as Indian, as casteized subjects, and so on. Instead, they were able to put on and take off their brown masks if and when they so decided, precisely because they could create "universal" technological tools to help those anywhere in the world, a conceit that had previously been reserved for white men as part of the colonizing project.[9]

But after observing Gooru's programs in East L.A., Krish was suspicious of the organization and its actual impact:

> You know the problem with technologists, they want everything to be how they imagine it in their heads. Gooru has a ton of funding because of their relationship to Google. I wondered, at first, why they hadn't been able to get into schools right here in Palo Alto, but then once I saw what was happening, it was obvious. I went into classrooms and started observing teachers. One student would have a question while they were looking at the screen, the teacher would go over and answer, and before she was done, another student would have the same question, then another, and another. Finally, the teacher would have to stop the entire class, explain the problem all at once, and then have them go back to their computers. But half the time, because they were all so focused on the computers, they wouldn't pay attention anyway. I suggested a small change, have an administrator button, where they can pause all of the computers at once. It was really simple. But nobody would really listen. And there were a ton of things like that. When I tried to talk to the teachers and principals, they would tell me flat out, "I don't think it's worth your time or my time to come all the way down here and meet. We really just have no use for the program." They are right; you have this sophisticated program, and a lot of teachers don't know how to use it, and it's so complicated that they feel like all of their fears of technology were justified. It's the same old story, no one goes and actually talks to the teachers. Before, I probably would have been excited about this type of opportunity. But now I can't. If it goes against what I believe, then how can I do it?

Krish began his critique by caricaturing the figure of the technologist, a person who wants everything to go just "how they imagine it in their heads" because they already know best. This demand for control was largely anticipatory, creating a self-fulfilling loop in which technologists' imaginations were tethered to the already expected future results of their interventions. Krish framed this problem of anticipatory technological control in relation to the fact that Gooru had been given significant funding from Google, demonstrating Gooru's power, and that the Gooru leadership nonetheless could not get into schools closer to their headquarters in the Bay Area. These schools, which were implicitly marked as having more resources, status, and affluence, which also likely meant they were marked as whiter (or at least more white adjacent), had the power to refuse the advances of Gooru's digital saviors. In turn, Krish hinted, Gooru moved to less affluent schools in the brown world that were perceived as "without agency and capacity to change their situation" and therefore were more susceptible to Gooru's control.[10]

Producing Techno-affective Communities
and Anticipatory Nostalgia

Krish saw his own experience with Sahaayaka, an organization that prided itself on the fact that they would "go there," that is, go to schools and communities, as an antidote to these kinds of technological visions, recognizing that digital integration must occur with the input of teachers and with some knowledge of the specificities of pedagogy. Otherwise, he noted, technology would only be feared. Krish went on to explain that he was now reading some texts in educational theory for the first time in his life. "I've been reading a lot by John Holt. Do you know him?" he asked. I nodded, yes, I did know Holt, who was the pioneer of the unschooling movement and a harsh critic of the American education system in the mid-twentieth century. I was pleasantly surprised that Krish was reading this kind of educational theory, especially given that up till this point he had had no training as an educator at all. That he and other digital brown saviors had been allowed to join and change education without having had any training in educational systems, pedagogy, or any similar area of study had always made me nervous, even angry, but was also an indicator of the exceptional global value that digital saviors had. Krish's critique of Gooru and his recognition that education was a deep art and science seemed, on the surface, to be an indicator of Krish's challenge to the technophilic impulse, a move away from the more trite ideologies associated with digital panaceas.

However, I was disconcerted when I realized that these observations about the edtech sector were *not* actually leading Krish away from digital interventions. Instead, Krish was even more convinced that he would go back to Bangalore in another year and try harder to find a digital strategy to make an impact on the schools and communities that Sahaayaka worked with. The only difference was that *he*, Krish, had understood the inadequacies of these other tech models, and *he* knew how to integrate these tools sensibly. Here Krish exhibited what Christo Sims calls a "disruptive fixation," in which "reformers and designers who meet moral calls to improve the world for others manage to produce and maintain their idealism despite having some knowledge of recurring failures."[11] Each time a project fails, the newest technologist believes that they have identified the problem with the last intervention and that *this time* they will be able to solve those problems. This fixation drives digital saviorism even though the saviors themselves are faced time and time again with the fact that "an app will not save us."[12]

In this case, Krish was driven toward new digital fixations because he felt that his experience with Sahaayaka had helped him to realize that getting teachers invested in technology and combating their technophobia was the first step for success and impact. To do this, Krish realized that he had to mobilize regional categories of belonging and already existing investments as part of his digital interventions. I noticed this for the first time when I saw Krish announce on Facebook the accomplishments of one of the teachers in Sahaayaka's network of schools, hailing the feat of translating a version of GCompris, an education learning software, into the Kannada language: "Please meet Shambu, one of our star teachers from Kanakapura who embraced our open source computer initiative since 2007. . . . [H]e has kept up with his passion for open source computing and Kannada and has now proudly contributed back . . . as his gift on Rajyotsava Day. Sahaayaka is proud of him and wishes him the best and hope it inspires other teachers." Krish here was referring to a new version of GCompris that Shambu had recoded completely in Kannada. GCompris's major feature, like the apps Sahaayaka would produce in the future, was that it was free and open access, which meant that there was little restriction on its use, improvement, or adaptation to any context. Sahaayaka's staff, especially Krish, were huge advocates for open-access software, believing that information ought to be free, maybe even *wanted* to be free. Yet, as Kimberly Christen has noted, information freedom and open access are not outside of the political.[13] That is to say, calls for open access require questioning *who* information is open to, *how* it is open to them, and what ideological constructs are reinscribed in the call for open information.

In this case, what struck me was that Shambu's open-access technological "gift" came on Rajyotsva Day, celebrated on November 1 of every year to commemorate the day in 1956 when Karnataka state was created to purportedly connect all the Kannada-speaking regions and people. Language politics in India has a long and affectively dense history as the creation of Indian states on linguistic grounds cemented the tie among ethnonationalism, language, and identity, especially in the southern states of India.[14] In a sense, the linking of software that promoted the learning of the Kannada language with the celebration of one's Kannadiga identity reanimated these discussions of region, language, and affect. It became a means to show one's allegiance to place while simultaneously assuming the value of technological innovation toward the development of Karnataka state, a technologically facilitated "affective excess marked by hyperperformative jingoism" that left out non-Kannada speakers in Karnataka, including, as I have discussed earlier, the Urdu-speaking Muslims in the region.[15]

In response to Krish's post, the teacher, Shambu, replied, "I miss my guru Ganesh sir. . . . Can I have his contact details." As Shambu's nostalgic words and Gooru's name reveal, these types of Hindu metaphors were part of the production of a global Hinduism: the "guru-shisha" (teacher-student) relationship being perhaps one of its most ubiquitous and generic markers. This ideology of Hindu teaching had been encoded in these open-access technologies, providing the foundational structuration of feelings for global savarna edtech creative makers, NGO personnel in Sahaayaka, and many teachers within Sahaayaka's network of Karnataka schools.[16] But what was most important about Shambu's statement was the way he situated himself vis-à-vis his "guru Ganesh." Shambu maintained the hierarchy between himself, a teacher in a Kannada-medium school, and Ganesh, a Tamil brahmin Sahaayaka board member who was a computer scientist by training. Here the guru-shisha relationship mimics the relationship between the savior and the saved, mediated by one's capacity to code *and* one's position within caste hierarchies.

Krish had recognized and wanted to maximize this affective connection among global Hindus in his other technological creations. For example, Krish was already imagining and coding a new phone app that he believed he could use to fund Sahaayaka programming. What he wanted to do, he told me, was find a way to make an app that would be accessible all over the world so that anyone, anywhere, could fund a school, taluk, or district of their choosing. In one sense, Krish's ideal felt like a more sophisticated, digitized form of Save the Children or the aforementioned Support My School campaign. In this case, a person could choose to fund a child or a school, and, in turn, they would be given data that showed the resulting impact. "It will be easy enough, we can just have some of the students in the school make a postcard, and we can scan it into the app, and it will be sent directly to the donor. We can also show them data about the school: how clean it is, how much student scores have improved." Rather than handwritten letters from thankful students to donors, now he could have these children's notes sent instantaneously while also demonstrating quantitatively the great impact of donations.

By imagining a model in which Sahaayaka relied on many single donors rather than a few large donor agencies, Krish was drawing from the crowdfunding and sharing-economy models that have come to define late capitalist digital accumulation. Websites like GoFundMe have become the hegemonic versions of this model in the help economy, allowing philanthropic giving to feel more personal and individualized. In this sense, Krish's innovations recognized how technological, economic, and emotional investments have come to define one another in the help economy.

Krish went on to explain that he got the idea for crowdsourced funding in part because he had taken a technologist friend to a school in a village. After going and seeing the school, the technologist, now living in faraway Connecticut, was moved to tears because it had reminded him of his own village school, and he then wanted to find a way to help the school. In this case, he was not moved to help because of his longings to help the long-suffering distant Other but, as Krish explained, by the possibility of helping Others supposedly like himself, who spoke the same language and came from a village like his but had not been given the same opportunities he had. In other words, the philanthropic impulse was about his tie to help those at home, an Indian diasporic affect that could be satiated only through the phone app's potential to direct his giving to those he cared for most.

This digitally enabled affective connection is predicated on a form of nostalgic temporality that Elisabeth Kirtsoglou characterizes as "anticipatory nostalgia."[17] In this case, the technologist experiences nostalgia after seeing a school that reminds him of his own past. In turn, the technologist feels an emotional connection to the village school as if it were his own school, collapsing the temporal distance between the past and the present. At the same time, this temporal collapse between the past and the present also collapses the present/past and the future in the impulse to produce a different kind of school that provides the kinds of opportunities that would allow students to become that which the technologist has already become. In other words, the technologist's nostalgia is anticipating that which will occur in terms of that which already was. Moreover, Krish was harnessing these temporalities of anticipatory nostalgia in his imaginary of the phone app.

In the next section, I continue in this exploration of the relation between digital technology and temporality in the help economies by attending to how Krish explicitly manipulates the experience of time through Sahaayaka's phone app.

14

DIGITAL TIME (AND ITS OTHERS)

It was 2016, and Krish and I sat in his apartment in Santa Clara, drinking tea and chatting. On this day, Krish wanted to reflect on "time"—the time that had passed since he joined Sahaayaka, the time to come, even the way he had come to appreciate time itself, primarily because he had had so much more of it over the past year, and he knew this excess time might soon come to an end if and when he embarked back to Bangalore. After Krish moved from Bangalore to Santa Clara in late 2014, his day-to-day work had changed dramatically. He no longer attended constant meetings, no longer was responsible for putting out organizational fires, and no longer traveled hours each day to visit schools. All these tasks were left to other members of Sahaayaka who were actually in Karnataka, allowing Krish to finally have the time to step back and reflect.

The time to think had also helped him process his previous ten years as CEO. After months of struggle, he had been able to recommit himself to his job, primarily because the physical distance had allowed him to do his work in the way he felt most comfortable: mediated by digital technologies. The computer screen was a part of Krish, a former computer engineer, in a way that those who are not digital makers can never quite experience.[1]

"It's great," he explained. "I can stay in contact with everyone over there in the evening into the night, say 3 or 4 a.m., when the school day is going on, have calls on Skype, over the phone, and in the daytime I can read, work on some of these tech projects, and figure out what to do." Krish then listed the many new technologies he was developing—a new phone app, a Kannada version of Wikipedia for children, databases to store student data—explaining how each of these innovations relied on attention to time and how he had learned to manipulate it.

It is almost a cliché at this point to speak of "time-space compressing technologies": information at our fingertips, the ability to communicate with people halfway around the world, the collapse of the traditional business cycle in the wake of technological outsourcing.[2] Digital technologies seem to "short-circuit or confound time itself," sometimes making us feel all too close to our fellows when connected on social media and sometimes making us feel, as Manoj reminded in chapter 10, as though we could potentially live forever as long as our digital footprints live on after our bodies have long since begun to decay.[3]

But when I listened to Krish describe his current position, there was no sense of this temporal collapse.[4] Even as digital time made instantaneous communication feasible and allowed for the storage and compression of massive amounts of archival data, it intersected with other structurings of time: the splitting of time zones that "duplicated" time for the Indian abroad; school time, which in Karnataka ran from 9 a.m. to 4:30 p.m. from June to March; and the time of urban-rural movement as fieldworkers shuttled back and forth between Bangalore headquarters and village schools. Krish made clear that these very real distances and multiplicities, in both time and space, provided him the opportunity to think and work. That is to say, the splitting of time by spatial distance was its own valuable commodity as cybernetic spacetime continued to place pressure on the physical world. Krish could even be considered an alchemist of digital time, ably manipulating it using the privileges of his translocality, working during times that no one else in his time zone worked and spending the rest of the day on other activities more appropriate to where he was physically located.[5]

I prefer *time-space manipulation* to *time-space compression* as an analytic for understanding technology's "temporal meaning" because it centers relations of power and avoids reifying a universal and singular experience of time in the digital age.[6] Historically, the ability to manipulate time has been a central tenet of accumulation, and the ability to determine temporal regimes and regulate how people should orient toward time has been a key mechanism by which to divide those with power from those without. Colonizers and their developmentalist successors constructed schizogenic notions of civilizational time that emplaced the colonized in a past time.[7] In some sense, those who code are the inheritors of this power to manipulate time in the digital age. In fact, for some of those who control the means of digital production, corporeal time is explicitly made to be manipulated. Casinos, for example, have pushed toward digital slot machines that are immersive, creating the illusion that one lives in the "machine zone" with no worries, no demands, and no awareness of the body's needs.[8] The casino's social games—poker, blackjack, and so on—have been slowly replaced by these virtual worlds, in which user experience is atomized and algorithms are created to measure one's "time on device," encoded on the assumption that the only time worth measuring is the constant and never-ending play from which capital is derived. Simultaneously, the only user experience worth producing is the illusion of stasis, the feeling that time is standing still for as long as the user keeps playing. These are the very same time-manipulating machines that Madhu told me her husband codes, manufactures, and sells to the United States, all with the purpose of helping India and her husband's company amass wealth in the process, as I mentioned in chapter 6.

But how does the brown savior's technological capacity to manipulate time shape the help economy? I turn to this question in the rest of this chapter.

Transaction Time and Lag Time

The way Krish thought about time and technology was linked to his past as a computer engineer. After completing his Master's in computer engineering at Texas A&M, Krish had lived in Austin, Texas, founding a start-up called TPSFutures that specialized in transaction processing systems (TPS). These systems are a form of information processing in which a series of operations are made indivisible, such that if one operation in the system fails, the entire transaction fails. This logic remains the basis for most contemporary transactions, manifesting in its current digital reformulation to facilitate online consumer practices.

Krish explained TPS using the example of buying a movie ticket online. "To pay and receive your ticket," he explained, "there are a number of intermediary operations, processing of the ticket with the store, checking the validity of the credit card you used, etc. If any one of those operations fails, then the entire transaction fails, and the transaction is only successful if all of the operations are completed successfully."

I found out later that TPS was a relatively old computer technology, first developed in 1960 as part of the American Airlines SABRE system, in order to create an automated system to better handle the incredible increase in passenger volume during the late 1950s. The system's early success with American Airlines expanded over the next fifty years, and the Sabre Global Distribution System became the TPS for American Express, Expedia, Frontier, JetBlue, and Travelocity, among others. This link between early information communication technologies and travel is more than just a coincidence: the global movement of capital required that these time-space–manipulating technologies emerge simultaneously.

Krish founded TPSFutures in 1998 in Texas to develop a more efficient digital TPS software. In his words, the innovation of his particular TPS software had nothing to do with technological advancement at all but rather lay in how he was able to manipulate a user's perception of time:

> You know, no matter what you do, it takes some twelve seconds from the time you swipe your credit card for the signal to reach the main office, usually in Nevada somewhere, and come back. You just can't change the amount of time it takes. It will always take that long. And so, for us, it wasn't about creating some highly complex new algorithm, it was finding the simplest solution. What we did was we looked at the client's needs, and one of ours was Chevron. For them, we figured out a user interface that asked a series of questions to a customer while they were waiting for the transaction to be processed. I'm sure you've seen it, when you're at the gas station and you swipe, it asks you for your zip code, whether you want to get a car wash, etc. We already know the zip code, we don't actually need that information, but it passes the waiting time. We did something similar for Safeway. We would create a system that would just track a customer's buying trends; if they were frequent customers, we would then just have a "local" approval so that they get approved faster and just have the "real" approval happen later. So it's always the simplest solution. Even in education it's that way.

This idea of the "simplest solution" was one of Krish's key values as CEO of Sahaayaka, one version of the technological regime that defined social processes as problems to be solved using the fewest resources while making the maximum impact.[9]

Behind the simplest-solution rhetoric is the question of time and the units used to measure time. In TPS logic, *transaction time*—that is, the time for an exchange to be completed, rather than seconds, minutes, hours, or any other standardized unit of time—is the base unit of measurement. Any partial task within that transaction system is relevant only insofar as it relates to this discrete packet of time. In the case of Chevron, Krish's strategy was based completely on shifting the user's perception of transaction time. Even though there was no way to speed up the transaction process, the process felt faster when users had to answer meaningless questions in the meantime. In the case of Safeway, the solution to the problem of transaction time was actually not to complete the entire transaction but to short-circuit the process such that someone who went to the grocery store had a shorter waiting time.

Each of these examples became Krish's way of explaining how he thought about digital integration in Sahaayaka and why, for him, it was not so much about making things go any faster using new technologies but instead about making everyone involved, especially those consumers who used his technologies, *feel* like the process was going faster. It wasn't about cutting twelve seconds to five, or thirteen minutes to six, but making it not matter whether it was twelve or five, thirteen or six. This power to shift how people perceived time was what gave Krish such great power and why I can't help but think of him as an alchemist of time.

To make this point, Krish showed me his newly minted phone app, replete with screens for inputting student and school performance data. The app was one of Sahaayaka's successes, the means by which Krish had made the organization indispensable to the Karnataka state education ministry. As I discuss later, the app would be integrated into the government bureaucracy. For now, however, Krish was testing the software on the mentors, seeking to discover whether and how the app would work when it was scaled up.

The smartphone and his app seemed to rely on the idea of instantaneous data collection—mentors could report what they were finding instantly and get information about schools and students instantly. It was the kind of instantaneous connectivity that has dominated discussions of digital technologies. Yet Krish knew better than to fall prey to this facile view of smart technologies. Instead, he reminded me that the mentors would not always have internet access, especially if they went to rural schools that still had little to no network connectivity or if they had limited data plans that would not allow them to use the internet all the time.

This fact, Krish explained, was what his app actually relied on. If all the mentors were on their phones and able to input data, and all of the data came to his servers at the same time, he might have a problem.

If that happened, our servers might be overtaxed. Probably not, but I don't want to take that chance. Because they don't have connectivity all the time, they input the data on their phone, so it looks as if they have already sent it, but the data is really still just stored on their device, and whenever they do get to the internet, then all that info will sync with the main server.

Because the data were not sent all at once, during the day, when thousands of bits of information were being collected, Krish did not need to worry about overworking his servers, that is, "taxing them." But even though Krish needed this *lag time*, this lag time was not perceived at all by the mentors. As they inputted data and completed their tasks, it felt as if they had completed the entire transaction process and had already sent their findings to Bangalore's central databases.

The Mentor's Labor, White Noise, and the Wasting of Time

As part of their jobs, mentors had to go from school to school and manually input data for every question on a checklist. Krish knew that the mentors were bored by the tedious task of data collection, a rote kind of labor that required no creative capacity. Here the task of data collection revealed the neocolonial stratification in labor value, in which the brown savior's capacity to innovate, create, and manipulate was juxtaposed with the "degraded" labor of the mentor, who was now forced to do robotic tasks that took them away from hands-on, face-to-face relational interactions.[10]

The mentors themselves were not oblivious to this fact. They regretted that they were no longer the change agents they used to be and were nostalgic for this past when they weren't merely collecting massive amounts of data but were doing something more. Even from the early days of the transition to the digital, the mentors were resentful and sought to manipulate their tasks in ways that might subvert the brown savior's authority to determine how they used their time.

For example, one afternoon I was sitting in the Sahaayaka office in Ramanagara waiting for Shiva and a few of the other mentors to get done with their weekly student progress reports. The task was mundane. The mentors were required to log the number of pages that students had filled out in notebooks distributed by the organization as part of a short-lived diary program. The by-product of the project, implemented in two hundred schools, was an enormous amount of data, which the mentors then were required to log in a Google spreadsheet once every two weeks. At the time, most of the mentors had some kind of informal log notebook, which they used to keep track of each school's page use. But even so, the numbers were always vague, at best.

Because there was only one computer in the office, each mentor had to wait their turn, slowly looking through each of their twenty-odd schools and in-putting the number of pages into the correct box in the spreadsheet. They were all visibly frustrated as six o'clock became seven and then eight. While waiting, the mentors entertained themselves by watching random Telugu and Kannada films. Shiva, bored even of this, started talking to me about his previous internship experience with the Deshpande Foundation, a Boston-based philanthropic organization.[11] "We had one very good exercise. We had to de-velop our own idea for an organization. Then we had to go and pitch the proj-ect and get some people to give funds for it. In two weeks we collected 25,000 rupees and won the competition. It was great learning. After that, Deshpande Foundation told me that I can get a job with them anytime I want." Shiva en-visioned himself as a global leader, one who had the skills to start and run his own organization if he so chose. That Shiva was still sitting in an office doing "paperwork" (albeit in a digital form) was a constant source of resentment. Re-gardless of his inclusion in the help economy, he was pigeonholed in a bureau-cratic time-space that made him feel immobile and static, useful only insofar as he functioned robotically, went to schools, collected data, and entered these data into a spreadsheet.

Shiva was even more frustrated when he looked on the Google spreadsheet and saw Manoj, one of his fellow mentors, typing from his home computer and having nearly completed his logging for the week. Eventually Shiva started urging the other mentors to fudge the data so they could get done faster, cal-culating random numbers of pages—5, 12, 3, 0—that seemed logical based on previous data inputs *and* that showed that the students had progressed. The task went much faster, and they were all soon done with their data-entry job.

In fudging the data, the mentors were taking away some of the authority over the ordering of this digital archive, queering these data by challenging the fixed, rigid bounds of these spreadsheet boxes and what they were intended to represent.[12] In one sense, they were participating in a practical act of jugaad, which Amit Rai argues is a unique form of Indian hacking that challenges pat-terns of casteized, classed, and gendered relations of labor: "Jugaad . . . as the idea of working around the point of sabotaging what's given as fixed, normal, formal, propertied, *suvarna* (upper caste), appropriate and right . . . destabilizes not only the value-form of commodity production of monopolistic control, but also the enforced dichotomy between intellectual and manual labor in several caste and class hierarchies."[13] The mentors as classed and casteized subjects whose roles had been reduced to manual labor were destabilizing these hierarchies by sabotaging transaction time, that is, producing the perception that all had gone well with the transaction even as they had completely messed with the data. In turn, they were producing new futures for students by changing how they were represented in these data sets, a shift in circumstance woven into the mentors' own resistance to their enforced predictability.

Krish was all too aware of the inefficiencies in Sahaayaka's old data system, which was the primary reason he had shifted the organization to a model in which mentors would input data directly into an app on their phones, a tool he knew they all had. Krish's training plan for the mentors was intended to make them excited about using the app so that they wouldn't be so obstinate about the long days of data inputting and would not try and fudge the data. While mentors were never included as participants in developing the app, Krish was constantly seeking to tweak the features of the app himself to enhance the "exciting" user experience. Krish flipped through the main menus on his new phone app, taking me step by step through the colorful interfaces. Using the app, mentors were expected to answer a series of questions about each school and student, at least sixty questions in total. These questions would, in turn, generate the necessary data for Sahaayaka to assess the performance of each school. Questions like "How many number of teachers have received Prerana training?" would help monitor the efficient implementation of the program, while questions like "Who checks the learning map?" were simple ways of determining the mechanism by which the program was implemented. Answering these questions on the app seemed more like playing a game than doing tedious data-collection work.

"I've made the questions really easy to answer, checkmarks in a user-friendly interface that I think they'll enjoy. But, even more than that, if they're excited to be part of Sahaayaka 2.0, to be part of India's digital future, they'll be more likely to *want* to do the work." In other words, Krish was seeking to create a user experience for mentors that made them feel differently about their work by also channeling their nationalist impulses through the evocation of the Digital India movement. He wanted them to experience the time of data collection as less burdensome, less time consuming, even if it ultimately was a less interactive (in the oxygenated sense) use of their time. In fact, Krish acknowledged that as they learned how to input data on the app, the process could actually take mentors *more* time. However, like the customer who was actively prevented from feeling how much time their transaction was taking, the mentors, too, were being manipulated by the app to make them experience their work time differently.

One idea for manipulating the mentors' sense of time came, inadvertently, from a conversation Krish had with me, which, in retrospect, has made me nervous about the ramifications of my fieldwork. Krish and I had had many discussions about what, exactly, qualitative research was. Having been trained in computer engineering, Krish generally associated research with quantitative data, and yet he listened with interest to my constant arguments regarding why and how long-term ethnographic study could generate insights both unexpected and highly useful for the world in which we lived. Because of this intrigue, I would provide further details about research design, field note-taking, and especially the use of images and film as part of research. Krish had seen me with my audio recorder or one of my digital cameras and would ask how and why I was taking so many photographs or pieces of footage while in the field.

During one of these chats, I had suggested to Krish that he might think about including a photo and audio feature in his app, a feature I believed would be a way of getting richer sorts of data that were not confined to standardized forms of measurement. Much to my delight, in 2016 Krish showed me a version of his app with a small button in the right-hand corner that would allow mentors to take photographs or record a short note about what they were seeing at the school site. I congratulated him on his new innovation, but Krish simply explained that including such a feature was nothing at all compared to the scale on which he had been working just a few short years prior with TPSFutures.

One year later, I finally met Krish again, this time in Bangalore in 2017. I had been unable to get the app, and especially the image feature, out of my mind since we had last met, admittedly because I had been salivating over the possibility of looking through the data myself at some point in the future. But Krish did not mention the image feature at all during our conversation. I finally could not wait any longer and blurted out a question about the image and audio feature, and he shruggingly told me, "It's mostly just noise." He compared it to a WhatsApp group that I had been added to a few years prior, on which mentors posted updates to the entire Sahaayaka staff, shared images with captions that were meant to inspire one another, and traded helpful tips while doing their work in schools. When he added me to the group, Krish had told me that once in a while, out of nowhere, there might be a post that was incredibly heartwarming, but almost all of it was "noise."

What Krish meant by noise was that the data he was getting both on WhatsApp and through the image feature of the Sahaayaka phone app were mostly *white noise*. Many have experienced white noise on their TV screens, the pixelated white, gray, and black dots with the accompanying sound of static when the signal is not coming through, and they have probably tried as quickly as possible to get rid of the white noise, to find the right cable connection or input in order to do so. In the most colloquial terms, white noise is the random, chaotic, and indecipherable signal that sounds and looks like static.[14] Krish's concept of white noise overlapped with this colloquial definition but really pertained to what coders call a "white noise time series," which is a time series where the variables are independent and identically distributed with a mean of zero. In simpler terms, it means that there are no correlations between any variables, and therefore the process is random and unpredictable over any given timescale.

For Krish, this kind of data set, in which there was no predictability, no ability to anticipate the result, was ultimately useless to him. Indeed, even though he admitted that there was some affective possibility in white noise—the image or sound that suddenly emerged out of the cacophony and struck an emotional note—it was not significant enough for him to consider it important for the formation of his app.

But then, I asked him, why include an image feature at all if he knew that this feature would do nothing to help him to collect the data he sought? Krish grinned when he saw my befuddlement and explained that he actually cared very little about the photographs themselves. Their real utility, he had realized, was that they would "motivate the mentors. Because when they feel like they are only inputting data, they don't feel like they are really participating in the process. But if they get to also add some unique features, images and such, they feel like their input is more valuable."

The white noise of the image was, in the end, another one of Krish's means to alchemically manipulate the mentors' experience of time, to keep them working optimally and collecting the "essential" data to drive the help economy, even though this extra process was actually just wasting their time when they already had so much labor to do.

Seen in this way, Krish's design of the phone app was really a way to discipline the mentors, preventing them from conducting work outside of the very specific protocols defined by the organization and channeling their bodily responses toward the organization's goals. In the next chapter, I draw out more of the ways that Sahaayaka's phone app was designed explicitly to surveil and monitor those using it, even as the rhetoric focused on the many ways that the app could help children achieve their best learning outcomes.

15

DIGITAL AUDIT CULTURE (OR METADATA)

One day in 2017, I met Krish, who had recently moved back to Bangalore. He invited me to join him at the Karnataka state education department to meet with a group focused on the nali kali program in Karnataka, one of the major initiatives of the Sarva Shiksha Abhiyan, the Indian government program aimed at the universalization of elementary education.

The nali kali program covers over 53,000 schools in Karnataka state and is a pedagogical model designed around play, intended for the youngest children attending government schools. It's a model that, on its surface, is one of the most innovative, child-centric learning strategies that has yet been devised for the Indian education system. I have gone into many of these nali kali class-rooms, mostly during my time in Adavisandra village. There are no rows in these classrooms, no expectation that children sit quietly or raise their hands before they speak. What I remember most is the music, songs that help students learn the alphabet, learn animal names, and begin the process of schooling. You can hear the music even one hundred meters away, in fifth-, sixth-, and seventh-standard classrooms that feel as if they exist in a separate dimension. It's jarring how different these classrooms feel from one another: younger students laughing, playing, and taking joy in their day while older students get on with the real business of education, sitting in rows, reading from textbooks, and following standardized curricula, a process that requires a literal rewiring of the child's nervous system in just a few short years.

My feelings about these nali kali classrooms came back to me as I sat in the Karnataka education office with Krish and two others, Rekha and Gururaj. As the meeting began, Rekha dominated the proceedings. When I looked and listened, I could not help but notice that she carried with her all the trappings of the brown savior. She was a relatively fair-skinned older Indian woman, perhaps in her early sixties, immaculately dressed in a sari that let us know that she was decidedly and traditionally Indian. She looked each of us in the eye as she spoke with the all-too-familiar sharp enunciation and accent of the well-traveled anglophile Indian, someone who had spent as much time elsewhere as in India itself and dripped with a civilized, cosmopolitan sensibility. I got an even better sense of who she was when she refused the kadle usli (black chickpeas) that was offered to all of us because, in her words, the oil in which it was made would not "sit well with her." Our stomachs always give us, the diasporic elite, away, so I decided to scarf down a few bites to prove my authenticity through commensality, though my stomach gave me away soon after. Rekha did not speak any Kannada and previous to this trip had spent very little time in Karnataka. However, even though she did not know much about the region and had never worked on a project in education in her life, what made her incredibly valuable was her expertise in the monitoring and evaluation of development programs.

Rekha had spent the majority of the past twenty-five years working for UNICEF, overseeing some of their biggest projects in health care in Africa. Her work with UNICEF had, for the most part, kept her traveling between Britain and Ghana during the 1990s. The brown savior was the perfect conduit between the white British subject and the Black Ghanaian subject, who were slotted into the most well-trodden global racist discourses of who could help and who was most in need. In this racist cosmology, as Adia Benton notes, "racialized perceptions of risk conjure notions of the human in which 'race' (generally) and blackness (specifically) are central mediators of risk."[1] Within this logic Rekha was heroized as the brown person willing and able to take the risk of helping supposedly abject and hypervulnerable Black peoples. Here her visible non-Blackness, nonwhiteness, relations to Western institutions, and class and caste positioning functioned to produce the boundaries within which Rekha could conduct her work and through which Rekha accrued value in relation to those Black peoples perceived as at risk.

Part of Rekha's privileged racialized slotting was her deep and total commitment to technocratic, universal, impersonal forms of intervention. For example, in Ghana, she was tasked with integrating the Tanahashi model into immunization projects. Even though the UNICEF Tanahashi model was purportedly a method to address the Millennium Development Goals related to health (especially with regard to the goal of combating HIV/AIDS, malaria, and other diseases), the model focused on analytic costing and budgeting strategies to assess which methods would have the quickest impact on health coverage.[2] "Make it all available, accessible, and used," Rekha said, underscoring the way the Tanahashi model reduced the problems of health and disease to problems of poor management, lack of accountability, and inefficiency, all of which could be corrected by the appropriate measurements, metrics, and accountability criteria "without the detailed particulars of context or history."[3] Rekha had since retired from UNICEF, but she continued to consult on various projects, including the nali kali project in India.

Next to Rekha sat Gururaj, an elderly gentleman, perhaps also in his sixties, soft-spoken and almost too nervous to introduce himself to us, primarily because he was far more comfortable speaking Kannada than English. Krish whispered to me, "He is the person who conceived of the nali kali program. He knows more about this than anyone else." Gururaj had spent his entire career in Karnataka's education system, and the nali kali program was the crowning achievement of his career. When he started talking about the program, he forgot all of his nerves, instead pulling out a six-page packet of almost sixty categories, each of which meticulously detailed one of the activities, objectives, or missions of the nali kali program. As I looked at this list, created to make sure that all of the teachers in nali kali schools were implementing the curriculum, I almost forgot that the nali kali program was actually about active, joyous learning. Instead, I was transported to a world steeped in the bureaucratic, neocolonial practices of categorization, a world in which even play must be divided into neat and isolated compartments and objectives.

As with almost every aspect of the Indian education system, a huge amount of bureaucratic processes had been tethered to the nali kali program. Local-level bureaucrats (called *block resource persons* [BRPs] and *cluster resource persons* [CRPs]) were expected to monitor and evaluate the functioning and implementation of the program. According to Gururaj, these CRPs and BRPs were intended to, "first, note how the schools are performing based on the quality scores I have outlined; second, observe the progress of implementation since the last visit; [and] third, identify the areas which are [preventing] teachers from implementing the curricula effectively." Gururaj's deepest anxiety was that all of his hard work, his years of commitment to primary education in India, would be for naught because those tasked with implementing and assessing his vision were failing.

But just as Gururaj finished, Rekha cut him off.

But we all know that these guys don't do their jobs right. They don't really care, they just want the paycheck. Sometimes they don't go, a lot of times they are just dishonest, or probably they may just be incompetent. They just fudge the data because they know that if they have poor results, then there will be more questions. You cannot have those whose performance is based on the success of the program *also* be the evaluators. What we need is a way of *monitoring the monitors*.

Monitoring the Monitors and Technologies of Antirelational Relationality

The language of "monitoring the monitors" describes a classic form of audit culture, a never-ending need to create new dimensions of accountability that layer on top of one another, creating ever more centralized and "meta" surveillance and control mechanisms that might, eventually, lead to the perfect system in which every human being follows the rules just as they are supposed to.

Audit culture has been a global "culture on the make" for a large part of the past two hundred years.[4] Historically, the audit's roots have been as a colonial technology of governance that was intended to help manage colonial populations by classifying them and then determining how resources ought to be allocated and extracted from the colony for the metropole.[5] With the rise of financial-managerial power, the audit has expanded, especially in postcolonial nation-states, into nearly every sphere of social life and functions as a taken-for-granted technology of contemporary neoliberal governance. In education, managerial ideas of standardization, quantification, and direct monitoring have replaced the many competing measures for how to hold educators and the educational bureaucracy accountable. As Marilyn Strathern writes:

Where audit is applied to public institutions—medical, legal, educational— the state's overt concern may be less to impose day-to-day direction than to ensure that internal controls, in the form of monitoring techniques, are in place. That may require the setting up of mechanisms where none existed before, but the accompanying rhetoric is likely to be that of help-ing (monitoring) people help (monitor) themselves, including helping people get used to this new "culture."[6]

Strathern is asking us to pay close attention to the everyday administrative and technical acts that may seem mind-numbingly tedious but that, taken as a whole, reveal quite a bit about contemporary governmentality and the systems of power that undergird it.[7] But Strathern is also focusing on the ethical basis for the audit. Those with power are seeking to *help*, but they cannot help if they cannot surveil. The audit, in other words, is premised on questions regarding who needs to be surveilled because they need to be helped, who is trustworthy to surveil/help them, who is rendered transparent, who is rendered opaque, and, most important, how these binary relations allow for particular people to accumulate ever more control and power—all questions that reproduce a version of the audit as a quintessential neocolonial technology of power that "actively document[s] *and* produce[s] . . . risks, problems, and uncertainties."[8]

Rekha wanted to audit the local government officials because, in her mind, their lack of ethics made them a constant risk for corruption and failure. Her problem, however, was that she had no way of properly holding them to ac-count. This was why she was interested specifically in exploring how digital tools might facilitate the monitoring of government officials and why she had enlisted the help of Krish, whose computational prowess had created an el-egant form of digital accountability.

Since 2016 Krish had been tweaking his new phone app, readying it for just such a moment when those working with the Indian educational bureaucracy might realize how beneficial his app might be. Each page of the app provided quick and easy checklist-based monitoring protocols, which Sahaayaka had unfolded and piloted over the past three years in its 50,000 or so schools. Ini-tially, the app's goal was to help Sahaayaka solve one of its biggest issues with funders: how to prove that they were making an impact in schools. As I've mentioned before, in its early years Sahaayaka relied heavily on the mentors and their ability to motivate students through in-person interactions. These interactions seemed to be creating large impacts, yet Sahaayaka struggled to communicate this to their funders, who wanted to know *how* exactly these very small interventions were producing such a large impact. The organization needed "hard" data (read: quantitative, metric-based data) to prove the impact of their programming.

Krish realized that the app would be the perfect solution. Data-driven intervention was what so many in the help economy were looking for, and now Krish had developed the technological key. But he had also realized that they could then analyze these metrics and present them back in easily digestible forms—bar graphs, Venn diagrams on a user dashboard—to teachers, mentors, government officials, and even parents.

Krish got the idea for this last aspect of his phone app after witnessing Manoj, one of Sahaayaka's mentors, as he was going to school sites: "The thing about Manoj was that while he was working in schools, he was also going on home visits. And what he would tell us is that when he would go on these home visits, he would get an SMS (text message) from these parents on his phone, stuff like 'I am going for coffee' and 'They [my children] are coming to school.'" Krish learned a few things from his observations of Manoj: first, that parents all had smartphones with at least a minimal amount of internet connectivity and bandwidth; and, second, that this form of communication seemed to create an emotional connection between the mentors and parents. In turn, Krish had decided to integrate parents into his app, making sure that they would be able to download it from the Android Play Store and access a parent interface that would show them their school's data as well as their student's data.

At the same time, Krish's interpretation of what he had witnessed seemed to almost completely erase the relational aspects of Manoj's story. Manoj had forged complex and long-lasting personal relationships, even friendships, with parents that produced and sustained these secondary digital relationships, all of which were eliminated in Krish's version of the phone app. When I spoke to Manoj about these interactions, he explained that he sent messages directly to families based on the specific things that were happening in their lives. In other words, Manoj's text messages and reminders were personal, tailored, familiar, and based on an ethics of care that arose from his commitment to getting these children to come to school and his sense of accountability to their parents to make sure that he kept up with this commitment. Texting back and forth about mundane aspects of day-to-day life was a central way of forging these types of accountable relationships. Even in Krish's retelling, it was the seemingly mundane and idiosyncratic act of telling a mentor about one's morning cup of coffee that signaled and created a closer interpersonal connection.

The app produced something quite different. The information that parents were getting stemmed from standardized measurements of student success and failure that did not include these personal bits of spontaneous daily connection. Moreover, Krish had mentors like Manoj, who had previously been working in schools in this relational way, use the phone app exclusively, documenting what they saw in the schools each time they went. This made the mentors' role much less about the personal connections they had forged and much more about being able to follow these simple procedures to collect more data. Now they would go through the app's "checklist," screens on which they could quickly document what was happening in the school: students are being awarded stars (CHECK); students are earning stickers (CHECK); students are completing workbooks (CHECK). In this process of documentation, students were transmuted into data, differentiated and hierarchized based on how they and their school had performed on Sahaayaka's metrics, which were then shared with parents as a data set that was accessible only on the app.

In this way, the phone app centered accumulations of information and transmuted an ethics of care into a kind of "antirelational relationality."[9] Here I am drawing explicitly from and applying the insights of Ruth Wilson Gilmore, who argues that racial capitalist systems require technologies of antirelationality, that is, technologies that reduce collective life to the racialized categories, demarcations, and divisions that sustain capitalist accumulation.[10] In this case, Manoj's everyday social relations with parents and students did not facilitate accumulation because these relations could not be flattened into generic, quantifiable, scalable patterns of data. It was only through the translation of these kinds of relationships into demographic categories (gender, school strength, etc.) and categories of achievement (attendance, test scores, etc.) that they could become valuable as information for proving things like academic growth and, therefore, proving the value of Sahaayaka's programming. This was why Krish wanted to reengineer the social relations among mentors, parents, teachers, and students such that they would use the phone app as their primary contact with one another and place excess value on the kinds of data that they consumed through the phone app. While the app still produced a form of relationality—in the sense that it was still a form of interpersonal communication mediated through technological datafication—it was an antirelational relationality in the sense that the app produced a form of social separateness out of what were once dense, complex social relations among mentors, students, and parents.

Metadata, Metasurveillance, and the Question of Who Can Think

In some ways, Krish had learned that his power came from his ability to harness the digital "platform" to reshape how people were doing their work.[11] Platforms can seem as if they facilitate flat, open interaction and communication.

However, in actuality this metaphor hides the fact that platforms are "shaped both by the contours provided by the platform and by the accretions of users and their activity—all of which can change at the whim of the designers."[12] Because he had developed and designed the platform on which Sahaayaka's new form of monitoring would occur, Krish was able to reorganize the entire help economy and the social relations therein based on his ability to tweak the Sahaayaka digital platform. Not surprisingly, then, the greatest shift was in the mentors' activities and habits, as their labor value was now completely tethered to their ability to collect data. "The mentors have become auditors," Krish admitted, something that he was not overly concerned about because he had anticipated that this would happen.

Krish's app had been so successful that the Karnataka state government had agreed to take over the majority of Sahaayaka's project. Even as we were sitting with Rekha and Gururaj, CRPs were being trained to use the app all over Karnataka state. It was a massive undertaking, and when I went to see some of these training sessions a few weeks later, I was amazed at just how meticulously each step of the app was discussed, reasoned through, and controlled. But given how these government bureaucrats were perceived, the overzealous stipulation of rules and procedures made sense. If Rekha saw them as incompetent, Krish's feelings were not so different. Krish told me, "You know the CRPs can input data, sure, but they have almost no ability to ask questions. They constantly struggle to think." It was this inability to think that Sahaayaka wanted to mitigate through these training programs, making the rules so clear, the protocols so transparent and easily understandable, that even these incompetent bureaucrats would not forget and would not try and innovate in ways that did not reflect the algorithmic reasoning encoded in the app.

This idea of "who can think" was steeped in neocolonial ideologies, which troped on the past idea that colonizers were the only ones capable of thinking but now incorporated those brown caste elites who possessed the perceived cognitive capacity to differentiate themselves from their fellows.[13] Krish was able to hide happily behind the app, the brown savior conferred the power to remain "outside" the surveillance infrastructure, enjoying the "epistemic privilege of classifying without being classified," because of his techno-cognitive capacity to create digital infrastructures even as those perceived to have lesser cognitive capacities—students, mentors, and bureaucrats—were further incorporated into the digital surveillance apparatus precisely because they did not have the capacity to create, or "think," digitally.[14]

However, regardless of what the brown savior thought about their cognitive capacities, bureaucrats were still human and actually *could* think and make decisions. In fact, Krish had already begun to witness this issue as his app was unfurled with the CRPs and BRPs. Krish laughed with resignation as he described the way that the government officials, despite having been trained on how to follow protocols, would still try to "innovate," short-circuiting the process of data entry they'd been tasked with and creating what seemed to them better methods. Krish's caricature followed almost directly from the way that Srinivasan had also articulated the problem of the Indian worker, as I discussed in chapter 4. In Srinivasan's caricature, Indian workers' inability to follow rules correctly was the foundation for their racialized incapacity. The digital, it seemed, did little to subvert the racialized politics of the "problem with Indians." Instead, the Indian problem disrupted the anticipated future of perfect digital predictability.

Krish knew that the solution to this problem was for the work being done by the bureaucrat to eventually be totally automated.[15] In this imaginary the degraded, racialized labor of data collection might eventually be done completely by robots in a human-less "postlabor" world.[16] Unfortunately, bureaucratic labor had not yet been replaced by automatons, and therefore, rather than initiating a postlabor world, the dream of automating actually was reproducing a regime of labor value that saw the bureaucrats' labor as even less valuable because their work was imagined as potentially "automatic," even as this labor was absolutely essential for the phone app to function properly and for the brown savior to be hailed for their digital innovations.[17]

Intrigued by Krish's phone app, Rekha asked, "See, one of the things that we can't do right now is find out exactly if the CRPs are fudging data. Like, we require them to take photographs of the field sites, but we don't know if they've actually done it when they're supposed to or if they just go and take the image later or if they are just uploading the same images over and over again."

The historical innovations in camera technology have been predicated on the romantic belief that the image can render the world more objective and transparent.[18] In the particular history of neocolonial strategies of help, the camera allowed help workers to "prove" the need for intervention by capturing the abject helplessness and impoverishment of in-need populations on-screen. However, for Rekha, the image itself was no longer enough because she knew that images were far too easy to manipulate on digital platforms. Now Rekha was more interested in finding ways to prove and verify who was behind the camera and when these photographs were taken, a kind of "corruption exposing X-ray machine" that posited a priori the potential criminality of the bureaucrat.[19]

For Krish, Rekha's question was almost too simple to respond to. He grinned sheepishly and explained that he could create a new interface on the app that was dedicated to the nali kali program that would make it extremely easy to know when and how the CRPs were conducting their work. If they tried to upload images at different times, he would know. If they tried to upload the same image twice, he would know. If Rekha wanted to make sure that the expected CRP had been the one to conduct the work, he could do that for her too. All he had to do was collect metadata from the EXIF file (exchangeable image file format) embedded in every digital photograph, which told him the date and time information, all of the camera settings at the time an image was taken, and even copyright information.[20]

It was this type of metadata that folks like Rekha and Gururaj were the most intrigued by because it seemed to be objective, unsullied proof that their programs were running without a human glitch. Of course, the metadata did not stop with the EXIF files. Krish went on to explain that he was also interested in when users log in, how frequently, and from where. He showed us a screen that could use GPS coordinates to identify exactly where individuals were at any given moment and where they were when they were inputting data. He could know when people were at school sites and when they were conducting their work, no matter how much they tried to fudge when and what they were inputting.

Best of all, Krish could collect these metadata even as he collected the "standard" school-based data, unbeknownst to the app's users. "What I sometimes do," he explained as he showed us the newest version of the app, "is just look at the OS which the user is using. They don't know, but I just wrote in a bit of code that allows me to see whether they're using Android 4.0 or whatever else. It's important for me because I can then figure out what system is most prevalent and how I might eventually target that system for updates." What Krish was describing was the closest he had been able to get to a system impervious to error in a world mediated by humans, primarily because metadata allowed him to surveil the human beings involved as they went about their daily labor tasks. In one sense, they were actually surveilling themselves, freeing the app administrators from any burdensome feeling of surveilling or controlling Others.

Krish let Rekha and Gururaj know that he could code all this within two weeks, maybe three weeks max, and everyone at the table sat silently for a while, before Rekha and Gururaj asked incredulously, "Can you do this? Are you sure???" Somehow they could not believe that all of this struggle to create the perfect system of monitoring would be solved with a few lines of code.

But then, perhaps feeling that this digital surveillance infrastructure and the conversations on monitoring were going too far, Rekha suddenly changed her approach. She looked at all of us and qualified everything that had been said in the conversation, emphasizing that she imagined these tools not just in this most draconian sense of metasurveillance. Instead, she said, she imagined that the app would be "an empowerment tool, rather than a monitoring tool."

How the app would be empowering was left unsaid, and for whom this app was empowering seemed even more ambiguous when everyone involved in the actual imagining and implementation of the project was an administrator. But this rhetoric remained so that those with power could continue to believe that digital monitoring was really just a way for all those who were being monitored to help themselves even if the humanity of their labor might have been stripped from them in the process. The digital platform was, Rekha reasoned, just a neutral intermediary that would help schools function better, meaning that children would find more joy as they went through the nali kali program.

Underlying Rekha's intrigue with the phone app was also the ease and efficiency with which it could scale up. If proven effective, Krish's platform would not just be implemented in one school or for one program but could actually be used to monitor bureaucrats all over Karnataka, India, and, perhaps, the world. In the next chapter, I turn to the contradictions (and abnormalities) inherent in Sahaayaka's approach to digital scaling.

DIGITAL SCALING (OR ABNORMALITIES)

I was sitting in the Sahaayaka office one afternoon in 2018, having just come back from a long visit to three schools where Sahaayaka had begun to integrate one of its new digital projects. I was contemplating how I was going to make sense of what I had seen—a seamless web of barcoded test sheets that had been passed out to students in every school in Karnataka state and scanned using Sahaayaka's phone app, soon to be collated and analyzed in Sahaayaka-developed databases—when Ranga, Sahaayaka's technology specialist, stopped me and asked if I would take a look at something.

He scrambled around his desk to pull out a math book. He handed it to me and asked me to look it over, and so I did, flipping through the pages, trying to discern what, if anything, he was trying to show me. The data Sahaayaka had collected using their phone app had allowed them to focus on "left-behind" children, and these math books had been designed to help them "catch up" with their classmates.

I looked and I looked at the math book while Ranga stared at me with a smile. He knew that I would not be able to see anything at all, untrained as my eye was for the algorithmic innovations he had made to the math textbook. Finally, he grabbed the book from me, turning to a page about midway through that showed two clocks side by side.

"Look at these. What do you notice?" he asked, deciding to extend this game just a bit longer.

"Two clocks . . ." I trailed off, waiting for him to explain why I should be so concerned about two clocks on a page of a math book.

"They're *identical!*" he finally yelled. I kept staring, not sure why that mattered whatsoever. Ranga sighed and just shook his head. "It's just like that, everyone is so 'IT' [information technology] ignorant. They can't even see what is in front of their eyes."

This had been an all-too-familiar critique by Ranga of those working in the education NGO space. The NGO personnel did not have the digital literacy (or was it digital vision?) necessary to decipher what was happening on the back end of the tools they were using and therefore could not understand how to use them in ways that could make their jobs easier. This knowledge gave Ranga his technocratic power. He was able to see behind the surface of the screen and "lift the veil" under which the code resided.

Ranga had spent the past month designing this math book using the free, open-source document preparation program LaTex. He had noticed that the formatting of the math books used in Karnataka's schools always seemed to be slightly off: the text wasn't quite aligned; the circles weren't quite perfect circles; the margins didn't always stay the same from page to page. The reason, he realized, was that those making these math books had been using formatted text software—Microsoft Word is a classic example—which only allows users to create on a pregiven interface. This book was written on Word and the advantage of that for the tech-ignorant like me is that I can see exactly how the text will look when printed ("what you see is what you get"). But what I can't see, and what those who were creating math books in Karnataka could not see, was the code behind the text. This meant, in simple terms, that they were bound to the rules of the user interface, and if they wanted to create tables or anything more complicated, this would likely be limited by the user interface.

LaTex, in contrast, is an automated typesetting system. It has been used by academics for a long time to display complex diagrams and is based entirely on macros, input commands that specify particular outputs. It's not a new technology: it was first created in the 1970s but developed into its current form in the early 1980s. For Ranga, it was not about the program's novelty—he knew that it was almost an archaic automated language—but about what it allowed him to do. He showed me the code he had used to create these clocks, which I have re-created in a very truncated form here:

```
\documentclass{article}
\usepackage{clock}
\usepackage[clock]{ifsym}
\begin{document}
\ClockFrametrue\ClockStyle=2\clock{8}{9}
\ClockFrametrue\ClockStyle=2\clock{8}{9}
\end{document}
```

The code is quite simple, a series of commands that initiates a document and incorporates a Tex package, which, with a few more lines of code, allows one to create images of analog clocks, perfectly round, in many different forms, in whatever size, showing whatever time, with numbers in any number of styles.

Ranga started explaining just how useful this ability to code in LaTex could be:

> I'm sure you've seen it before, a math book where you have a problem, but when you go to the answer section in the back of the book, it doesn't have the right solution. That's because all of the data was inputted manually. I don't have to do that. I can just input a command such that that particular problem will automatically generate the exact solution I want in the answer section. It's so simple—but in this work I don't need it to be complex, I need it to work. When you move from manual work to automated work, the possibilities are endless.

These endless possibilities are really about precision: small errors, minor variability, almost completely eliminated. When I mentioned that this seemed to allow for a much more efficient set of processes, he cut me off immediately. "No, it's not about efficiency, it's about *productivity*. I don't want it to just be faster, but I want there to be fewer mistakes and to know what the final result will be beforehand."

In the rest of this chapter, I want to tease out a few of the neocolonial ideologies embedded in Sahaayaka's incessant drive to find more precise, productive, and predictable ways of scaling.

Testing, QR Codes, and Datafication

Ranga's math book was just the tip of the iceberg in Sahaayaka's imagining of digital scaling. Just moments before speaking to Ranga, I had visited Adavisandra school while Sahaayaka had been administering their newly minted test, a generic version of the Census State Achievement Survey (CSAS), a standardized accountability metric to assess student learning. For years, Sahaayaka had wanted to find an efficient and accurate way of gathering achievement data in every subject for every student in every school in Karnataka state, over 3.6 lakhs (360,000) of students in 56,000 schools. To do this, Sahaayaka needed to administer at least two separate tests, each of which assessed three subjects, which, in turn would produce more than 7.2 lakh (720,000) student answer sheets in total. They had struggled to figure out how to do this for quite some time because the process of administering tests was time-consuming, and they had never been able to find an efficient way to collect these data. Any method that relied too much on people administering and grading tests was prone to error, and Sahaayaka was trying to avoid this at all costs because it was imprecise and not scalable. This CSAS test and the new procedure they were deploying were the solution to their problem of testing at scale.

Three people were in the front of the classroom, one of Adavisandra's teachers, a government official, and one of Sahaayaka's mentors. The classroom was typical of rural schools—four long benches with a large chalkboard and small desk and chair at the front of the room. The classroom was as far as possible from the kind of digital worlds I had imagined when agreeing to observe the implementation of Sahaayaka's digital testing program. Where were the computers, the smart tablets, the virtual reality goggles? If I could just start to see and listen algorithmically, I kept thinking, this whole classroom should blossom with digital life, despite its appearance.

It was the government official who gave the final instructions on how to fill out the attached answer sheet, a series of boxes that students were to fill in with checkmarks on a standardized form that could be processed digitally. Filling in boxes (or bubbles) has become a generic part of the educational experience in many parts of the world, including India, as schools have increasingly relied on optical mark recognition (OMR) or image-scanning technologies. These technologies allow for tests to be standardized, scanned, and assessed in a single step, making them an easy source of instantaneous data. The seemingly innocuous process of placing a check in the appropriate box in a rural classroom will eventually render students into data and initiate a network of "micro-translations that link bodies to machines, information to databases, and statistics to policies, and . . . [foster] particular regimes of inclusion and exclusion."[1]

What Sahaayaka had done was leverage these earlier OMR technologies for the data analytics age. Krish explained that Sahayaaka had created their own kinds of answer sheets because most OMR and image-scanning technologies—like the popular testing technology Scantron—were proprietary. Instead, Sahaayaka utilized an entirely open-source optical imaging system called SDAPS (scripts for data acquisition with paper-based surveys) that would start with these checkmarks on paper, which would then be scanned into a computer and converted into PDFs. This conversion process could then be read by an open-source OMR conversion software and, eventually, end in the databases they had created to store all this student information.

The start was again LaTex, which allowed Ranga to create the answer sheets that students were filling out in Adavisandra. The innovation, as Ranga would explain, was that these answer sheets could be completed without having to fill in the entire box—no worries about filling inside or outside the lines of the box—and they could be filled using either pencil or pen, which made the process less prone to errors when scanning and digitizing later.

But the second, and perhaps more important, innovation was how Sahaayaka dealt with tracking each student. On the right side of the page was a small QR code, a kind of matrix bar code, mostly unnoticed by anyone in the classroom. In this barcode all of the vital information about this test was stored, the key to Sahaayaka's efforts to scale. When the barcodes were scanned, the student would, eventually, be translated into a barcode, an obligatory "passage point" that would abstract from the complexity of their lived experience and then result in new forms of encounter and intervention.[2]

The barcode, like LaTex and OMR, is an old technology being reenergized by Sahaayaka in the digital age. We witness its current use all the time, in, for example, the now-ubiquitous use of barcodes to view menus on smartphones at many restaurants to prevent touch in the age of pandemics. We also experience the barcode in how we send, track, and receive packages. We can track our packages online at any time because all mail carriers, whether the postal service or private services like FedEx, UPS, and DHL, use barcodes encoded with two vital pieces of information—primarily the mailing address and a tracking number that allows us to follow the package until it arrives. In its version of the barcode, Sahaayaka has encoded all the information about the school, the subject, and each student's grade. Once Sahaayaka processed the tests and stored the information in their database, each student would be forever linked to this barcode. "Students as barcodes" evokes the same kind of tracking process used for the UPS package, initiated at the point of entry into school testing and ending when they reach the databases created to store all their information.

Krish wanted each student's barcode to be mapped to their Aadhaar ID, a twelve-digit unique identity number that has become a near requirement for all residents of India.[3] The Aadhaar project is considered the largest biometric ID system in the world and has already brought 1.2 billion Indian enrollees into its fold. Perhaps not surprisingly, the primary spearheader of the project was Nandan Nilekani, one of the most powerful of the digital brown saviors. Nilekani, best known as the billionaire CEO of Wipro, had imagined a technocratic solution for one of India's biggest problems, the lack of identification of citizens, which he believed prevented the poor and the marginal from joining India's economic growth and prosperity. Regarding Nilekani's framing, Ursula Rao and Vijayanka Nair write:

> Like many others, the authors pose the lack of identification as a root problem that hampers development, echoing a global trend emphasising the need for every human being to possess a recognised identity. According to UNESCO's "Sustainable Development Goals 16.9," access to "legal identity, including birth registration" is an important requirement to build "peaceful and inclusive societies . . . provide access to justice for all and build effective, accountable and inclusive institutions at all levels." In the Indian case . . . Aadhaar would allow better access to the human right of identity and bring "the benefits of technology to India's social protection system."[4]

Here the problem of underdevelopment, social welfare, and human rights is a problem of lack of national identification, and the technological fix is to identify every single individual and therefore produce an organized, efficient system at scale by which all Indians can be connected to the public and private institutions that can confer on them social goods and integrate them into the economy. In this sense, Aadhar's identification system is a gateway platform that will connect individuals to other platforms and services they need.[5] This was, in part, why Krish imagined that Sahaayaka's new student database would and should be tethered to Aadhar. He believed that the individual ID would allow him to target each student exactly for specific educational help.

At the same time, those students who were transformed into data through the barcode (or by being given a biometric ID) were now slotted into categories determined by those with the power to create these categories, in an almost classical form of governmentality and population management. In Sahaayaka's case, Krish was using the CSAS test to slot each student into predetermined stereotypes regarding "need" based on the ability to do well (or not) on subject tests. I use the word *stereotype* purposely here to evoke the way that this digital categorizing actually mimics the usage of the term stereotype to describe older forms of mechanical reproduction.[6] In printing, the stereotype was a solid plate of metal that allowed for the consistent reproduction of typeface and images, not unlike how Ranga described his use of LaTex earlier. Scaling, by definition, then, requires the stereotype for (re)production. In this case, however, the process of moving from barcode into database also transmuted the individual student into a stereotype based on their test scores. This process of stereotyping dehistoricized students, predetermining the categories that mattered while occluding those that were too messy for consideration. For example, historically situated social stratifications such as caste, class, and linguistic background, which may have been part of each student's "inherited possibility," were rendered invisible in the datafication of the student.[7] In this way, the datafication of the student produced stereotypes that may actually have been linked to other relevant categories (or might actually reflect older stereotypes) but that were not recognized as part of the considerations for the future mobility of the child. In some sense, this was precisely what the digital savior sought: a technocratic solution that erased the complexity of the past and the social stratifications that produced current inequities, while being able to determine and anticipate the categories through which to save those in need in the future.

The Abnormalities of the Start-Up State

It took Sahaayaka about a month and a half to get all of the data into their system, methodically shipping packages of tests to each school, making sure all the tests were administered, and, finally, scanning all of the tests into their centralized databases. Once this was done, they were able to get all of the baseline data on student achievement, which they could then share with the government, a huge coup for a bureaucracy that had not, until that point, had a way of assessing student data over time. As Krish told me, "This sort of information was not too useful for us, but for the state government, getting such an efficient testing and database system is hugely valuable. That's why they will pick up my call anytime."

By way of proof, Krish took me on a visit to meet the state project director of Sarva Shiksha Abhiyan in Bangalore later in 2018. It was a quiet office, with a few people sitting in a group in a small room. We waited there for a while until an official came in and took us to his office. Krish kindly made small talk with him as the official was visibly excited about the opportunity to chat. He told us that he was very proud of his daughter because she had been admitted to engineering school in the United States in a school called California Polytechnic State University. I made a note in my head that the global Indian IT class now had a new member. Finally, the state project director greeted us and apologized for being late. "You'll have lunch?" he asked and then went on to praise Krish, Sahaayaka, and their programming during the course of our meal together.

"You see," he explained, "we know that we have to make many changes here. But we think that people like him [pointing to Krish] can do it. We have struggled to understand the needs of children in this country. Testing needs to be done better. Right now, it is really terrible. But we are starting over."

The state project director imagined a state apparatus that could be precise and scalable, a rupture from India's inefficient postcolonial past, which had been caricatured as corrupt, bogged down by protocols and a never-ending stream of paperwork. This shift marked a move to what Nair calls the emerging "start-up state" in which the state is an "entity born anew."[8] Here, just as the databases produced by the digital savior are perceived to break students from their pasts, so, too, will the government suddenly be washed clean of its previous inadequacies as it imagines a completely new approach predicated on the potentials of "cybertime."[9] Critically, however, the state can succeed in its new vision only if it brings in those digital saviors who already understand this form of start-up culture and can ably help retrain the government bureaucrat for this future. This was why, in order to start over, the Karnataka state government had announced that Sahaayaka would become "the IT backbone" for education, incorporating all of their scalable testing mechanisms into the process of state governance.

As Krish got further into his partnership with Karnataka state, however, he recognized quite soon that the government's inefficient "past" had not receded into the background quietly and that it would not be easy to bring it into this newly imagined "start-up" culture. Because he had agreed to partner with the state government, he was forced to include government officials in the administering of tests. It was one of these test-administering sessions that I had witnessed in Adavisandra. But government officials were in the middle of other parts of the process as well: Sahaayaka had to send hundreds of packets of tests to each local government official, labeled with the correct schools, grades, and students, with the expectation they would then administer them, repackage them, and send them back to Sahaayaka.

Krish laughed as he told me that the government officials, despite having been trained on how to follow protocols, did not really know what the

QR codes' purpose was and that therefore they would sometimes just get rid of the codes when they were administering the tests, scratching them out or covering them up, which meant that tests could not be processed when they reached Sahaayaka's main office. More often, they would need extra tests for "ghost students" who were in school but who had not been accounted for, and they would just scratch out a name on a test and make copies of it, then have a student write their own name on it. This meant that when it came time to process these tests using the QR code, there could be hundreds of the "same" student since they all had the same student and school information encoded in the barcode. Krish joked that there were somehow fifty Patils and seventy-two Supriyas who came back from certain schools. There ended up being some six thousand of these "ghost students" who had taken tests but did not actually have individualized IDs—"abnormalities," as Krish called them.

Anthropologists have had a unique interest in the abnormal as a way to analyze the social and cultural imaginaries that produce normativity and those who fall into the categories of the strange, unfamiliar, and occult.[10] In this case, Krish was explicitly producing an imaginary in which two different ideas of reproduction are placed on opposite sides of the normal/abnormal divide: it was abnormal to have seventy-two Supriyas in a database, but it was not abnormal to have ten thousand students stereotyped to be in need of more math worksheets. Presumably, abnormality was linked to the types of information that confounded the attempt at prediction, which was also conceived as a de facto moral good because normative predictive understandings would, supposedly, allow for a solution to the problem of educational inequality.

But for Krish, even more than the abnormalities produced by these government bureaucrats, it was the inadequacies of government databases that were deleterious to the implementation of his program. He explained that he had encountered major delays when he wanted to use government databases for the storage of test data:

> So, we wanted to store all of this information on the government servers, but there was some issues of privacy. Just right before we were going to launch, the Chief Minister had a data hack, and there was a huge controversy. So right now all the information is stored on Amazon Web Services. Eventually what we want to do is create randomized numbers that will only make sense when mapped on the back end—meaning on the FTP server.

If the Indian bureaucracy hoped to become a new "start-up state," it still had a long way to go: shoddy servers and privacy breaches would not do for the productive, stable data storage and analysis necessary for the future. But then, while Krish was speaking, I paused just to clarify, "Did you just say Amazon Web Services"?

As a solution to the inadequacies of the government stood the global tech giant, invisible, stable, secure, and ably facilitating the needs of its digital clients, including the digital brown savior. We often associate Amazon with tangible products—bottles, computer parts, or really anything else we want to buy. But Amazon Web Services is what gives Amazon its true power by providing businesses the server space, security, and all of the infrastructure necessary to operate on the internet. It dominates the cloud computing industry and shapes the entire digital platform economy. In 2017 it held over 50 percent of the global market share, providing server space to companies like Netflix, Airbnb, Adobe, and Spotify, just to name a few. But what struck me when hearing Krish was how he was building his own digital platform with Amazon Web Services functioning as its "backbone." In some sense, Sahaayaka's version of the help economy reproduced technocapitalist domination on a global scale, reorganizing how the help economy must function in the process. While Krish was concerned about ghost students and open-source software, he seemed completely unconcerned about the ghost of global cloud computing that underlay the entire process and perhaps subverted the moral efficacy of doing "help work" under the premise of digitally scaling. In 2018 global data centers likely consumed around 205 terawatt-hours (TWh), or 1 percent of global electricity use, a significant energy footprint in its own right.[11] At the same time, by placing student data onto Amazon servers, Krish was inadvertently incorporating them into a global system that could, potentially, allow other private actors to target these students in the future for either consumption or worse.

What digital scaling seemed to make clear, at least to me, was that the work of helping Others has slowly but surely moving farther into the clouds, finding new ways to abstract from the complex realities of those who continue to struggle in communities in India and elsewhere in the world. In fact, Krish's approach to data seemed to be dovetailing with the ongoing project of "data colonialism."[12] Here I am drawing from the work of Jenny Reardon and Kim TallBear, who write specifically about the way that Indigenous people's DNA in North America is appropriated under the guise that it will both better the lives of those who provided these data *and* benefit other people as well. As they argue, "Such claims are not made on the ground that European culture and practices are superior but on the grounds of justice."[13] Digital datafication is seen as a novel form of "doing good" because it regards the transparent extraction of data as a requirement for innovation and new discoveries despite the fact that these processes seem to take for granted the same slots, divisions, and directionalities of extraction as earlier colonial practices that were also justified as part of economies of salvation.

In this case, converting and privatizing the data appropriated from student work is understood as the best and most effective means for Sahaayaka and the state together to better the lives of children who otherwise would be left behind. However, the very process of datafication actually creates a situation in which the students who are generating so much data have almost no rights or control over their data. In fact, the only people who benefit from this data collection are those given the powerful role to implement change and intervene. What is "normalized," then, is a global-digital neocolonial order that requires student data for the accumulation of ever more power to save.

In the final chapter of this text, I analyze one interface of Sahaayaka's phone app dedicated to collecting data on the production of clean schools and clean students. In this last analytic salvo, I showcase how this form of data collection is predicated on and reproduces colonial-caste relationships.

DIGITAL DUSTBINS

It's June 2014, and I'm ambivalently scouring my Facebook page when I see a new post by Krish reflecting on Prime Minister Narendra Modi's Swachh Bharat, or Clean India, campaign, a campaign that Modi claimed would bring a complete and radical change to Indian sanitation.[1]

The problem of India's uncleanliness continues to be a persistent discourse that shapes its developmentalist visions. As Anand Teltumbde writes, "There is little doubt that India stands as a uniquely unclean country."[2] According to the World Health Organization, it is in the top ten most polluted countries in the world and includes eleven of the top twelve most polluted cities.[3]

This is the problem Modi sought to solve with his Swachh Bharat campaign. Riffing on the Quit India Movement, the iconic civil disobedience movement Mohandas Gandhi launched in August 1942 against the British colonial government, Modi said, "Bapu gave us the message 'Quit India. Clean India', but his 'Clean India' dream is still unfulfilled. . . . I am confident that Clean India will give us as much joy as Quit India."[4]

But Krish was deeply critical of Swachh Bharat back in 2014, especially in how Modi was going about it, using his own learnings with Sahaayaka to explain why. He posted on Facebook:

> Seeing pictures of so many celebrities and politicians including our PM [prime minister] cleaning streets with a broom takes me back to 2007. During my first week in Sahaayaka when we went to a school . . . the teacher was proud to show that the kids all come early and clean up the classrooms. In one room where they were cleaning it was mostly bits of paper! Our founder asked a very simple question: why is there so much garbage in the first place? Why can't you [the teacher] keep a waste basket in the corner! I wish Modi had asked such a simple question and got the entire country thinking! Instead of the broom cleaning video I wish he had eaten a chocolate, kept the wrapper in his pocket and then later on thrown it in a garbage can when he came across one. I wish he talked about buying products with minimal packaging, composting, recycling, etc . . . etc.

For Krish, Modi's strategy is merely one of branding and optics, a publicity stunt rather than a project with a vision to enact substantive change. In particular, Krish was disturbed by Modi's strategic alliance with prominent Indian celebrities, including Aamir Khan, Priyanka Chopra, Salman Khan, and Anil Ambani, among others.[5] These celebrities were filmed sweeping the streets with Modi to make the act of sweeping roads into something glamourous and worthy of commitment.

By contrast, Krish had a different pedagogical vision, one that started with "asking simple questions" that could habituate people into a new culture of cleanliness: throwing a wrapper into a dustbin, learning about composting and other environmental sustainability practices, and so on. Over the next three years, Krish began to seek his own solution to the problem of uncleanliness, eventually creating a monitoring interface of the Sahaayaka app dedicated to school cleanliness, called Swachh Shale (Clean School), shown in figure 17.1. On its surface, it seemed uncontroversially innovative and promoted a social good—helping schools to promote cleanliness by diligently documenting how they performed on each of four metrics. In some ways, the app functioned like a wastebasket, a digital dustbin that would allow everyone in a school to dump

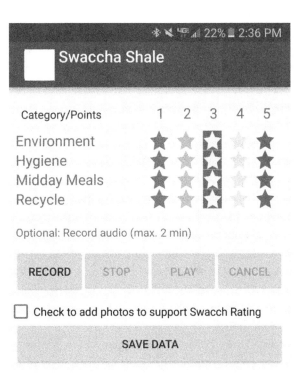

FIGURE 17.1. One user interface of the Sahaayaka phone app prototype.
(Photo by Arjun Shankar)

data about school cleanliness into it. The data would then get appropriately organized and categorized (read: cleaned) and, in turn, would allow them to ask simple questions at scale and anticipate how to change the behaviors of students and teachers. This was Krish's "simple" technological solution to the problem of uncleanliness.

Digital technologies, like Krish's app, can delude the uninitiated with their perceived novelty. The fetishizing of the digital surface erases, whether purposely or not, that which came before it, enticing with the idea that the app might actually be a break from the past and initiate a future not tethered to the inequities of this past. Yet, as Ruha Benjamin writes, "Technical fixes too often reinforce and even deepen the status quo. . . . [They] reflect and reproduce existing inequities but . . . are promoted and perceived as more objective or progressive than the discriminatory systems of a previous era."[6] The Swacch Shale interface created by Sahaayaka was no different: even as Krish sought to create an app that would replace the supposedly archaic and facile solutions to uncleanliness promoted by Modi, excavating the ideologies embedded in the app reveals a folding of the past into the present, perhaps reproducing hierarchy in ways that the brown savior neither intended or realized. In this case, as I explain, the Swacch Shale app not only hid but actually reinforced historically situated colonial, racial, casteist, and neoliberal structurings of the help economy.

The Feeling of Cleanliness and the Measurement of Colonial Reproduction

When I met Krish in 2018, he explained that he was keen to develop the new Swachh app because school cleanliness and student cleanliness were two of the most important criteria by which one could know whether a school would be successful or not. He was always grappling with a feeling he would get when he went into different schools on visits: "I just know a good school when I see the surroundings. If it's clean, then it's definite that the students will be doing well academically. It means they have care, and it means they have a sense of ownership of their school."

Krish's "feeling" linked discourses of hygiene and cleanliness with educational success or failure—imagined here as passing tests and moving to the next standard successfully. Krish was also making a series of assumptions about value and cleanliness as a savarna, middle-class, cosmopolitan global Indian, using his own cultural sensibilities to determine a universal idea regarding what cleanliness should look like and why it was important. A "sense of ownership" took this idea a step further, mapping private-property ideologies onto cleanliness such that a clean student not only was academically successful but also was being inculcated with the appropriate values that would potentially bring them into the propertied classes.

Part of Krish's frustration was that he had not been able to back up this feeling with data, and the app was Krish's solution to this problem of measurement. The interface for the phone app allowed Sahaayaka mentors to rate schools on four cleanliness criteria on a scale of 1–5 stars: (1) environment, (2) hygiene, (3) midday meals, and (4) recycling. In Sahaayaka's conceptualization, each of these criteria was seen as a proxy for cleanliness. As part of these inputs, mentors were able to include audio recordings or photographs taken at school sites. While, as I have mentioned, visual and aural data were viewed as more distracting than useful, these bits of data still relied on a priori assumptions that cleanliness was visually objective and universal. That is to say, it was assumed that the mentors' assessment of school cleanliness would match Krish's (or anyone else's) imagination of how cleanliness looked and felt.

Yet the criteria were quite different in type. One criterion, midday meals, fit neatly within national and state-level policy that all government schools should provide a midday meal to students.[7] Recycling, in contrast, mimicked Krish's comments "about buying products with minimal packaging, composting, recycling." In making this wish an explicit part of Sahaayaka's phone app, Krish was channeling a global liberal consciousness that viewed the problem of cleanliness as related to the contemporary push to green the environment through sustainable change.

In practice, the Swacch app also reproduced the category of the impoverished as those responsible for the lack of environmentally sustainable practices and as the core group that needed to be socially reengineered. As D. A. Ghertner has argued, the poor, lacking in social infrastructures (housing, sanitation, and so on), are the visible and obvious markers of uncleanliness.[8] Even if their actual energy consumption in India is less than 1 percent of total energy consumption, they are considered a "nuisance," aesthetically displeasing to the middle-class eye because they look "unclean" and practice such things as open defecation.[9] If the poor would just learn to be clean, the logic goes, then India would be clean. It is not surprising, then, that a phone app on cleanliness was targeted at relatively poor rural children.

Photographing students during the act of cleaning inculcated the students in a bootstrap performativity that would define their successes based on their ability to comport themselves in these universally imagined, digitally visualized "clean ways." Most of the photographs I looked through showed students in movement: planting trees, sweeping floors, and cleaning toilets. But all of these assessments of cleanliness were also part and parcel of a whole set of assumptions about students based on their caste, class, and gendered positions, which greatly influenced how they could be seen as clean and how they might participate in the act of cleaning. First, take a look at the photograph in figure 17.2, taken by a mentor to demonstrate the process of "cleanliness" in schools. It shows girls (redacted here) at the front of their school, hard at work sweeping the floors. While Modi's version of sweeping was about the celebrity, this version looks like girls learning to do gendered labor, sweeping the floors just as they might be expected to do in the traditional patriarchal home. In this sense, Sahaayaka's cleanliness criteria were not merely "descriptive" but produced gendered ideologies regarding the appropriately clean girl and boy.

The criteria regarding hygiene surveilled and regulated the students' bodies — do they come to school well dressed; do they appear to have dirt on their feet, hands, or face; and so on. Students ought to come to school dressed appropriately, or else their value to the school community was lower. In the app's

FIGURE 17.2. Redacted image of girls sweeping the floor at their school.
(Photo by Arjun Shankar)

assessment, then, a school's environment and the student's body were entangled, assuming that a student's personal hygiene was a reflection of school cleanliness and, further, the school's success or failure.

The appropriately clean student was also a student who was easily commodifiable, and images like the preceding could be shared with those at NGO headquarters, funders living elsewhere in India or in the United States, or government officials interested in the program. Indeed, the Swacch app was also a response to a highly visible stream of global funding and philanthropic giving through corporate social responsibility projects. The Gates Foundation, for example, strongly endorsed the Swachh Bharat project and had been a vocal advocate for safe sanitation projects, especially the building of toilets. Their website noted, "Investing in better sanitation can yield significant economic and social benefits, by reducing the incidence of infectious diseases and preventing disability and early death. Better sanitation can also reduce health care costs, increase productivity, and lead to better educational outcomes."[10] Here the Gates Foundation's rationale for cleanliness resembled Krish's, linking sanitation concerns not just with health outcomes but with productivity and economic mobility.

The fundability of Swachh programs in India is an inheritance of its colonial past and builds on the history of racialized colonial and postcolonial concerns about hygiene, dirt, and filth in India beginning in the early 1800s.[11] Take, for example, Katherine Mayo's (1927) Indophobic and racist *Mother India*, a text I have mentioned before. Central to Mayo's critiques were the filthiness of Indians and Indian society: "How perfectly the habits of the Indian peoples favor the spread of the disease. . . . [D]irt, bad sanitation, confinement, lack of air and exercise, make a perfect breeding-place for the White Death. Between nine hundred thousand and one million persons, it is estimated, die annually of tuberculosis in India."[12] This racist critique was also a critique of the institutions of education in India and the Indians who attended these institutions of higher education:

> In 1923–4 thirteen universities of British India put forth a total of 11,222 graduates. Of these, 7,822 took their degrees in arts and sciences, 2,046 in law, 446 in medicine, 140 in engineering, 546 in education, 136 in commerce, and 86 in agriculture. . . . The high figures consistently stand opposite the arts and law courses, while such vital subjects as agriculture, hygiene and sanitation, surgery, obstetrics, veterinary science and commerce, under whatever aegis offered, still attract few disciples.[13]

In Mayo's reasoning, a lack of hygiene and sanitation was related almost directly to a lack of scientific education among Indians. At the same time, such ideas regarding hygiene and sanitation were associated with particular affective regimes—disgust, fear, anxiety—which were linked to the habits of the colonial subject.[14] Taken with this historical view in mind, cleanliness becomes a sign of order and progress—a measure of civilizationalism in India.

This is why being clean mattered so deeply for nation builders in postcolonial contexts. Gandhi, for example, saw "filth" in relation to his own encounters with the West:

> I shall have to defend myself on one point, namely, sanitary conveniences. I learnt 35 years ago that a lavatory must be as clean as a drawing-room. I learnt this in the West. I believe that many rules about cleanliness in lavatories are observed more scrupulously in the West than in the East. The cause of many of our diseases is the condition of our lavatories and our bad habit of disposing of excreta anywhere and everywhere. I, therefore, believe in the absolute necessity of a clean place for answering the call of nature and clean articles for use at the time.[15]

What Gandhi's remarks reveal are the kinds of inadequacies that the brown postcolonial subject felt after years of colonization, the feeling that the West was a place of cleanliness and sanitation while the East was a place of uncleanliness.

Caste Society and the Digital Politics of Purity and Pollution

What is veiled, yet obvious, in Gandhi's reference to the disposing of excreta is the issue of caste and sanitation. Those who "learned" about the importance of sanitation were the very same savarna classes who received British educations in higher numbers and took on technical roles in the British colonial apparatus. In this sense, the brown savior as savarna elite is the inheritor of this civilizational notion of cleanliness and the technocratic ideologies for solving the problem of cleanliness. At the same time, the technocratic disposition toward sanitation, latrines, and hygiene also occluded the links to India's caste society. As Sudipta Kaviraj writes, brahminical notions of purity created a conceptual boundary between the private and public spheres that rendered the public a space of impurity, neglect, garbage, and untouchability.[16] In this context, the cleaning of excreta is an especially fraught sign of impurity within this cultural politics of caste. Even into the present, the cleaning of toilets and the disposing of waste have largely been left to manual scavengers from a subcaste of Dalits, who continue to be forced into these jobs despite the fact that this has been ruled illegal.[17] Because the cleaning of excreta has been seen as a sign of caste impurity and left to manual scavengers, the cleaning of filth is a moral question, based as much in the history of caste in India as it is in economic considerations regarding India's future.

Here Gandhi is again instructive. Even as he spoke of his learning regarding the use of latrines, he also recognized that in India the cleaning of shit was left to the Bhangi, a caste associated with manual scavenging. He infamously wrote in his publication the *Harijan*, "A bhangi does for the society what a mother does for her baby. A mother washes her baby of the dirt and ensures his health. Even so the bhangi safeguards the health of the entire community by maintaining sanitation of it."[18] Rather than condemning and seeking to eradicate a dehumanizing casteist practice, Gandhi sought to change how the practice was valued and, therefore, how the people who did this work might be valued. "To clothe the Bhangi with the dignity and respect due to him," Gandhi goes on to say, "is the especial task and privilege of the educated class. Some members of the class would first themselves master the science of sanitation to educate Bhangis around them in the same."[19] Here Gandhi is placing the responsibility to change the social value of the practice of cleaning excreta on "educated" castes and classes, who are expected to learn and then teach those from a caste community whose job it has been for hundreds of years. In so doing, he idealizes the benevolence and capacity of the caste elite and treats the Bhangi community with paternalistic and patronizing hubris, while sidestepping entirely the need to protect manual scavengers through law. When Modi linked Swachh to Gandhi, this was the ethos to which he was linking the project.

Sahaayaka's brown saviors also drew from this logic in how they undertook their work in the help economy. From the early days of their intervention, they had struggled to deal with the issue of school cleanliness in relation to caste. Srinivasan was especially concerned with the problem of why schools remained in shabby condition and had tried to figure out how to change it. For him, toilets were the most direct example of this issue. He would angrily explain how every single toilet in rural schools either was locked up or remained extremely dirty. We would walk together through a school, and he would point to such toilets and remark, "You know why these toilets are so dirty. Because none of these people will clean them themselves." On one occasion, while visiting a school in rural Karnataka, he pulled aside the headmaster and began lambasting him about the toilets. When he did, the headmaster meekly remarked that there was no one in the entire village who would do this work because none of them wanted to defile their caste position.

The solution that emerged in Sahaayaka's phone app actually individualized caste responsibility, seeking to change the "value" of such practices in the Gandhian sense rather than producing a systemic critique of the caste system itself. Take, for example, the criterion about the "environment," which was meant to assess the space of the school: is there garbage on the ground, are the classrooms kept organized, and so on. This system of monitoring was meant to produce a new way of valuing the space of the school. But this spatial reengineering, perhaps not surprisingly, focused extensively and continuously on toilets. Of the hundreds of photographs I collected from Sahaayaka's database, more than a quarter were photographs of toilets: was the toilet locked or unlocked, was the toilet functional, clean, or unclean. These photographs revealed the mentors' way of assessing "environmental" cleanliness.

Take a look at the photograph in figure 17.3, taken by a mentor using the app to demonstrate the process of "cleanliness" in schools. It shows a boy (redacted here) standing in front of a toilet that he has recently cleaned. The doors are open, and though we cannot see clearly inside, the primary point is that students should be proud of their school toilets and should take on the individual responsibility, as this boy has, to learn to clean them.

FIGURE 17.3. Redacted image of boy standing in front of toilet.
(Photo by Arjun Shankar)

Notice the location of the toilet in the photograph: a separate building spatially disconnected from the school itself, which is not visible within the frame. This separation is not accidental but based on the confluence of caste histories, which enforced extreme segregation of latrines from homes, and the reproduction of such ideologies in the built infrastructure of colonial homes by the colonizers, who learned these architectural features from savarna architects in India.[20] These features of spatial segregation have continued into the present, also reinforcing the separation of the person who is cleaning the toilet from the rest. Therefore, in the picture shown here, it matters quite a bit that both the toilet is separate and the person cleaning the toilet is separated, which is why, unlike in other photographs of "cleanliness" taken by the mentors—showing the sweeping of floors or planting of trees—this child is not seen with anyone else. In other words, what is documented as cleanliness here is a reproduction of the cultural politics of spatialized caste-colonial relations into the present. But in assessing the cleanliness of toilets, Sahaayaka was *also* unwittingly assessing just how casteist a school was without actually being explicit and intentional about it. The cleaner the toilet, the more likely it was that someone within the school community who was *not* from a manual scavenging caste was willing to clean it.

The focus on toilets has even more sinister consequences: in September 2019 two Dalit boys were beaten to death by savarna Hindu supremacists after they had supposedly defecated in public. In the aftermath, more attention was paid to the need for more toilets than to the need to eradicate the caste-based violence that continues to exist in India, allowing a supremacist system to hide in plain sight under the guise of public infrastructure. For example, references to the Gates Foundation emerged yet again in the reporting; during the same week as the atrocity, the foundation praised Swachh Bharat as "a model for other countries around the world that urgently need to improve access to sanitation for the world's poorest."[21] Here an attention to toilets as the technocratic solution to the universal and urgent problem of poverty abstracts from India's specific issue of uncleanliness as it is directly linked to its caste supremacist society.

As such, when we see the discourse on Swachh rendered in this phone app, what should ring in our ears is not the unmediated, unquestioned good of cleaning India but instead the colonial racial anxieties and casteist supremacies, which, while safely hidden from view, are reproduced in the brown savior's digital creations and technocratic ambitions to solve the problem of India's unhygienic lifestyles and "filthy" public spaces. The digital infrastructure, in its hailing of individual student responsibility for cleanliness, prevents the country from "thinking," to use Krish's phrase, about "the fact that India cannot be swachh without the system of castes being completely annihilated."[22]

Part IV Is Done: In Sum and What's to Come

The chapters in part IV have focused on the way that digital technologies mediate brown saviorist interventions. Specifically, these chapters have drawn from my observations of Sahaayaka's new digital integration strategy to show how the fetishizing of technology as an assumed social good and anticipated harbinger of progressive social changes allows Sahaayaka's leadership to accrue excess value in India. Here the technophilic impulse intersects with a need to produce networks of kin- and blood-based forms of digital saviorism. For example, in chapter 13, I showed how Krish's phone app extracted funds by playing on the affective relations among savarna Hindu Indians.

The ensuing chapters revealed the way that Sahaayaka thinks of digital technologies as precise and effective technocratic tools to scale, show impact, and hold workers accountable to their expected roles in the organizational and state labor hierarchies. In this sense, I have tried to highlight the way that technological integration requires a reinscription of graded labor value, which inevitably places the brown savior in the position of control, surveillance, and disciplining while further devaluing the everyday work conducted by mentors and even government officials. These assumptions regarding labor were predicated on a universalizing, ahistorical view of technology that veiled the way that technologies like Sahaayaka's phone app assumed categories that further entrenched the very divisions on which racial and caste capitalism function.

It's worth a reminder that these types of technological innovations and integrations in the nonprofit sector are assumed to be ideal and important forms of care. But when we excavate under the surface of the screen, what becomes clear is that this kind of datafied help work can be far more fraught than meets the eye. Even as technologically mediated forms of help are seen as the only way to get the impoverished the help they need, in actuality, tech solutions are a process of neocolonial predation that relies on massive quantification, abstraction, and the ongoing categorization and movement of people's data into the cloud. Those who stand to benefit from this kind of datafication are those we might expect: NGO leaders, state bureaucracies, and the big tech companies that need to make sure that everyone's data continues to be under their control. Here it becomes more and more evident that the nonprofit-industrial complex is tethered to the big tech *and* national security apparatuses that shape current imperial relations.

I conclude by returning to a consideration of nervousness as a multiscalar analytic by which to understand the project of brown saviorism I have excavated thus far in this text.

Conclusion: Against Saviorism

I have framed this entire text as a *nervous ethnography*, and, therefore, it is inevitable that the ending, too, would be a cause for nerves. Endings make me nervous because I cannot help but feel a kind of finality to this whole project even though people tell me to remember that "this is a living object" and that "every story begets its sequel."[1] They say I should free myself of the dread of letting this document go. But it's not that easy for me. I'm not that enlightened.

Endings make me nervous because I know that there is some expectation that I will end with a way forward and an answer to some version of the question of "Well, what, then, should we do?": *What should we do, for example, if the help economies are so profoundly colonial?*

I wish I knew. The fact that I don't know frustrates the would-be savior in me. That person wants to be able to say with moral certitude that there is a "right" way forward. That person even wants to provide a five-part program that might save us partially because he knows that deep down inside it will give him pleasure and will massage his masculine ego.

In all honesty, my only sincere and incomplete answer to the question "What should we do?" stems from my attention to nervousness. In the rest of this conclusion, I want to undertake a very provisional analysis of nervousness that moves beyond individual affect to recognize the multiscalar political economies within which nervousness functions. The contradictory, tense, historically induced vibratory states that link political and economic institutions locally, nationally, and globally create the nervous conditions that those who seek change must nervously navigate. Let me turn now to some of these scales of nervousness to think one last time about my fieldwork in India.

India, the so-called largest democracy in the world, is, without question, falling toward authoritarianism. The country is currently ranked 142 out of 180 countries in the Press Freedom Index, and the need to silence dissent has gotten more overt. In Karnataka, where much of this ethnography took place, the rise of Hindu supremacists was announced most viciously with the assassination of the activist journalist Gauri Lankesh in 2017.[2] Lankesh, who had started her own periodical, the *Gauri Lankesh Patrike*, was an outspoken critic of Hindutva and also sought grounds for solidarity across leftists, Muslims, Dalits, women, and the Adivasi communities of India. Perhaps most important, Lankesh wrote *in Kannada*, which allowed her to forge local solidarities in a way that was especially threatening to supremacists, who, tacitly backed by the Indian state, showed that they would do whatever was in their power to keep these groups divided and under their control.

The stories somehow only get worse as horrific anti-Muslim racism continues to take over the country. For example, in 2022 the Karnataka state court ruled that it was legal for a government school to bar Muslim girls wearing hijabs from entering classrooms because the hijab was not "essential" to Islam. The ruling furthers India's move toward an apartheid state that legally sanctions the exclusion of the nearly 200 million Muslims in the country. At the same time, on New Year's Day of 2022, hundreds of Muslim women in India, including journalists, social workers, and other prominent personalities, found their images along with derogatory slander about them on an app called Bulli Bai. The app offered an online "auction" of Muslim women, meant to humiliate and dehumanize them.[3] Such apps and the people who create them are part of the extreme alt-right that draws straight from the scientific racist past. Shweta Singh, one of the alleged perpetrators in the incident, infamously posted a Hindutva propaganda poster that mimicked a Nazi propaganda poster exhorting "Aryans" to have more children. These supremacist elements characterize savarna Hindus as those with the purest of blood, who must regain their strength by cleansing India of all "backward" castes, Muslims, and Christians, who are "browning" and therefore impurifying the blood of the body politic.

One way of understanding these violent proliferations is to see them as phenomena tethered to the Indian state's neocolonial nervous condition. In the preface of this text, I evoked Nancy Rose Hunt's idea of the "nervous state" and Jean-Paul Sartre's characterization of the native as living in a "nervous condition" to acknowledge and draw out the way that colonized subjects and systems live in a kind of contradiction that emerges from the specificity of colonial/precolonial subjugations as they enter into the present.[4] In India specifically, even as the "liberal democratic nation-state" was conjured (by the colonizers and the colonized elite) as the antithesis to the past—the obliteration of communal forms of living and the inception of a constitutional order of things—it has primarily functioned as the racialized home of perceived primordial blood-kin-native peoples that is always already associated exclusively with the Hindu religion and dominant-caste groups. The contradictions therein create a constant sense of nervousness, instability, and potential for extreme forms of violence, including the kinds of ethnic-cleansing projects we are seeing today.[5]

But even as India continues toward an overt fascist future, we also know, as Toni Morrison so perfectly captured, that "before there is a final solution, there must be a first solution, a second one, even a third."[6] This book has been about these earlier stages that also warrant nervous excavation. Indeed, when we are closer to the action, living everyday lives, things can feel different, less about extreme violence and more about our everyday complicities, our naive desire to be on the right side of history and find salvation (for ourselves and Others) while drawing from and engaging in practices that actually only reinscribe the same categories and ideologies on which fascism builds. When we observe the political economy of nervousness in these everyday workings of liberal subjects and liberal institutions, we might notice all those nervous conditions that arise precisely because of the contradictions and collusions that come with an inability to move beyond neocolonial institutional, material, and ideological configurations.

These complicities take so many forms and produce so much jittery, nervous energy. They take the form of Sarathi's racist anti-Muslim joke told when he went on a school visit to an Urdu-medium school in Karnataka; or the form of Ranga's flippant and irritated comment regarding the excess attention to caste in India while sitting at a bar in Bangalore that catered to the global Indian elite; or the form of Srinivasan's fatally pragmatic decision to work with business schools in the United States despite his knowledge that they do not value the work he does; or the form of Vishnu's resigned decision to follow his accumulationist impulses after he realized that Sahaayaka's work is not quite what it seemed; or the form of Ragu trying not to give a damn while also reinscribing the racial capitalist hierarchies he so loathed in his previous job; or the form of Krish's building of a phone app that surveils, based on and reinventing racialized categories despite his belief that it will beget better futures for children all over India; or the form of Swati and Sweta's enthusiastic embrace of doing good in a way particular to brown savarna women even as they require that doing good leave no dent in their pocketbooks; or the form of my decision to write a white paper for Sahaayaka or suggest new features for their phone app or teach in a village that belied my saviorist tendencies or stay silent at so many moments when I should have refused the impulse toward complicity.

For me, these are the kinds of insights that ethnography, and a nervous ethnography especially, can reveal if we are willing to be so brave as to follow our nerves and excavate those everyday conditions of nervousness that aren't already at the level of catastrophe but that can nevertheless lead to the places where we don't want to go.

Most specifically, in this text I have focused on the help economies and the NGO as a (neo)liberal institutional formation whose nervous condition hinges on a very real commitment to making the world a better place. Nearly every member of Sahaayaka whom I met on this journey came to work every day wanting to change India by figuring out better ways to help rural children. None of them is trying to do harm, and therefore this book is centered less on any individual person's morality and more on the systems that produce them. In other words, the problem with Sahaayaka's personnel is not really about some internal psychological state of extreme villainy; rather, they, like so many others I have met, have imbibed the illusion of (neo)liberalism's promise of salvation. As I have argued in the introduction and chapter 1 of this text, the help economies emerged as part of Western imperialism's solution to the "problem" of decolonization. If Frantz Fanon recognized that a different, more humane future in the brown world required a form of extreme expunging of the values, ideologies, practices, and people associated with colonization, the liberal mid-century compromise promised that the brown world could find salvation and ascend if it just learned from, assimilated into, and embodied their masters' technocratic teachings.[7] Sahaayaka, too, assumed and deployed the same old categories while also characterizing their interventions under the technocratic rubric of universal solutions. In this sense, Sahaayaka consents to, even advocates for, the neocolonial world order even as they seek to reform it. This contradiction produces the kind of (neo)liberal institutional nervousness I have sought to reveal in this text.

Here I am reminded yet again of B. R. Ambedkar's words in *Annihilation of Caste* about reformists in general. Ambedkar was deeply critical of savarna reformists who thought they could find a solution to the problem of caste atrocity in and through the logic of Hindu cosmologies. He wrote presciently, "All reform consists in a change in the notions, sentiments and mental attitudes of the people. . . . If new notions are to be inculcated in the minds of people, it is necessary to give them new names. To continue the old names is to make the reform futile."[8] In this book I have taken Ambedkar's critique to heart and have tried to show, as best I am capable, how the reinscription of value based on caste, race, and gendered categories along with rural/urban and technological distinctions renders reform efforts largely futile. But Ambedkar's story also teaches us how nervousness is built into the liberal reformist effort because reformers refuse to reckon with or even acknowledge the material destruction and reconstruction required to produce a more equitable society. The result, inevitably, is instability, tension, nerves.

Still, this national condition of nervousness does not quite capture the kinds of movements and projects that produce our current global nervous condition. For example, I have spent a large part of this text focusing on the fetish of technology as the harbinger of salvation for those in India and across the world. In the bluntest terms, the project of technocratic liberal modernity has morphed into a contemporary global project of racialized neoliberal, digitized technocracy. J. Khadijah Abdurahman explains, "The joke I always make is that techno-capitalism puts people who have never taken the humanities in charge of humanity."[9] As I noted in chapter 7, a joke can tell us so much: about complicity or about the way we try to find joy within a system meant to crush us. But the joke can also be the way we deal with a truth that might be too scary to confront, a truth that reveals our society's nervous condition so clearly that we laugh with a hiccup in our throat. Abdurahman's joke takes me to Sahaayaka's leadership, all of whom came from the world of computer science and engineering, had no training in any social science or humanities field, but had been given the keys to solving the problems of poverty through education. In excavating Sahaayaka's practices, especially in part IV, I have tried to show how a utopic, rabid form of technophilia is at the center of the contemporary global saviorist imagination, assuming so much about what technology can do and assuming so much about those who supposedly possess the gift of technological creation. This turn to digitized technophilia is one of the sinister tricks of neocolonial modernity's nervous condition because it at once promises salvation from its past colonial violence, while hiding so many neocolonial reconfigurations behind the slick veneer of the screen. This problem looms especially large because digital projects also double down on a (neo)liberal version of "equality for all" that invisibilizes all those power asymmetries that precede the moment of digital encounter. The result has been a constant state of nervousness as new technologies seem to offer opportunities for radical social movements and global political possibility before finding themselves in the hands of those with fascist intentions.

In fact, the real trick of contemporary technophilic saviorism is its ability to enfold into itself the twenty-first-century global representational politics of multicultural racial inclusion, in this case by drawing the brown subject into its ranks. As I have argued, brownness emerges in the clashes of colonization, when British, Spanish, Portuguese, French, German, and American imperial histories rub against each other as "browned" people continue to move across the world. Therefore, brownness sits at the nexus of contradictory racialized (in)capacities: deficiency, poverty, underdevelopment, impurity, on the one hand, *and* assimilability, postracial brown futures, on the other hand. This brown in-betweenness is what has created the nerve-racking global politics of brown saviorism. For me, the multiple, contradictory, clashing racial geographies of brownness have been an essential way to trace the movement from midcentury global racial reordering to twenty-first-century technocapitalist saviorism. In fact, I might say that technophilia and the fetish for brown blood have cross-pollinated, making it feel as if the brown savior has just the right blood type to "save" neoliberal technocapitalism from its own fascistic tendencies and effects.

Of course, brownness also, by definition, obfuscates other operations of power. While these operations of power are regionally and historically specific, and because this book has focused on the case of the Indian and the Indian diaspora as brown subjects, I have focused on the relation between race and caste. I have argued that the brown savior's value hinges on assumptions related to their "capacity" for technological labor that is tied to their global race and caste capital along with their perceived urbanity and globality. This fact holds true whether brown savarnas were born in the United States or in India. As such, the case I have presented here pushes against any simplistic "nation-centric" story by forcing us to see the Indian diaspora and those within the borders of the Indian nation-state *within the same frame*, as connected and shaped by intimate histories of, at minimum, India as a caste-colonial society, the United States as a settler colonial and imperial society, and Britain as a franchise colonial society growing out of the transatlantic slave trade.[10]

The unstated but obvious fact is, of course, that the supposed racial "capacity" of the brown savior is actually but a mirage, an illusion brought on by colonial racist mythologies that continue to be passed down and reinforced. Therefore, being positioned as a brown savior cannot but produce excess nervous energy: when an ideology is based on fiction, it is extremely unstable and therefore needs to be constantly reasserted through control and hierarchy, whether the subjects involved are conscious of this or not. The brown savior's nervous condition was most easily observed in juxtaposition with Sahaayaka's mentor class, whose aspirations to mobility were constantly undermined because of assumptions regarding their feminized labor capacities as related to their caste position, rurality, nonelite education, and the like. Here the technoracial politics of brown saviorism is quite clearly heteropatriarchal. As I have shown, this plays out both in the way that women in Sahaayaka end up being slotted neatly into normative gendered class and caste expectations and in the way that NGO labor regimes eliminate traditional care work, while relying on the fact that relational labor is feminized and therefore understood as freely extractable.

These insights are also why I have come to believe that global racial, caste, and gender capitalist critique is so fundamental to understanding our current world order. Such critique can reveal the continuities between Sahaayaka and other forms of technofascistic accumulation. For example, it is not surprising that the rabid proliferation of digital infrastructures has become the panacea for Indian statecraft at the very moment that Hindutva forces have been rising all over the country. The Bharatiya Janata Party (BJP), after all, articulates almost all of its claims, including its Digital India movement, through the rhetoric of universal, technocratic economic development—the means for the nation to continue to accumulate capital. Digitized technocracy as a means for accumulation works equally well under authoritarian and liberal regimes. This is why Sahaayaka's leaders continued, if nervously, to partner ever more concretely with the current government in order to maintain their programming and grow despite the fact that they were unhappy with the regime change and the new political order. The question, for me, is if and when they, too, will be cast aside as outsiders to the fascist state.

Here, then, is what I mean when I say that we are living in a sustained global nervous condition, a world that teeters on the edge because it refuses to reckon with the neocolonial futures we continue to produce and the contradictions that emerge when we do not confront our complicities in the production of these neocolonial futures.

Annihilationist Impulses

Okay. We are at the end. What, then, should we do?

When I try to answer this question, I think about my classroom and my students, both in India and in the United States, especially those who want to join an NGO. I think about this book and what they might take away from it if they read it. What I want them to take away is that there is no time to give up or be frozen in guilt. I want them to be able to sit with discomfort and recognize that their discomfort is a call to action. Whether they work within the help economies or not, they will still be living in a racial, gendered, and caste capitalist world. There is no "outside," and there is no "pure" position, and there will be work to be done no matter which life path they choose. What I want them to take away is that whatever their position is within this system, the system itself requires annihilation and a radical reimagining. Most important, I want them to extend their imagination beyond the very limited confines of the nonprofit-industrial complex to engage with the vast number of radical solidarity movements that *already* recognize the inseparability of (neo)liberalism and fascism and are working to create futures that don't yet exist.

Saviorism undermines solidarity because it requires the kind of individualistic, abstract, binaristic thinking that produces, at best, paternalistic forms of care. Solidarity, in contrast, requires relationships; empathy across difference; multiscalar political, economic, and historical analysis; and the real work of learning from one another to advocate together to annihilate the violent system we live in. Here I am drawing on Roseann Liu and Savannah Shange's conception of "thick solidarity." For them, thick solidarity is "a kind of solidarity that mobilizes empathy in ways that do not gloss over difference, but rather push into the specificity, irreducibility, and incommensurability of racialized experience."[11] Thick solidarity resists the superficial urge to connect with others under the universalizing rubric that "we have all experienced suffering." Instead, thick solidarity asks us to take radical political and economic histories seriously so that we can move toward the much more nerve-racking, uncomfortable conversations that help us to learn how to show radical care for one another. While Liu and Shange are writing with reference to the particularities of interracial solidarity in the United States, Goldie Osuri and Ather Zia expand on this type of solidarity by drawing together the specific global histories of colonization in Palestine and Kashmir.[12] This project does not collapse the differences between these distinct colonial histories but instead begins with an excavation of "archives of solidarity" that attends to all those global relationships and connections that set the stage for how we can find embodied connections with one another in our struggles against contemporary manifestations of imperial power.

These kinds of solidarities move well beyond the classroom, especially the liberal classroom, and certainly beyond the limited imaginations of the help economies. This is why, most of all, I want my students to learn from all those activists and organizers who have shaped and continue to shape our world. I want students to learn how to organize themselves and, as Charisse Burden-Stelly advocates, to "join an organization, contribute to that organization, and strive to embody and concretize its ethics and principles."[13] I wish I had undertaken the rigorous study to join and contribute to radical organizations earlier in my life, and it is a task I am only now fully embracing.[14] In this process of learning from those who have done this work better for longer, I want my students to slowly but surely cultivate their annihilationist impulses. An annihilationist impulse refuses any romantic mythologies regarding salvation and embraces the labor-intensive, fraught, and ever-expanding solidarities and coalition building that might push us toward a world as yet to come.

By bringing the discussion back to annihilation, I am evoking two strands of thought that have influenced this book most profoundly and have set the foundation for what I hope students receive in the classroom as they start to expand their imaginations of what might be possible in the future. First, and most directly, I use *annihilation* in the Ambedkarite sense to refer to the project to annihilate the evil and violent system of global caste. While I am still learning the many ways to take global caste critique seriously, I start with the premise that annihilating global caste systems requires a constant focus on the way that laborers in various institutional settings are graded above one another or excluded entirely. In this text I have applied this type of caste critique to focus specifically on the way that laborers within the help economy have been placed in a graded hierarchy based on interlocking regimes of global value.

However, if we are to take the struggle against caste seriously, this project must start in the home, the family, and the other spaces in which caste exclusionary politics play out every day. In this sense, the everyday of the annihilation of caste also intersects with feminist-of-color critiques of political economy and domesticity. The everyday and the domestic, as Maria Mies has reminded us, is directly connected to and structured by neocolonial patriarchal political economies and histories.[15] Therefore, even if we annihilate the help economies entirely, it will matter very little if the same racist, sexist, casteist logics continue to operate in our other spheres of life. I have so many Indian American students who have no idea just how rooted their lives are in casteist reproduction. Some of them have sidestepped any thought of India at all, embracing a singular American identity under the sign of "brown," while others have idealized India and want to have a greater relation to India both personally and professionally. In both cases, there is a uniform neglect and erasure of any discussion of caste culture and caste position. I try to explain my own embarrassingly slow process of realizing how deeply rooted in caste my cosmology was and is, and how difficult the task of annihilating these cosmologies continues to be, especially when I am faced with so many family members who either consciously or unconsciously refuse to engage with my ongoing critiques. If they want to help the world, I explain, they can start right at home.

To start at home, however, does not mean one has to start alone. Instead, part of the sincere work I want my students to engage in is to recognize those "archives of solidarity" that already exist but have been submerged within the status quo of our (neo)liberal teachings. To follow this path requires remembering people like Muslim feminist activist Fatima Sheikh, who provided the space for Savitribai Phule to open her school for girls of all castes, or remembering the way that Jyotiba Phule dedicated his book *Gulamgiri* to the abolitionist struggle in the United States.[16] Learning from, building, and contributing to these archives of solidarity offer alternative understandings of the present and the everyday. More important, such learning, I hope, will provide a foundation to join the long history of struggle that continues in India and all over the world. Such projects are anything but romantic or easy. The powerful and inspiring protests against the National Register of Citizens and the Citizenship Amendment Act in 2019 and the farmers' protests in 2020 *both* required multi-scalar caste, class, religious, and linguistic coalitions to succeed even as these coalitions were fractured and extremely fraught.[17] In the case of the farmers' protests in particular, the most prominent faces of the protests were landowning jat farmers' organizations.[18] Yet so many other, less visibilized groups also joined the fight, including some leftist Dalit organizations, especially in Punjab, who supported the farmers' struggle despite the fact that in previous struggles they had been adversaries, primarily because landless laborers have been especially exploited by dominant-caste farmers. There is little doubt that without this broad-based caste coalition, the Indian state would not have repealed the draconian laws they proposed. However, while the three farm laws were repealed, Dalit agricultural activists were also advocating for higher wages, pushing against the rise of the BJP regime, and making the violent hierarchies of caste in Punjab visible to a mainstream public. This annihilationist struggle still continues.

Second, I use annihilation in the Césairean decolonial sense to refer to the project to annihilate the evil that is colonial Western civilizationalism and its knowledge formations. This annihilationist impulse requires a constant reckoning with the way that categories and capacities get fixed. If there is one colonial inheritance that feels exceptionally ubiquitous, it's the scientific racist legacies that fix human beings to particular, narrow bodily capacities. The logic of colonial racial capitalism, as I argued in the introduction, *required* the fixing of labor capacities in order to determine the global pathways of accumulation through exploitation and expropriation. This legacy continues in a global political economic system that separates people based on their perceived labor capacities but *also*, as important, perpetuates an almost impossibly deep-rooted cultural ideology that our capacities are natural, inherited, pregiven, and fixed.[19]

When I start to observe and trace fixedness, I find manifestations everywhere, and I am coming to believe that it is one of the most difficult things for me to challenge in myself, in my conversations with students in the classroom, and in conversations with family and friends—in how we think about race, nation, ethnicity, caste, capital, ability, gender, sexuality, education, health, science and, of course, in how we think about development: who needs it, where needs it, and so on. The fixing of capacities is, for me, so pernicious because it makes us feel that nothing can be different and that who we are is who we are forever. Indeed, despite all its good intentions, what I find fatal about Sahaayaka's approach to interventions is that they, like so many others, assume the very same categories that perpetuate so much inequality and, implicitly or explicitly, fix these categories in place. I think about this when I remember Srinivasan's flippant story about "Indian" deficiency or his beliefs about corruption and the rural mentor class. I also think about this when I look back on Krish's phone app and the way that it reproduces the very same categories of student deficiency, educational lack, and perceptions of uncleanliness and fixes them further through the process of datafication.

Therefore, what I think we require, as students and as people, are strategies to keep questioning our assumptions, to make us radically curious, and to unsettle the categories that we take for granted to characterize ourselves and Others.[20] Here I am drawing on Yarimar Bonilla's excellent insight that because we are all touched by colonial legacies, there is no way of finding our way to the pure "outside." Instead, our task is to constantly denaturalize the colonial categories, logics, and institutions we have inherited and to use this process of unsettling to imagine something different.[21] This process proves especially hard in liberal institutions that are not equipped for the kind of materialist analyses that would awaken our annihilationist impulses partially because they hold on to the pernicious ideology of meritocracy. "Merit" assumes the naturalness of our social, economic, and political order by hiding material inequities behind the individualized bootstrap rhetoric of hard work, aspiration, and mobility.

This is why an annihilationist impulse requires a different kind of curiosity, one that, as Perry Zurn describes, is a "curiosity at war."[22] This kind of warring curiosity is predicated on a constant state of radical nervousness. Radical nervousness keeps me aware of those complicities, those ideologies, those learnings that I must recognize, question, unlearn, and challenge. It also keeps me humble, knowing that whatever reckoning I've had today will reveal some new unsettling I have to do tomorrow. I lean once again on the brilliance of Sara Ahmed, who set the frame for this nervous, sweaty text by reminding that "it is good to think of life as always potentially in crisis, to keep asking the question: how to live?"[23] In other words, if I am taking my annihilationist impulses seriously, I should be nervous until the day I die.

This way of thinking about radical nervousness is *not* about individualized growth or aspiration. This fact is sometimes hard for students to wrap their heads around after going through a liberal education that requires truths already known in order for them to move up the prescripted accumulationist hierarchy. In fact, if anything, students are taught to fear the unknown, the as-yet-imagined, and to see their struggles as purely and wholly individual.[24] They are even taught to submerge their nerves or, if their nerves do happen to manifest, to see them as a by-product of their own psychological deficiencies rather than a by-product and useful indicator of a broken system that is producing a whole slew of nervous conditions.

This is why questions like *how to live* are questions that we cannot ask alone and that we cannot know the answers to already. Instead, such questions require collective study, collective questioning, collective learning, collective challenging of one another outside of the confines of our colonized institutional frameworks.[25] This slow, hard work gets easier when we start to cultivate our annihilationist impulses and recognize that many more of us feel the agitations that come with the oppressive system we live in than we originally thought. I cannot imagine cultivating any of my still-nascent annihilationist impulses without the constant, nerve-racking challenges that came from hundreds of people who have learned more, struggled longer, and were willing to believe that I, too, could join them if I was willing to begin to alter how I understood and interacted in the world. Therefore, our annihilationist impulses are a way to build our capacities, our collectives, our coalitions, our pathways, our annihilationist blocs, so that we can together learn how to strike at all those contradictions that come with the nervous conditions produced within the neocolonial state. It is a way of expanding our awareness of alternative ways of living, of together building our collective body without knowing what is to come but knowing full well, as Fanon reminds us, "The more the people understand, the more vigilant they become, and the more they realize in fact that everything depends on them and their salvation lies in their solidarity, in recognizing their interests and identifying their enemies. The people understand that wealth is not the fruit of labor but the spoils from an organized protection racket."[26]

Acknowledgments

This book has been a series of stops, starts, trials, failures, rejections, rewrites, self-doubts, anxieties, sorrows, monotonies, more rewrites, epiphanies, and small joys. It is absolutely not an exaggeration to say this book almost did not get written at all. For those in the process of writing a book right now, I feel for you. For those who have written books in the past, I have more admiration for you now than I ever did before. It's really, really hard. And the one thing I know for certain is that you can't do it alone. I certainly couldn't. When I was at my lowest and ready to give up, I had many who reminded me that my ideas mattered, that things would get easier, and that I needed to find that place of love again—love for the project, love for writing, love for myself. When I was overzealous and overconfident, I had many who kept me grounded and pushed me to be better and do better; to stop being so comfortable with what I was writing and to slow down and question every word, every idea; to get back to the political project at hand with humility rather than conceit.

First and foremost, thanks to all of those in Karnataka who opened up their lives and work to me. Special thanks to those students, teachers, and NGO personnel who were my first and most trusted guides. While we may not have always agreed, they were always willing to share openly and honestly. Without them there could truly be no ethnography. Thanks also go to Azim Premji University, which gave me a second home during my fieldwork. The faculty and students whom I learned from and taught during my time there were truly special. Two of my students, Sripriya Pratinidhi and Lekha Adavi, came on many a fieldwork trip with me, working with students, taking photographs, and conducting interviews. It was a pleasure working with both of them.

Thank you to the small group of people—Gajendran Ayyathurai, E. Gabriel Dattatreyan, Mariam Durrani, Daria Krisnovos, Shiloh Krupar, Andrew Milne,

Derek Pardue, Diana Pardo Pedraza, and Mubbashir Rizvi—who read drafts (and redrafts and redrafts) of this book and gave careful, caring feedback at various stages of its unfolding.

Portions of this book were presented at a number of conferences, workshops, and invited talks over the course of ten years, during which I met some incredible scholars, who, in many cases, probably do not remember me but had an indelible impact on how this project took shape. In 2012, just before I began fieldwork, I attended the workshop "The City and Village" in Göttingen, during which I met Rupa Viswanath, Anupama Rao, Arvind Rajagopal, Katy Hardy, Andrew Liu, and reconnected with Sahana Udupa, among many others. The workshop left an especially important mark on me because it was the first time I met Palagummi Sainath, with whom I eventually audited the mindblowing "Reporting Inequality" at Princeton University. In 2017 I presented on the "Brown Savior Industrial Complex" for the first time at the American Anthropological Association conference. There I had the opportunity to present in front of Deborah A. Thomas, Nell Gabiam, Erica Caple James, Adia Benton, and Ezgi Guner, all of whose work on humanitarianism and development has shaped how I conceptualize the help economies. In 2018 I presented on brown saviorism at the annual conference of the Association for Asian American Studies, where I finally met scholars—Vivek Bald, Tamara Bhalla, and Pawan Dhingra among them—who have come to define the study of race and South Asian America. I have never been around that many progressive desi American scholars all at once, and it felt both grounding and so damn inviting. Most important, I got the opportunity to think with Stanley Thangaraj, who kindly but directly told me that I needed to theorize brown racialization far more robustly by engaging with the field of South Asian American studies in earnest. I hope this book has done some of that work. In 2018 I had the opportunity to organize a Wenner-Gren funded workshop in Austin, Texas, with the Writing with Light collective (Vivian Choi, Lee Douglas, Craig Campbell, and Mark Westmoreland), during which I had the opportunity to grapple with the politics and possibilities of my participatory image-making work. What a wonderful experience that was. In 2019 I presented a paper called "Brown Saviors and the Politics of Help" at the Racial Orders, Racial Borders conference in Amsterdam. I won't lie, I was nervous as fuck given the people I knew would be there, and I practiced that presentation at least one hundred times. After that talk I had the incredible opportunity to get critical questions and feedback from Gargi Bhattacharyya, Barnor Hesse, and Nishant Upadhyay, who pushed me to be even more precise in my theorizing of brownness, caste, and capitalism. In 2020, during the wave of protests in India and *just* before the pandemic, I attended the workshop "Education and Society," hosted by Leya Methew (a friend from the University of Pennsylvania), Karishma Desai, and Maryann Chacko at Ahmedabad University. There I workshopped my ideas with P. Sanal Mohan, Sangeeta Kamat, Aradhana Sharma, Carol Upadhyay, and my dissertation committee member, Ritty Lukose (among many other brilliant people). Going into the workshop, I felt as if I had to present my work in India one more time before I could feel good about what I was writing. Thankfully, the world gave me that chance before it completely shut down. I also presented versions of my research at Colgate University, the University of Houston, Goldsmiths University, Aarhus University, the University of Puget Sound, and Georgetown University. Each presentation gave me that much more assurance that people were excited about what I had to say. But to be honest, after all these presentations, I'm conferenced out. I'm not sure I will ever present a paper again.

Finally, I had the incredible opportunity to organize the 2020 Society for Cultural Anthropology (SCA)/Society for Visual Anthropology (SVA) virtual conference Distribute, together with Mayanthi Fernando, Andrea Muehlebach, and E. Gabriel Dattatreyan. What a wild learning experience that was, fighting over how to decolonize time, struggling to make sure panels and panelists understood our technology, and navigating a pandemic that was in full force. At a time when I was ready to leave the academy, being embraced by these intellectual peers meant a whole lot to me. Most important, it was during Distribute that I met Elizabeth Ault, my incredible editor.

Thank you to Elizabeth and Duke University Press. It is an understatement to say that at the time I met Elizabeth, this project was barely hanging on. But Elizabeth, in a random, informal, lucky four-minute virtual encounter, got what I was trying to do and immediately gave my work new life. She has constantly made sure I know how much she believes in this project while telling me when I haven't gotten my structure, writing, or theory quite right. Thanks also to the anonymous reviewers who took the time to give thoughtful, engaged feedback that has made this book much, much better.

Thank you to all of those from my Philly life, who started my journey in the academy and have expanded how I think and create in the world. First and foremost, thank you to John L. Jackson Jr., whose encouragement and generosity I could not have survived without. When I thought it might be time to quit, he reminded me that it was just a matter of time before things started to come together for me (though I definitely did not believe him) and, in his very particular way, he managed to share the exact ideas to push my thinking only when I was ready to receive them. Thank you to Deborah A. Thomas, who quietly has steered how I think, giving me unexpected opportunities to see the world and always supporting me and my work. Our travels to the UK and South Africa to make the metafilm for *Bad Friday* is perhaps the greatest experience I had as a graduate student. Thank you also to my other University of Pennsylvania faculty and colleagues who helped me along the way: Amit Das, Kathleen Hall, Stanton Wortham, and committee members, Lisa Mitchell and Sharon Ravitch. Thank you to my fellow members of CAMRA, OreOluwa Badaki, Sofia Chaparro, Tali Ziv, Matt Tarditi, Sandra Ristovska, Kate Zambon, Andrew Hudson, Juan Castrillon, and Melissa Skolnick, among many others. I still miss the creative, unencumbered vibrancy of our attempt to create a world of multimodality none of us had seen before. Thank you to Maori Karmael Holmes, whose Taurean spirit and passion as a filmmaker, curator, and artist-activist has changed how I see; thank you to Ra'anan Alexandrowicz, whose political filmmaking vision has been indispensable to my own intellectual growth; thank you to Perry Zurn, who embarked on the journey of radical curiosity with me during our days as postdocs at Penn. Thank you especially to Mariam Durrani, who, despite the epic roller coaster we have been on, pushed me to produce a project that met the highest ethical and creative standards. She never stopped believing in my capacity to do better.

Thank you to my slowly growing DC and Georgetown community—Diana Pardo Pedraza, Leniqueca Welcome, Kwame Edwin Otu, Tariq Ali, Melyssa Haffaf, Shiloh Krupar, Shelbi Nawhilet Meissner, Katrin Sieg, Mubbashir Rizvi, Mariangela Mihai, Scott Taylor, Fida Adely, and Heath Pearson—who have shepherded me into a new, hopeful stage of my life.

Thank you to my students at Azim Premji University, the University of Pennsylvania, Hamilton College, Colgate University, and Georgetown University. You all are truly what sustains me.

Thank you to the excellent therapists and spiritual teachers who have blessed me with coping mechanisms, strategies to balance myself, and new ways to see my future as one of possibility rather than inevitable tragedy.

Thank you to my sister, who is on her own journey of self-discovery and shares with me a commitment to forever-nervous growth. Thank you to my mother, who supports me unconditionally and really, genuinely tries to understand and learn from what I write even when it is uncomfortable or challenging. Without her, the preface of this book would have never been completed. As for my father, I wonder what he would have thought of this work and how he might have changed and grown over the twenty-five years that never were. Thank you for being in my memories.

I can't believe this is finally done. It feels really good, and I've learned a whole fucking lot. It also makes me incredibly nervous to feel such a wave of finality. But then I try to remind myself that every journey only begins at the end. My journey, too, is beginning at the end.

Notes

1   I have anonymized the names of the villages in which I worked, along with all the names of the individuals and organizations with whom I worked.

2   See the introduction for a discussion/definition of *savarna*. I have chosen not to capitalize *brahmin* throughout this text in order to follow those critical anti-caste scholars who refuse to recognize, valorize, and contribute to the power asymmetries and violent exploitation of the caste system emplaced historically through brahminical patriarchy. I also do not capitalize the kshatriya and vaishya castes, whose positions within the caste hierarchy facilitate its ongoing violence. However, I do capitalize some specific caste groups within the Shudra castes in Karnataka, specifically that of the Vokkaliga and Lingayat caste groups, and Dalit, the general term chosen by those who were deemed "outside" of the varna system. This is intended to draw from the Bahujan tradition which sees caste not simply as a "Dalit problem" but links the struggles of "the majority of the people" in India, comprised of Dalits, Shudras, and Adivasis. This decision is itself fraught. I recognize that there are a number of fissures between and within these caste groupings as well, and some of the complicities of Vokkaligas and Lingayats emerge during the rest of the text.

3   I elaborate on the specificity of caste and race and the sometimes contradictory relationship between them in the introduction. Also see the introduction for a definition of the help economies.

4   *Kannadiga* is a term used to describe those who speak Kannada and is also associated with a shared set of cultural practices. Kannada is one of the four primary South Indian languages and is the official language spoken in Karnataka state. It is spoken by approximately 65 percent of the state's population.

5   For example, nearly 50 percent of the population of Ramanagara city, also known as the "silk city," is Muslim. This religious distribution differs quite dramatically from villages in South Karnataka, which are predominantly Hindu.

6   A *sattvic diet* is one that includes only vegetarian recipes without onions or garlic. Such recipes are viewed as spiritually pure within one version of brahminical Hindu cuisine.

7   See A. Shankar, "Participation, Reception, Consent, and Refusal," for a thorough exploration of my thoughts on consent and ethics, including how I negotiated questions of consent with my participants during fieldwork.

8   Ferguson, *Global Shadows*. I am drawing explicitly from the theoretical work in Simpson, "Consent's Revenge"; Jackson, *Thin Description*; and Glissant, *Poetics of Relation*, which, in very different contexts, theorize the ethics of refusal and opacity. John Jackson Jr. critiques the history of "thick description" in anthropology, which traffics in a colonial ideology that requires the complete transparency of postcolonized, mostly brown and Black, subjects. Audra Simpson writes that Indigenous peoples' refusal emerged as "the very deliberate, willful, intentional actions that people were making in the face of the expectation that they consent to their own elimination as a people, that they consent to having their land taken, their lives controlled, and their stories told for them." Simpson, "Consent's Revenge," 327. Édouard Glissant argues that the previously colonized have "the right to opacity" and should be allowed to exist without the demand for transparency imposed by the colonizer. Glissant, *Poetics of Relation*, 190.

9   Muñoz, *Sense of Brown*.

10 My research in Adavisandra would not have happened without Sripriya Pratinidhi, a former student at Azim Premji University, where I briefly taught university courses during my time in Karnataka. While she did not always accompany me on my trips to Adavisandra, when she did join, her careful and caring questioning changed what and how I learned while there.

11 Thirty-one districts in four states (Andhra Pradesh, Maharashtra, Karnataka, and Kerala) have been characterized as suicide-prone, and Karnataka has the second-highest number of farmers' suicides, behind Maharashtra. The term *farmers' suicide* is itself highly controversial given that the patriarchal capitalist definition by which the government determines who is a "real" farmer is based on title to land. This leaves out all but landowning male heads of agricultural households. See Nagaraj, *Farmers' Suicides in India*, 5–6.

12 I am deeply indebted to the work and teachings of Palagummi Sainath, with whom I had the opportunity to take a Media and Inequality class while a PhD student. Sainath's continuous focus on the tragic results of capitalism and agrarian crisis has guided some of my own attentions in this project. See Sainath, *Everybody Loves a Good Drought*.

13 For a more elaborate explanation of the phenomenon and its sociohistorical antecedents, see Münster, "Farmers' Suicides and the State in India." In addition, Suraj Yengde points out that the question of farmers' suicides in India is not just related to the neoliberal economic restructuring of the nation-state but also must be understood vis-à-vis India's caste society. See Yengde, *Caste Matters*, 18.

14 Nancy Scheper-Hughes and Carolyn Sargent make the powerful point that children are typically seen in social science, and in broader imaginaries in neoliberal societies,

as incapable of thinking for themselves, of reasoning, and therefore of changing the world in which they live. See Scheper-Hughes and Sargent, *Small Wars*; and Hecht, *At Home in the Street*.

15 Similarly, Liisa Malkki shifts the focus "from humanitarian intervention and its effects on the *recipients* of aid to a more intimate set of questions about 'humanitarians' themselves." Malkki, *Need to Help*, 2. I return to Malkki's argument at the end of chapter 1.

16 Hunt, *Nervous State*, 5.

17 My thoughts on nervousness also have a strong relation to the conception of postcolonial disorders in Good et al., *Postcolonial Disorders*. Nervousness can be understood as a historical category of medicalized pathology, especially for women and the colonized, related to affects like "hysteria." See also Briggs, "Race of Hysteria."

18 For example, see Taussig, *Nervous System*.

19 Madison, *Critical Ethnography*.

20 Ginsburg, "Parallax Effect."

21 Simpson, "Consent's Revenge"; Jackson, *Thin Description*; and Dattatreyan, "Waiting Subjects."

22 Jackson, "On Ethnographic Sincerity," S284–85.

23 See M. Gonzalez, "Methods of Motherhood."

24 I am also drawing from Zurn, "Cripping Curiosity," in Zurn, *Curiosity and Power*. Zurn critiques an intrusive curiosity that objectifies those with disabilities. In turn, those with disabilities are not recognized as practitioners and critical questioners from whom we should learn. Beyond the fetish of those with disabilities as objects consumable for entertainment, Zurn also writes, "Such curiosity deeply informs the social construction of disability—perhaps especially in the case of supercrip narratives—as well as its analysis. With supercrip narratives, certain people with disabilities are singled out as exemplars of resilience, while disability itself is reinscribed as something to be overcome." See Zurn, *Curiosity and Power*, 149. As a response, Zurn argues that cripping curiosity "resists the compulsion of ablebodymindedness. It is an insistent refusal to comply. . . . It celebrates the 'unnatural' bodymind and disrupts the repeated enforcement of its normate counterpart. And it does so across multiple temporal vectors." See Zurn, *Curiosity and Power*, 159.

25 Ahmed, *Living a Feminist Life*, 13.

26 Williams argues that radical honesty hinges on three key foci—telling the truth, valuing narrative and personal experience, and acting—that seek to challenge racist and patriarchal institutional cultures in the academy. See B. Williams, "Radical Honesty," 73. In her 2021 American Anthropology Association meeting comments as part of the panel "Beyond Crisis," Williams noted that many of her graduate students challenge the framework of radical honesty by pointing out that this kind of emotional openness is being conscripted and commodified within the university, only further reinforcing emotional labor regimes that disproportionality impact women of color, especially Black feminist scholars. B. Williams, "Beyond Crisis," 2021. This insight reminds me that nervous ethnography cannot be and should not be enacted in identical ways by all scholars but must emerge from

our situated positions within institutional power regimes. As another example of a very different decision when it comes to personal narrative in writing, Max Liboiron explicitly argues that they will not be telling stories of self because of the way that neocolonial academic violence is invested in forcing those who have been violated to reveal themselves. See Liboiron, *Pollution Is Colonialism.* I've decided on a different approach here partly because I am embarking on an excavation of the complex registers of complicity and partly because I am unable to make a stark distinction between the academy and the rest of the world, especially when nearly every social relation that I am part of is no more "outside" the colonial than is academia.

27 Jackson, "On Ethnographic Sincerity," S284–85.

28 Ahmed reminds us, "Caring is anxious—to be full of care, to be careful, is to take care of things by becoming anxious about their future, where the future is embodied in fragility of an object whose persistence matters. . . . But we would not end up with a liberal notion. . . . To attend to something that has become more easily breakable is to attend to its history, with love, and with care." Ahmed, *Living a Feminist Life,* 266.

29 Ahmed writes, "We need to start with our own complicity. . . . To be complicit should not become its own reproductive logic: that all we can do is to reproduce the logics of the institutions that employ us. In fact those who benefit from unjust systems need to work harder to expose that injustice." Ahmed, *Living a Feminist Life,* 263.

30 Here I am thinking with two scholars. First, Gloria Wekker shows how claims to white innocence allow for the ability to perform racist violence, while also allowing the performer of such violence to claim "innocence" and therefore shun any culpability for their acts. Second, Dia Da Costa argues that savarna academics traffic in caste innocence as they pretend to be progressive scholars but still find ways to invisibilize their caste position and/or utilize their powerful academic positions to sidestep their participation in explicit or implicit caste violence. See Wekker, *White Innocence*; and Da Costa, "Caste-Ignorant Worlds of Progressive Academics."

31 See A. Shankar, "Silence and Privilege Renegotiated." Some notable exceptions include Brodkin, *How Jews Became White Folks*; Walley, *Exit Zero*; Hartigan, "Establishing the Fact of Whiteness"; and Pearson, "Prickly Skin of White Supremacy."

32 The "problem of pleasure" has been well documented in visual research, especially when focused on Black and brown Others. In Deborah Poole's work, the violent power of colonial pleasure, what she refers to in Edward Said's terms as "the pleasure of empire," becomes embedded in the imagination of imperial subjects. See Poole, *Vision, Race, and Modernity*, 17.

33 See also Lipsitz, *Possessive Investment in Whiteness.*

34 See Ayyathurai, "It Is Time for a New Subfield"; Rawat and Satyanarayana, *Dalit Studies*; and S. Thomas, *Privileged Minorities.*

35 For example, Subramanian Shankar writes, "Postcolonial theory is peculiar. In startling ways it is not postcolonial at all. Consider, for example, caste and how little postcolonial theory has to say about it. On the one hand, caste has been the

object of intense scholarly scrutiny for centuries. At least from the time of the British entry into India as a colonizing power, it has been steadily made into the very identity of India—its essential nature. Yet in *The Weapon of the Other*, Kancha Ilaiah records his sense that 'caste was not a category of socio-historical analysis' in contemporary scholarship. . . . Certainly, in the tens of thousands of pages of 'postcolonial' commentary on India (that is, from within institutional postcolonialism, or the academic formation known most frequently as 'postcolonial studies'), caste is largely absent." S. Shankar, *Flesh and Fish Blood*, 28.

36 See Ambedkar Age Collective, *Hatred in the Belly*, for a critique of the savarna position in telling stories of Dalit-Bahujans. The term *Dalit-Bahujan* references movements that recognize that caste is not just a Dalit problem. Valliammal Karunakaran writes, "For example, I believe the term *Bahujan*, simply meaning 'the majority of the people,' brings to attention to the reality that caste is not a 'Dalit problem.' While Dalit and Adivasis are some of the most vulnerable communities in a caste society, the majority of the people of the subcontinent are caste-bound and ruled by "upper"-caste minorities. The term *Bahujan* refers to present day Scheduled Castes (Dalits), Scheduled Tribes (Adivasis/indigenous) and Shudra (peasant) castes—cutting across religion, ethnicities and geographies." Karunakaran, "The Dalit-Bahujan Guide to Understanding Caste in Hindu Scripture." Similarly, see Guru, "How Egalitarian Are the Social Sciences in India?," for a critique of the dichotomy between "theoretical brahmins" and "empirical shudras" that assumes brahmins as somehow solely capable of theoretical contributions, even when it comes to the lives of the oppressed castes. My text emerges from these considerations.

37 Here I take seriously the critique made by Shailaja Paik, who writes that savarna scholars, while focusing quite a bit of attention on Dalit communities, are "remarkably silent on Suvarna anxieties about caste sociality, which serve to mark other Indian communities as violent, anti-national, and foreign. They are thus complicit in perpetuating the myth of perceived unmarkedness as castelessness and thereby becoming casteless and burdening Dalits with caste." Paik, "Dalit Feminist Thought."

38 Manan Ahmed Asif writes, "The majorities of the subcontinent have accumulated power to govern, and they have condemned the minorities to be marginalized or to be expunged. . . . The majoritarian Sunni or Hindutva projects ask that we, as historians, consider them inevitable and immutable. . . . Undoubtedly, as postcolonized historians we have inherited the colonial episteme. . . . It is our collective task to re-imagine the past." Asif, *Loss of Hindustan*, 225.

39 Sharmila Rege writes, "Except for a few notable exceptions, women's studies scholars did not seriously engage with dalit feminist critiques. . . . This lack of engagement cannot be dismissed easily, either by savarna feminist justification of being 'frozen in guilt' . . . or by a resigned dalit feminist position that sees a 'fit of caste identities and ideological positions' (brahman and 'upper caste' women will be brahmanical). The former assumes that caste is solely the concern of dalit women. . . . The latter resigns itself to assuming the impossibility of transcending

caste identities." Rege, *Writing Caste, Writing Gender*, 4–5. See also C. Gupta, *The Gender of Caste*, for the possibilities of new ways of thinking and researching when one takes seriously "auto-critique" (xi).

With regard to being a caste traitor, I draw on the terms instantiated by Noel Ignatiev and the journal *Race Traitor*. See Ignatiev and Garvey, *Race Traitor*. I see caste treason similarly to the way that they argued as the slogan for each of the issues of their journal that "treason to whiteness is loyalty to humanity." This set of ideas resonates with ideas emerging from anticaste scholars. For example, Yengde calls for savarnas and Ambedkarite brahmins to serve as "a 'cultural suicide bomber' willing to blow up the oldest surviving edifice of discrimination." Yengde, *Caste Matters*, 30. While I agree with his sentiment, given my own relationship to suicide, I am less eager to use this phrasing to describe the work of annihilating caste.

40 The story of this project might actually start after college, when, not having any career direction, I joined Teach for America (TFA), thinking that I might enjoy teaching. A nonprofit organization, TFA recruits college graduates who have attended elite institutions in the United States to teach in many of the United States' most underresourced schools. At the time, I knew absolutely nothing about just how problematic TFA's project of salvation was, and my time at TFA was an absolute disaster. I left after teaching in New York City having no love for that organization but having cultivated a real love for teaching and an understanding that the education system was horrifically unequal. I came back to study at a graduate school of education with a conviction that I needed to know more about the systemic inequities perpetrated by these kinds of institutions.

41 I owe a great debt to Gajendran Ayyathurai, who, while I was an undergraduate student, pulled me aside to mention that my use of Tamil (one of the South Indian languages) marked me as a brahmin. He then handed me a copy of Kancha Ilaiah's *Why I Am Not a Hindu*. I devoured the text and suddenly was able to recognize why I had been so disturbed by the brahmin community I had grown up in. Professor Ayyathurai, in no uncertain terms, changed my life.

42 Zwick-Maitreyi et al., "Caste in the United States."

43 Let me not get into the endless savarna stories of struggle, rags-to-riches, and "coming to the USA with only $5 in their pockets" that give the illusion that the savarna in the United States fits snugly within the brown immigrant story.

44 Charania, review of *The Sense of Brown*.

45 I was inspired by a tweet by Discourse Hacker (@shudraism), who reminded on Twitter, "The most difficult Savarna Savior to combat with is the one within me." January 8, 2021, https://twitter.com/shudraism/status/1347459654624768003.

INTRODUCTION: BROWN SAVIORISM

Early versions of certain sections of this text were published in "The Making of the Brown Savior: Race, Caste, Class, and India's (Global) Help Economy," *Current Anthropology* 63, no.4 (2022): 431–53; "On Brown Blood: Race, Caste, and the Bhagat

Singh Thind Case," *Ethnic Studies Review* (2023): forthcoming; "Air-Conditioners and the Talk of the Middle Class," *City and Society* 33, no. 1 (2021), https://anthro source.onlinelibrary.wiley.com/doi/10.1111/ciso.12379; "Participation, Reception, Consent, and Refusal," in *The Routledge International Handbook of Ethnographic Film and Video*, ed. Phillip Vannini (London: Routledge, 2020), 204–13.

1   Nundy, "Accelerating Family Philanthropy."

2   Women and girls have been one primary target for these types of interventions in the brown world. See, for example, Khoja-Moolji, "Death by Benevolence"; Wilson, "Towards a Radical Re-appropriation"; A. Sharma, *Logics of Empowerment*; and Bernal and Grewal, *Theorizing NGOs*.

3   Kannada brahmins are brahmins whose mother tongue is Kannada.

4   Tamil brahmins are brahmins whose mother tongue is Tamil. For more on Tamil brahmins, see Fuller and Narasimhan, *Tamil Brahmans*.

5   Teach for India is modeled on Teach for America and also recruits college graduates to work for two years in India's most underresourced schools. Teach for India was founded by Shaheen Mistri, who was born in India but who moved along with her father, a senior manager for Citigroup, to Lebanon, Greece, Britain, Indonesia, and the United States. She, too, might be considered within the conceptual frame of the brown savior.

6   See Irani, *Chasing Innovation*, 11, for a discussion of the "global Indian." See also Radhakrishnan, *Appropriately Indian*.

7   Jacob Copeman and Dwaipayan Banerjee excavate blood politics in India. Especially important to my own work here is their recognition of the historical intersections of nation, race, caste, and blood. In the Indian context, they show how blood mixing is seen as a way of transcending caste—"using blood to go beyond blood"—even though it constantly coagulates around these very same racialized categories of nation and caste. See Copeman and Banerjee, *Hematologies*, 37.

8   Ferreira da Silva, *Toward a Global Idea of Race*, xix.

9   As Amy Bhatt has written, this migration of Indians was part of the massive reconfiguration of the global system of racial capitalism that accompanied the end of World War II and continued in the postneoliberal era of H1B visas for educated workers from India. See Bhatt, *High-Tech Housewives*.

10 Sara Ahmed writes that those "who embody diversity . . . are assumed to bring whiteness to an end by virtue of [their] arrival." Ahmed, *Living a Feminist Life*, 5. See also Táíwò, "Identity Politics and Elite Capture," on "elite capture"; and Haider, *Mistaken Identity*, on the commodification of "identity politics" in a way that completely strips the term of its radical, intersectional, anticapitalist meaning as set forth by the Combahee River Collective. Jared Sexton has characterized this phenomenon as "people-of color-blindness." See Sexton, "People-of-Color-Blindness."

11 Escobar, *Encountering Development*.

12 See Du Bois, *Souls of Black Folk*, 13. Du Bois wrote, "The problem of the twentieth century is the problem of the color-line; the relation of the lighter to the darker

races of men in Asia and Africa, in America and the islands of the sea" Du Bois, *Souls of Black Folk*, 13.

13 Subramanian, "Making Merit."

14 See also Jobson, "The Case for Letting Anthropology Burn."

15 Amrute, *Encoding Race, Encoding Class*; and Subramanian, *Caste of Merit*.

16 I began my first phase of fieldwork in March 2013 and continued in the field until June 2014. I took follow-up trips during the summers of 2015, 2016, and 2018. I also traveled to Bangalore in the winters of 2016/17 and 2019/20.

17 Bornstein and Sharma, "The Righteous and the Rightful."

18 The terms *liberalism* and *liberal* can be ambiguous in their usage and meaning. Traditionally, *liberalism* has been used as a catchall term for a set of Western governance ideals that are associated with the ambiguously defined values of liberty, freedom, individuality, equality, rationality, rule of law, separation of church and state, and the like. Secularism, in particular, is an ideology that maintains that the state can govern without a formal affiliation with a particular religious doctrine/majority; it functions as a fulcrum for liberal governance strategies because it opens up the constant negotiation of majoritarian versus minoritarian rights claims. I prefer the term *late liberalism* when thinking about current liberal-secular projects, which, as Elizabeth Povinelli argues, are the "formal or informal policies of cultural recognition (or cognate policies such as multiculturalism) as a strategy for addressing the challenge of internal and external difference." Povinelli, *Economies of Abandonment*, 25. In other words, managing difference became key to the economic and political projects in the late liberal state, bringing into its ambit institutional actors as diverse as government technocrats, market researchers, scholars, and humanitarian actors. *Liberals* in this definitional context might best be understood as those tasked, either formally or informally, with managing difference in neoliberal, secular societies. See also Chow, *The Protestant Ethnic and the Spirit of Capitalism*; and Jobson, "The Case for Letting Anthropology Burn." One way of understanding the relationship between "liberals" and "fascists" is that liberals—whether pursuing profit, care, or oppression—reproduce categories, oftentimes colonial, to manage difference. These, in turn, become the very same categories that are reappropriated by fascists toward their own draconian ends. However, many scholars have reminded that these ideologies need to be studied in culturally and historically specific contexts precisely because they come to mean very different things in, for example, the United States versus a place like India. For example, liberalism and secularism in the Indian case pivot on the postcolonial condition initiated by the end of British colonialism and the beginning of a constitutional democracy founded against the backdrop of religious violence (Hindu/Muslim), caste violence (dominant caste/oppressed caste), regional variation (North/South India and urban/rural), and the obvious fact that those building this so-called liberal democracy were part of a Western-educated elite minority.

19 In this narrative, both British colonialism and previous Mughal rule are conflated to produce a mythology in which all Hindus have been oppressed by outside invad-

ers for the past five hundred years, while also erasing the fact that India's caste society existed before these imperial regimes and continues to violently oppress Dalit communities.

20 Calling someone a brown sepoy is meant to suggest that a person looks Indian but is actually colonized with a white Anglo mindset. Historically, the sepoy was a soldier serving in the British army. However, it has come to be used for anyone perceived as elite, including anyone who may have been part of colonial bureaucracies or who currently inhabits positions that likely require interfacing with communities outside of India and involve the use of the English language. Primarily, however, the pejorative is focused on those who critique the erosion of Indian democracy and the rise of supremacist elements. I, for example, would be a classic example of the brown sepoy for Hindutva given my politics and the fact that I live in the United States.

21 See Kelley, foreword to *Border and Rule*; and Walia, *Border and Rule*.

22 Scheduled Caste is the government-sanctioned term to characterize those castes who had previously been considered "untouchable." People from these castes generally prefer the term *Dalit*. Rupa Viswanath writes, "'SC' and 'Dalit' simply refer to different sets of people. Where 'Dalit' refers to all those Indians, past and present, traditionally regarded as outcasts and untouchable, 'SC' is a modern governmental category that explicitly excludes Christian and Muslim Dalits." See Viswanath, "Textbook Case of Exclusion."

With regard to the percentages of populations in Karnataka, these numbers are shrouded in controversy, and the populations of Muslims and Scheduled Castes could actually be even higher. A Caste Census report in 2018 suggested that the Muslim and Scheduled Caste populations in India were both higher than the Vokkaliga or Lingayat populations, creating extreme concern for dominant-caste politicians. See Satish, "Dalits, Muslims Outnumber Lingayats and Vokkaligas in Karnataka?"

23 Povinelli has termed this phenomenon liberalism's "cunning of recognition." See Povinelli, *Cunning of Recognition*.

24 See Annavarupa, "Risky Routes, Safe Suspicions," for a slightly different, middle class women's perspective on the potential for sexual violence while in cabs and on roads in South India.

25 B. R. Ambedkar argues that caste as a division of labor is accompanied by a "gradation of labourers." Ambedkar, *Annihilation of Caste*, 234.

26 I am drawing from and extending Gayatri Chakravorty Spivak's critique of colonialism through the excavation of the native informant. She writes, "I shall docket the encrypting of the name of the 'native informant' *as the name of Man*— the name that carries with it the inaugurating affect of being human. . . . I borrow the term from ethnography, of course. In that discipline, the native informant, although denied autobiography as it is understood in Northwestern European tradition (codename 'West'), is taken with utmost seriousness. He (and occasionally she) is a blank, though generative of a text of cultural identity that only the West (or a Western-model of discipline) could inscribe. The practice of some

benevolent cultural nativists today can be compared to this, although the cover story there is of a fully self-present voice-consciousness. Increasingly, there is a self-marginalizing and self-consolidating migrant or postcolonial masquerading as a 'native informant.'" Spivak, *Critique of Postcolonial Reason*, 5–6.

27 See Robb, *Concept of Race in South Asia*, for a general overview of various conceptions of race in India. Most recently, Jesús Cháirez-Garza and colleagues developed a conceptual framework for the study of India and global racialization in "Rethinking Difference in India through Racialization."

28 Wimmer and Schiller, "Methodological Nationalism."

29 Mariam Durrani argues that methodological nationalism constrains how researchers construct their studies, binding their field sites in ways that prevent analyses that reveal interlocking forms of imperial power. See Durrani, "The Imperial Optic." However, Durrani has also pointed out to me on many occasions that grant-conferring agencies facilitate these rigid, conservative, unimaginative, bounded projects by funding only those whose work fits into neat national boundaries and already existing religious, ethnic, and linguistic ways of seeing particular communities. For example, while my own project has changed quite a bit from its initial articulations, it was funded by the Fulbright-Hays Program precisely because it fit the simplistic criteria of nation-centric research that also seemed to focus on already fundable categories associated with India, including rurality and poverty.

30 On Twitter, historian Isabel H. Alonso wrote, "I have to say this bc it has to be said and bc waiting for tenure will kill something in me: South Asia-related US academia is not diverse: it is Brahmin (and upper-caste) and white, and the gatekeeping is so strong. For those facing it, I am here for you. YouAreNotAlone" (@tarikhistorias, July 8, 2020).

31 This critique of postcolonial theory has been made many times over. See S. Shankar, *Flesh and Fish Blood*. See also Good et al., *Postcolonial Disorders*; McClintock, "Angel of Progress"; and Grosfoguel, "Decolonizing Post-colonial Studies." Finally, I would be remiss if I did not at least mention the elitism of subaltern studies, which supposedly opened up a sphere of discourse critiquing colonialism from below, while safely maintaining all of the simplistic strictures of nationalist savarna ideologies of difference.

32 Texts that have greatly influenced my thinking on the colonial inception of race thesis include Harrison, *Decolonizing Anthropology*; Hesse, "Im/plausible Deniability"; Rodney, *How Europe Underdeveloped Africa*; Gopal, *Insurgent Empire*; Lowe, *Intimacies of Four Continents*; Ferreira da Silva, *Toward a Global Idea of Race*; D. Thomas, *Political Life in the Wake of the Plantation*; Carby, *Imperial Intimacies*; and Du Bois, *Black Reconstruction in America*.

The term *franchise colonialism* is used here to distinguish it from other forms of colonialism, such as settler colonialism. Franchise colonialism, especially as it was practiced by the British in India, is marked by its extractivist orientation, in which the colony is perceived as a site for resources (diamonds, spices, textiles, etc.) as well as a site to sell manufactured goods (therefore extracting hard money from the colonies as well). Utsa Patnaik argues that the British extracted nearly

$45 trillion from India from 1765 to 1938, a number that she also cautions is a massive underestimate. U. Patnaik, "How the British Impoverished India." I am also drawing from Deborah Thomas's framing of the history of global racialization: "The 'settling' of the New World . . . saw the twin transformative processes of racial fixing (of diverse African peoples into *negros* and diverse indigenous New World populations into *indios*) and racial flexibility (the various configurations of creolization, transculturation, and hybridity that emerged). . . . The initial racialized elaborations of what it means to be human would be subsequently mobilized to serve late nineteenth-century projects of indirect imperial rule throughout Africa and South Asia, as well as the emergent imperialist project of the United States." D. Thomas, *Political Life in the Wake of the Plantation*, 3–4.

33 Du Bois, *Black Reconstruction in America*, 16.

34 Du Bois, *Black Reconstruction in America*, 15.

35 Du Bois wrote, "Americans saw throughout the world the shadow of the coming change of the philanthropic attitude which had dominated the early nineteenth century, with regard to the backward races. International and commercial imperialism began to get a vision. Within the very echo of that philanthropy which had abolished the slave trade, was beginning a new industrial slavery of black and brown and yellow workers in Africa and Asia." Du Bois, *Black Reconstruction in America*, 632. See also Khan, "Indebted among the 'Free,'" for one example of how the abolition of slavery produced new circuits of exploited, bonded coolie labor from India.

36 Lowe, *Intimacies of Four Continents*, 150.

37 I also find Sareeta Amrute's definition of *racialization* helpful here. Drawing on Frantz Fanon, she writes that racialization directs our attention to how "the capacity to labor in particular ways and cultural knowledge are 'epidermalized'— mapped onto the skin, clothing, smell, and mannerisms of living bodies." I would add essentializing discourses regarding blood, DNA, and national belonging to Amrute's definition of that which is epidermalized. See Amrute, *Encoding Race, Encoding Class*, 14.

38 Moon Charania makes the excellent point that scholars come to "brownness" from a number of different intellectual traditions which shape how they understand its valences. She writes, "I come to brownness through women of color feminisms and queerness, thinking here of how Muñoz—learning from Audre Lorde, Gloria Anzaldua, Barbara Christian, Combahee River Collective to name a few—furthered the notion of a queerness that is always and already in relation to blackness and brownness. And this route to brownness versus other routes (say W.E.B Dubois's color line, Stuart Hall's floating signifier, Gayatri Spivak's subalternity) is another sort of reckoning." Charania, review of *The Sense of Brown*. I come to brownness most directly through Du Bois and Spivak.

39 Sharma writes, "Brown's work as an adjective ('brown bird'), verb ('to brown'), and noun parallels its references to multiple groups of people, including those from Africa, Asia, Europe, the Pacific, and Latin America. Given that many people have 'brown' skin, 'Brown' of course refers to much more than skin color and

phenotype . . . The unsettled and untethered uses of 'Brown' illustrate the ambiguity and contestation that define its history." N. Sharma, "Brown," 18.

40 See Mohammed, "But Most of All Mi Love Me Browning." As another example, writing from a perspective that is rooted in Filipino, Mexican, and Latin American racial theorizings, Anthony Ocampo argues that "Brown is not a fixed racial label, but rather an indexing of a shared relationship to a dominant order." Ocampo, *Brown and Gay in LA*. See also Guzman, "Brown."

41 Indians migrated to a vast number of places based on specific histories of movement. They traveled to the United Kingdom, Uganda, Ethiopia, Mauritia, Guyana, Trinidad and Tobago, Australia, Belgium, France, and the United States, among many other places. Each of these migratory patterns has specific relations to caste, class, religion, language, and labor.

42 In much of the Orientalist scholarship on India, *brown* has been perceived as "foreign" to the subcontinent because it is an "English" term. As such, brown has not often been considered a useful category for analyzing Indians or South Asians more broadly, except as it pertains to a narrow diasporic population living in the United States. However, because English became the language of the elite after British colonialism in its colonies and has continued to accrue value with the rise of American imperial regimes, there is an expanding association between brownness, mobility, and the speaking of English.

43 Muñoz, *Sense of Brown*, 122.

44 Here I am evoking Carby, *Imperial Intimacies*; and Lowe, *Intimacies of Four Continents*.

45 Nehru, *Autobiography*, 500.

46 Charania, review of *The Sense of Brown*.

47 For a further elaboration on the politics of Red and Black blood in the United States, see TallBear and Tuck, "Red and Black DNA, Blood, Kinship and Organizing." See also Hannabach, *Blood Cultures*. With regard to the politics of blood in relation to Blackness and Indigeneity, Flores writes, "In the United States. . . . there is the well-known black-white binary with its infamous 'one-drop rule,' enacted during the era of slavery and continuing well into the twentieth century, stipulating that anyone with African ancestry, however remote, is considered Black. Although these attitudes might suggest that miscegenation is anathema, the US American position toward Indigenous Americans has been starkly different. As opposed to the 'expansive' understanding of Black, 'Native Americanness is subtractive.' The disappearance of the Native was sought at all costs because 'the goal of settler colonialism is to diminish claims to land over generations (or sooner, if possible).'" Flores, "Latinidad is Cancelled," 58. In this quote, Flores is citing Tuck and Yang, "Decolonization Is Not a Metaphor," 12.

48 Lee Baker argues that in the context of North American racial politics, a supposed progressive racial agenda required that "the Negro needed to amalgamate by 'encouraging the gradual process of lightening up this large body of people by the influx of white blood.'" Baker, "Racist Anti-racism of American Anthropology," 127. Here I want to argue that the ideology of assimilation can be understood as

browning one's blood, even as the values, ideologies, and understandings of self were rendered white. In Latin America, especially, the romance of mixing has been used to argue that Spanish colonialism was less, or even not, racist because they were not concerned with blood purity. See Martinez, *Genealogical Fictions*, 8.

49 See Macaulay, "Minute on Indian Education." However, lest we imagine that the ideology of assimilation was a purely British notion, Walter Rodney reminds us that assimilationist ideologies and civilizing educational projects were also central to French, Portuguese, and Belgian colonialism. See Rodney, *How Europe Underdeveloped Africa*, 302.

50 I draw on Deborah Thomas's definition of *modernity*: "By 'modernity', I mean to signal the particular arrangement of political and economic life that emerged during the late 15th century as mercantile capitalism came to dominate new understandings of the relationship between economic activity and social and political hierarchies, and as imperialism and the trans-Atlantic slave trade became the foundation of new political and juridical arrangements." D. Thomas, "End of the West," 124.

51 Du Bois famously outlined the way that British colonialism in India was inherently racist. He wrote, "The situation in India is another case of racial conflict. . . . The basic reason for this, openly or by inference, is the physical difference of race which makes it, according to British thought, impossible that these peoples should within any reasonable space of time become autonomous or self-governing." Du Bois, "Prospect of a World without Racial Conflict," 451.

52 Sylvia Wynter discusses how neoliberal, secular, biologized ideologies regarding humanity replace earlier religious forms *and yet* remain as intransigently dogmatic and self-assured in the belief that all humans, for any hope of salvation, must follow in line. See Wynter and McKittrick, "*Unparalleled Catastrophe for Our Species?*," 26. See also Mignolo, *Darker Side of Western Modernity*, 14; and Rist, *History of Development*.

53 The Bretton Woods institutions were initially created to help with the post–World War II reconstruction of Europe. In that capacity, their policy suggestions were largely geared toward rebuilding infrastructures and national economies in Keynesian-style redevelopment terms that also restricted the flow of speculative capital. By contrast, the same institutions famously imposed structural adjustment policies for those nation-states that were emerging in the "Global South" and/or the "Third World," placing them in unequal financial relationships with the Global North and preventing the kind of institutional developments necessary to begin to join and prosper in a world economy.

I also want to note that the history of the term *Third World* is quite a bit more complicated than its pejorative connotation vis-à-vis developmentalist discourse. Third Worldism was a project of postcolonized nation-states to generate unity among themselves and challenge their position in the global racial and economic order. See Prashad, *Darker Nations*.

54 Muñoz is speaking primarily about the Latinx populations in the Americas when he is describing the poverty of brownness. However, in taking up his concepts and placing them in relation to the production of the "Third World," I see the relation

between poverty and brownness as a global postcolonized condition. See Muñoz, *Sense of Brown*.

55 P. Patnaik, "Why Is India's Wealth Inequality Growing So Rapidly?"

56 See Gidwani, *Capital, Interrupted*, for an excellent discussion of this shift in developmentalist reason.

57 Ananya Roy coins the term *poverty capital* to discuss the circulation of financial resources as they pertain to microfinance. Erica Caple James uses the term *compassion economies* to discuss the way that Haitian people, especially women, reorganize themselves into the category of *viktim* as a strategy to partake in international aid. Kalyan Sanyal argues that the "need economy" is the NGO-state solution to the problem of surplus population. See Ananya Roy, *Poverty Capital*; James, *Democratic Insecurities*; and Sanyal, *Rethinking Capitalist Development*.

58 "Old tyrants" is from Césaire, *Discourse on Colonialism*, 43.

59 Fanon writes, "The more the black Antillean assimilates the French language, the whiter he gets. . . . Going one step further we shall enlarge the scope of our description to include every colonized subject. All colonized people—in other words, people in whom an inferiority complex has taken root . . . —position themselves in relation to the civilizing language. . . . After a fairly long stay in the metropole, many Antilleans return home to be deified." Fanon, *Black Skin, White Masks*, 2–3.

60 While Fanon is speaking specifically about Black Antilleans who have been colonized by the French, his analysis lends itself to reconsidering these elites as being *browned*, as his "phenotype undergoes an absolute mutation" that indexes an ascension within the colonial racist hierarchy but that *can never achieve whiteness*. Fanon, *Black Skin, White Masks*, 3.

61 Gajendran Ayyathurai writes, "Colonial racial capitalism depended for its success (and stability) on comprador privileged caste groups. . . . The brahmins—who are not even five percent of India's population, then and now—through the propagation of their caste-power and by predominantly working the British colonial apparatuses reaped maximum benefits. Such caste groups not only viciously appropriated the labor and land of the oppressed communities but also normalized their dependency on the colonialist-casteist structures." Ayyathurai, "Emigration against Caste," 46. See also Slate, *Colored Cosmopolitanism*, for an example of a work that hails racial solidarities between civil rights activists in the United States and independence leaders in India in ways that can obfuscate material differences between Black civil rights activists and savarna elites like Nehru and Gandhi in India.

62 There has been a robust discussion on development in India, both as it began postindependence and as it has been reshaped in the postliberalization period. Three books that have influenced my work are Gidwani, *Capital, Interrupted*; A. Gupta, *Postcolonial Developments*; and A. Sharma, *Logics of Empowerment*.

63 Algerian feminist scholar Melyssa Haffaf mentioned in conversation with me that the "brown sahib" figure reminded her of a similar figure called the Harki in Algeria. *The Harki* is a term for those Muslim Algerians who served as auxiliaries in the French army during the Algerian War of Independence from 1954 to 1962, but

it can also be glossed as a term for any Algerian Muslims who supported French Algeria during the war. What strikes me about this figure and the discussion we had was the way that various colonial encounters produce different versions of brown in-betweenness that reflect the specific ways that colonized people, especially elites, imbibed colonial values, ideologies, and the like.

64 Charania, review of *The Sense of Brown*. Nitasha Sharma also makes this point, arguing, "As a racial category forged through racialist ideologies and colonization, Brown often reflects the intermediary hierarchal position of those who are neither Black nor (fully) White." N. Sharma, "Brown," 18.

65 Charania, review of *The Sense of Brown*.

66 Burton, *Africa in the Indian Imagination*.

67 Ministry of Foreign Affairs, "Brown Man's Burden," 16. This discussion was included in the first *Asian-African Conference Bulletin*, issued by the Ministry of Foreign Affairs, the Republic of Indonesia, in March 1955.

68 One important outgrowth of this brown man's burden was a massive post-1947 bursary project in India to bring East African students to India to study. African students continue to migrate to India for educational opportunities and, when they do, face the intense anti-African, anti-Black sentiment of Indian nationals. See Burton, *Africa in the Indian Imagination*; and Dattatreyan, "Desiring Bollywood," for more on this subject.

69 Rosa, *Looking Like a Language, Sounding Like a Race*, 3.

70 Ruha Benjamin argues, "Tech advances are sold as morally superior because they purport to rise above human bias and are therefore considered neutral solutions to global problems that occlude the histories of exclusion and discrimination" that get encoded into new digital technologies. See R. Benjamin, *Race after Technology*, 11.

71 Ajantha Subramanian writes of this phenomenon in her study of the Indian Institute of Technology (IIT), stating, "Such patterns of racialization for the market are strikingly evident within the global 'knowledge economy.' The 2003 episode of *60 Minutes* is just one example of the current fetishizing of the IITian as today's 'global Indian.' IITians themselves have been particularly adept at forging diasporic networks that shore up the value of Brand IIT." Subramanian, "Making Merit," 315.

72 See Rana, *Terrifying Muslims*.

73 S. Thomas, *Privileged Minorities*; Kikon, "Hello Chinky"; Jegathesan, *Tea and Solidarity*; Durrani, "The Imperial Optic"; and Dattatreyan, *Globally Familiar*.

74 Bald, *Bengali Harlem*; Thangaraj, *Desi Hoop Dreams*; Upadhyay, "Making of 'Model' South Asians on the Tar Sands"; and Amrute, *Encoding Race, Encoding Class*.

75 See Wilson, "Re-centring 'Race' in Development."

76 Cháirez-Garza et al., "Rethinking Difference in India through Racialization," 194.

77 Soundararajan, "How Brown Girl Solidarity Harms Us." Similarly, referencing the hashtag #Unfairandlovely, which was meant to challenge white beauty standards, Shaista Patel writes, "Claiming pride in our shades of brown skins is admirable, and urgently needed. . . . However, we have to center the fact that lower caste and

Dalits, associated with impurity, dirt and inhumanity have informed our fear of Blackness and Black or dark brown skin in South Asia." S. Patel, "Complicating the Tale of 'Two Indians.'"

78 Subramanian explains that B. R. Ambedkar set educational reservations in place to rectify the historical legacy of untouchability in India, which included a 20 percent reservation of seats in educational institutions for Scheduled Castes and Scheduled Tribes. In 1979, after the Mandal Commission Report, reservations were expanded to include Other Backward Classes. The expanded reservations were met with protests by savarnas against the "unfair" advantages received by the oppressed castes despite the fact that dominant castes were still disproportionately attending India's most prestigious institutions. This shift was occurring at the very moment that the reservation system was producing some upward mobility for the oppressed castes in the public sector, resulting in brahmin (and savarna) migrations to urban centers and abroad for private-sector jobs, in which caste was not a protected category. Ultimately, what emerged was a cultural politics related to educational attainment and caste that further marked the lower castes while allowing the dominant castes to see themselves as meritorious entrants into higher education despite their massive historical accumulation of caste capital. This version of racialized merit discourse propelled savarna men into global roles as the techno-cognitariate by transforming caste capital into modern forms of "casteless" capital while perpetuating the myth that savarna Hindus, especially brahmins, had a primordial disposition toward service and the unique cognitive capacities to fix any of society's ailments. See Subramanian, *Caste of Merit*.

79 Ambedkar wrote, "The caste system is not merely a division of labourers—which is quite different from division of labour—it is a hierarchy in which the divisions of labourers are graded one above the other." Ambedkar, *Essential Writings*, 263. "Untouchability" is rooted in ideas regarding occupations that were deemed "polluting" and therefore spiritually "impure" and therefore outside the varna system. By contrast, in trying to argue for a cross-cultural approach to caste, Berreman defined a caste system as "a hierarchy of endogamous divisions in which membership is hereditary and permanent." Berreman, "Caste in India and the United States," 120.

80 See, for example, Fields and Fields, *Racecraft*.

81 See Thomas, "Cox's America: Caste, Race, and the Problem of Culture" for a thorough discussion of Oliver Cox's ideas and its relation to the "racial caste" school. See also Berreman, "Caste in India and the United States" for a comparative perspective.

82 Ambedkar, *Annihilation of Caste*, 236.

83 For discussions of both Wilkerson's text and the relation of race and caste, see Burden-Stelly, "Caste Does Not Explain Race"; Carby, "Limits of Caste"; Dutt, "Feeling Like an Outcast"; and A. Rao, "Work of Analogy."

84 See Burden-Stelly, "Caste Does Not Explain Race," for an excellent racial capitalist critique of Wilkerson's book as it pertains to the United States.

85 See D. Thomas, "Cox's America"; and Berreman "Caste in India and the United States." See also Visweswaran, *UnCommon Cultures*.

86   Chinnaiah Jangam, for example, argues, "One of the limitations of Ambedkar's understanding of caste is that he doesn't investigate the role of colonialism in strengthening . . . caste and also strengthening . . . Brahminism. Jyotiba Phule . . . sees this interconnection between Brahminism and colonialism . . . they are working in alliance with each other in reinforcing the caste system. In this context what you see is that if you really want to see what should be the project of decolonizing caste . . . we have to look at this whole idea of interconnection between race, caste and gender, and its invisible epistemological interconnections, particularly with white supremacy, with Brahminical Hindu supremacy." Jangam, "Decolonizing Caste."

87   In 2001, for example, a contingent of Dalit scholars and activists who attended the UN-led Durban World Conference against Racism, Racial Discrimination, Xenophobia, and Related Intolerance argued that caste should be understood, at least in part, as a form of racial discrimination because it hinges on questions of blood, descent, and labor, postcolonization. This claim was challenged by the Indian state, which sought to argue that caste was a social problem of religion and an "internal matter" to India and therefore not a problem of global racial discrimination. See Rawat and Satyanarayana, *Dalit Studies*, 7; and Pinto, "UN Conference against Racism."

88   Suraj Yengde argues, "Caste has been thought of as an institution intimately tied to the Indian past and present. However, caste as a social system invested in purity, pollution, endogamy, hierarchy, and inflexibility locked in the rigidity of birth, is found in major societies across the world." Yengde, "Global Castes," 340.

89   *Jati* refers to one of the thousands of endogamous clans, tribes, communities, and subcommunities in India. Each jati typically has an association with a traditional job function. The British categorized the many thousands of jatis into either one of the four varnas (brahmin, kshatriya, vaishya, Shudra) or the avarna (outcastes) of the brahminical varna classification system. See Bayly, *Caste, Society and Politics in India*; and Dirks, *Castes of Mind*, for extensive discussions of the relation between colonialism and caste. See also Carby, "Limits of Caste"; and Jangam, "Decolonizing Caste."

90   Trauttman, *Aryan Debate*.

91   Shankar, "On Brown Blood."

92   *United States v. Bhagat Singh Thind*, 261 U.S. 204 (1923), at 261 U.S. 215.

93   Jangam, "Decolonizing Caste."

94   In fact, in some cases, colonial modernity may have actually punctured the institutional forms of savarna supremacy and therefore benefited the caste oppressed. For one extremely important example, see P. Sanal Mohan's *Modernity of Slavery*, which argues that the "slave castes" of Kerala converted in large numbers to Christianity during their encounter with European missionaries in the nineteenth and early twentieth centuries. These experiences reshaped what Dalit consciousness looked like in Kerala and how equality and mobility were imagined afterward. In his review of Mohan's text, Uday Chandra writes, "The single most important lesson of Sanal Mohan's finely-crafted book is to rethink the nature of colonial

modernity and its implications for historically subordinated groups in ex-colonial territories.... [C]olonialism may ... have, paradoxically, been central to the efforts of Dalits and other subaltern groups to overcome the historical conditions of their subordination." Chandra, review of *Modernity of Slavery*, 211.

95 Ambedkar had argued that Dalits should be allowed to choose their own separate representatives to the legislature independently and *also* vote in the general constituency. He argued that this "double vote" would eventually lead to the full dignity of and respect for Dalits as political actors over time. However, when the double vote was to be enshrined as part of the Communal Award (1932), Gandhi, who was steadfastly opposed to anything but a single voting block for all whom he considered Hindu, announced a fast unto death. While Ambedkar tried to hold his ground against this form of coercion, eventually he signed the Poona Pact, which gave up the double vote and the separate electorate while leaving the reserved seats for Dalits within the general electorate. See S. Anand, "A Note on the Poona Pact."

96 Subramanian, *Caste of Merit*.

97 Over the past five years, caste-based discrimination in the United States has finally come under scrutiny and become a cause for policy change. For example, in November 2021 the University of California (UC), Davis, added caste to its antidiscrimination policy, making it the first UC institution to acknowledge the existence of caste discrimination in the United States and on its campus. In 2019 Brandeis University became the first US institution of higher education to ban caste-based discrimination. Chopra and Subramanian, "Caste Discrimination Exists in the U.S., Too—But a Movement to Outlaw It Is Growing."

98 Ayyathurai, "It Is Time for a New Subfield." Another response has been the field of Dalit studies, which has centered the movements, narratives, and histories of struggle against caste-based oppression by Dalit communities. See, for example, Rawat and Satyanarayana, *Dalit Studies*. Others include P. Mohan, *Modernity of Slavery*; Guru, "How Egalitarian Are the Social Sciences in India?"; A. Rao, *Gender and Caste*; Jaffrelot, *Dr. Ambedkar and Untouchability*; Omvedt, *Understanding Caste*; Paik, *Dalit Women's Education in Modern India*; and Rege, *Writing Caste, Writing Gender*.

99 Yengde, *Caste Matters*, 33.

100 Minai and Shroff, "Yaariyan, Baithak, Gupshup."

101 See the preface for detailed discussion of my approach to "nervous ethnography."

102 As the title suggests, part 1 is *by far* the most theoretically (in the academic sense) burdened part of the book.

103 Ong and Roy, *Worlding Cities*.

104 R. Benjamin, *Race after Technology*; and Noble, *Algorithms of Oppression*.

1. GLOBAL HELP ECONOMIES AND RACIAL CAPITALISM

1 Suraj Yengde argues, "The networks that become the lingua franca of a capitalist society are nothing but caste-based ties, wherein a person from a specific caste ensures that his fellow caste people are given opportunities." Yengde, *Caste Matters*,

1. See also Mosse, "Caste and Development"; and Chakrovorty, Kapur, and Singh, *Other One Percent*.

2 Shailaja Paik writes, "Despite India's more accessible and much improved education system, the Indian economy has failed to create large numbers of secure jobs for those it educates. This has created a serious problem of unemployment among educated Dalit youth in North India." While Paik is writing specifically about Dalit youth in North India, this insight is valuable to my study of Karnataka state, where the number of youth who graduate without jobs is also high. See Paik, *Dalit Women's Education in Modern India*, 16. Siddharth Anil Nair, in "More Than Half the Graduates Not Getting Employed," reports that "Karnataka's combined 600+ Engineering and Management institutions have produced an average placement rate of 30% (at best) between 2012–17, while 277 post-graduate institutions have produced an average placement rate of 40% for the same."

3 David Harvey reenergized the question of primitive accumulation in relation to landlessness with his framework of "accumulation by dispossession." However, the expropriation of land, as Savannah Shange makes explicit in her rephrasing of "neocolonial-cum-neoliberal dispossession," was and is never random; it is based on neocolonial categorizations and differentiations. See Harvey, "'New' Imperialism"; and Shange, *Progressive Dystopia*, 9.

4 Jeffrey, *Timepass*. Jeffrey, Jeffrey, and Jeffrey, *Degrees without Freedom?*

5 Enloe, *Curious Feminist*, 215.

6 One struggle I continue to face given the fact of "good intentions" is how to continue to make sharp critiques of how participants, friends, and colleagues uphold oppressive systems without incorrectly collapsing personhood with systemic forces.

7 Prabhat Patnaik explains how and why global poverty has not gone down anywhere in the world (except China) between 1990 and 2010 when using any reasonable metric for measuring standard of living. See P. Patnaik, "Decline in Poverty Rate."

8 "25 Facts and Stats about NGOs Worldwide," Volunteers.org, June 15, 2016. See also Giridharadas, *Winners Take All*.

9 Elyachar, *Markets of Dispossession;* Manzo, "Imaging Humanitarianism."

10 Wilde, *The Soul of Man Under Socialism*, 2.

11 Shange, *Progressive Dystopia*, 158.

12 Cole, "White-Savior Industrial Complex."

13 Here I draw from the definition offered by Shange: "Late liberal . . . is a modifier that attempts to index the changing global landscape after the collapse of Fordist-Keynesianism, while also calling attention to the *continuities* between the neoliberal era and the age of globalization ushered in by transatlantic slavery and franchise colonialism." Shange, *Progressive Dystopia*, 6.

14 Arundhati Roy summarizes this well: "The Privatization of Everything has also meant the NGO-ization of Everything. As jobs and livelihoods disappeared, NGOs have become an important source of employment, even for those who see them for what they are. And they are certainly not all bad. Of the millions of NGOs, some do remarkable, radical work, and it would be a travesty to tar all NGOs with

the same brush. However, the corporate or foundation-endowed NGO are global finance's way of buying into resistance movements. . . . They sit like nodes on the central nervous system, the pathways along which global finance flows." Arundhati Roy, *Capitalism*, Kindle loc. 408 of 1319.

15 See Bernal and Grewal, *Theorizing NGOs*, 8, for a comprehensive framing of the NGO as part of the neoliberal state project, specifically in relation to feminist struggle.

16 In discussing microcredit in India, Smitha Radhakrishnan notes, "According to a 2016 report, India is the second-most unequal country in the world, after South Africa, with millionaires controlling 54 percent of the country's wealth. Economic indicators suggest that these staggering levels of inequality have been accompanied by rising unemployment since the early 2000s, with a spike in 2018, especially among urban women." Radhakrishnan, *Making Women Pay*, 4.

17 See Tukdeo, *India Goes to School*, for a comprehensive look at the current state of the Indian education system; Ladousa, *Hindi Is Our Ground, English Is Our Sky*, for more on English education; and Kumar, "Against Neoliberal Assault on Education in India," for how markets and privatization have impacted India's education system.

18 Manash Pratim Gohain reports that the primary shift has been from government schools to unaided private schools, which require fees and purport to be English medium but have shown no statistically significant benefit for students, even by traditional metrics of test scores or graduation rates. Rural India, while not seeing as dramatic a shift to unaided private schools as urban areas, still has seen a steady rise in private schools as well, from 9 percent in 1978, to 27 percent in 2017. See Gohain, "Why Half of India Prefers Private Schools."

19 Dustin Jenkins and Justin Leroy write that just as "the invasion of indigenous lands is not a single moment in time but an ongoing structuring logic in all settler societies, our conception of racial capitalism frames primitive accumulation as an ongoing organizing principle of capitalist social order." Jenkins and Leroy, *Histories of Racial Capitalism*, 11.

20 There are several potential reasons that racial capitalist critique has not fully emerged in scholarship on global help economies. First, because theorizings of racial capitalism have, sometimes problematically, assumed abject (neo)colonial violence—enslavement, incarceration, militarization, land dispossession, and the like—the moralizing projects associated with help and care work seem to fit quite uneasily. See Ralph and Singhal, *Racial Capitalism*. Second, part of the scholarly fissure over the past fifty years has been a pernicious separation of the United States, and its conversation on race and racialization, from the rest, creating a situation in which the humanitarian, developmentalist, and human rights imaginaries continue to draw from neocolonial racial paradigms without attention to how they emerged as part of the production of the global color line(s). See Johnson, "Racial Capitalism and Human Rights."

21 I am deeply indebted to the work of Nell Gabiam, who has shown how humanitarianism (as a short-term urgent response to crisis) and development (as long-

term modernist infrastructural and human projects) have merged in most of the postcolonized world. See Gabiam, "When 'Humanitarianism' Becomes 'Development.'" On development as "colonialism in disguise," see U. Kothari, "Agenda for Thinking about 'Race' in Development"; Wilson, *Race, Racism and Development*; and A. Kothari et al., *Pluriverse*.

22 Ferreira da Silva, "Race and Development," 39. With regard to humanitarian projects, see Benton, "Risky Business." See also White, "Thinking Race, Thinking Development"; and Lowe, *Intimacies of Four Continents*.

23 K. Patel, "Race and a Decolonial Turn in Development."

24 Benton, "Risky Business," 190.

25 As Ferreira da Silva writes, social scientific scholarship on the help economies may occlude race because scholars implicitly assume the same racialized power differentials that undergird the project of help (First World/Third World, developed/underdeveloped, etc.), which inadvertently naturalizes these differentials. Kothari writes that this process of naturalization "masks the profound material implications of 'race' in terms of its impact upon the unequal distribution of resources that shape dynamics of poverty and exclusion." Ferreira da Silva, "Race and Development"; and U. Kothari, "Agenda for Thinking about 'Race' in Development," 10.

26 Escobar, *Encountering Development*.

27 This move conveniently sidestepped more complicated discussions about reparations to the many people dispossessed by colonial extraction. See, for example, Táíwò, *Reconsidering Reparations*.

28 Chakrabarty, *Provincializing Europe*.

29 Escobar, *Encountering Development*, xvi.

30 For example, Cedric Robinson argues, "The development, organization, and expansion of capitalist society pursued essentially racial directions, so too did social ideology. As a material force, then, it could be expected that racialism would inevitably permeate the social structures emergent from capitalism." This argument challenges traditional theorizings of capitalism (by mostly white men), in which capitalist relations are abstracted from other demographic markers, demonstrating that accumulation necessarily requires differentiation and hierarchy based on race, gender, ability, and even age. Moreover, while some neo-Marxist scholars have argued that primitive accumulation ended when capitalism emerged in its modern form, scholars of the racial capitalist and settler colonial traditions show that capitalism continues to differentiate between those whose labor will be exploited and those whose land, labor, and lives will be expropriated. See C. Robinson, *Black Marxism*, 2.

31 Ong and Roy, *Worlding Cities*, 6.

32 Sanyal, *Rethinking Capitalist Development*.

33 See Trouillot, *Global Transformations*. Some post-Marxist scholars have quibbled about whether Karl Marx's wording has been mistranslated into English as "primitive" or "original" accumulation. For me, this is an irrelevant debate because the process of *primitivizing* is central to accumulation. See N. Singh, "On Race, Violence, and So-Called Primitive Accumulation." In her classic definition in *Caliban*

and the Witch, Sylvia Federici argues that "primitive accumulation . . . was not simply an accumulation and concentration of exploitable workers and capital. It was also accumulation of differences and divisions . . . whereby hierarchies built upon gender, as well as 'race' and age, become constitutive of class rule," 63–64. Even Marx himself, who spent very little time considering the colony or race, wrote, "The discovery of gold and silver in America, the extirpation, enslavement and entombment in mines of the indigenous population of that continent, the beginnings of the conquest and plunder of India, and the conversion of Africa into a preserve for the commercial hunting of blackskins, are all things which characterize the dawn of the era of capitalist production. These idyllic proceedings are the chief moments of primitive accumulation." Marx, *Capital*, 915. Here Marx is showing how processes of dispossession are differentiated in Indian, African, or American contexts.

34 Bhattacharyya, *Rethinking Racial Capitalism*, 26. Ruth Wilson Gilmore has argued that the prison-industrial complex is one way that capital has solved the problem of surplus, while Abigail Boggs and colleagues have theorized the way that institutions of higher education have been used to solve the problem of surplus. See Gilmore, *Golden Gulag*; and Boggs et al., "Abolitionist University Studies."

35 Melamed, "Racial Capitalism," 78. Melamed's argument is a distillation of Ruth Wilson Gilmore's ideas regarding racial capitalism and how it functions.

36 Rodney writes, "All of the countries named as 'underdeveloped' in the world are exploited by others; and the underdevelopment with which the world is now preoccupied is a product of capitalist, imperialist, and colonialist exploitation." Rodney, *How Europe Underdeveloped Africa*, 16.

37 Wilson, *Race, Racism and Development*.

38 Pierre, "The Racial Vernaculars of Development," 86. Similarly, Elisa Pascucci shows how racialized and classed relations undergird humanitarian labor stratifications. See Pascucci, "Local Labour Building the International Community."

39 Soniya Munshi and Craig Willse write, "The non-profit and the school are two key sites in which neoliberal social and economic reforms are both constituted and contested. These two realms are not distinct but are deeply implicated in one another, often in joint projects of producing for neoliberalism—producing knowledge and producing communities." Munshi and Willse, foreword to *The Revolution Will Not Be Funded*, xiv. This idea of the NGO producing fundable communities became an analytic theme in my work.

40 For example, Chandra Talpade Mohanty writes, "A homogeneous notion of the oppression of women as a group is assumed, which, in turn, produces the image of an 'average third world woman.' This average third world woman leads an essentially truncated life based on her feminine gender (read: sexually constrained) and her being 'third world' (read: ignorant, poor, uneducated, tradition-bound, domestic, family-oriented, victimized, etc.)." Mohanty, "Under Western Eyes," 56.

41 Spivak, "Can the Subaltern Speak?," 93.

42 Abu-Lughod, *Do Muslim Women Need Saving?*

43 Khoja-Moolji, "Death by Benevolence."

44 Radhakrishnan, *Making Women Pay*, 6. See also Ananya Roy, *Poverty Capital;* Karim, *Microfinance and Its Discontents*; and Kilby, *NGOs in India.*

45 Mies explains, "It is my thesis that capitalism cannot function without patriarchy, that the goal of this system, namely the never-ending process of capital accumulation, cannot be achieved unless patriarchal man-woman relations are maintained or newly created. . . . As capitalism is necessarily patriarchal it would be misleading to talk of two separate systems." Mies, *Patriarchy and Accumulation on a World Scale*, 38. See also Federici, *Caliban and the Witch*; and Bhattacharyya, *Rethinking Racial Capitalism.*

46 Bhattacharyya writes, "Racial capitalism describes a set of techniques and a formation, and in both registers the disciplining and ordering of bodies through gender and sexuality and dis/ability and age flow through what is happening. I continue to call this 'racial capitalism' because these techniques of othering and exclusion utilize the logics of race, regardless of the targeted population." Bhattacharyya, *Rethinking Racial Capitalism*, x.

47 Mosse, "Modernity of Caste and the Market Economy."

48 Mosse and Nagappan, "NGOs as Social Movements."

49 Yengde, *Caste Matters*, 33.

50 Mosse, "Modernity of Caste and the Market Economy," 1237.

51 Cynthia Stephen has argued that the NGO sector has systematically silenced Dalit, Tribal, and Bahujan voices, especially in relation to discussions of gender-based violence, by taking up the sign of "women" as a universal category even as it centers the ideologies of dominant-caste women. See Stephen, "#MeToo."

52 Malkki, *Need to Help*, 51.

53 Grace Kyungwon Hong's work on Asian American racialization and economic value proves especially useful here for its relational emphasis on how "ideological determinations of value can devalue surplus populations . . . [and] confer value—and therefore some protection from precarity—to others." My study intends to show the historical processes through which the brown savior accrues value in relation to the surplus populations they are tasked with saving. Hong, "Speculative Surplus," III.

2. THE RACIAL POLITICS OF THE SAVARNA HINDU (OR THE WOULD-BE SAVIOR)

1 Amrute, *Encoding Race, Encoding Class*; and Immerwahr, "Caste or Colony?"

2 Macaulay, "Minute on Indian Education."

3 See Gould, *Mismeasure of Man.*

4 The anthropological study of human remains has been defined by violent expropriative histories in which the ancestors of people from around the world were/are stolen in the name of "science." Laws like the Native American Graves Protection and Repatriation Act (NAGPRA, 1990) attempt to force museums to take some responsibility for the atrocities of the past by repatriating Native ancestral remains.

Of course, such laws have been limited to Native American tribes and Native Hawaiian communities, and therefore the majority of the crania in Morton's collection can still be used however the Penn museum deems fit. Laws like NAGPRA, in other words, reveal that recognition of settler colonial extractivism still only extends as far as the borders of the nation-state.

5 I was not a *pure* anthropologist because I received a joint PhD in anthropology and education. I did not believe, therefore, with heart and soul in the four-field approach to the discipline. In some ways, I wish I had taken Physical Anthropology, only because I have taken enough biology classes in my life to enjoy the study of the human body (albeit in less racist colonial forms than that espoused in most anthropology departments).

6 Diaz, "Penn Museum to Relocate Skull Collection of Enslaved People."

7 A. Shankar, "Primitivism and Race in Ethnographic Film."

8 I am drawing from Tina Campt's work in *Listening to Images*, to imagine the redaction as a way to draw our attention to "instances of rupture and refusal." Campt, *Listening to Images*, 5. That is to say, by redacting the image, I hope to remind that, even in death, these people may be refusing our gaze or our "scientific" readings of their value to the present.

9 Rana, *Terrifying Muslims*. In other words, their blood, too, was "browned."

10 Quoted in Altman, *Heathen, Hindoo, Hindu*, 1. Mather was a New England Puritan minister and influential author who lived from the late seventeenth to the early eighteenth century. Mather became one of the most important intellectual figures in English-speaking colonial America, attempting to become the president of Harvard as his father had (which he failed to do). Along with being a racist, Mather also supported the notorious Salem witch trials, enshrining violent sexism against any woman who did not conform to the white puritanical heteronormative family structure.

11 Prashad, *Karma of Brown Folk*, 1.

12 S. Patel, "'Indian Queen' of the Four Continents," 417 and 429.

13 Morton, *Crania Americana*, 32.

14 Morton, *Crania Americana*, 35.

15 S. Patel, "'Indian Queen' of the Four Continents," 427. Patel's discussion of the "Indian Queen" reveals the way that the undifferentiated Indian was central to perpetuating European anti-Black and anti-Muslim cosmologies, while valorizing the figure of the brahmin. *Ethiop*, along with *Aethiops* and *Ethiope*, were pejorative terms used to refer to a dark-skinned person, or to anyone from Africa.

16 Müller wrote, "Those men were the true ancestors of our race; and the Veda is the oldest book we have in which to study the first beginnings of our language, and all that is embodied in language. We are by nature Aryan, Indo-European, not Semitic; our spiritual kith and kin are to be found in India, Persia, Greece, Italy and Germany; not in Mesopotamia, Egypt, or Palestine." Müller, *Essential Max Müller*, 171. Essentially, Müller positioned European peoples within a non-Semitic set of traditions, in line with anti-Jewish sentiments pervading western Europe at the time.

17 Ghurye, *Caste and Race in India*, 126.

18 Jacob Copeman and Dwaipayan Banerjee argue, "As early as 1936, the foremost Dalit leader of the twentieth century, B. R. Ambedkar, used ethnological accounts of regional consanguinity to argue that the caste system had come into being after Indians were already commingled in blood, and therefore to confuse caste with race was scientifically incorrect." Copeman and Banerjee, *Hematologies*, 37.

19 Tilak was a Hindu supremacist who sought to make India into an explicitly Hindu nation.

20 Thapar, "Theory of Aryan Race and India," 6.

21 At the same time, prominent Dalit activists of the early and mid-twentieth century used this same mythology to subvert understandings of who had the right to the land that had become India, arguing that, as outsiders to India, dominant-caste Hindus did not have a legitimate right to remain rulers of India (see, for example, *Jyotiba Phule's critiques of caste supremacy, Gulamgiri*).

22 Vanaik, *Rise of Hindu Authoritarianism*.

23 Ayyathurai, "Foundations of Anti-caste Consciousness," 1; Nehru, *An Autobiography*, 274–75.

24 Subramanian, *Caste of Merit*. The perceived hierarchy between intellectual and manual labor propagated within brahminical systems, and the special stigma associated with manual scavenging especially, has been a consistent critique by anticaste activist and intellectuals.

25 Gail Omvedt points out that this historical unfolding meant that one strand of Hindu reform over the next sixty years would focus on encouraging occupational mobility for brahmin women. Omvedt, *Understanding Caste*. See also Chandra, *The Sexual Life of English*.

26 See Viswanath, *Pariah Problem*, 7, for a detailed discussion of how elite reformers, Mohandas Gandhi in particular, sought to position a project of Dalit salvation outside the remit of the state.

27 Erica Bornstein explains how ideas of dāna continue and sometimes clash with other ideas of service and giving in contemporary India. One understanding of dāna is that it is "as a noninstrumental and nonattached gift, is a sacred directive to give to strangers scripturally regulated by dharma, or duty, but is not a reciprocal relationship. . . . According to these expressions of dān, liberation and renunciation of the material world are orienting directives." See Bornstein, *Disquieting Gifts*, 29.

28 See Arundhati Roy, "The Doctor and the Saint," 89; and Bornstein, *Disquieting Gifts*, 35.

29 The 1920s to 1950s brought, as Mrinalini Sinha writes, "a crucial imperial restructuring: that is, a shift from the illusion of permanence that characterized the high imperialism of the late nineteenth century to the recognition of the conspicuously altered state of metropolitan-colonial ties at the advent of what has been called the 'American century.'" Sinha, *Specters of Mother India*, 4.

30 S. Patel, "Complicating the Tale of 'Two Indians.'"

31 Rana, *Terrifying Muslims*.

32 The Immigration and Nationality Act was itself a product of the civil rights movement; therefore, as Vijay Prashad explains, savarna Indians benefited both

from the Indian nationalist movements and from the liberatory struggles of Black Americans. See Prashad, *Karma of Brown Folk*.

33 Rosa, *Looking Like a Language, Sounding Like a Race*, 3. See also Thangaraj, *Desi Hoop Dreams*; Thangaraj, "We Share the Same Ancestry"; Treitler, *The Ethnic Project*; Gualtieri, *Between Arab and White*; and Maghbouleh, *Limits of Whiteness*.

34 Immerwahr, "Caste or Colony?"

35 See Prashad, *Karma of Brown Folk*, for a thorough examination of the racial politics of guru-fication.

36 Stanley Thangaraj, in "Sipping on the Indian Haterade," writes, "South Asian Americans come from various nations, various diasporic locations (such as the Indo-Guyanese, Trinidadians, and from Africa), a wide spectrum of religious backgrounds, and many ethnic groups, while speaking multiple languages and dialects. In addition, people hailing from South Asia and its many diasporic locations have not migrated to the United States at the same time and do not all share the same capital, social status, and access to resources and wealth. . . . In contrast, Hindu fundamentalists and Hindu nationalists present a starkly different political position and alliance. As a result of their financial clout and representational power in government and business, they have monopolised the conversation about South Asia by conflating South Asia, India, and Hindu."

37 These groups reproduce caste discriminations in the United States. Maari Zwick-Maitreyi and colleagues, in "Caste in the United States," find that nearly one in three Dalit Americans experience caste-based discrimination.

38 Thangaraj, *Desi Hoop Dreams*, 17–18.

39 See Lukose, *Liberalization's Children*, for the impact of liberalization on the global aspirations of youth in India.

40 Yashica Dutt writes, "The overwhelmingly higher-caste Indian-American community is seen as a 'model minority' with more than an average $100,000 median income and rising cultural and political visibility. But it has engendered a narrative that is as diabolical as it is in India: insisting that they live in a 'post-caste world' while simultaneously upholding its hierarchical framework that benefits the higher-caste people." Dutt, "Specter of Caste in Silicon Valley." See also Mishra, *Desis Divided*.

41 Dhingra, "Indian Americans and the 'Brain Sport' of Spelling Bees," 127.

42 Kapur, *Diaspora, Development, and Democracy*.

43 Maira, "Flexible Citizenship/Flexible Empire"; and Vora, *Impossible Citizens*.

44 Mishra, "Not Quite Home."

45 Tanuschree Basuroy, "Internet Penetration Rate in India from 2007 to 2021," Statistica, June 9, 2002, https://www.statista.com/statistics/792074/india-internet-penetration-rate/. See also Dattatreyan, *The Globally Familiar*.

46 See the discussion of reservations in the introduction. Karnataka state had already, previous to the 1979 Mandal Commission report, included Other Backward Class (OBC) reservations, which allowed for the political mobility of the Vokkaliga and Lingayat castes and continues to have major impacts on Karnataka state politics today.

47 Baas, "IT Caste," 286. See also Fuller and Narasimhan, *Tamil Brahmans*.

48 Amrute, *Encoding Race, Encoding Class*.

49 See Irani, *Chasing Innovation*; Mazzarella, "Beautiful Balloon"; and Tacchi, "Digital Engagement."

3. POVERTY'S MOTIVATIONAL DOUBLE BIND (OR NEO-MALTHUSIAN VISIONS)

1   Sherry Ortner famously wrote of "key symbols" as a way of unlocking the world of the native, when "the investigator observes something which seems to be an object of cultural interest, and analyzes it for its meanings." Ortner, "On Key Symbols," 1339. This makes me nervous because the entire key symbol project is predicated on the racist idea of a bounded and cohesive native culture awaiting discovery by the brilliant anthropological investigator.

2   See Pandian, "Devoted to Development."

3   Du Bois, *Souls of Black Folk*, 1.

4   Piketty, *Capital in the Twenty-First Century*.

5   C. Robinson, *Black Marxism*, 26.

6   See Malthus, *Essay on the Principle of Population*, 20 and 95.

7   This was also true in the French colonies. See Vergès, *Wombs of Women*, for an excellent excavation of the long history of French colonial state intervention focused on Black women's wombs.

8   Wilson, "Re-centering 'Race' in Development," 437.

9   Vergès, *Wombs of Women*, 2.

10 Wilson, "Re-centering 'Race' in Development," 443.

11 Tarlo, *Unsettling Memories*.

12 Vergès, *Wombs of Women*, 3.

13 Refer to Ross, *Malthus Factor*, for examples of neo-Malthusian thinking, especially pertaining to environmental degradation and overpopulation.

14 Foucault, *Technologies of the Self*, 16.

15 Shange, *Progressive Dystopia*, 8.

16 A. Sharma, "State and Women's Empowerment in India," 108.

17 Sarva Siksha Abhiyan is the Education for All Movement, which was meant to universalize elementary education in India by providing free and compulsory education to all elementary-age children. This quote by the state project director is from one of Sahaayaka's press releases.

18 Ferguson, *Anti-politics Machine*.

19 In scholarship on affect, *intensity* is conceived as both a measurement and a synonym for *affect*. Brian Massumi most notably refers to intensity as the body's response to stimuli, filling the body with "vibratory motion, resonation." Massumi, "Autonomy of Affect," 85. See also Stewart, *Ordinary Affects*.

20 Elysée Nouvet suggests that affects are neither good nor bad and that all affects are produced from within the same environments. Either way, motivation is *never just a psychological* phenomenon but always a social one. See Nouvet, "Some Carry

On, Some Stay in Bed." Crowd theory, too, builds on this idea, the affective effervescence of the crowd spilling out on itself and resulting in a groupthink that might be directed anywhere and anyhow. See Mazzarella, "Beautiful Balloon."

21 See Harrelson, "Intensity."

22 See Mazzarella, "Affect" for more on the affect generated by crowds

23 In *A Fine Balance*, Rohinton Mistry's dark commentary on Indian life during the Emergency, one character, Rajaram, aka the hair collector, takes a job as a family planning motivator.

4. FATAL PRAGMATISM (OR THE POLITICS OF "GOING THERE")

1 Freire, *Pedagogy of Freedom*, 40.

2 Though its history dates back to the mid-1960s, when Jawaharlal Nehru's nationalist industrial growth model was at its peak, BHEL began to manufacture power equipment in 1982 for industrial sectors including transportation, oil, and gas—a moment that marked BHEL's transition into one of India's preeminent national electronics companies, employing almost fifty thousand employees. Srinivasan ran BHEL's Electronics Divisions, which was based out of Bangalore and was the original reason for Srinivasan's move to Bangalore in the 1970s.

3 Ferreira da Silva, *Toward a Global Idea of Race*, xix.

4 Unlike in Srinivasan's caricature—which links lack of "ability" to underdevelopment, inadequacy, and lack—Michele Ilana Friedner examines how "deaf development" rearticulates economic development through the spiritual, moral, and emotional development of deaf peoples. Friedner, *Valuing Deaf Worlds in Urban India*.

5 Gramsci, *Antonio Gramsci Reader*, 288.

6 The Secondary School Leaving Certificate (SSLC) is a certification obtained by a student on the completion of their grade-ten public examination. Passing this exam signals that the student has completed their basic education. The SSLC is commonly used in Kerala, Karnataka, and Tamil Nadu.

7 At the same time, Mirca Madianou and Daniel Miller argue that "the situation of polymedia is one in which the media are mediated by the relationship as well as the other way around." Madianou and Miller, *Migration and New Media*, 148.

5. THE CASTE OF LIBERAL INTERVENTION

1 Birla was an Indian industrialist who, as Arundhati Roy points out, came from the same Gujarati bania (vaishya) caste as Gandhi: "G. D. Birla was a wealthy man who was chafing at the bit, offended by the racism he had personally encountered at the hands of the British. He had several run-ins with the colonial government. He became Gandhi's chief patron and sponsor and paid him a generous monthly retainer to cover the costs of running his ashrams and for his Congress party work." Arundhati Roy, "Doctor and the Saint," 89.

2 Ayyathurai, "It Is Time for a New Subfield"; and Yengde, *Caste Matters*.

3 Subramanian, *Caste of Merit*.

4 Indian railways provide a 75 percent ticket concession for SC or ST (Scheduled Tribe) youth for educational tours and for travel back home from schools located away from their homes.

5 Grace Kyungwon Hong argues that financial capital requires populations who are able to disavow and abstract from actual historical racialized positions in order for them to imagine a future premised only on cost-benefit analyses. The wielders of this ability to abstract within particular historical and regional contexts are conferred "value—and therefore some protection from precarity." Here the ability to abstract from caste, in the context of India and for those of Indian origin, produces their particular excess capital. See Hong, "Speculative Surplus," 111.

6 Deshpande, "Caste and Castelessness."

7 Subramanian, *Caste of Merit*, 19.

8 Jayanagar is a neighborhood in the southern part of Bangalore. It used to be considered the farthest-south area of the city and initially came to prominence because it was Asia's first planned neighborhood.

9 The term atrocity was defined within the act as "an expression commonly used to refer to crimes against Scheduled Castes (SCs) and Scheduled Tribes (STs) in India . . . [that] denotes the quality of being shockingly cruel and inhumane, whereas the term 'crime' relates to an act punishable by law. . . . [C]rimes which have ingredients of infliction of suffering in one form or the other . . . should be included for reporting. . . . ." Ministry of Social Justice and Empowerment, "Scheduled Castes and Scheduled Tribes (Prevention of Atrocities) Act, 1989," Casemine, January 29, 1990, https://www.casemine.com/act/in/5a979df74a93263ca60b770c.

10 "Statement of Objects and Reasons," in "Scheduled Castes and Scheduled Tribes (Prevention of Atrocities) Act, 1989."

11 See Subramanian, *Caste of Merit*; and Deshpande, "Caste and Castelessness," for further discussion of castelessness.

12 *Times of India*, "Can't Stay Provisions of SC/ST (Amendment) Act."

13 *Times of India*, "Can't Stay Provisions of SC/ST (Amendment) Act."

14 Ambedkar, *Annihilation of Caste*, 189.

15 The Jat-Pat-Todak Mandal was founded in Lahore in 1922 as an offshoot of the Arya Samaj. Members pledged themselves to a program of anticaste propaganda, coupled with interdining and intermarriage. The Arya Samaj was a monotheistic Indian Hindu reform movement founded in 1875.

16 Ambedkar, *Annihilation of Caste*, 199.

17 Said, *The World, the Text, and the Critic*, 243.

18 Ambedkar, *Annihilation of Caste*, 294.

19 Ambedkar argues that this is a by-product of the caste system's antisocial spirit. He writes, "The literature of the Hindus is full of caste genealogies in which an attempt is made to give a noble origin to one caste and an ignoble origin to other castes. . . . This anti-social spirit is not confined to caste alone. It has gone deeper and has poisoned the mutual relations of the sub-castes as well. . . . This anti-social spirit, this spirit of protecting its own interests, is as much a marked feature

of the different castes in their isolation from one another as it is of nations in their isolation." Ambedkar, *Annihilation of Caste*, 245–46.

20 I am drawing from Prabhat Patnaik, who writes, "It would appear, therefore, that capitalism in our society, far from obliterating caste, actually strengthens it; that caste is not just a hangover from the past that is insufficiently effaced, but an institution that is reinforced by our capitalist development. Borrowing a phrase from [Karl] Marx, one can even say that Indian capitalism is characterized by an 'expanded reproduction' of caste prejudice." P. Patnaik, "New Casteism," n.p.

21 See Rajesh Veeraraghavan's *Patching Development* for an example of how the powerful Reddy community controls much of the land in Andhra Pradesh and "creates a fundamental asymmetry in social relations" which have serious negative impacts on the young Dalit men in the area.

22 In Amar Diwakar's "A Silicon Valley Lawsuit Reveals Caste Discrimination Is Rife in the US," Gajendran Ayyathurai is cited to describe the Indian Institutes of Technology (IITs) as "'the fiefdom of Brahmins in independent India' . . . function[ing] as a vector for what he [Ayyathurai] designates as 'Global Brahminism,' or the 'global ascendance of local racism and casteism' to take root in international firms," n.p.

23 Ambedkar, *Annihilation of Caste*, 264.

6. HINDU FEMINIST RISING AND FALLING

1 Khoja-Moolji, "Death by Benevolence"; Bernal and Grewal, *Theorizing NGOs*; and A. Sharma, *Logics of Empowerment*.

2 Marwa Arsanios writes, "Gender essentialism—'women's empowerment'—overtakes any class or race discourses, which are at the core of internationalist feminist politics. 'Global womanhood' becomes a category or a class in itself. Hunger is separated from class and from the failure of states to provide and distribute wealth equally." Arsanios, "Who's Afraid of Ideology?" https://www.e-flux.com/journal/93/215118/who-s-afraid -of-ideology-ecofeminist-practices-between-internationalism-and-globalism/.

3 Françoise Vergès argues, "Women are often put in the position of cleaning and caring for what is broken. There are fifty-three million domestic workers in the world who are cleaning the city for the white middle class. . . . We must think about waste and the production of waste as a capitalist mode of production. Women are now expected to clean and care for what has been broken in the earth, for the damage that has been done to the earth, to the land. But before rushing and doing the naturalized work of 'repair' and care, let's take a moment to think about how it was broken, why it was broken, and by whom." Vergès comments made during panel discussion at the Colonial Repercussions conference, Akademie der Künste, Berlin, June 23–24, 2018, quoted in Arsanios, "Who's Afraid of Ideology?" https://www.e-flux.com/journal/93/215118/who-s-afraid-of-ideology-ecofemi nist-practices-between-internationalism-and-globalism/.

4 Khoja-Moolji, "Girl-Focused Development Campaigns." https://www.huffpost .com/entry/girlfocused-development-c_b_12283066.

5   While feminist movements in India were purportedly based on universal frameworks for women's equality and uplift, Sharmila Rege writes, "The writings and manifestoes of different dalit women's groups underlined the fact that the unmarked feminism of the 1970s had, in fact, been in theory and praxis a kind of brahmanical feminism." Rege, *Writing Caste, Writing Gender*, 4.

6   Mayo, *Mother India*, 84.

7   Mayo, *Mother India*, 129.

8   Sinha, *Specters of Mother India*.

9   Mohanty, Russo, and Torres, *Third World Women and the Politics of Feminism*; Mohanty, "Under Western Eyes"; Jayawardena, *Feminism and Nationalism in the Third World*; and Chatterjee, *Nation and Its Fragments*.

10 Kumari Jayawardena sums this position up well: "Even before the nationalist movement had become politically active in India, the social reformers had started to agitate on two of these issues—the practice of *sati* and the ban on widow remarriage. These could safely be tackled because they had not existed in very early times, were confined to the upper castes and classes and, if remedied, would have given India the appearance of being 'civilized' without endangering the traditional family structures." Jayawardena, *Feminism and Nationalism in the Third World*, 80. See also C. Gupta, *Sexuality, Obscenity, Community*.

11 Savitribai Phule is considered the first Indian woman teacher and was the first to found a school for girls, which also allowed Dalit children to attend. Fatima Sheikh is considered India's first Muslim woman teacher. She worked in Savitribai Phule's school but also provided the housing for the school itself. See S. Mohan, "Remembering Fatima Sheikh."

12 As Vivek Bald and colleagues argue, "They [Third World feminist scholars] revealed the ways that model minority South Asianness in the diaspora was built upon confining women to the role of the home, family, and community." Bald et al., *Sun Never Sets*, 5.

13 Bhatt is drawing from Maria Mies's brilliant theorizing of colonization and housewification. See Bhatt, *High-Tech Housewives*; and Mies, *Patriarchy and Accumulation on a World Scale*.

14 Jayawardena, *Feminism and Nationalism in the Third World*, 91.

15 Gargi Bhattacharyya writes, "One outcome of this innovation is that there is a considerable literature describing the role of the poor and migrant women in enabling the entry of middle-class women in the workforce. . . . In brief, what this debate posits is the paid work of (relatively) class-privileged women from the affluent world as sufficiently lucrative to warrant the subsidy of bought-in domestic labour. In an internalization of market rhetoric, such women are considered to have been bought out of domestic work in order to be free to engage in better-paid and higher-status work." Bhattacharyya, *Rethinking Racial Capitalism*, 47.

16 Vergès, *Wombs of Women*.

17 Bhatt discusses the problems faced by Indian women migrants to the United States, who struggle to maintain their occupations. Here the reverse movement back to India actually creates the same issues, which the NGO resolves. See Bhatt, *High-Tech Housewives*.

7. GATEKEEPERS (OR THE ANTI-MUSLIM POLITICS OF HELP)

1 Jackson, "On Ethnographic Sincerity," S286.
2 For more on Muhammad Jaunpuri, see Balkhi, *The Biography of Imam Mahdi Maud Hazrat Syed Muhammad Jaunpuri AS.*
3 Kalam, *Ignited Minds*, 157.
4 Durrani, "Gendered Muslim Subject"; and Thapar, "Theory of Aryan Race and India."
5 A report entitled *The Status of Urdu Medium Schools in Karnataka* states, "'Government schools are in distress while Urdu schools are in shambles.' . . . There is an essential difference between Government Urdu and Kannada medium schools in that a Kannada speaking student becomes at least a Kannada literate and can effectively integrate with the life and development in the State. . . . It is generally observed that Muslims are a ghettoized minority. Ghettoisation is an essential corollary of education, language one speaks, worries and concerns a community is engrossed with and residential and housing pattern in which he physically exists. In a multicultural society like India, one could break the shibboleths and cultural monoliths only by coming out of his/her own shell, questioning absolutes inherited from his own faith and culture, and through exposing himself to the ideas and ideals of the larger society." M. A. Siraj, *The Status of Urdu Medium Schools in Karnataka: Imparting Inclusive Orientation to Instructions*, accessed February 2, 2023.
6 Durrani, "Gendered Muslim Subject."
7 Thapar, "Theory of Aryan Race and India."
8 Charu Gupta historicizes this crisis of Hindu masculinity and specifically discusses the violent 1920s Hindu-Muslim riots by arguing, "These movements constructed Hindu masculinity as a contrast to the colonial image of the emasculated, effeminate and militarily incompetent Hindu male. For militant Hindu organizations, a show of physical strength was their psychological defense, their reply to the images of the powerful, rational British and the lustful Muslim." C. Gupta, *Sexuality, Obscenity, Community*, 234.
9 Thangaraj, "Sipping on the Indian Haterade"; and Vanaik, *Rise of Hindu Authoritarianism.*
10 Rana, "Racial Infrastructure of the Terror-Industrial Complex." See also Bhattacharyya, *Dangerous Brown Men.*
11 Abu-Lughod, *Do Muslim Women Need Saving?*; Khoja-Moolji, *Forging the Ideal Educated Girl*; and Idris and Ahmad, "Muslim Women Do Not Need Saving."
12 Rana, "Racial Infrastructure of the Terror-Industrial Complex"; and Durrani, "Gendered Muslim Subject."
13 Mariam Durrani writes, "In studies about anti-Muslim discourse, the gendered character of the racialized Muslim subject remains an underexamined area. Analyzing the construction of the racialized Muslim subject without an attention to gender can obscure how racialized violence, similar to ethnic violence, is enacted 'in and through gender.'" Durrani, "Gendered Muslim Subject," 344.

14 Lowe, *Intimacies of Four Continents*.

15 Mathew and Lukose, "Pedagogies of Aspiration," 692. See also Appadurai, *The Future as Cultural Fact*.

8. THE ROAD TO ACCUMULATION

1   Frazier, "Urban Heat."

2   Frazier, "Urban Heat."

3   Heitzman, *Network City*; and J. Nair, *Promise of the Metropolis*.

4   Gilmore, *Golden Gulag*. See also Williams, *The Country and the City*.

5   See Tsing, *Friction*, 6; and Larkin, "Politics and Poetics of Infrastructure," 333. Dimitris Dalakoglou uses the term *road to capitalism*, which does not quite describe the actual process underway of "accumulation through dispossession." Dalakoglou, "'Road from Capitalism to Capitalism.'"

6   See Sheller, *Mobility Justice*, 95. Mubbashir Rizvi defines the politics of infrastructure as "the social-cultural impact of modern technologies of communication, transportation, and utilities on integrating spaces by incorporating and differentiating disparate populations within the modern state." Rizvi, *Ethics of Staying*, 3.

7   For additional scholarship on infrastructural politics outside of South Asia, see Ference, "Joyriding"; Mains, *Under Construction*; Pardue and Amaral de Oliviera, "City as Mobility"; and Simone, "People as Infrastructure."

8   Ananthamurthy, "Ooru and the World."

9   See Udupa, *Making News in Global India*, for an excavation of language politics in Karnataka state media publics. See also Mitchell, *Language, Emotion, and Politics in South India*; and Srinivasan, *Passions of the Tongue*, for examples from Tamil Nadu.

10 The NICE road was especially controversial because the 130-kilometer expressway would catalyze regional urbanization and turn agricultural, village, and forested land into private townships and industrial parks. See Goldman, "Speculating on the Next World City," 243, for a thorough discussion of nice within the context of eminent domain laws in India.

11 Similar protests erupted in March 2016 as farmers demanded redress of several connected issues: (1) diminished subsidies for agricultural goods, (2) lack of drought compensation by the government for farmers during severe drought years, and (3) unpaid debts for farmers' suicides, which had totaled a record 1,002 over a nine-month period between 2015 and 2016. Shree, "Why Did Farmers Protest in Bengaluru, and What You Can Do about It."

12 *Al Jazeera*, "India Unemployment Rate Highest in 45 Years."

13 See Rizvi, *Ethics of Staying*, for an excellent analysis of the relation between colonial irrigation and canal policies and the ongoing conflict over farmland in the Punjab region.

14 Lloyd and Wolfe, "Settler Colonial Logics and the Neoliberal Regime," 112. See also Guha, *Dominance without Hegemony*, on permanent settlement in Bengal.

15 While all three of these systems made land into a commodity, each system had its own specificities and therefore resulted in different regional agricultural relations. In the zamindari system, intermediaries known as zamindars collected land revenue from farmers. Under the mahalwari system, village headmen, on behalf of the whole village, collected farmers' land revenue. Under the ryotwari system, farmers paid land revenue directly to the state. Karnataka was almost exclusively under the ryotwari system. Some have argued that the specific forms of indebtedness in Karnataka are a direct result of the colonial ryotwari system, because the direct farmer-state tax relationship prevented village-level and community-level protections and collective strategies. Instead, this model allowed for the emergence of a class of moneylenders who facilitated farmers' debt and loss of land. At the same time, all three systems invariably concentrated land in the hands of fewer landowning male caste elites, who exploited marginalized landless farmers, typically from Dalit communities, while passing on land via patrilineal inheritance.

16 See Bhander, *Colonial Lives of Property*, for exploration of global settler colonial land policies. See Appadurai, "Modi and His Brand of Hindutva," for further elaboration on Hindutva as a settler colonial project.

17 Here I am troping on the words of Mohawk anthropologist Audra Simpson, who writes of North America, "The matter of postcolonial frankly eludes the North American case: 'They' never left; the Native never disappeared." Simpson, "Consent's Revenge," 330. While the case is quite different, what I want to emphasize here is that they, that is, the settler, never left the so-called postcolony either, and that reading a place like India as a settler colonial state might help us better understand the ongoing modalities of dispossession. For a different example of settler colonial border creation, the ideology of the frontier, and ongoing neocolonial resource extraction regimes in Northeast India, see Kikon, *Living with Oil and Coal*.

18 Gidwani, *Capital, Interrupted*.

19 A. Gupta, *Postcolonial Developments*.

20 In 2013 the national government finally replaced the 1894 Land Acquisition Act to better protect farmers from the current regime of accumulation through dispossession by requiring the government to provide appropriate compensation for land. However, by 2019 Karnataka state had amended the law to again create exceptions for what they deemed crucial public-private infrastructural projects. Ram, "K'taka Amends Land Acquisition Act to Speed Up Projects."

21 U. Patnaik, "Agrarian Question in the Neoliberal Era," 49.

22 Jeffrey, *Timepass*.

23 Whitehead, "John Locke," 3.

24 Seema Purushothaman and Sham Kashyap write, "The emergence of modern industries and increasing opportunities for the literate households to find jobs in the government sector resulted in these dominant caste groups to reinvest in land and agriculture in the rural areas. . . . The first half of the 20th century witnessed educated Brahmins migrating into cities. This was followed by Lingayat and Vok-

kaliga migration to cities in search for better opportunities, which continues to this day. However, as M. N. Srinivas notes, land as a permanent asset was always a prized possession and hence, these migrated households did not give up their land." Purushothaman and Kashyap, "Historical Analysis of Land Ownership and Agroecology," 10.

25 The social scientist Louis Dumont famously surmised that India could and should only be studied as a caste society. Dumont, *Homo Hierarchicus.* See also Mines and Yazgi, *Village Matters.*

26 Irani, *Chasing Innovation*, 10. See also Dattatreyan, "Diasporic Sincerity." In the context of Karnataka, this split is also articulated as Bangalore/Bengaluru.

27 González, Wyman, and O'Connor, "Past, Present, and Future of 'Funds of Knowledge,'" 482.

28 Iyko Day describes the way commodities "are above all the representations (carriers) of social processes that are objectified in things." Aimé Césaire argued that the human body can be thingified and function as commodity. The mentors are one example of how this process plays out in help economies, revealing rearticulations of race in the era of global multicultural "diversity." See Day, *Alien Capital*, 11; and Césaire, *Discourse on Colonialism*, 42.

29 U. Patnaik, "Agrarian Question in the Neoliberal Era," 50.

30 See Chakravarti, "Conceptualising Brahmanical Patriarchy in Early India," on brahmanical patriarchy.

31 Uma Chakravarti explains that streedharma is "the idea that women should strive to be desirable, which actually ensures women's participation in their own subordination." Chakravarti, "Building Blocks of Brahmanical Patriarchy."

32 Irani, *Chasing Innovation*, 1.

9. URBAN ALTRUISM/URBAN CORRUPTION

1 Baaz, *Paternalism of Partnership*, 163.

2 See A. Gupta, *Red Tape*, for more on the politics of corruption.

3 Gidwani, *Capital, Interrupted*, xx. Vinay Gidwani characterizes development as liberalism's justification for colonial rule and civilizing projects tied to "waste."

4 See Kamat, *Development Hegemony*, for a detailed discussion of NGO-State relations.

5 Gidwani, *Capital, Interrupted*, xxi.

6 Lukose, *Liberalization's Children*, 67.

7 Gidwani, *Capital, Interrupted*, xx.

8 David Harvey argues that "freedom is just a word" in neoliberal societies because, rather than take seriously social inequities, neoliberal governance requires the fetish of "choice" and the fetish that markets will allow for freedom of choice, which further reinscribes inequality. See Harvey, *Brief History of Neoliberalism*, 7.

10. A GLOBAL DEATH

1 See Srinivas, *Caste in Modern India and Other Essays*, 48. While M. N. Srinivas terms this phenomenon "Sanskritization," I prefer the term *brahminization* to locate these shifts in practices within caste society and brahminical supremacy in particular.

2 J. Nair, *Promise of the Metropolis*.

3 Das, *Life and Words*.

4 Liu and Shange, "Toward Thick Solidarity," 190.

5 In some sense, Manoj's story and the other stories told by the mentors are examples of Berlant's concept of cruel optimism in which late liberal societies continue to convince us that we can find upward mobility despite structural constraints that render that impossible. In this sense, "A relation of cruel optimism exists when something you desire is actually an obstacle to your flourishing." Berlant, *Cruel Optimism*, 1.

6 U. Patnaik, "Agrarian Question in the Neoliberal Era," 11, 40.

7 Ana Ramos-Zayas reminds that emotion and affect carry the "illusion of immediacy and intimacy" and can function "as powerful tools in advancing neoliberal objectives." Ramos-Zayas, *Street Therapists*, 7.

8 Nouvet, "Some Carry On, Some Stay in Bed"; and Povinelli, *Economies of Abandonment*.

9 Moore, *Still Life*; and Chua, *In Pursuit of the Good Life*.

10 Bourgois, "Recognizing Invisible Violence," 18.

11 N. Kumar, *Unraveling Farmer Suicides in India*, 273.

12 Povinelli, *Economies of Abandonment*, 33.

13 Maddrell and Sidaway, *Deathscapes*.

14 Mankekar, *Unsettling India*, 9.

15 Shukla, *India Abroad*, 4.

16 See Ramos-Zayas, *Street Therapists*, for a discussion of the racialized "emotional commonsense" of Latinx communities in Newark.

17 The places that those with Indian passports can travel to without a visa (for various time limits) include Barbados, the British Virgin Islands, the Cook Islands, Dominica, El Salvador, Fiji, Grenada, Haiti, Indonesia, Jamaica, Macau, Maldives, Mauritius, Micronesia, Montserrat, Niue, Northern Cyprus, Palestine, the Pitcairn Islands, Qatar, Saint Kitts and Nevis, Saint Vincent and the Grenadines, Senegal, Serbia, Svalbard, Transnistria, Trinidad and Tobago, Tunisia, the Turks and Caicos Islands, and Vanuatu.

11. THE INSULT OF PRECARITY (OR "I DON'T GIVE A DAMN")

1 See my discussion of the Yadav caste in part 1.

2 Jasbir Puar writes, "I develop the conceptual frame of 'homonationalism' for understanding the complexities of how 'acceptance' and 'tolerance' for gay and lesbian subjects have become a barometer by which the right to and capacity for national sovereignty is evaluated." Puar, "Rethinking Homonationalism," 336–37.

3 See M. Prasad, "Imagined Village." See also Srinivas, *The Remembered Village*; and Pandian, "The Remembering Village."
4 Federici, *Caliban and the Witch*; Fraser, "Contradictions of Capital and Care"; Virno, *Grammar of the Multitude*.
5 See Appadurai's *Modernity at Large* for earlier theorizings of the cultural politics of globalization.
6 The image and the hashtag are especially interesting given that the woman had come to Bangalore and Karnataka, a region whose culinary culture is not at all associated with chicken tikka masala, and that the dish itself, though associated with North India (specifically Punjabi cuisine), may actually find its roots in an Indian restaurant in the United Kingdom.
7 A taluk is an administrative district defined for taxation purposes, typically comprising a number of villages.
8 Similarly, Nancy Scheper-Hughes has argued that the global organ trade creates global stratifications between disposable and valuable lives. These stratifications typically reproduce the colonial geographic racialized distinctions between the First and Third Worlds. Scheper-Hughes, "Global Traffic in Human Organs."

12. AC CARS AND THE HYPERREAL VILLAGE

1 For example, Wipro, the India-based tech giant, pledged $2 billion in 2010 to the Azim Premji Foundation, named after Wipro founder Azim Premji.
2 Smith, Preface to *Revolution Will Not Be Funded*, 3.
3 Petras, "NGOs."
4 I discuss this phenomenon in more detail in chapter 6.
5 "Support my School Campaign," NDTV.com, accessed August 20, 2017, https://www.ndtv.com/supportmyschool.
6 RT, "Coca-Cola Forced to Close India Bottling Factory."
7 "Newly-Weds Sidharth Malhotra and Alia Bhatt Break the Ice over the Great, Refreshing Taste of Coca-Cola," Coca-Cola, May 4, 2015 (last accessed July 15, 2017), https://www.coca-colaindia.com/newsroom/newly-weds-siddharth-malhotra-alia-bhatt-break-ice-great-refreshing-taste-coca-cola.
8 "Support My School Campaign." https://www.ndtv.com/supportmyschool. Last accessed: August 20, 2017.
9 Lowry, "Book Review: 'The Ironic Spectator,'" 3, in reference to Chouliaraki, *Ironic Spectator*.
10 Madianou and Miller, *Migration and New Media*.
11 Shipley, "Selfie Love"; and Dattatreyan, "Waiting Subjects."
12 See Chouliaraki, *The Ironic Spectator*, for more on celebrity and humanitarianism.
13 See Benton, "Risky Business," for a fascinating argument regarding institutionalized racism in humanitarianism, as she analyzes an image of Salma Hayek, the Mexican American Hollywood actress, breastfeeding an African baby.
14 See Minj, "Zen and the Art of Anjali Patil," for an explanation of race, colorism, and caste in Indian cinema.

15 Epstein, "Hyper in 20th Century Culture," 10–11.

16 Eco, *Travels in Hyperreality*, 14.

17 A. Robinson, "Jean Baudrillard."

18 The Abhayamudrā is considered the gesture of fearlessness, reassurance, and safety, which accords divine protection and bliss in the Hindu, Buddhist, Jain, and Sikh traditions. The right hand is held upright, and the palm is facing outward. You can see this mudrā depicted in many of the images of the Buddha, for example. More generally, mudrās are symbolic or ritual gestures or poses in Hinduism, Jainism, and Buddhism.

19 H. Gupta, "Testing the Future."

13. DIGITAL SAVIORS

1 Eubanks, *Automating Inequality*, 11, 9.

2 R. Benjamin, *Race after Technology*, 10.

3 Ananya Roy, *Poverty Capital*. See also Mazzarella, "Beautiful Balloon."

4 Similarly, in 2017 the billionaire Mukesh Ambani told reporters at the launch of a massive project to digitize 90 percent of India, "Anything and everything that can go digital is going digital—at an exponential rate. . . . Life is going digital." See "World is at the Beginning of a Digital Revolution," News18, March 30, 2016, https://www.news18.com/news/india/world-is-at-the-beginning-of-a-digital -revolution-mukesh-ambani-1223046.html.

5 "Text of Modi's Address at 'Digital India' Dinner" Daijiworld.com, September 27, 2015. https://daijiworld.com/index.php/news/newsDisplay?newsID=357582.

6 "Mark Zuckerberg Changes His Profile picture to Support 'Digital India,'" *Times of India*, September 27, 2015. https://timesofindia.indiatimes.com/tech-news/mark -zuckerberg-changes-his-profile-picture-to-support-digital-india/articleshow /49128369.cms.

7 Zuckerberg instrumentalizes the rhetoric of "social good" to support an "unbiased" view of content. Many argue that he takes this view because restricting content would restrict users and therefore curb profits.

8 See Amrute, *Encoding Race, Encoding Class*, for comprehensive discussion of the history of technology and computers in India.

9 This is why Benjamin writes, in the context of technological design thinking, that "design is a colonizing project." R. Benjamin, *Race after Technology*, 176.

10 Irani and Silberman, "Stories We Tell about Labor," 4573.

11 Sims, *Disruptive Fixation*, 171.

12 Noble, *Algorithms of Oppression*, 165.

13 Christen, in "Does Information Really Want to Be Free?," shows how "free information" is tethered to nation-centric ideologies that invisibilize other cultural ideas of openness, including indigenous ones.

14 See, for example, Mitchell, *Language, Emotion, and Politics in South India*; and Srinivasan, *Passions of the Tongue*.

15 Rai, *Jugaad Time*, xv.

16 Sahaayaka is drawing from the "salience of religious discourse and practice to regimes of production in software" and "the spirituality of Bangalore, gives to the operations there an entirely different feel, conducive to broad thinking and to world-encompassing ideas." Amrute, "Producing Mobility," 208.

17 Kirtsoglou writes of "anticipatory nostalgia" as "a future-oriented affective state of longing for what has already been accomplished and at once yet to be achieved." Kirtsoglou, "Anticipatory Nostalgia and Nomadic Temporality," 159.

14. DIGITAL TIME (AND ITS OTHERS)

1 See Coleman, *Coding Freedom*, for more on coding culture.

2 Harvey, *Condition of Postmodernity*, 260; and Nadeem, *Dead Ringers*.

3 Jackson, *Thin Description*, 26.

4 See Virilio's *Art of the Motor* and *Speed and Politics* for more on technology and temporal collapse.

5 See Bell, "The Secret Life of Big Data," 23, for more on technologists as alchemists.

6 See Munn, "Cultural Anthropology of Time"; Thompson, *Making of the English Working Class*; and Rovelli, *Order of Time*, for other examples of the links between time and global stratifications of labor.

7 Fabian, *Time and the Other*; and Rifkin, *Beyond Settler Time*.

8 Schull, *Addiction by Design*.

9 Ruha Benjamin writes, "Problem solving is at the heart of tech. An algorithm, after all, is a set of instructions, rules, and calculations designed to solve problems." Benjamin, *Race after Technology*, 11.

10 Atanasoski and Vora, *Surrogate Humanity*, 16.

11 Started in 1996 by two Boston residents with affiliations to MIT, the philanthropic organization Deshpande Foundation, per their website, "has supported sustainable, scalable social and economic impact through innovation and entrepreneurship in the United States, Canada, and India." Deshpande Foundation, https://www .deshpandefoundation.org/.

12 Manalansan, "'Stuff' of Archives."

13 Rai, *Jugaad Time*, 20.

14 For an audio signal, the relevant range is the band of audible sound frequencies (between 20 and 20,000 hertz).

15. DIGITAL AUDIT CULTURE (OR METADATA)

1 Benton, "Risky Business," 188.

2 For more on how "Africa" and HIV/AIDS have been conflated to justify interventions in African nation-states, even where cases are low, read Benton, *HIV Exceptionalism*.

3 Merry, "Measuring the World," s84.

4 Strathern, "Introduction: New Accountabilities," 2.

5 Pels, "What Has Anthropology Learned from the Anthropology of Colonialism?"; and Cohn, *Colonialism and Its Forms of Knowledge*.

6   Strathern, "Introduction: New Accountabilities," 4.

7   See also Shore and Wright, "Audit Culture Revisited," 421.

8   Lowe, *Intimacies of Four Continents*, 4. For another fascinating example of audit culture and aid, see James, *Democratic Insecurities*.

9   Melamed, "Racial Capitalism."

10 Ruth Wilson Gilmore, "Race and Globalization," 261–74.

11 Steinberg, *Platform Economy*; and Gillespie, "Platform Metaphor, Revisited."

12 Gillespie, "Platform Metaphor, Revisited."

13 Dabashi, *Can Non-Europeans Think?*

14 Mignolo, foreword to *Can Non-Europeans Think?*, xvii.

15 See H. Gupta, "Testing the Future," for another example of labor stratification in the start-up city.

16 Atanasoski and Vora, *Surrogate Humanity*, 28.

17 See Atanasoski and Vora, *Surrogate Humanity*, for an exploration of the links among the ideology of menial labor, the imaginary of automation, and racialized stratification.

18 Galison, "Objectivity Is Romantic."

19 Mazzarella, "Internet X-Ray," 475.

20 In *Believing Is Seeing*, documentarian Errol Morris uses EXIF file data to discover the timeline and relation of the now-infamous Abu Ghraib photographs.

16. DIGITAL SCALING (OR ABNORMALITIES)

1   U. Rao and Nair, "Aadhaar," 478.

2   In his work on Aadhar, India's mass ID system, Ranjit Singh argues that ID systems actually function as passage points, a two-step translation that renders humans into data and then, in turn, into a new kind of human. See R. Singh, "Give Me a Database and I Will Raise the Nation-State."

3   U. Rao and Nair, "Aadhaar."

4   U. Rao and Nair, "Aadhaar," 474.

5   Not surprisingly, those who have challenged the legitimacy of the Aadhar system have seen it as a veiled attempt at the expansion of a massive surveillance state and feared that data might be accessed and used by private actors. See U. Rao and Nair, "Aadhaar."

6   See Benjamin, *Illuminations*.

7   Dixon-Roman, *Inheriting Possibility*.

8   V. Nair, "Governing India in Cybertime," 523.

9   V. Nair, "Governing India in Cybertime."

10 See Benedict, "Anthropology and the Abnormal."

11 Masanet et al., "Recalibrating Global Data Center Energy-Use Estimates."

12 Couldry and Mejias, "Data Colonialism."

13 Reardon and TallBear, "'Your DNA Is Our History'," S234.

1 While Modi claimed that he would get India clean by 2019, 2022 has come and gone with no real change to India's cleanliness problem.

2 Teltumbde, *Republic of Caste*, 319. Teltumbde explains, "There is no official index of uncleanliness to compare countries. There are rankings for cleanliness but they seem to be based on the cleanliness of the environment" (319).

3 Teltumbde, *Republic of Caste*, 319.

4 Rukmini S. "Modi launches 'My Clean India' campaign."

5 Aamir Khan, Salman Khan, and Priyanka Chopra are some of Bollywood's biggest film stars. Anil Ambani is the chairman of the Reliance Group.

6 R. Benjamin, *Race after Technology*, 7.

7 A. Shankar, "Moral Economies."

8 Ghertner, "Rule by Aesthetics."

9 Ghertner, "Rule by Aesthetics."

10 "Sanitation," Bill and Melinda Gates Foundation, accessed December 4, 2022, https://www.gatesfoundation.org/our-work/places/india/sanitation.

11 Bashford, *Imperial Hygiene*, 30.

12 Katherine Mayo, *Mother India*, 157.

13 Katherine Mayo, *Mother India*, 195.

14 S. Prasad, *Cultural Politics of Hygiene in India*.

15 Gandhi, *The Collected Works of Mahatma Gandhi*, 390.

16 Kaviraj, "Filth and the Public Space."

17 "The Protection of Civil Rights Act, 1955, prohibits compelling anyone to practice manual scavenging. In 2013, the Indian parliament enacted The Prohibition of Employment as Manual Scavengers and Their Rehabilitation Act (the 2013 Act) outlawing all manual excrement cleaning. The 2013 Act also recognized a constitutional obligation to correct the historical injustice and indignity suffered by these communities by providing alternate livelihood and other assistance." Human Rights Watch, "India: Caste Forced to Clean Human Waste."

18 Gandhi, "Ideal Bhangi," 336, quoted in Teltumbde, *Republic of Caste*, 324.

19 Gandhi, "Ideal Bhangi," 336.

20 With regard to this caste culture, Teltumbde writes, "It is nothing but caste-culture—which is inimical to having in-house toilets—that explains the uniquely enduring practices of uncleanliness in India. A culture based so strongly on ideas of ritual purity that it resists both, access to toilets and the evidence of disease as backed by research." Teltumbde, *Republic of Caste*, 320. See also Muhammad, "Contemporary Practices of Pollution and Space"; and Viswanath, "Textbook Case of Exclusion."

21 *Al Jazeera*, "Dalit Children Beaten to Death for Defecating in Public."

22 Teltumbde, *Republic of Caste*, 339.

CONCLUSION: AGAINST SAVIORISM

1   With regard to "every story begets its sequel," see John Jackson Jr.'s statement in the documentary film by Mariam Durrani and me, *Bad Friday Goes to South Africa: Rights and Reparations*. With reference to "this is a living object," I am thinking about books as living objects that circulate; get interpreted, marked up, and discussed; and change as they encounter new readers.

2   Deb, "Killing of Gauri Lankesh."

3   Jafri and Barton, "Explained."

4   Hunt, *Nervous State;* Sartre, preface to *The Wretched of the Earth.*

5   Mamdani, *Neither Settler nor Native,* 3–4.

6   Morrison, "Racism and Fascism," 384.

7   Fanon, *Wretched of the Earth*

8   Ambedkar, *Essential Writings,* 278.

9   In Abdurahman and Smythe, "Technologies of Black Freedoms."

10   On intimate histories, see Carby, *Imperial Intimacies;* and Lowe, *Intimacies of Four Continents.*

11   Liu and Shange, "Toward Thick Solidarity," 190.

12   Osuri and Zia, "Kashmir and Palestine," 249.

13   Burden-Stelly, "On Joining an Organization."

14   Currently, I am most excited to have joined Bol, a worker-owned cooperative bookstore dedicated to holding space for those working toward global justice. I look forward to learning from all the challenges we will face as we explore and imagine what this project could be.

15   Mies, *Patriarchy and Accumulation on a World Scale.*

16   Mohan, "Remembering Fatima Sheikh"; Phule, *Gulamgiri.*

17   See Dubal and Gill, "Governments are Invincible Until They're Not"; and Dubal and Gill, "Long Live Farmer-Labor Unity."

18   For almost two years between 2020 and 2021, Indian farmers sustained one of the longest and largest protests in the world during a global pandemic, focusing their resistance on agricultural policy changes that were being enacted by the BJP government. Three agricultural bills that were passed into law in September 2020 were designed to deregulate and privatize the agrarian economy and therefore tie farmers further to markets in a way that would have exponentially increased their ongoing dispossession.

19   Allen and Jobson, "The Decolonizing Generation."

20   See my work with Perry Zurn, *Curiosity Studies,* for more on this. Also see Zurn, *Curiosity and Power.*

21   Bonilla, "Unsettling Sovereignty."

22   Zurn, "Curiosities at War."

23   Ahmed, *Living a Feminist Life,* 196.

24   A. Shankar, "'Campus Is Sick.'"

25   Moten and Harney, *Undercommons.*

26   Fanon, *Wretched of the Earth,* 133.

Bibliography

Abdurahman, J. Khadijah, and SA Smythe. "Technologies of Black Freedoms: Calling on Black Studies Scholars, with SA Smythe." Beacons. Special issue, *Logic*, no. 15 (2021). https://logicmag.io/beacons/technologies-of-black-freedoms-calling-on-black-studies-scholars-with-sa/.

Abu-Lughod, Lila. *Do Muslim Women Need Saving?* Cambridge, MA: Harvard University Press, 2013.

Ahmed, Sara. *Living a Feminist Life*. Durham, NC: Duke University Press, 2017.

Al Jazeera. "Dalit Children Beaten to Death for Defecating in Public." September 26, 2019. https://www.aljazeera.com/news/2019/09/Dalit-children-beaten-death-india-defecating-public-190926110658711.html.

Al Jazeera. "India Unemployment Rate Highest in 45 Years: Report." January 31, 2019. https://www.aljazeera.com/economy/2019/1/31/india-unemployment-rate-highest-in-45-years-report.

Allen, Jafari Sinclaire, and Ryan Jobson. "The Decolonizing Generation: (Race and) Theory in Anthropology since the Eighties." *Current Anthropology* 57, no. 2 (2014): 129–48.

Altman, Michael J. *Heathen, Hindoo, Hindu: American Representations of India, 1721–1893*. Oxford: Oxford University Press, 2017.

Ambedkar, B. R. *Annihilation of Caste*. New York: Verso, 2016.

Ambedkar, B. R. *The Essential Writings of B. R. Ambedkar*. Edited by Valerian Rodrigues. New Delhi: Oxford University Press, 2002.

Ambedkar Age Collective, ed. *Hatred in the Belly*. Hyderabad: Shared Mirror, 2015.

Amrute, Sareeta. *Encoding Race, Encoding Class: Indian IT Workers in Berlin*. Durham, NC: Duke University Press, 2016.

Amrute, Sareeta. "Of Techno-ethics and Techno-affects." *Feminist Review* 123, no. 1 (2019): 56–73.

Amrute, Sareeta. "Producing Mobility: Indian ITers in an Interconnected World." PhD diss., University of Chicago, 2008.

Anand, S. "A Note on the Poona Pact." In B. R. Ambedkar, *Annihilation of Caste*. New York: Verso, 2016.

Ananthamurthy, U. R. "Ooru and the World." In *Multiple City: Writings on Bangalore,* edited by Aditi De, 63–68. London: Penguin, 2012.

Annavarupa, Sneha. "Risky Routes, Safe Suspicions: Gender, Class, and Cabs in Hyderabad, India." *Social Problems* 69, no. 3 (2022): 761–80.

Appadurai, Arjun. *The Future as Cultural Fact: Essays on the Global Condition.* New York: Verso, 2013.

Appadurai, Arjun. *Modernity at Large: Cultural Dimensions of Globalization.* Minneapolis: University of Minnesota Press, 1996.

Appadurai, Arjun. "Modi and His Brand of Hindutva Are Direct Descendants of the British Raj and Its Policies." *Wire,* December 13, 2021. https://thewire.in/politics /narendra-modi-hindutva-british-raj.

Arsanios, Marwa. "Who's Afraid of Ideology? Ecofeminist Practices between Internationalism and Globalism." *e-flux Journal,* no. 93 (2018). https://www.e-flux.com/journal /93/215118/who-s-afraid-of-ideology-ecofeminist-practices-between-internationalism -and-globalism/.

Asif, Manan Ahmed. *The Loss of Hindustan: The Invention of India.* Cambridge, MA: Harvard University Press, 2020.

Atanasoski, Neda, and Kalindi Vora. *Surrogate Humanity: Race, Robots, and the Politics of Technological Futures.* Durham, NC: Duke University Press, 2019.

Ayyathurai, Gajendran. "Emigration against Caste, Transformation of the Self, and Realization of the Casteless Society in Indian Diaspora." *Essays in Philosophy* 22, nos. 1–2 (2021): 45–65.

Ayyathurai, Gajendran. "Foundations of Anti-caste Consciousness: Pandit Iyothee Thass, Tamil Buddhism, and the Marginalized in South India." PhD diss., Columbia University, 2011.

Ayyathurai, Gajendran. "It Is Time for a New Subfield: 'Critical Caste Studies.'" *SouthAsia@LSE* (blog), July 5, 2021. https://blogs.lse.ac.uk/southasia/2021/07/05/it-is-time -for-a-new-subfield-critical-caste-studies/.

Baas, Michiel. "The IT Caste: Love and Arranged Marriages in the IT Industry of Bangalore." *South Asia: Journal of South Asian Studies* 32, no. 2 (2009): 285–307.

Baaz, Maria Eriksson. *The Paternalism of Partnership: A Postcolonial Reading of Identity in Development Aid.* London: Zed Books, 2005.

Baker, Lee D. "The Racist Anti-racism of American Anthropology." *Transforming Anthropology* 29, no. 2 (2021): 127–42.

Bald, Vivek. *Bengali Harlem and the Lost Histories of South Asian America.* Cambridge, MA: Harvard University Press, 2015.

Bald, Vivek, Miabi Chatterji, Sujani Reddy, and Manu Vimalassery, eds. *The Sun Never Sets: South Asian Migrants in an Age of U.S. Power.* New York: New York University Press, 2013.

Balkhi, Al-Haj Syed Munawar Husain. *The Biography of Imam Mahdi Maud Hazrat Syed Muhammad Jaunpuri AS.* Hyderabad: Al-Haj Syed Munawar Husain Balkhi, 1989.

Bashford, Alison. *Imperial Hygiene: A Critical History of Colonialism, Nationalism and Public Health.* London: Palgrave, 2003.

Bayly, Susan. *Caste, Society and Politics in India from the Eighteenth Century to the Modern Age.* Cambridge: Cambridge University Press, 1999.

Bell, Genevieve. "The Secret Life of Big Data." In *Data, Now Bigger and Better*, edited by Tom Boellstorff and Bill Maurer, 7–26. Chicago: Prickly Paradigm, 2015.

Benedict, Ruth. "Anthropology and the Abnormal." *Journal of General Psychology* 10, no. 1 (1934): 59–82.

Benjamin, Ruha. *Race after Technology: Abolitionist Tools for the New Jim Code*. New York: Polity, 2019.

Benjamin, Walter. *Illuminations: Essays and Reflections*. Edited by Hannah Arendt. Translated by Harry Zohn. New York: Schocken Books, 1968.

Benton, Adia. *HIV Exceptionalism: Development through Disease in Sierra Leone*. Minneapolis: University of Minnesota Press, 2015.

Benton, Adia. "Risky Business: Race, Nonequivalence and the Humanitarian Politics of Life." *Visual Anthropology* 29, no. 2 (2016): 187–203.

Berlant, Lauren. *Cruel Optimism*. Durham, NC: Duke University Press, 2012.

Bernal, Victoria, and Inderpal Grewal. *Theorizing NGOs: States, Feminisms, and Neoliberalism*. Durham, NC: Duke University Press, 2014.

Berreman, Gerald. "Caste in India and the United States." *American Journal of Sociology* 66, no. 2 (1960): 120–27.

Bhander, Brenna. *Colonial Lives of Property: Law, Land, and Racial Regimes of Ownership*. Durham, NC: Duke University Press, 2018.

Bhatt, Amy. *High-Tech Housewives: Indian IT Workers, Gendered Labor, and Transmigration*. Seattle: University of Washington Press, 2018.

Bhattacharyya, Gargi. *Rethinking Racial Capitalism: Questions of Reproduction and Survival*. London: Rowman and Littlefield International, 2018.

Boggs, Abigail, Eli Meyerhoff, Nick Mitchell, and Zach Schwartz-Weinstein. "Abolitionist University Studies: An Invitation." *Abolition Journal*, August 28, 2019. https://abolitionjournal.org/abolitionist-university-studies-an-invitation/.

Bonilla, Yarimar. "Unsettling Sovereignty." *Cultural Anthropology* 32, no. 3 (2017): 330–39.

Bornstein, Erica. *Disquieting Gifts: Humanitarianism in New Delhi*. Palo Alto, CA: Stanford University Press, 2012.

Bornstein, Erica, and Aradhana Sharma. "The Righteous and the Rightful: The Technomoral Politics of NGOs, Social Movements, and the State in India." *American Ethnologist* 43, no. 1 (2016): 76–90.

Bourgois, Phillipe. "Recognizing Invisible Violence: A Thirty-Year Ethnographic Retrospective." In *Global Health in Times of Violence*, edited by Barbara Rylko-Bauer, Linda Whiteford, and Paul Farmer, 17–40. Santa Fe, NM: School for Advanced Research Press, 2010.

Briggs, Laura. "The Race of Hysteria: 'Overcivilization' and the 'Savage' Woman in Late Nineteenth-Century Obstetrics and Gynecology." *American Quarterly* 52, no. 2 (2000): 246–73.

Brodkin, Karen. *How Jews Became White Folks and What That Says about Race in America*. New Brunswick, NJ: Rutgers University Press, 1998.

Burden-Stelly, Charisse. "Caste Does Not Explain Race." Review of *Caste: The Origins of Our Discontents*, by Isabel Wilkerson. *Boston Review*, December 15, 2020. https://www.bostonreview.net/articles/charisse-burden-stelly-tk/.

Burden-Stelly, Charisse. "On Joining an Organization." *The Last Dope Intellectual* (blog), June 27, 2022. https://www.charisseburdenstelly.com/blog/entry-7-on-joining-an -organization.

Burton, Antoinette. *Africa in the Indian Imagination: Race and the Politics of Postcolonial Citation*. Durham, NC: Duke University Press, 2016.

Campt, Tina. *Listening to Images*. Durham, NC: Duke University Press, 2017.

Carby, Hazel V. *Imperial Intimacies: A Tale of Two Islands*. New York: Verso, 2019.

Carby, Hazel V. "The Limits of Caste." Review of *Caste: The Origins of Our Discontents*, by Isabel Wilkerson. *London Review of Books*, January 21, 2021.

Card, Kenton, dir. *Geographies of Racial Capitalism with Ruth Wilson Gilmore*. Cardiff, UK: Antipode Foundation, 2019. 16 min.

Carnegie, Dale. *How to Win Friends and Influence People*. New York: Simon and Schuster, 1936.

Césaire, Aimé. *Discourse on Colonialism*. Translated by Joan Pinkham. New York: Monthly Review Press, 2001.

Cháirez-Garza, Jesús F., Mabel Denzin Gergan, Malini Ranganathan, and Pavithra Vasudevan. "Introduction to the Special Issue: Rethinking Difference in India through Racialization." *Ethnic and Racial Studies* 45, no. 2 (2021): 193–215.

Chakrabarty, Dipesh. *Provincializing Europe: Postcolonial Thought and Historical Difference*. Princeton, NJ: Princeton University Press, 2007.

Chakravarti, Uma. "Building Blocks of Brahmanical Patriarchy: An Interactive." EPW Engage, 1993. https://www.epw.in/engage/article/building-blocks-brahmanical -patriarchy.

Chakravarti, Uma. "Conceptualising Brahmanical Patriarchy in Early India: Gender, Caste, Class and State." *Economic and Political Weekly* 28, no. 14 (1993): 579–85.

Chakrovorty, Sanjay, Devesh Kapur, and Nirvikar Singh. *The Other One Percent: Indians in America*. Oxford: Oxford University Press, 2016.

Chandra, Shefali. *The Sexual Life of English: Languages of Caste and Desire in Colonial India*. Durham, NC: Duke University Press, 2011.

Chandra, Uday. Review of *Modernity of Slavery: Struggles against Caste Inequality in Colonial Kerala*, by P. Sanal Mohan. *Social Sciences and Missions* 30, no. 1–2 (2017): 209–11.

Charania, Moon. Review of *The Sense of Brown*, by José Esteban Muñoz. *Society and Space*, June 28, 2021. https://www.societyandspace.org/articles/sense-of-brown.

Chatterjee, Partho. *The Nation and Its Fragments: Colonial and Postcolonial Histories*. Princeton, NJ: Princeton University Press, 1993.

Chopra, Rohit, and Ajantha Subramanian. "Caste Discrimination Exists in the U.S., Too—But a Movement to Outlaw It Is Growing." *TIME*, February 11, 2022. https://time .com/6146141/caste-discrimination-us-opposition-grows/.

Chouliaraki, Lilie. *The Ironic Spectator: Solidarity in the Age of Post-humanitarianism*. Cambridge, UK: Polity, 2013.

Chow, Rey. *The Protestant Ethnic and the Spirit of Capitalism*. New York: Columbia University Press, 2002.

Christen, Kimberly A. "Does Information Really Want to Be Free? Indigenous Knowledge Systems and the Question of Openness." *International Journal of Communication* 6 (2012): 2870–93.

Chua, Jocelyn. *In Pursuit of the Good Life: Aspiration and Suicide in Globalizing South India.* Berkeley: University of California Press, 2014.

Cohn, Bernard. *Colonialism and Its Forms of Knowledge: The British in India.* Princeton, NJ: Princeton University Press, 1996.

Cole, Teju. "The White-Savior Industrial Complex." *Atlantic,* March 21, 2012. https://www.theatlantic.com/international/archive/2012/03/the-White-savior-industrial-complex/254843/.

Coleman, Gabriella. *Coding Freedom: The Ethics and Aesthetics of Hacking.* Princeton, NJ: Princeton University Press, 2013.

Copeman, Jacob, and Dwaipayan Banerjee. *Hematologies: The Political Life of Blood in India.* Ithaca, NY: Cornell University Press, 2019.

Couldry, Nick, and Ulises A. Mejias. "Data Colonialism: Rethinking Big Data's Relation to the Contemporary Subject." *Television and New Media* 20, no. 4 (2018): 336–49.

Cox, Oliver. *Caste, Class, and Race.* Garden City, NY: Doubleday, 1948.

Dabashi, Hamid. *Can Non-Europeans Think?* London: Zed Books, 2015.

Da Costa, Dia. "Caste-Ignorant Worlds of Progressive Academics: Academically-Transmitted Caste Innocence." *RAIOT: Challenging the Consensus,* August 24, 2018. https://raiot.in/academically-transmitted-caste-innocence/.

Dalakoglou, Dimitris. "'The Road from Capitalism to Capitalism': Infrastructures of (Post)socialism in Albania." *Mobilities* 7, no. 4 (2012): 571–86.

Das, Veena. *Life and Words: Violence and the Descent into the Ordinary.* Berkeley: University of California Press, 2007.

Dattatreyan, E. Gabriel. "Desiring Bollywood: Re-staging Racism, Exploring Difference." *American Anthropologist* 122, no. 4 (2020): 961–72.

Dattatreyan, E. Gabriel. "Diasporic Sincerity: Tales from a 'Returnee' Researcher." *Identities: Global Studies in Culture and Power* 21, no. 2 (2014): 152–67.

Dattatreyan, E. Gabriel. *The Globally Familiar: Digital Hip Hop, Masculinity, and Urban Space in Delhi.* Durham, NC: Duke University Press, 2020.

Dattatreyan, E. Gabriel. "Waiting Subjects: Social Media–Inspired Self-Portraits as Gallery Exhibition in Delhi, India." *Visual Anthropology Review* 31, no. 2 (2015): 134–46.

Day, Iyko. *Alien Capital: Asian Racialization and the Logic of Settler Colonial Capitalism.* Durham, NC: Duke University Press, 2016.

Deb, Siddhartha. "The Killing of Gauri Lankesh." *Columbia Journalism Review,* Winter 2018. https://www.cjr.org/special_report/gauri-lankesh-killing.php.

Deshpande, Satish. "Caste and Castelessness: Towards a Biography of the 'General Category.'" *Economic and Political Weekly* 48, no. 15 (2013): 32–39.

Dhingra, Pawan. "Indian Americans and the 'Brain Sport' of Spelling Bees." In *Asian American Sporting Cultures,* edited by Stanley Thangaraj, Constancio Arnaldo Jr., and Christina Chin, 127–51. New York: New York University Press, 2016.

Diaz, Johnny. "Penn Museum to Relocate Skull Collection of Enslaved People." *New York Times,* July 27, 2020. https://www.nytimes.com/2020/07/27/us/Penn-museum-slavery-skulls-Morton-cranial.html.

Dirks, Nicholas B. *Castes of Mind: Colonialism and the Making of Modern India.* Princeton, NJ: Princeton University Press, 2001.

Divakaruni, Chitra Banerjee. *The Palace of Illusions*. New York: Anchor Books, 2008.

Diwakar, Amar. "A Silicon Valley Lawsuit Reveals Caste Discrimination Is Rife in the US." *TRT World*, September 15, 2020. https://www.trtworld.com/magazine/a-silicon -valley-lawsuit-reveals-caste-discrimination-is-rife-in-the-us-39773.

Dixon-Roman, Ezekiel. *Inheriting Possibility: Social Reproduction and Quantification in Education*. Minneapolis: University of Minnesota Press, 2017.

Dubal, Veena, and Navyug Gill. "Governments Are Invincible Until They're Not: On the Farmers' Victory in India." LPE Project, January 18, 2022. https://lpeproject.org /blog/governments-are-invincible-until-theyre-not-on-the-farmers-victory-in-india/.

Dubal, Veena, and Navyug Gill. "Long Live Farmer-Labor Unity: Contextualizing the Massive Resistance Going on in India." LPE Project, December 12, 2020. https:// lpeproject.org/blog/long-live-farmer-laborer-unity-contextualizing-the-massive -resistance-going-on-in-india/.

Du Bois, W. E. B. *Black Reconstruction in America, 1860–1880*. New York: Free Press, 1992.

Du Bois, W. E. B. "Prospect of a World without Race Conflict." *American Journal of Sociology* 49, no. 5 (1944): 450–56.

Du Bois, W. E. B. *The Souls of Black Folk*. New York: Penguin Books, 1903.

Dumont, Louis. *Homo Hierarchicus: The Caste System and Its Implications*. Chicago: University of Chicago Press, 1980.

Durrani, Mariam. "The Gendered Muslim Subject: At the Intersection of Race, Religion, and Gender." In *The Oxford Handbook of Language and Race*, edited by Samy Alim, Angela Reyes, and Paul Kroskrity, 342–46. Oxford: Oxford University Press, 2020.

Durrani, Mariam. "The Imperial Optic: Mapping the Impact of the Global War on Terror on Higher Education in the US and Pakistan." *Transforming Anthropology* 30, no. 1 (2022): 66–79.

Durrani, Mariam, and Arjun Shankar. *Bad Friday Goes to South Africa: Rights and Reparations*. 2013. Vimeo, uploaded March 8, 2014. https://vimeo.com/88529275.

Dutt, Yashica. "Feeling Like an Outcast." Review of *Caste: The Origins of Our Discontents*, by Isabel Wilkerson. *Foreign Policy*, September 17, 2020. https://foreignpolicy.com/2020 /09/17/caste-book-india-dalit-outcast-wilkerson-review/.

Dutt, Yashica. "The Specter of Caste in Silicon Valley." *New York Times*, July 14, 2020. https://www.nytimes.com/2020/07/14/opinion/caste-cisco-indian-americans -discrimination.html.

Eco, Umberto. *Travels in Hyperreality: Essays*. New York: Harcourt Brace, 1986.

Elyachar, Julia. *Markets of Dispossession: NGOs, Economic Development, and the State in Cairo*. Durham, NC: Duke University Press, 2005.

Enloe, Cynthia. *The Curious Feminist: Searching for Women in a New Age of Empire*. Berkeley: University of California Press, 2004.

Epstein, Michael. "Hyper in 20th Century Culture: The Dialectics of Transition from Modernism to Postmodernism." *Postmodern Culture* 6, no. 2 (1996). https://www .pomoculture.org/2013/09/22/hyper-in-20th-century-culture-the-dialectics-of -transition-from-modernism-to-postmodernism/.

Escobar, Arturo. *Encountering Development: The Making and Unmaking of the Third World*. Princeton, NJ: Princeton University Press, 2011.

Eubanks, Virginia. *Automating Inequality: How High-Tech Tools Profile, Police, and Punish the Poor*. New York: St. Martin's, 2018.

Fabian, Johannes. *Time and the Other: How Anthropology Makes Its Object*. New York: Columbia University Press, 1983.

Fanon, Frantz. *Black Skin, White Masks*. Translated by Charles Lam Markmann. New York: Grove, 1967.

Fanon, Frantz. *The Wretched of the Earth*. New York: Grove, 2005.

Federici, Sylvia. *Caliban and the Witch: Women, the Body and Primitive Accumulation*. New York: Autonomedia, 2004.

Ference, Meghan. "Joyriding: Making Place in Nairobi's Matatu Sector." *City and Society* 31, no. 2 (2019): 188–207.

Ferguson, James. *The Anti-politics Machine: Development, Depoliticization, and Bureaucratic Power in Lesotho*. Cambridge: Cambridge University Press, 1994.

Ferguson, James. *Global Shadows*. Durham, NC: Duke University Press, 2006.

Ferreira da Silva, Denise. "Race and Development." In *The Companion to Development Studies*, edited by Vandana Desai and Robert B. Potter, 39–41. 3rd. ed. New York: Routledge, 2014.

Ferreira da Silva, Denise. *Toward a Global Idea of Race*. Minneapolis: University of Minnesota Press, 2007.

Fields, Karen Ellis, and Barbara J. Fields. *Racecraft: The Soul of Inequality in American Life*. New York: Verso, 2014.

Flores, Tatiana. "'Latinidad Is Cancelled': Confronting an Anti-Black Construct." *Latin American and Latinx Visual Culture* 3, no. 3 (2021): 58–79.

Foucault, Michel. *Technologies of the Self: A Seminar with Michel Foucault*. Edited by Luther H. Martin, Huck Gutman, and Patrick H. Hutton. Amherst, MA: University of Massachusetts Press, 1988.

Fraser, Nancy. "Contradictions of Capital and Care." *New Left Review*, no. 100 (2016): 99–117.

Frazier, Camille. "Urban Heat: Rising Temperatures as Critique in India's Air-Conditioned City." *City and Society* 4, no. 3 (2019): 441–61.

Freire, Paolo. *Pedagogy of Freedom: Ethics, Democracy, and Civic Courage*. Lanham, MD: Rowman and Littlefield, 2001.

Friedner, Michele Ilana. *Valuing Deaf Worlds in Urban India*. New Brunswick, NJ: Rutgers University Press, 2015.

Fuller, C. J. and Haripriya Narasimhan. *Tamil Brahmans: The Making of Middle-Class Caste*. Chicago: University of Chicago Press, 2014.

Gabiam, Nell. "When 'Humanitarianism' Becomes 'Development': The Politics of International Aid in Syria's Palestinian Refugee Camps." *American Anthropologist* 114, no. 1 (2012): 95–107.

Galison, Peter. "Objectivity Is Romantic." In *The Humanities and the Sciences*, edited by Jerome Friedman, Peter Galison, Susan Haack, and Billy Eugene Frye, 15–43. New York: American Council of Learned Societies, 2000.

Gandhi, M. K. "The Ideal Bhangi." *Harijan* 336 (November 28, 1936).

Gandhi, Mahatma. *The Collected Works of Mahatma Gandhi*, vol. 31. New Delhi: Publications Division, Ministry of Information and Broadcasting, Government of India, 2000.

Ghertner, D. A. "Rule by Aesthetics: World-Class City Making in Delhi." In *Worlding Cities: Asian Experiments and the Art of Being Global*, edited by Ananya Roy and Aihwa Ong, 279–306. Oxford: Blackwell, 2011.

Ghurye, G. S. *Caste and Race in India*. London: K. Paul, Trench, Trubner, 1922.

Gidwani, Vinay. *Capital, Interrupted: Agrarian Development and the Politics of Work in India*. Minneapolis: University of Minnesota Press, 2008.

Gillespie, Tarleton. "The Platform Metaphor, Revisited." *Culture Digitally*, August 24, 2017. https://culturedigitally.org/2017/08/platform-metaphor/.

Gilmore, Ruth Wilson. *Golden Gulag: Prisons, Surplus, Crisis, and Opposition in Globalizing California*. Berkeley: University of California Press, 2007.

Gilmore, Ruth Wilson. "Race and Globalization." In *Geographies of Global Change: Remapping the World*, edited by R. J. Johnston, Peter J. Taylor, and Michael Watts, 261. New York: Wiley-Blackwell, 2002.

Ginsburg, Faye. "The Parallax Effect: The Impact of Aboriginal Media on Ethnographic Film." *Visual Anthropology Review* 11, no. 2 (1995): 64–76.

Giridharadas, Anand. *Winners Take All: The Elite Charade of Changing the World*. New York: Penguin, 2018.

Glissant, Édouard. *Poetics of Relation*. Ann Arbor: University of Michigan Press, 1997.

Gohain, Manash Pratim. "Why Half of India Prefers Private Schools." *Times of India*, July 23, 2020. https://timesofindia.indiatimes.com/india/why-half-of-india-prefers -private-schools/articleshow/77107620.cms.

Goldman, Michael. "Speculating on the Next World City." In *Worlding Cities: Asian Experiments and the Art of Being Global*, edited by Aihwa Ong and Ananya Roy, 229–59. Chichester, UK: Wiley-Blackwell, 2011.

Gonzalez, Melinda. "Methods of Motherhood: The Borderlands of Scholarship, Motherhood, and Trauma." *Anthro{dendum}*, August 13, 2019. https://anthrodendum.org/2019/08 /13/methods-of-motherhood-the-borderlands-of-scholarship-motherhood-and-trauma/.

González, Norma, Leisy Wyman, and Brendan H. O'Connor. "The Past, Present, and Future of 'Funds of Knowledge.'" In *A Companion to the Anthropology of Education*, edited by Bradley A. U. Levinson and Mica Pollock, 481–95. Chichester, UK: Wiley-Blackwell, 2011.

Good, Mary-Jo DelVecchio, Sandra Teresa Hyde, Sarah Pinto, and Byron J. Good. *Postcolonial Disorders*. Berkeley: University of California Press, 2009.

Gopal, Priyamvada. *Insurgent Empire: Anticolonial Resistance and British Dissent*. London: Verso, 2019.

Gould, Stephen Jay. *The Mismeasure of Man*. New York: W. W. Norton, 1980.

Gramsci, Antonio. "Americanism and Fordism." In *Antonio Gramsci*, edited by Steven Jones and Robert Eaglestone, 1–12. London: Routledge, 2006.

Gramsci, Antonio. *The Antonio Gramsci Reader: Selected Writings, 1916–1935*. Edited by David Forgacs. New York: New York University Press, 2000.

Grosfoguel, Ramon. "Decolonizing Post-colonial Studies and Paradigms of Political-Economy." *Transmodernity: Journal of Peripheral Cultural Production of the Luso-Hispanic World* 1, no. 1 (2011): 1–38.

Gualtieri, Sarah. *Between Arab and White: Race and Ethnicity in the Early Syrian American Diaspora*. Berkeley: University of California Press, 2009.

Guha, Ranajit. *Dominance without Hegemony: History and Power in Colonial India*. Cambridge, MA: Harvard University Press, 1997.

Gupta, Akhil. *Postcolonial Developments: Agriculture in the Making of Modern India*. Durham, NC: Duke University Press, 1998.

Gupta, Akhil. *Red Tape: Bureaucracy, Structural Violence, and Poverty in India*. Durham, NC: Duke University Press, 2012.

Gupta, Charu. *Sexuality, Obscenity, Community: Women, Muslims, and the Hindu Public in Colonial India*. New York: Palgrave, 2001.

Gupta, Charu. *The Gender of Caste: Representing Dalits in Print*. Seattle: University of Washington Press, 2016.

Gupta, Hemangini. "Testing the Future: Gender and Technocapitalism in Start-Up India." *Feminist Review* 123, no. 1 (2019): 74–88.

Guru, Gopal. "How Egalitarian Are the Social Sciences in India?" *Economic and Political Weekly* 37, no. 50 (2002): 5003–9.

Guzman, Joshua Javier. "Brown." *Keywords for Latina/o Studies*, edited by Deborah R. Vargas, Nancy Raquel Mirabal, and Lawrence M La Fountain-Stokes, 25–28. New York: New York University Press, 2017.

Haider, Asad. *Mistaken Identity: Race and Class in the Age of Trump*. New York: Verso, 2018.

Hannabach, Cathy. *Blood Cultures: Medicine, Media, and Militarisms*. New York: Palgrave Macmillan, 2015.

Harrelson, Stephanie. "Intensity." *affectsphere: keywords and reviews in affect theory*, April 2, 2014. https://affectsphere.wordpress.com/2014/04/02/intensity/.

Harrison, Faye V., ed. *Decolonizing Anthropology: Moving Further toward an Anthropology for Liberation*. 2nd ed. Arlington, VA: American Anthropological Association, 2008.

Hartigan, John, Jr. "Establishing the Fact of Whiteness." *American Anthropologist* 9, no. 3 (1997): 495–505.

Harvey, David. *A Brief History of Neoliberalism*. New York: Oxford University Press, 2005.

Harvey, David. *The Condition of Postmodernity: An Enquiry into the Origins of Cultural Change*. Cambridge, MA: Blackwell, 1990.

Harvey, David. "The 'New' Imperialism: Accumulation by Dispossession." *Socialist Register* 40 (2004): 63–87.

Hecht, Tobias. *At Home in the Street: Street Children of Northeast Brazil*. Cambridge: Cambridge University Press, 1998.

Heitzman, James. *Network City: Planning the Information Society in Bangalore*. Oxford: Oxford University Press, 2004.

Hesse, Barnor. "Im/plausible Deniability: Racism's Conceptual Double Bind." *Social Identities* 10, no. 1 (2004): 9–29.

Hong, Grace Kyungwon. "Speculative Surplus: Asian American Racialization and the Neoliberal Shift." *Social Text* 36, no. 2 (2018): 107–22.

Human Rights Watch. "India: Caste Forced to Clean Human Waste." August 25, 2014. https://www.hrw.org/news/2014/08/25/india-caste-forced-clean-human-waste#.

Hunt, Nancy Rose. *A Nervous State: Violence, Remedies, and Reverie in Colonial Congo*. Durham, NC: Duke University Press, 2016.

Idris, Afrin Firdaus, and Heba Ahmad. "Muslim Women Do Not Need Saving." *First Post*, April, 21, 2017. http://www.firstpost.com/long-reads/muslim-women-do-not-need-saving-3392516.html. Last accessed June 20, 2020.

Ignatiev, Noel, and John Garvey. *Race Traitor*. New York: Routledge, 1996.

Ilaiah, Kancha. *Why I Am Not a Hindu*. Calcutta, India: SAMYA, 1996.

Immerwahr, Daniel. "Caste or Colony? Indianizing Race in the United States." *Modern Intellectual History* 4, no. 2 (2007): 275–301.

INCITE!, ed. *The Revolution Will Not Be Funded: Beyond the Non-profit Industrial Complex*. Durham, NC: Duke University Press, 2007.

Irani, Lilly. *Chasing Innovation: Making Entrepreneurial Citizens in Modern India*. Princeton, NJ: Princeton University Press, 2019.

Irani, Lilly C. and M. Six Silberman, ed. 2016. "Stories We Tell about Labor: Turkopticon and the Trouble with 'Design.'" *Proceedings of the 2016 CHI Conference on Human Factors in Computing Systems* (May 2016): 4573–86. https://doi.org/10.1145/2858036.2858592.

Jackson, John L., Jr. "On Ethnographic Sincerity." *Current Anthropology* 51, no. S2 (2010): S279–87.

Jackson, John L., Jr. *Thin Description: Ethnography and the African Hebrew Israelites of Jerusalem*. Cambridge, MA: Harvard University Press, 2013.

Jaffrelot, Christophe. *Dr. Ambedkar and Untouchability: Fighting the Indian Caste System*. New York: Columbia University Press, 2005.

Jafri, Alishan, and Naomi Barton. "Explained: 'Trads' vs 'Raitas' and the Inner Workings of India's Alt-Right." *Wire*, January 11, 2022. https://thewire.in/communalism/genocide-as-pop-culture-inside-the-hindutva-world-of-trads-and-raitas.

James, Erica Caple. *Democratic Insecurities: Violence, Trauma, and Intervention in Haiti*. California Series in Public Anthropology. Berkeley: University of California Press, 2010.

Jangam, Chinnaiah. "Decolonizing Caste and Rethinking Social Inequality in South Asia." Paper presented at Virtual CASI Seminar, University of Pennsylvania, April 8, 2020. https://casi.sas.upenn.edu/events/chinnaiahjangam.

Jayawardena, Kumari. *Feminism and Nationalism in the Third World*. New York: Verso, 2016.

Jeffrey, Craig. *Timepass: Youth, Class, and the Politics of Waiting*. Stanford, CA: Stanford University Press, 2010.

Jeffrey, Craig, Patricia Jeffery, and Roger Jeffery. *Degrees without Freedom? Education, Masculinities, and Unemployment in North India*. Stanford, CA: Stanford University Press, 2007.

Jegathesan, Mythri. *Tea and Solidarity: Tamil Women and Work in Postwar Sri Lanka*. Seattle: University of Washington Press, 2019.

Jenkins, Dustin, and Justin Leroy. *Histories of Racial Capitalism*. New York: Columbia University Press, 2021.

Jobson, Ryan. "The Case for Letting Anthropology Burn: Sociocultural Anthropology in 2019." *American Anthropologist* 122, no. 2 (2020): 259–71.

Johnson, Walter. "Racial Capitalism and Human Rights." *Boston Review*, February 21, 2018. https://www.bostonreview.net/forum_response/walter-johnson-racial-capitalism-and-human/.

Kalam, A. P. J. *Ignited Minds: Unleashing the Power Within India.* New Delhi: Penguin Books, 2002.

Kamat, Sangeeta. *Development Hegemony: NGOs and the State in India.* New Delhi: Oxford University Press, 2002.

Kapur, Devesh. *Diaspora, Development, and Democracy: The Domestic Impact of International Migration from India.* Princeton, NJ: Princeton University Press, 2010.

Karim, Lamia. *Microfinance and Its Discontents: Women in Debt in Bangladesh.* Minneapolis: University of Minnesota Press, 2011.

Karunakaran, Valliammal. "The Dalit-Bahujan Guide to Understanding Caste in Hindu Scripture." Velivada: Educate, Agitate, Organize. Accessed February 7, 2023, https:// velivada.com/2017/04/07/dalit-bahujans-guide-understand-caste-hindu-vedas-scriptures/.

Kaviraj, Sudipta. "Filth and the Public Space: Concepts and Practices about Space in Calcutta." *Public Culture* 10, no. 1 (1997): 83–113.

Kelley, Robin D. G. Foreword to *Border and Rule: Global Migration, Capitalism, and the Rise of Racist Nationalism,* by Harsha Walia, 1–4. Chicago: Haymarket Book, 2021.

Khan, Mishal. "The Indebted among the 'Free': Producing Indian Labor through the Layers of Racial Capitalism." In *Histories of Racial Capitalism,* edited by Destin Jenkins and Justin Leroy, 85–110. New York: Columbia University Press, 2021.

Khoja-Moolji, Shenila. "Death by Benevolence: Third World Girls and the Contemporary Politics of Humanitarianism." *Feminist Theory* 21, no. 1 (2019): 1–26.

Khoja-Moolji, Shenila. *Forging the Ideal Educated Girl: The Production of Desirable Subjects in Muslim South Asia.* Berkeley: University of California Press, 2018.

Khoja-Moolji, Shenila. "Girl-Focused Development Campaigns: Two Steps Forward, One Step Back." The Blog. *HuffPost,* December 6, 2017. https://www.huffpost.com /entry/girlfocused-development-c_b_12283066.

Kikon, Dolly. "Hello Chinky." Fieldsights, Hot Spots. *Society for Cultural Anthropology,* March 16, 2021. https://culanth.org/fieldsights/hello-chinky.

Kikon, Dolly. *Living with Oil and Coal: Resource Politics and Militarization in Northeast India.* Seattle: University of Washington Press, 2019.

Kilby, Patrick. *NGOs in India: The Challenges of Women's Empowerment and Accountability.* New York: Routledge, 2011.

Kirtsoglou, Elisabeth. "Anticipatory Nostalgia and Nomadic Temporality: A Case Study of Chronocracy in the Crypto-Colony." In *The Time of Anthropology: Studies of Contemporary Chronopolitics,* edited by Elisabeth Kirtsoglou and Bob Simpson, 159–86. ASA Monograph Series 52. London: Routledge, 2021.

Kothari, Ashish, Ariel Salleh, Arturo Escobar, Federico Demaria, and Alberto Acosta, eds. *Pluriverse: A Post-development Dictionary.* New Delhi: Tulika Books, 2019.

Kothari, Uma. "An Agenda for Thinking about 'Race' in Development." *Progress in Development Studies* 6, no. 1 (2006): 9–23.

Kumar, Nilotpal. *Unraveling Farmer Suicides in India: Egoism and Masculinity in Peasant Life.* Oxford: Oxford University Press, 2016.

Kumar, Ravi. "Against Neoliberal Assault on Education in India: A Counternarrative of Resistance." *Journal of Critical Education Policy Studies* 6, no. 1 (2008). http://www.jceps .com/archives/563.

LaDousa, Chaise. *Hindi Is Our Ground, English Is Our Sky: Education, Language, and Social Class in Contemporary India*. New York: Berghahn Books, 2014.

Larkin, Brian. "The Politics and Poetics of Infrastructure." *Annual Review of Anthropology* 42 (2013): 327–43.

Liboiron, Max. *Pollution Is Colonialism*. Durham, NC: Duke University Press. 2021.

Lipsitz, George. *Possessive Investment in Whiteness: How White People Profit from Identity Politics, Twentieth Anniversary Edition*. Philadelphia: Temple University Press, 2018.

Liu, Roseann, and Savannah Shange. "Toward Thick Solidarity: Theorizing Empathy in Social Justice Movements." *Radical History Review* 2018, no. 131 (2018): 189–98.

Lloyd, David, and Patrick Wolfe. "Settler Colonial Logics and the Neoliberal Regime." *Settler Colonial Studies* 6, no. 2 (2015): 109–18.

Lowe, Lisa. *The Intimacies of Four Continents*. Durham, NC: Duke University Press, 2015.

Lowry, Elizabeth. Review of *The Ironic Spectator: Solidarity in the Age of Post-humanitarianism*, by Lilie Chouliaraki. *Diffractions*, no. 4 (2015): 1–6.

Lukose, Ritty A. *Liberalization's Children: Gender, Youth, and Consumer Citizenship in Globalizing India*. Durham, NC: Duke University Press, 2009.

Macaulay, Thomas Babington. "Minute on Indian Education," 1835. http://www.columbia .edu/itc/mealac/pritchett/00generallinks/macaulay/txt_minute_education_1835 .html.

Maddrell, Avril, and James D. Sidaway. *Deathscapes: Spaces for Death, Dying, Mourning and Remembrance*. Farnham, UK: Ashgate, 2010.

Madianou, Mirca, and Daniel Miller. *Migration and New Media: Transnational Families and Polymedia*. New York: Routledge, 2012.

Madison, Soyini D. *Critical Ethnography: Method, Ethics, and Performance*. Los Angeles: Sage, 2011.

Maghbouleh, Neda. *The Limits of Whiteness: Iranian Americans and the Everyday Politics of Race*. Palo Alto, CA: Stanford University Press, 2017.

Mains, Daniel. *Under Construction: Technologies of Development in Urban Ethiopia*. Durham, NC: Duke University Press, 2019.

Maira, Sunaina. "Flexible Citizenship/Flexible Empire: South Asian Muslim Youth in Post-9/11 America." *American Quarterly* 60, no. 3 (2008): 697–720.

Malkki, Liisa. *The Need to Help: The Domestic Arts of International Humanitarianism*. Durham, NC: Duke University Press, 2015.

Malthus, Thomas. *An Essay on the Principle of Population: Or, A View of Its Past and Present Effects on Human Happiness*. London: Ward, Lock, 1890.

Mamdani, Mahmood. *Good Muslim, Bad Muslim: America, the Cold War, and the Roots of Terror*. New York: Pantheon Books, 2004.

Mamdani, Mahmood. *Neither Settler nor Native: The Making and Unmaking of Permanent Minorities*. Cambridge, MA: Harvard University Press, 2020.

Manalansan, Martin F. "The 'Stuff' of Archives: Mess, Migration, and Queer Lives." *Radical History Review* 2014, no. 120 (2014): 94–107.

Mankekar, Purnima. *Unsettling India: Affect, Temporality, Transnationality*. Durham, NC: Duke University Press, 2015.

Manzo, Kate. 2008. "Imaging Humanitarianism: NGO Identity and the Iconography of Childhood." *Antipode* 40, no. 4 (2008): 632–57.

Martinez, Maria Elena. *Genealogical Fictions: Lipieza de Sangre, Religion, and Gender in Colonial Mexico*. Palo Alto, CA: Stanford University Press.

Marx, Karl. *Capital*. Vol. 1, *A Critique of Political Economy*. New York: Penguin Classics, 1992.

Masanet, Eric, Arman Shehabi, Nuoa Lei, Sarah Smith, and Jonathan Koomey. "Recalibrating Global Data Center Energy-Use Estimates." *Science* 367, no. 6481 (2020): 984–86.

Massumi, Brian. "The Autonomy of Affect." *Cultural Critique*, no. 31 (1995): 83–109.

Mather, Cotton. *India Christiana: A Discourse, Delivered Unto the Commissioners, for the Propagation of the Gospel Among the American Indians, which Is Accompanied with Several Instruments Relating to the Glorious Design of Propagating Our Holy Religion, in the Eastern as Well as the Western Indies: an Entertainment which They that are Waiting for the Kingdom of God Will Receive as Good News from a Far Country*. Boston: B. Green, 1721. http://name.umdl.umich.edu/N01899.0001.001.

Mathew, Leya, and Ritty Lukose. "Pedagogies of Aspiration: Anthropological Perspectives on Education in Liberalising India." *South Asia: Journal of South Asian Studies* 43, no. 4 (2020): 691–704.

Mayo, Katherine. *Mother India*. 1927. Ann Arbor: University of Michigan Press, 2000.

Mazzarella, William. "Affect: What Is It Good For?" In *Enchantments of Modernity: Empire, Nation, Globalization*, edited by Saurabh Dube, 291–309. New York: Routledge, 2009.

Mazzarella, William. "Beautiful Balloon: The Digital Divide and the Charisma of New Media in India." *American Ethnologist* 37, no. 4 (2010): 783–804.

Mazzarella, William. "Internet X-Ray: E-Governance, Transparency, and the Politics of Immediation in India." *Public Culture* 18, no. 3 (2006): 473–505.

McClintock, Anne. "The Angel of Progress: Pitfalls of the Term 'Post-colonialism.'" *Social Text*, no. 31/32 (1992): 84–98.

McKittrick, Katherine, ed. *Sylvia Wynter: On Being Human as Praxis*. Durham, NC: Duke University Press, 2015.

McKittrick, Katherine, and Sylvia Wynter. "Unparalleled Catastrophe for Our Species? Or, to Give Humanness a Different Future: Conversations." In *Sylvia Wynter: On Being Human as Praxis*, edited by Katherine McKittrick, 15–17. Durham, NC: Duke University Press, 2015.

McLaverty-Robinson, Andrew. "Jean Baudrillard: Hyperreality and Implosion." *Ceasefire*, August 19, 2012. https://ceasefiremagazine.co.uk/in-theory-baudrillard-9/.

Melamed, Jodi. "Racial Capitalism." *Critical Ethnic Studies* 1, no. 1 (2015): 76–85.

Merry, Sally Engle. "Measuring the World: Indicators, Human Rights, and Global Governance: With CA Comment by John M. Conley." *Current Anthropology* 52, no. S3 (2011): S83–95.

Mies, Maria. *Patriarchy and Accumulation on a World Scale: Women in the International Division of Labour*. London: Zed Books, 2014.

Mignolo, Walter D. *The Darker Side of Western Modernity: Global Futures, Decolonial Options*. Durham, NC: Duke University Press, 2011.

Mignolo, Walter. Foreword to *Can Non-Europeans Think?*, by Hamid Dabashi, vii–xiii. London: Zed Books, 2015.

Minai, Naveen, and Sara Shroff. "Yaariyan, Baithak, Gupshup: Queer Feminist Formations and the Global South." *Kohl: A Journal for Body and Gender Research* 5, no. 1 (2019): 31–44.

Mines, Diane P., and Nicolas Yazgi, eds. *Village Matters: Relocating Villages in the Contemporary Anthropology of India*. New Delhi: Oxford University Press, 2010.

Ministry of Foreign Affairs, Republic of Indonesia. *Asian-African Conference Bulletin*, no. 1 (March 1955). https://bandung60.wordpress.com/bandung-bulletin/.

Minj, Nolina S. "Zen and the Art of Anjali Patil." The Cinema Issue: Seeing Is Believing. *Verve*, December 2020. https://vervemagazine.in/cinemaissue/#/anjali-patil-cover-story.

Mishra, Sangay. *Desis Divided: The Political Lives of South Asian Americans*. Minneapolis: University of Minnesota Press, 2016.

Mishra, Sangay. "Not Quite Home." *Indian Express*, July 3, 2020. https://indianexpress.com/article/opinion/not-quite-home-covid-international-travel-restriction-oci-6488925/.

Mistry, Rohinton. *A Fine Balance*. New York: Knopf, 1995.

Mitchell, Lisa. *Language, Emotion, and Politics in South India: The Making of a Mother Tongue*. Bloomington: Indiana University Press, 2009.

Mohammed, Patricia. "'But Most of All Mi Love Me Browning': The Emergence in Eighteenth and Nineteenth-Century Jamaica of the Mulatto Woman as the Desired." *Feminist Review* 65, no. 1 (2000): 22–48.

Mohan, P. Sanal. *Modernity of Slavery: Struggles against Caste Inequality in Colonial Kerala*. Oxford: Oxford University Press, 2015.

Mohan, Siddhant. "Remembering Fatima Sheikh, the First Muslim Teacher Who Laid the Foundation of Dalit-Muslim Unity." *TwoCircles.net*, April 7, 2017. http://twocircles.net/2017apr07/407472.html.

Mohanty, Chandra Talpade. "Under Western Eyes: Feminist Scholarship and Colonial Discourses." In *Third World Women and the Politics of Feminism*, edited by Chandra Talpade Mohanty, Ann Russo, and Lourdes Torres, 333–58. Bloomington: Indiana University Press, 1991.

Mohanty, Chandra Talpade, Ann Russo, and Lourdes Torres, eds. *Third World Women and the Politics of Feminism*. Bloomington: Indiana University Press, 1991.

Moore, Henrietta. *Still Life: Hopes, Desires and Satisfactions*. Cambridge, UK: Polity, 2011.

Morris, Errol. *Believing Is Seeing (Observations on the Mysteries of Photography)*. New York: Penguin, 2011.

Morrison, Toni. "Racism and Fascism." *Journal of Negro Education* 64, no. 3 (1995): 384–85.

Morton, Samuel. *Crania Americana, or, A comparative view of the skulls of various aboriginal nations of North and South America: to which is prefixed an essay on the varieties of the human species; illustrated by seventy-eight plates and a colored map*. Philadelphia: J. Dobson, 1839.

Mosse, David. "Caste and Development: Contemporary Perspectives on a Structure of Discrimination and Advantage." *World Development* 110 (2018): 422–36.

Mosse, David. "The Modernity of Caste and the Market Economy." *Modern Asian Studies* 54, no. 4 (2020): 1225–71.

Mosse, David, and Sundara Babu Nagappan. "NGOs as Social Movements: Policy Narratives, Networks and the Performance of Dalit Rights in South India." *Development and Change* 52, no. 1 (2020): 134–67.

Moten, Fred, and Stefano Harney. *The Undercommons: Fugitive Planning and Black Study.* New York: AK Press, 2013.

Muhammad, Raees. "Contemporary Practices of Pollution and Space Part 3-3." Dalit Camera, June 20, 2020. https://www.dalitcamera.com/contemporary-practices-of -pollution-and-space-part-3-3/. Last accessed July 1, 2020.

Müller, Max. *The Essential Max Müller: On Language, Mythology, and Religion.* Edited by Jon R. Stone. New York: Palgrave Macmillan, 2002.

Munn, Nancy. "The Cultural Anthropology of Time: A Critical Essay." *Annual Review of Anthropology* 21 (1992): 93–123.

Muñoz, José Esteban. *The Sense of Brown.* Durham, NC: Duke University Press, 2020.

Munshi, Soniya, and Craig Willse. Foreword to *The Revolution Will Not Be Funded: Beyond the Non-profit Industrial Complex,* edited by INCITE!, xii–xxii. Durham, NC: Duke University Press, 2007.

Münster, Daniel. "Farmers' Suicides and the State in India: Conceptual and Ethnographic Notes from Wayanad, Kerala." *Contributions to Indian Sociology* 46, nos. 1–2 (2012): 181–208.

Nadeem, Shehzad. *Dead Ringers: How Outsourcing Is Changing the Way Indians Understand Themselves.* Princeton, NJ: Princeton University Press, 2011.

Nagaraj, K. *Farmers' Suicides in India: Magnitudes, Trends and Spatial Patterns.* Chennai: Bharathi puthukalayam, 2008.

Nair, Janaki. *The Promise of the Metropolis: Bangalore's Twentieth Century.* Oxford: Oxford University Press, 2005.

Nair, Siddarth Anil. "More Than Half the Graduates Not Getting Employed: What Are the Challenges?" *Bangalore Citizen Matters,* July 3, 2018. https://bengaluru .citizenmatters.in/bangalore-employability-problems-25907.

Nair, Vijayanka. "Governing India in Cybertime: Biometric IDs, Start-Ups and the Temporalised State." *South Asia: Journal of South Asian Studies* 42, no. 3 (2019): 519–36.

Nehru, Jawaharlal. *An Autobiography.* New Delhi: Oxford University Press, 1936.

Noble, Safiya Umoja. *Algorithms of Oppression.* New York: New York University Press, 2018.

Noble, Safiya Umoja. "Social Inequality Will Not Be Solved by an App." *Wired,* March 4, 2018. https://www.wired.com/story/social-inequality-will-not-be-solved-by -an-app/.

Nouvet, Elysée. "Some Carry On, Some Stay in Bed: (In)convenient Affects and Agency in Neoliberal Nicaragua." *Cultural Anthropology* 29, no. 1 (2014): 80–102.

Nundy, Neera. "Accelerating Family Philanthropy Will Drive India's Socio-economic Growth." *Forbes India,* April 8, 2021. https://www.forbesindia.com/blog/giving /accelerating-family-philanthropy-will-drive-indias-socio-economic-growth/.

Ocampo, Anthony. *Brown and Gay in LA: The Lives of Immigrant Sons.* New York: New York University Press, 2022.

Omvedt, Gail. *Understanding Caste: From Buddha to Ambedkar and Beyond*. New Delhi: Orient Blackswan, 2011.

Ong, Aihwa, and Ananya Roy. *Worlding Cities: Asian Experiments and the Art of Being Global*. Oxford: Blackwell, 2011.

Ortner, Sherry B. "On Key Symbols." *American Anthropologist* 75, no. 5 (1973): 1338–46.

Osuri, Goldie, and Ather Zia. "Kashmir and Palestine: Archives of Coloniality and Solidarity." *Identities* 27, no. 3 (2020): 249–66.

Paik, Shailaja. "Dalit Feminist Thought." Paper presented at University of Pennsylvania CASI Seminar, November 5, 2020. https://casi.sas.upenn.edu/events/shailajapaik.

Paik, Shailaja. *Dalit Women's Education in Modern India: Double Discrimination*. New York: Routledge, 2014.

Pandian, Anand. "Devoted to Development: Moral Progress, Ethnical Work, and Divine Favor in South India." *Anthropological Theory* 8, no. 2 (2008): 159–79.

Pandian, Anand. "The Remembering Village: Looking Back on Louis Dumont from Rural Tamil Nadu." *Contributions to Indian Sociology* 43, no. 1 (2009): 121–33.

Pardue, Derek, and Lucas Amaral de Oliviera. "City as Mobility: A Contribution of Brazilian *Saraus* to Urban Theory." *Vibrant Virtual Brazilian Anthropology* 15, no. 1 (2018). https://journals.openedition.org/vibrant/2982.

Pascucci, Elisa. "The Local Labour Building the International Community: Precarious Work within Humanitarian Spaces." *Environment and Planning A: Economy and Space* 51, no. 3 (2018): 743–60.

Patel, Kamna. "Race and a Decolonial Turn in Development." *Third World Quarterly* 41, no. 9 (2020): 1463–75.

Patel, Shaista. "Complicating the Tale of 'Two Indians': Mapping 'South Asian' Complicity in White Settler Colonialism along the Axis of Caste and Anti-Blackness." *Theory and Event* 19, no. 4 (2016). https://muse.jhu.edu/article/633278.

Patel, Shaista. "The 'Indian Queen' of the Four Continents: Tracing the Undifferentiated 'Indian' through Europe's Encounters with Muslims, Anti-Blackness, and Conquest of the 'New World.'" *Cultural Studies* 33, no. 3 (2019): 414–36.

Patnaik, Prabhat. "Decline in Poverty Rate Is a Farce Perpetuated by World Bank's Poverty Line." *People's Dispatch*, July 19, 2020. https://mronline.org/2020/07/24/decline-in-global-poverty-is-a-farce-perpetuated-by-world-banks-poverty-line/.

Patnaik, Prabhat. "The New Casteism." *Telegraph India*, February 8, 2016. https://www.telegraphindia.com/opinion/the-new-casteism/cid/1446922.

Patnaik, Prabhat. "Why Is India's Wealth Inequality Growing So Rapidly?" *Al Jazeera*, January 28, 2018. https://www.aljazeera.com/opinions/2018/1/26/why-is-indias-wealth-inequality-growing-so-rapidly.

Patnaik, Utsa. "The Agrarian Question in the Neoliberal Era." In *The Agrarian Question in the Neoliberal Era: Primitive Accumulation and the Peasantry*, edited by Utsa Patnaik and Sam Moyo, 7–60. Oxford: Pambazuka Press, 2011.

Patnaik, Utsa. "How the British Impoverished India." *Hindustan Times*, October 20, 2018. https://www.hindustantimes.com/analysis/how-the-british-impoverished-india/story-zidAo8pKyIrmO7UnBkcjfJ.html.

Pearson, Heath. "The Prickly Skin of White Supremacy: Race in the 'Real America.'" *Transforming Anthropology* 23, no. 1 (2015): 43–58.

Pels, Peter J. "What Has Anthropology Learned from the Anthropology of Colonialism?" *Social Anthropology* 16, no. 3 (2008): 280–99.

Petras, James. "NGOs: In the Service of Imperialism." *Journal of Contemporary Asia* 29, no. 4 (1999): 429–40.

Phule, Jyotiba. *Gulamgiri*. n.p., 1885.

Pierre, Jemima. *The Predicament of Blackness: Postcolonial Ghana and the Politics of Race.* Chicago: University of Chicago Press, 2012.

Pierre, Jemima. "The Racial Vernaculars of Development: A View from West Africa." *American Anthropologist* 122, no. 1 (2019): 86–98.

Piketty, Thomas. *Capital in the Twenty-First Century*. Cambridge, MA: Harvard University Press, 2014.

Pinto, Ambrose. "UN Conference against Racism: Is Caste Race?" *Economic and Political Weekly* 36, no. 30 (2001): 2817–20.

Poole, Deborah. *Vision, Race, and Modernity: A Visual Economy of the Andean Image World.* Princeton, NJ: Princeton University Press, 1996.

Povinelli, Elizabeth. *The Cunning of Recognition: Indigenous Alterities and the Making of Australian Multiculturalism*. Durham, NC: Duke University Press, 2002.

Povinelli, Elizabeth. *Economies of Abandonment: Social Belonging and Endurance in Late Liberalism*. Durham, NC: Duke University Press, 2010.

Prasad, M. Madhava. "The Imagined Village: Representations of Rural Life in Indian Cinema." In *Village Matters: Relocating Villages in the Contemporary Anthropology of India*, edited by Diane P. Mines and Nicolas Yazgi, 256–71. New Delhi: Oxford University Press, 2010.

Prasad, Srirupa. *Cultural Politics of Hygiene in India, 1890–1940: Contagions of Feeling*. London: Palgrave Macmillan, 2015.

Prashad, Vijay. *The Darker Nations: A People's History of the Third World*. New York: New Press, 2007.

Prashad, Vijay. *The Karma of Brown Folk*. Minneapolis: University of Minnesota Press, 2000.

Puar, Jasbir. "Rethinking Homonationalism." *International Journal of Middle East Studies* 45, no. 2 (2013): 336–39.

Purushothaman, Seema, and Sham Kashyap. "A Historical Analysis of Land Ownership and Agroecology, in the Erstwhile Mysore Region of South India." Working paper, Azim Premji University, 2017. https://www.iss.nl/sites/corporate/files/2017-11/BICAS%20CP%205-60%20Purushothaman.pdf.

Radhakrishnan, Smitha. *Appropriately Indian: Gender and Culture in a New Transnational Class*. Durham, NC: Duke University Press, 2011.

Radhakrishnan, Smitha. *Making Women Pay: Microfinance in Urban India*. Durham, NC: Duke University Press, 2022.

Rai, Amit. *Jugaad Time: Ecologies of Everyday Hacking in India*. Durham, NC: Duke University Press, 2019.

Ralph, Michael, and Maya Singhal. "Racial Capitalism." *Theory and Society* 48, no. 6 (2019): 851–81.

Ram, Theja. "K'taka Amends Land Acquisition Act to Speed Up Projects, Activists Call It 'Dangerous.'" *News Minute*, March 12, 2019. https://www.thenewsminute.com/article /k-taka-amends-land-acquisition-act-speed-projects-activists-call-it-dangerous-98166.

Ramos-Zayas, Ana Y. *Street Therapists: Race, Affect, and Neoliberal Personhood in Latino Newark*. Chicago: University of Chicago Press, 2012.

Rana, Junaid. "The Racial Infrastructure of the Terror-Industrial Complex." *Social Text* 34, no. 4 (2016): 111–38.

Rana, Junaid. *Terrifying Muslims: Race and Labor in the South Asian Diaspora*. Durham, NC: Duke University Press, 2011.

Rao, Anupama. "The Work of Analogy: On Isabel Wilkerson's 'Caste: The Origins of Our Discontents.'" *Los Angeles Review of Books*, September 1, 2020. https:// lareviewofbooks.org/article/the-work-of-analogy-on-isabel-wilkersons-caste-the -origins-of-our-discontents/.

Rao, Anupama. *Gender and Caste*. New Delhi: Kali for Women, 2003.

Rao, Ursula, and Vijayanka Nair. "Aadhaar: Governing with Biometrics." *South Asia: Journal of South Asian Studies* 42, no. 3 (2019): 469–81.

Rawat, Ramnarayan S., and K. Satyanarayana. *Dalit Studies*. Durham, NC: Duke University Press, 2016.

Reardon, Jenny, and Kim TallBear. "'Your DNA Is Our History': Genomics, Anthropology, and the Construction of Whiteness as Property." *Current Anthropology* 53, no. S5 (2012): S233–45.

Rege, Sharmila. *Writing Caste, Writing Gender: Reading Dalit Women's Testimonios*. New Delhi: Zubaan Books, 2006.

Resnick, Mitchel. *Turtles, Termites, and Traffic Jams: Explorations in Massively Parallel Microworlds*. Cambridge, MA: MIT Press, 1994.

Rifkin, Mark. *Beyond Settler Time: Temporal Sovereignty and Indigenous Self-Determination*. Durham, NC: Duke University Press, 2017.

Rist, Gilbert. *The History of Development: From Western Origins to Global Faith*. New York: Zed Books, 1997.

Rizvi, Mubbashir A. *The Ethics of Staying: Social Movements and Land Rights Politics in Pakistan*. Palo Alto, CA: Stanford University Press, 2019.

Robb, Peter, ed. *The Concept of Race in South Asia*. Delhi: Oxford University Press, 1995.

Robinson, Cedric. *Black Marxism: The Making of the Black Radical Tradition*. Chapel Hill: University of North Carolina Press, 2000.

Rodney, Walter. *How Europe Underdeveloped Africa*. New York: Verso, 2018.

Rosa, Jonathan. *Looking Like a Language, Sounding Like a Race: Raciolinguistic Ideologies and the Learning of Latinidad*. Oxford: Oxford University Press, 2018.

Ross, Eric B. *The Malthus Factor: Poverty, Politics and Population in Capitalist Development*. London: Zed Books, 2000.

Rovelli, Carlo. *The Order of Time: Seven Brief Lessons on Physics*. New York: Riverhead Books, 2018.

Roy, Ananya. *City Requiem*. Minneapolis: University of Minnesota Press, 2002.

Roy, Ananya. *Poverty Capital: Microfinance and the Making of Development*. London: Routledge, 2010.

Roy, Arundhati. *Capitalism: A Ghost Story*. London: Haymarket Books, 2014.

Roy, Arundhati. "The Doctor and the Saint." In B. R. Ambedkar, *Annihilation of Caste: The Annotated Critical Edition*, edited by S. Anand, 11–143. New York: Verso, 2016.

RT. "Coca-Cola Forced to Close India Bottling Factory over Excessive Water Use, Pollution." June 18, 2014. http://www.rt.com/news/167012-coca-cola-factory-closed-india/.

Rukmini, S. "Modi launches 'My Clean India' campaign." *The Hindu*, October 2, 2014. https://www.thehindu.com/news/national/Modi-launches-My-Clean-India-campaign/article60391303.ece.

Said, Edward. *The World, the Text, and the Critic*. Cambridge, MA: Harvard University Press, 1983.

Sainath, Palagummi. *Everybody Loves a Good Drought: Stories from India's Poorest Districts*. New Delhi: Penguin, 1996.

Sanyal, Kalyan. *Rethinking Capitalist Development: Primitive Accumulation, Governmentality and Post-colonial Capitalism*. London: Routledge, 2014.

Sartre, Jean-Paul. Preface to *The Wretched of the Earth*, by Frantz Fanon. New York: Grove, 2005.

Satish, D. P. "Dalits, Muslims Outnumber Lingayats and Vokkaligas in Karnataka? 'Caste Census' Stumps Siddaramaiah Govt." *News18*, March 15, 2018. https://www.news18.com/news/politics/dalits-muslims-outnumber-lingayats-and-vokkaligas-in-karnataka-caste-census-stumps-siddaramaiah-govt-1689531.html.

Scheper-Hughes, Nancy. "The Global Traffic in Human Organs." *Current Anthropology* 41, no. 2 (2000): 191–224.

Scheper-Hughes, Nancy, and Carolyn Sargent. *Small Wars: The Cultural Politics of Childhood*. Berkeley: University of California Press, 1998.

Schull, Natasha Dow. *Addiction by Design: Machine Gambling in Las Vegas*. Princeton, NJ: Princeton University Press, 2012.

Sexton, Jared. "People-of-Color-Blindness: Notes on the Afterlife of Slavery." *Social Text* 28, no. 2 (2010): 31–56.

Shange, Savannah. *Progressive Dystopia: Abolition, Antiblackness, and Schooling in San Francisco*. Durham, NC: Duke University Press, 2019.

Shankar, Arjun. "Air-Conditioners and the Talk of the Middle Class." *City and Society* 33, no. 1 (2021). https://anthrosource.onlinelibrary.wiley.com/doi/10.1111/ciso.12379.

Shankar, Arjun. "'The Campus Is Sick': Capitalist Curiosity and Student Mental Health." In *Curiosity Studies: A New Ecology of Knowledge*, edited by Perry Zurn and Arjun Shankar, 106–25. Minneapolis: University of Minnesota Press, 2020.

Shankar, Arjun. "Moral Economies, Developmentalist Sovereignty, and Affective Strain." In *Sovereignty Unhinged: An Illustrated Primer for the Study of Present, Intensities, Disavowals, and Temporary Derangements*, edited by Joe Masco and Deborah Thomas, 162–84. Durham, NC: Duke University Press, 2023.

Shankar, Arjun, "On Brown Blood: Race, Caste, and the Bhagat Singh Thind Case." *Ethnic Studies Review*, forthcoming.

Shankar, Arjun. "Participation, Reception, Consent, and Refusal." In *The Routledge International Handbook of Ethnographic Film and Video*, edited by Phillip Vannini, 204–13. London: Routledge, 2020.

Shankar, Arjun. "Primitivism and Race in Ethnographic Film: A Decolonial Revisioning." *Oxford Bibliographies*, 2020. https://www.oxfordbibliographies.com/view /document/obo-9780199766567/obo-9780199766567-0245.xml.

Shankar, Arjun. "Silence and Privilege Renegotiated." Fieldsights, Member Voices. *Society for Cultural Anthropology*, December 8, 2016. https://culanth.org/fieldsights /silence-and-privilege-renegotiated.

Shankar, Subramanian. *Flesh and Fish Blood: Postcolonialism, Translation, and the Vernacular*. Berkeley: University of California Press, 2012.

Sharma, Aradhana. *Logics of Empowerment: Development, Gender, and Governance in Neoliberal India*. Minneapolis: University of Minnesota Press, 2008.

Sharma, Aradhana. "The State and Women's Empowerment in India: Paradoxes and Politics." In *Theorizing NGOs: States, Feminisms, and Neoliberalism*, edited by Victoria Bernal and Inderpal Grewal, 93–113. Durham, NC: Duke University Press, 2014.

Sharma, Nitasha Tamar. "Brown." In *Keywords for Asian American Studies*, edited by Cathy Schlund-Vials, Linda Trinh Vo, and K. Scott Wong, 18–19. New York: New York University Press, 2015.

Sheller, Mimi. *Mobility Justice: The Politics of Movement in an Age of Extremes*. New York: Verso, 2018.

Shipley, Jesse. "Selfie Love: Public Lives in an Era of Celebrity Pleasure, Violence, and Social Media." *Visual Anthropology* 117, no. 2 (2015): 403–13.

Shore, Cris, and Susan Wright. "Audit Culture Revisited: Rankings, Ratings, and the Reassembling of Society." *Current Anthropology* 56, no. 3 (2015): 421–44.

Shree, D. N. "Why Did Farmers Protest in Bengaluru, and What You Can Do about It." *Bangalore Citizen Matters*, March 24, 2016. https://bengaluru.citizenmatters.in/farmers -problems-solutions-from-cities-8143.

Shukla, Sandhya. *India Abroad*. Princeton, NJ: Princeton University Press, 2003.

Simone, AbdouMaliq. "People as Infrastructure: Intersecting Fragments in Johannesburg." *Public Culture* 16, no. 3 (2004): 407–29.

Simpson, Audra. "Consent's Revenge." *Cultural Anthropology* 31, no. 3 (2016): 326–33.

Sims, Christo. *Disruptive Fixation: School Reform and the Pitfalls of Techno-idealism*. Minneapolis: University of Minnesota Press, 2017.

Singh, Nikhil Pal. "On Race, Violence, and So-Called Primitive Accumulation." *Social Text* 34, no. 3 (128) (2016): 27–50.

Singh, Ranjit. "Give Me a Database and I Will Raise the Nation-State." *South Asia: Journal of South Asian Studies* 42, no. 3 (2019): 501–18.

Sinha, Mrinalini. *Specters of Mother India: The Global Restructuring of an Empire*. Durham, NC: Duke University Press, 2006.

Siraj, M. A. *The Status of Urdu Medium Schools in Karnataka: Imparting Inclusive Orientation to Instructions*. Centre for Study of Social Exclusion and Inclusive Policy, National Law School of India University, Bengaluru, 2012. https://dom.karnataka.gov.in/storage

/pdf-files/Sir%20Syed%20Ahmed%20Khan/Status%20of%20Urdu%20Medium%20
School%20 -%20M%0A%20Siraj.pdf.

Slate, Nico. *Colored Cosmopolitanism: The Shared Struggle for Freedom in the United States and India*. Cambridge, MA: Harvard University Press, 2017.

Soundararajan, Thenmozhi. "How Brown Girl Solidarity Harms Us." *Wear Your Voice Mag*, February 20, 2020. https://wearyourvoicemag.com/identities/how-brown-girl -solidarity-harms-us. Last accessed February 27, 2021.

Soundararajan, Thenmozhi. *The Trauma of Caste: A Dalit Feminist Meditation on Survivorship, Healing, and Abolition*. Berkeley, CA: North Atlantic Books, 2022.

Spivak, Gayatri. "'Can the Subaltern Speak?'" In *Colonial Discourse and Post-colonial Theory: A Reader*, edited by Patrick Williams and Laura Chrisman. New York: Columbia University Press, 1994.

Spivak, Gayatri Chakravorty. *A Critique of Postcolonial Reason: Toward a History of the Vanishing Present*. Cambridge, MA: Harvard University Press, 1999.

Srinivas, M. N. *Caste in Modern India and Other Essays*. Bombay: Asia Publishing House, 1962.

Srinivasan, Sumathi. *Passions of the Tongue: Language Devotion in Tamil India, 1891–1970*. Berkeley: University of California Press, 1997.

Steinberg, Marc. *The Platform Economy: How Japan Transformed the Consumer Internet*. Minneapolis: University of Minnesota Press, 2019.

Stephen, Cynthia. "#MeToo: The NGO Sector Systematically Silences Dalit, Tribal and Bahujan Voices." *Wire*, October 29, 2018. https://thewire.in/caste/metoo-the-ngo -sector-systematically-silences-dalit-tribal-and-bahujan-voices.

Stewart, Kathleen. *Ordinary Affects*. Durham, NC: Duke University Press, 2007.

Strathern, Marilyn. "Introduction: New Accountabilities." In *Audit Cultures: Anthropological Studies in Accountability, Ethics and the Academy*, edited by Marilyn Strathern, 1–18. London: Routledge, 2000.

Strathern, Marilyn, ed. *Audit Cultures: Anthropological Studies in Accountability, Ethics and the Academy*. London: Routledge, 2000.

Subramanian, Ajantha. *The Caste of Merit: Engineering Education in India*. Cambridge, MA: Harvard University Press, 2019.

Subramanian, Ajantha. "Making Merit: The Indian Institutes of Technology and the Social Life of Caste." *Comparative Studies in Society and History* 57 (2015): 291–322.

Tacchi, Jo. "Digital Engagement: Voice and Participation in Development." In *Digital Anthropology*, edited by Heather Horst, and Daniel Miller, 225–41. Oxford: Berg, 2012.

Táíwò, Olúfẹ́mi O. "Identity Politics and Elite Capture." *Boston Review*, May 7, 2020. https://www.bostonreview.net/articles/olufemi-o-taiwo-identity-politics-and-elite -capture/.

Táíwò, Olúfẹ́mi O. *Reconsidering Reparations*. Oxford: Oxford University Press, 2021.

TallBear, Kim, and Eve Tuck. "Red and Black DNA, Blood, Kinship and Organizing." *Henceforward* (podcast), July 25, 2016. https://thehenceforward.libsyn.com/episode-3 -red-and-black-dna-blood-kinship-and-organizing-with-kim-tallbear.

Taussig, Michael. *The Nervous System*. New York: Routledge, 1992.

Teltumbde, Anand. *Republic of Caste: Thinking Equality in the Time of Neoliberal Hindutva*. New Delhi: Navayana, 2018.

Thangaraj, Stanley. *Desi Hoop Dreams: Pickup Basketball and the Making of Asian American Masculinity*. New York: New York University Press, 2015.

Thangaraj, Stanley. "Sipping on the Indian Haterade: Hindu American Whiteness and Support for Trump." *Tropics of Meta: Historiography of the Masses*, January 30, 2017. https://tropicsofmeta.com/2017/01/30/sipping-on-the-indian-haterade-hindu-american-whiteness-and-support-for-trump/.

Thapar, Romila. "The Theory of Aryan Race and India: History and Politics." *Social Scientist* 24, nos. 1–3 (1996): 3–29.

Thomas, Deborah. "The End of the West and the Future of Us All." *African Diaspora* 11, nos. 1–2 (2019): 123–43.

Thomas, Deborah A. "Cox's America: Caste, Race, and the Problem of Culture." *Canadian Journal of Latin American and Caribbean Studies* 30, no. 3 (2014), 364–81.

Thomas, Deborah A. *Political Life in the Wake of the Plantation: Sovereignty, Witnessing, Repair*. Durham, NC: Duke University Press, 2019.

Thomas, Deborah, and M. Kamari Clarke. "Globalization and Race: Structures of Inequality, New Sovereignties, and Citizenship in a Neoliberal Era." *Annual Review of Anthropology* 42 (2013): 305–25.

Thomas, Sonja. *Privileged Minorities: Syrian Christianity, Gender, and Minority Rights in Postcolonial India*. Seattle: University of Washington Press, 2018.

Thompson, E. P. *The Making of the English Working Class*. New York: Vintage, 1963.

Tilak, Lokmanya. *The Arctic Home in the Vedas: Being Also a Key to the Interpretation of the Many Vedic Texts and Legends*. Poona: The Manager, 1903.

Times of India. "Can't Stay Provisions of SC/ST (Amendment) Act as It Is Legislation Now: SC." September 7, 2018. https://timesofindia.indiatimes.com/india/cant-stay-provisions-of-sc/st-amendment-act-as-it-is-legislation-now-sc/articleshow/65722440.cms.

Trautmann, Thomas R. *The Aryan Debate*. Oxford: Oxford University Press, 2008.

Tsing, Anna. *Friction: An Ethnography of Global Connection*. Princeton, NJ: Princeton University Press, 2005.

Tuck, Eve, and K. Wayne Yang. "Decolonization Is Not a Metaphor." *Decolonization, Indigeneity, Education and Society* 1, no. 1 (2012): 1–40.

Udupa, Sahana. *Making News in Global India: Media, Publics, Politics*. Cambridge: Cambridge University Press, 2015.

Upadhyay, Nishant. "Making of 'Model' South Asians on the Tar Sands: Intersections of Race, Caste, and Indigeneity." *Journal of the Critical Ethnic Studies* 5, nos. 1–2 (2019): 152–73.

Vanaik, Achin. *The Rise of Hindu Authoritarianism: Secular Claims, Communal Realities*. New York: Verso, 2017.

Veeraraghavan, Rajesh. *Patching Development: Information Politics and Social Change in India*. Oxford: Oxford University Press, 2021.

Vergès, Françoise. *The Wombs of Women: Race, Capital, Feminism*. Durham, NC: Duke University Press, 2020.

Virilio, Paul. *The Art of the Motor*. Minneapolis: University of Minnesota Press, 1995.

Virilio, Paul. *Speed and Politics: An Essay on Dromology*. New York: Semiotext(e), 1986.

Virno, Paolo. *Grammar of the Multitude: For an Analysis of Contemporary Forms of Life*. Los Angeles: Semiotext(e), 2004.

Viswanath, Rupa. *The Pariah Problem: Caste, Religion, and the Social in Modern India*. Cambridge: Cambridge University Press, 2014.

Viswanath, Rupa. "A Textbook Case of Exclusion." *Indian Express*, July 20, 2012. http://archive.indianexpress.com/news/a-textbook-case-of-exclusion/973711/.

Visweswaran, Kamala. *Un/common Cultures: Racism and the Rearticulation of Cultural Difference*. Durham, NC: Duke University Press, 2010.

Vora, Neha. *Impossible Citizens: Dubai's Indian Diaspora*. Durham, NC: Duke University Press, 2013.

Walia, Harsha. *Border and Rule: Global Migration, Capitalism, and the Rise of Racist Nationalism*. Chicago: Haymarket Books, 2021.

Walley, Christine J. *Exit Zero: Family and Class in Postindustrial Chicago*. Chicago: University of Chicago Press, 2013.

Wekker, Gloria. *White Innocence: Paradoxes of Colonialism and Race*. Durham, NC: Duke University Press, 2016.

White, Sarah. "Thinking Race, Thinking Development." *Third World Quarterly* 23, no. 3 (2002): 407–19.

Whitehead, Judith. "John Locke, Accumulation by Dispossession and the Governance of Colonial India." *Journal of Contemporary Asia* 42, no. 1 (2012): 1–21.

Wilde, Oscar. *The Soul of Man under Socialism*. 1900. CreateSpace Independent Publishing Platform, 2016.

Wilkerson, Isabel. *Caste: The Origin of Our Discontents*. New York: Random House, 2020.

Williams, Bianca. "Radical Honesty: Truth-Telling as Pedagogy for Working through Shame in Academic Spaces." In *Race, Equity, and the Learning Environment: The Global Relevance of Critical and Inclusive Pedagogies around the Globe*, edited by Frank Tuitt, Chayla Haynes, Saran Stewart, and Lori D. Patton, 71–82. Sterling, VA: Stylus, 2016.

Williams, Bianca. "Beyond Crisis: Temporalities, Epochal Shifts and Colonial Currents." Paper presented at the American Anthropological Association meeting, Baltimore, MD, November 17–21, 2021.

Williams, Raymond. *The Country and the City*. New York: Oxford University Press, 1973.

Wilson, Kalpana. *Race, Racism and Development: Interrogating History, Discourse and Practice*. London: Zed Books, 2012.

Wilson, Kalpana. "Re-centring 'Race' in Development: Population Policies and Global Capital Accumulation in the Era of the SDGs." *Globalizations* 14, no. 3 (2017): 432–49.

Wilson, Kalpana. "Towards a Radical Re-appropriation: Gender, Development and Neoliberal Feminism." *Development and Change* 46, no. 4 (2015): 803–32.

Wimmer, Andreas, and Nina Glick Schiller. "Methodological Nationalism, the Social Sciences, and the Study of Migration: An Essay in Historical Epistemology." *International Migration Review* 37, no. 3 (2003): 576–610.

Yengde, Suraj. *Caste Matters*. New Delhi: India Viking, 2020.

Yengde, Suraj. "Global Castes." *Ethnic and Racial Studies* 45, no. 2 (2021): 340–60.

Zurn, Perry. "Curiosities at War: The Police and Prison Resistance after Mai '68." *Modern and Contemporary France* 26, no. 2 (2018): 179–91.

Zurn, Perry. *Curiosity and Power: The Politics of Inquiry*. Minneapolis: University of Minnesota Press, 2021.

Zurn, Perry, and Arjun Shankar. *Curiosity Studies: A New Ecology of Knowledge*. Minneapolis: University of Minnesota Press, 2020.

Zwick-Maitreyi, Maari, Thenmozhi Soundararajan, Natasha Dar, Ralph Bheel, and Prathap Balakrishnan. "Caste in the United States: A Survey of Caste among South Asian Americans." Equality Labs, 2018. https://static1.squarespace.com /static/58347d04bebafbb1e66df84c/t/603ae9f4cfad7f515281e9bf/1614473732034 /Caste_report_2018.pdf.

Index

Page locators in italics indicate figures

Britain, and overpopulation fears, 65–66

British colonialism, 16, 53–54, 98, 124, 264–65n19, 269n51; civilizationalism, rhetoric of, 126–27

brown, as term, 13–14, 267–68n39, 268n42

"brown man's burden," 18, 271n68

brownness, 268n40, 270n60; brown blood, 14–15, 23, 244; commodifiable form of, 18–20; dilution of, 80–81; as illegible in United States, 56; in-betweenness of, 18, 244, 270–71n63; miscegenation, 13–14, 268–69n47; and multiculturalism, 243–44; multiple hierarchies of, 20; racial capitalism and politics of, 11–15; resilience attributed to brown poor, 2, 37, 41, 259n24; romanticization of, 15, 56, 268–69n48

brown saviorism: brown savior complex, 177; fascist regimes, pacts with, 8; globalizing the liberal erasure of caste-based discrimination, 90–93; and historic conditions, xi–xii, 5, 25, 59; moral sensibility attributed to, 150; neocolonial-cum-neoliberal-cum-neofascist salvation, 240–45; and potential loss of status, 87–90; regionally specific versions of, 13; strategies of, 16. *See also* brahmins; mentors (Sahaayaka); Sahaayaka (NGO); savarna castes

brown saviors, vii–viii, xi, 3–5; abstraction by, 83; from agricultural castes, 157–58; binaries required by, 83; caste dismissed by, 92; as conduits between white British and Black Ghanaian subjects, 204; defined, vii; disillusionment with, 175–77; occlusion of mentors' aspirations, 134; paternalism of toward mentors, 134–35; racialized values and ideologies upheld by, 5; savarna women as, 101–2; as secular, liberal, and nonpartisan, 109–10; in United States, 181–82; US overvalued by, 80, 83; valorization of, 147, 155–56, 158, 204–5; and valuable death, 155–56

brown sepoy/sahib, 7, 17, 265n20, 270–71n63

Bulli Bai app, 240

Burden-Stelly, Charisse, 246

Byrd, Jodi, 49

call centers, 140–41

capitalism: dependent on graded stratification, 39; dispossession rooted in settler colonial praxis, 32, 36; employment, constrictions on, 32–33, 72; gendered capitalist critique of NGO labor, 38–43; global racial and caste system of, xv, 5–6, 12–13, 19, 27, 73, 77, 115–16, 122, 165, 184, 238, 245–46; late liberal capitalist period, 7, 11, 28n29, 292n5; patriarchal, 10, 33, 169, 279n45. *See also* neoliberal capitalism; racial capitalism

care, ethic of, xiii–xv, 208–9, 260n28

Caribbean, 13–14

Carnegie, Dale, 139

casino time, 195

casta, as term, 22

caste: abstraction of, 42–43, 86, 90, 285n5; annihilation of, 90, 237, 245–50, 262n39; Bahujan tradition, 257n2, 261n36; brown occlusions of, 20–24; caste-as-blood, 21–23; colonial construction of, 22, 273n86; conservative discourses on, 92; digital caste system, 183–84; globality of, xv–xvi, 3–4, 10, 17, 22, 85–86, 90–93, 97, 162–64, 247; global racial and caste system of capitalism, xv, 5–6, 12–13, 19, 27, 73, 77, 115–16, 122, 165, 184, 238, 245–46; invisibilizing of, 42, 87, 93, 102, 114, 221, 243, 260n30; jati system, 22, 273n89; neocolonial stratification, 11, 26, 143, 149, 156, 198; patriarchal system of, 54, 96, 98–100; and perceived capabilities, 9–10; purity/impurity politics, 15, 22, 42, 234–37; racialization of, 5, 9–10, 20–22, 51, 273n87; varna system, 20, 22, 91, 257n2, 272n79, 273n89. *See also* agricultural castes; brahmins; caste capital; graded stratification; savarna castes; violence

Caste, Class, and Race (Cox), 21

Caste and Race in India (Ghurye), 51

caste capital, xviii, 4, 58, 63–64, 79–80, 89, 92, 244–46, 272n78; transformed into modern capital, 86–87

castelessness, 24, 58, 87, 90–92, 261n37, 272n78

caste networks, 91–93, 142, 271n71; exclusionary nature of, 85–86; global, 162–64; Non-Resident Indian networks, 57

caste supremacy, 19–20, 23, 53, 99, 237; Hindu, 19, 106, 108–11, 273n86

Caste: The Origin of Our Discontents (Wilkerson), 21

caste traitor, xvi, 262n39

celebrities, 170–71, *171*, 228, 293n13

digital infrastructures, 103, 183–84, 210, 224, 237, 245

digital saviorism, 26, 181–91, 222–24, 237; Digital India movement, 8, 178, 184–85, *185*, 200, 245; "disruptive fixation," 188; Gooru, 59, 182–83, 186–89; and "kin" connections, 185–86; techno-affective communities and anticipatory nostalgia, 187–91; technophilia, technopanacea, and solutions "imagined in their heads," 184–87

digital scaling, 215–25; and abnormalities of the start-up state, 221–25; and "ghost student problem," 223; QR codes, 219–20, 222–23; student loss of rights over their data, 223–25; testing, QR codes, and datafication, 217–21

digital solutions, 5–6, 8, 58; anticipatory technological control, 187; colonial structures reinforced by, 198, 206, 210–11, 217, 224–25, 229–30, 237–38; critique of, 186–87; crowdfunding and sharing-economy models, 189; difficult questions erased, 185, 221–22, 229–30, 235–36, 242–43; "digital dustbin," 229; and graded stratification, 183–84, 199, 221, 237–38; as morally superior, 19; open-access software, 188–89, 216, 219; parents and smartphone apps, 208; and racialized caste hierarchy of labor, 10–11, 26. *See also* apps; data collection; Swachh Shale (Clean School) app

digital time, 193–202; jugaad practiced by mentors, 199–200; mentor's labor, white noise, and the wasting of time, 198–202; time-space manipulation, 194–95, 200–201; transaction time and lag time, 195–98. *See also* technology

dispossession, 26; accumulation through, 72, 289n5, 290n20; benefit to NGOs from, 32, 36, 39, 128, 169; deficiency-based paradigms, 128; due to farmer suicides, 148; in Europe, 148; exacerbation of potential for, 65, 178; global hierarchies of disposability, 164–66; neoliberal rooted in settler colonial praxis, 32, 36; psychological effects of, 151; of rural areas, 122; through education, 65, 72; and urban-rural distinction, 116

"disruptive fixation," 188

Divakaruni, Chitra Banerjee, 102

Du Bois, W. E. B., 12, 263–64n12, 267n35, 269n51

Durrani, Mariam, 266n29, 288n13

Eco, Umberto, 172

education, 1–2, 26; cleanliness mapped onto, 230; datafication of students, 209, 217–21, 224–25, 238, 249; dispossession through, 65, 72; of gay men, 159; inequality in, 182–83; of Muslim girls, idealized, 41; nali kali program, 203–6, 212–13; need for racial capitalist critique of NGOs, 35–38; privatization of, 4, 35–36; Sarva Shiksha Abhiyan (Education for All Movement), 69, 203, 221–22, 283n17; skepticism, of students, x–xi, 64–65, 68, 72; skepticism, of teachers, 162; "students as barcodes," 219–21; and uplift of women, 99–100; Urdu-medium schools, 109, 110–11, 288n5. *See also* digital audit culture; digital scaling; digital solutions; help economies; nongovernmental organizations (NGOs); Sahaayaka (NGO)

EkStep Foundation, 58

Emergency (1970s), 67, 72, 284n23

employment, capitalist constrictions on, 32–33, 72

empowerment, 69–73; focus on students' emotional states, 69–70; monitoring as, 213; women's and girls,' 93, 95–97, 103–6

Enloe, Cynthia, 33

entrepreneurship, 2, 132, 150–52

Epstein, Mikhail, 172

Escobar, Arturo, 37, 38

Europe: Christian clashes with with Jewish and Muslim peoples, 48–49; global imperial regimes of extraction, 40; migration from, 148; racialization of difference within, 66; surplus peasants, 148

expropriation, 270n61; of agricultural land, 116, 123–25; British rationalizations for, 16; eminent domain laws, 124–25; land-use policy and tax revenue systems, 124, 290n15; masked by corporate funding, 168, 169, 174; naturalized- by binaries, 37; poverty produced by global imperial regimes of, 40; and settler and franchise colonialism, 36, 38, 124–25, 276n19, 277n30; and surplus value, 12. *See also* violence

Facebook [Meta], 184–85

family planning and sterilization programs, 66–67

Karnataka state (India), vii–viii; "authentic," 123; caste- and race-based violence in, 240; Dalits and Muslims in, 8–9, 110; expropriation of rural land from, 26; Hindutva influence in, 109; Rajyotsva Day, 188, 189; Ramanagara, 129, 147–48, 161–62, 164, 257n5. *See also* Bangalore (India); Hindutva (Hindu nationalist) state

Kaviraj, Sudipta, 234

KFC protest (1995), 123, *123*

Khoja-Moolji, Shenila, 41, 97

"kin" connections, 9–10, 31–32, 237, 241; and digital saviorism, 185–86; Muslims as "outside" of, 111; Overseas Citizens of India scheme, 57; and "trust" networks, 85

King, Martin Luther, Jr., 56

Kirtsoglou, Elisabeth, 190, 295n17

Kothari, Uma, 37, 277n25

Kuruba caste, 20

labor: ability to "follow directions," 77–78; affective, 10–11, 42, 162; digital solutions and racialized caste hierarchy of, 10–11, 26; doubling of, 135–40; emotions regulated by, 149; feminized, 8–11, 100, 244–45; funds-of-knowledge approach to, 127–28; gendered, 98–100, 103–6, 129–32; manual scavenging, 234–35, 281n24, 297n17; perceived capacities of savarna women, 98–100; perceived problem with Indians' labor capacity, 77–80, 211; precincts of precarious, 39; "primordial," 8–11, 126, 272n78; racialization of perceived capacity for, 5–8, 77–80, 244, 248–49; technoracial capacity, presumption of, 5–8, 18–19, 25, 53–54, 125, 281n27. *See also* surplus labor

Land Acquisition Act of 1894, 124, 290n20

language politics, 189, 270nn59, 60, 288n5

Lankesh, Gauri, 240

late liberal capitalist period, 7, 11, 28n29, 292n5

late liberalism, 7, 27, 264n18

LaTex, 216–17, 219, 221

Latinx communities, 182, 183

laughter, cultural politics of, 108, 113, 243

liberal, as term, 6–7, 264n18

liberal values, 87–93; globalizing the erasure of caste-based discrimination, 90–93; used to oppose Prevention of Atrocities Act, 88–89

Liboiron, Max, 260n24

limpieza de sangre ("blood purity"), 22

Lingayat caste, 8, 20, 91, 126–27, 257n2, 282n78

literacy, 67–68

Liu, Roseann, 147, 246

Lloyd, David, 124

"local," the, 37–38, 110–11

"looking after," rhetoric of, 2, 109, 127

Lowe, Lisa, 12–13, 116

Lukose, Ritty, 117

Lytton, Lord (Viceroy of India), 66

Macaulay, Thomas, 15, 45–46, 269n49

Mahabharata epic, 102, 107–8

Maldives Education Department, 73

Malthus, Thomas, 65–66

Malthusian population control theory, 25

Mankekar, Purnima, 155

Marx, Karl, 277–78n33

masculinist discourse, xiii–xiv, xviii, 10, 18, 78, 93

masculinity: entrepreneurial, 150–52; Hindu crisis of, 113, 288n8

Mather, Cotton, 49, 280n10

Mathew, Leya, 117

Mayo, Katherine, 98–99, 233

media, 161–64; and hyperreality, 172–73; social media, 164, 170, 184–85, *185*

Melamed, Jodi, 39–40

mentors (Sahaayaka), 2; and altruism/corruption discourse, 134; ambivalence of, 128–29; and anti-Muslim racism, 109–15; caste problem displaced onto, 91; and digital time, 198–202; doubling of labor of, 135–40; economic need, moral obligation, and impossible dreams of saviorism, 140–43; funds-of-knowledge approach to, 127–28; gendered labor and mobility regimes, 129–32; jugaad practiced by mentors, 199–200; mobility, aspirations to, 26, 39, 43, 116–17, 126–29, 134, 158–59; NGO start-ups as aspiration for, 141–42, 159; paternalism of brown saviors toward, 134–35; and racialization of rural difference, 125–29; reengineering of, 135–40; as representative of target populations, 128; self-objectification of as source of value, 128; women as, 129–32. *See also* brown saviorism

"merit," 2, 5, 86, 249–50, 272n78

Michael and Susan Dell Foundation, 96, 101

Mies, Maria, 41, 247, 279n45

Millennium Development Goals (United Nations), 205

Minai, Naveen, 24–25

mobility: aspirations to, 12, 26, 39, 43, 93, 116–17, 126–29, 158–59; gendered, 10, 129–32, 149; horizontal and vertical, 149; limitations on, 128–33; and limited on physical movement, 131–32; and material precarity, 158–59; narratives of as dupes, 132, 142, 152; neocolonial stratifications of, 143, 148–49, 152, 156; regimes of, 43, 122, 129–32; and visibility, 162–63. *See also* aspiration

"model minority" narrative, 55–56, 282n40, 287n12

modernity, 15, 17, 89, 243, 269n50, 273–74n94

Modi, Narendra, 6, 108, 109; and Clean India campaign, 227–28, 235; and Digital India movement, 178, 184–85

moral ambitions, 9–10

moral discourse, 132, 145–46, 150, 271n70; of cleaning of excreta, 234; and digitized solutions, 19; and "discovery" of poverty, 37; double bind for savior, 68; immediate need, rhetoric of, 33; of obligation, discourse of, 140–43, 177; post-Fordist, 78

Morrison, Toni, 241

Morton, Samuel, 47, 49–50

Mosse, David, 42

Mother India (Mayo), 98–99, 233

motivation, 2, 65, 69–73; bodily intensity, 70–71; "learning tree" analogy, 71–72; neo-Malthusian logic reproduced by, 25–26; prerana program, 69

Muhammad Jaunpuri, 109

Müller, Max, 51, 52, 280n16

multiculturalism, 243–44

Mumbai Taj Hotel bombings (2008), 113

Munoz, Jose Esteban, 1, 16, 269n54

Muñoz, José Esteban, 15

Muslims, xvi, 8–9, 265n22; Algerian, 270–71n63; and anti-Muslim racism, 6, 19, 51, 57, 109, 111–16; in Channapatna, 108–9; everyday practices against, 111–16; as focus of saviorism, 41; "good" secular, 115–16; as "illiberal," 18; Mahdavia sect, 109; Urdu-medium schools, 109, 110–11, 288n5; violence against, 113–14, 240, 288n8, 288n13; and war on terror, 41, 57, 113

Nair, Vijayanka, 220, 222

nali kali program, 203–6, 212–13

naming, cultural politics of, 122–23

National Democratic Alliance, 109–10

National Register of Citizens (NRC), 57, 114, 248

national security apparatuses, 238

"native informant," 11, 83, 265–66n26

NDTV (New Delhi Television Limited), 167–76

Nehru, Jawaharlal, 14–15, 17, 18, 53–55, 100, 127

neocolonial-cum-neoliberal saviorism, 69, 240–45

neocolonial haunting, 152

neocolonialism: academic disciplining, 11–12, 46; in Bangalore, 123; cultural reeingineering, 139; "data colonialism," 224; digital solutions as reinforcement of, 198, 206, 210–11, 217, 224–25, 229–30, 237–38; "femo-neocolonialism," 102; as gendered, 149; global-digital order, 225; and graded stratification, 11, 26, 143, 149, 156, 198; hierarchies in, 26, 73, 77; internalization of values of, 149, 151, 156; and the "local," 37; and mobility, 143, 148–49, 152, 156; racialized difference, 16–17, 59–60; "who can think," question of, 210–11

neocolonial saviorism, 25, 61

neoliberal capitalism: and empowerment discourse, 69–70; financial resources deployed to help economies, 16–17; and increase in inequality, 35; individualism of, 5, 65, 143, 147, 235, 242, 249–50; "merit" and "hard work," 2, 5, 249–50; privatization, 4, 35–36, 124; universalizing method of, 110. *See also* capitalism

nervous ethnography, xi–xv, 25, 48, 239, 242, 259–60n26; and blood talk, 3–4; and representation of villages, 161

nervousness, xi–xx, 7, 33; among bureaucrats and NGO workers, 42–43, 244; and annihilationist impulses, 245–50; and complicity, xv–xvi, 43; and multiscalar political economies, 238, 239; and neocolonial-cum-neoliberal-cum-neofascist salvation, 240–45; postcolonial disorders, 259n17

"nervous state," 240–41

NICE (US corporation), 124

Nilekani, Nandan, 58, 220

Noble, Safiya Umoja, 179

noble savage rhetoric, 134

nongovernmental organizations (NGOs), viii, 275–76n14; and accumulation, 126; benefit of dispossession to, 32, 36, 39, 128, 169; caste discussions excluded from, 42; empowerment as strategy of, 69; far-right attacks on, 6; girls'/women's empowerment as focus, 96–97; NGOization of voluntary sector, 1–2, 17; proliferation of, 1–2, 34, 55; savarna women's mobility in, 100–101. *See also* Sahaayaka (NGO)

nonprofit-industrial complex, 34–35, 40–41, 97, 238, 246. *See also* help economies

Non-Resident Indians (NRIs), 57, 182

nostalgia, 185; anticipatory, 187–91, 295n17; politics of, 172

Ocampo, Anthony, 268n40

open-source software, 188–89, 216–17, 219

optical mark recognition (OMR) technologies, 218–19

organism, idea of, 71

Osuri, Goldie, 246

Others, 13; and anticipatory nostalgia, 190; capacity of former colonizers to help, 37; and corruption discourse, 134–35; of Europe, 49; as hyperindustrious, 2, 37, 69; Othering, anthropological, xii–xiii; precariat, appropriate, 159; and savior complex, 34; and savior/saved binary, 39–40; as unassimilable, 19, 106

Overseas Citizens of India (OCI) scheme, 57

Paik, Shailaja, 261n37

"Pakistani ancestry," 57

The Palace of Illusions (Divakaruni), 102

Patel, Kamna, 36

Patel, Shaista, 49, 51, 271–72n77

paternalism, xix, 2, 33, 54–55, 127, 235, 246; of brown saviors toward mentors, 134–35; and motivational strategies, 69; "trusteeship," 55

pathology, social, 147–50

Patnaik, Prabhat, 275n7, 286n20

Patnaik, Utsa, 125, 148, 266–67n32

patriarchy: and capitalism, 10, 33, 169, 279n45; and household, 54, 96, 98–100, 129–30; linked to caste supremacy, 99–100; and stratification of mentor class, 129

pedagogies of aspiration, 117

Phule, Jyotiba, 99, 248, 273n86

Phule, Savitribai, 99, 248, 287n11

Pierre, Jemima, 40

platform metaphor, 209–10

playground, imaginary of, 172

pleasure, problematic, xiv, xv, 163, 165, 239, 260n32

population control, 65–68

postcolonial theory, 260–61n35

postdevelopment critique, 37–38

post-Fordist societies, 78

poverty: cleanliness mapped onto, 231; double bind for liberal savior, 68; illiteracy linked with population control, 67–68; Malthusian population control theory, 25; neocapitalist characterization of, 37–38; non-white reproduction blamed for, 66–67; population control, 65–68; produced by global imperial regimes of extraction, 40; racialization of, 16. *See also* inequality

Povinelli, Elizabeth, 152, 264n18

pragmatism. *See* fatal pragmatism

Prasad, M. Madhava, 161

precarity: global hierarchies of disposability, 164–66; hierarchy, and the pedagogy of the insult, 158–61; racialized and gendered image of social (media) mobility, 161–64. *See also* inequality

Press Freedom Index, 240

primitivizing discourse, 37, 39, 98, 114, 277–78n33

privatization, 4, 35–36, 124, 172, 275n14, 276n18, 298n18

productivity: attributed to caste, 20, 40; and digital scaling, 216; literacy and population control linked to, 67–68; "motivation" strategies for, 2; sanitation linked to, 232–33

protests, 248, 298n18; Bangalore, *123*, 123–24, 132, 289nn10, 11

Puar, Jasbir, 292n2

purity/impurity politics, 15, 22, 42; digital politics of, 234–37

Quit India Movement, 228

racial capitalism, 276n20, 277n30, 279n46; brownness, politics of, 11–15; as gendered, 41–42; materiality of, 38–43; and politics of brownness, 11–15; savior/saved binary, 13;

technologies of antirelationality required for, 209; in United States, 11–12, 21. *See also* capitalism

"racial caste" school, 21

racialization, 267n32, 267n37; of altruism, 134; of caste, 5, 9–10, 20–22, 51, 273n87; conflation of Hindu, Indian, and Brahmin, 48–52; of difference, 16–18, 39, 59–60; evolutionary typologies, 126; and graded stratification, 13, 20, 126, 177–78, 293n8; intersecting processes of, 5; and Orientalist exoticism, 126; of perceived labor capacity, 5–8, 77–80, 244, 248–49; of poverty, 16; of rural difference, 125–29; savior/saved binary, 13; scientific racism, *46*, 47–52; United States and transnational reorderings, 16, 55–59

radical honesty, xiv, 259n26

Rai, Amit, 199–200

Rai Bachchan, Aishwarya, 170–71, *171*

Rajyotsva Day, 188, *189*

Ramanagara (Karnataka state), 129, 147–48, 161–62, 164, 257n5

Rana, Junaid, 48–49, 55

Rao, Ursula, 220

Reardon, Jenny, 224

Reddy caste, 92, 286n21

reformists, 242–43

refusal/resistance, x, 37, 258n8, 259n24, 280n8

Rege, Sharmila, 261–62n39, 286–87n5

religion, racialization of, 48–51, 98; Hindu supremacy, 19, 106, 108–11, 240–41, 273n86; spiritual capacity attributed to brahmins, 53–55, 58

Resnick, Mitchel, 139

revitalization, discourse of, 169–70, *173*

The Revolution Will Not Be Funded (INCITE! Collective), 40–41

Rizvi, Mubbashir, 289n6

Robinson, Cedric, 277n30

Rodney, Walter, 40, 61, 269n49, 278n36

Roy, Ananya, 119, 270n57

Roy, Arundhati, 55, 275–76n14

Sabre Global Distribution System, 196

Sahaayaka (NGO): caste-based discrimination alleged against leadership, 86–87, 91; caste gradation reproduced in, 8–10, 13, 24, 26, 43, 110–11, 134, 149, 158, 166, 238; "exit

strategy" graduate student project, 81–83; funding for, 96, 101, 137, 167–68, 207; Girl Empowerment Program, 95–96; Kalam valorized by, 109–10; leadership of, 2–3, 24, 31–33, 76, 83, 85, 243; motivation as focus of, 2, 25–26, 65; partnerships with US funders and universities, 25–26, 73, 81–83; partnership with NDTV/Coke, 167–76; private and public spaces in field offices, 137; prosperity during early Hindutva ascension, 7–8; scaling up, 76–77; student trips sponsored by, 86; and Support My School campaign, 167–76, *171*; transnational influence of, 58–59, 73, 162–63; women in leadership positions, 85, 97. *See also* brown saviorism; digital solutions; nongovernmental organizations (NGOs)

Said, Edward, 90, 260n32

salvation, economies of, 13; brown form of, 15–20; colonial roots of, 15

Sanskrit, 51

Sanyal, Kalyan, 39

Sartre, Jean-Paul, vii, 240

Sarva Shiksha Abhiyan (Education for All Movement), 69, 203, 221–22, 283n17

savarna castes, 1–4; in academia, 266nn30,31; and Aryan theory of race, 22–23, 51–52; ascension during post/colonial period, 5, 57; ascension of, 5, 13, 15, 18, 23, 38, 185–86; brown delineation used by, 14; and castelessness, 24, 58, 87, 90–92, 261n37, 272n78; diasporic, xvi, xix, 2–4, 14, 19, 26, 57, 97, 127, 170, 185–86, 204, 244, 282n36; and digital politics of purity, 234–37; globality of, vii–viii, xv–xvi, 3–4, 10, 17; Hindus "indigenized," 52; and nationalist movements, 17, 51–52; and national uplift, 52–55; objection to Prevention of Atrocities Act, 88–89; perceived preternatural racial capacity of, 6, 10–11, 12, 26, 53–54, 56–57; racial politics of, 45–60; rural India as nostalgic for, 127; self-fashioning of, 14, 23, 87, 117; technoracial labor capacity in the wake of fascism, 5–8; transnational class, Indian technocrats as, xvi, 4, 8, 11, 19, 35, 38, 55–59, 80–81, 183–84; in United States, 1–2, 19–20, 55–59, 181–82. *See also* brahmins; brown saviorism; savarna women

urban saviorism, 117
Urdu language, 110, 189

value, 279n53, 285n5; cleanliness as, 230; excess, 20, 27, 158, 178, 209, 237; shared regime of, 89
varna system, 20, 22, 91, 257n2, 272n79, 273n89
Vergès, Françoise, 61, 286n3
violence: anthropological, 48, 260n26, 279-80n4; caste-based, 23, 54, 87, 90, 237, 240-41, 248, 257n2, 260n30, 264-65n19, 264n18; colonial, 12, 14; epistemic, xii-xiii; erasure of savarna complicity in, 260n30, 264-65n19, 264n18; against Muslims, 113-14, 240, 288n8, 288n13; neocolonial, xii-xiii, 48, 260n26, 276n20. *See also* caste; expropriation
visibility, 162-63, 230
Vokkaliga caste, viii, 8, 11, 20, 91, 126-27, 257n2, 282n78

war on terror, 41, 57, 113
Warren, William F., 52
waste, rhetoric of, 135, 136
Whitehead, Judith, 126
white noise, 201-2
"white noise time series," 202
white saviorism, 5, 25, 35
white supremacist imperialism, 17-18
"Who is in the room?" question, 4-5

Wilde, Oscar, 34
Wilkerson, Isabel, 21
Williams, Bianca, xiv, 259n26
Wilson, Kalpana, 40, 66
Wipro (Indian technology company), 220
Wolfe, Patrick, 124
women and girls, 278n40, 286n3, 287n10; brown, as focus of saviors, 41, 96-97; constructed as saviors, 41, 95-97; economic mobility, 100; and empowerment, 93, 95-97, 103-6, 286n2; Indophobic discourses on, 98-99; and internalization of market rhetoric, 287n15; as mentors, 129-32; patriarchal constraints on, 10, 99-100; as preternaturally capable of care, 96-97, 286n3; streedharma ideology, 130, 291n31; and sustainable development discourse, 96; as universal category, 279n51; women conflated with girls, 98. *See also* savarna women
World Health Organization (WHO), 227

Yadav caste, 91, 158
Yengde, Suraj, 1, 23n887, 24, 42, 258n13, 262n39, 274n1

Zia, Ather, 246
Zuckerberg, Mark, 184-85, 294n7
Zurn, Perry, 249, 259n24